Lecture Notes in Computer Science 6503

Commenced Publication in 1973
Founding and Former Series Editors:
Gerhard Goos, Juris Hartmanis, and Jan van Leeuwen

Editorial Board

T0074225

David Hutchison
Lancaster University, UK

Takeo Kanade
Carnegie Mellon University, Pittsburgh, PA, USA

Josef Kittler
University of Surrey, Guildford, UK

Jon M. Kleinberg
Cornell University, Ithaca, NY, USA

Alfred Kobsa
University of California, Irvine, CA, USA

Friedemann Mattern
ETH Zurich, Switzerland

John C. Mitchell
Stanford University, CA, USA

Moni Naor
Weizmann Institute of Science, Rehovot, Israel

Oscar Nierstrasz
University of Bern, Switzerland

C. Pandu Rangan
Indian Institute of Technology, Madras, India

Bernhard Steffen
TU Dortmund University, Germany

Madhu Sudan
Microsoft Research, Cambridge, MA, USA

Demetri Terzopoulos
University of California, Los Angeles, CA, USA

Doug Tygar
University of California, Berkeley, CA, USA

Gerhard Weikum
Max Planck Institute for Informatics, Saarbruecken, Germany

Somesh Jha   Anish Mathuria (Eds.)

Information Systems Security

6th International Conference, ICISS 2010
Gandhinagar, India, December 17-19, 2010
Proceedings

 Springer

Volume Editors

Somesh Jha
University of Wisconsin
Computer Sciences Department
Madison, WI 53706, USA
E-mail: jha@cs.wisc.edu

Anish Mathuria
Dhirubhai Ambani Institute of Information
and Communication Technology
Gandhinagar 382007, Gujarat, India
E-mail: anish_mathuria@daiict.ac.in

Library of Congress Control Number: 2010940624

CR Subject Classification (1998): C.2.0, C.2, E.3, D.4.6, K.6.5, K.4.4, H.2.4

LNCS Sublibrary: SL 4 – Security and Cryptology

ISSN   0302-9743
ISBN-10   3-642-17713-1 Springer Berlin Heidelberg New York
ISBN-13   978-3-642-17713-2 Springer Berlin Heidelberg New York

This work is subject to copyright. All rights are reserved, whether the whole or part of the material is
concerned, specifically the rights of translation, reprinting, re-use of illustrations, recitation, broadcasting,
reproduction on microfilms or in any other way, and storage in data banks. Duplication of this publication
or parts thereof is permitted only under the provisions of the German Copyright Law of September 9, 1965,
in its current version, and permission for use must always be obtained from Springer. Violations are liable
to prosecution under the German Copyright Law.

springer.com

© Springer-Verlag Berlin Heidelberg 2010
Printed in Germany

Typesetting: Camera-ready by author, data conversion by Scientific Publishing Services, Chennai, India
Printed on acid-free paper   06/3180

Message from the General Chairs

It is our pleasure to welcome you to the proceedings of the 6th International Conference on Information Systems Security. ICISS was first held in 2005 in Kolkata, and has been successfully organized every year in different parts of India. Even within a short span of its life, the conference has left its mark in the field of information systems security.

There is a long list of people who have volunteered their time and energy to put together this conference and who deserve acknowledgement. Our thanks go to the Program Chairs, Somesh Jha and Anish Mathuria, along with the Program Committee members for an excellent job in completing a rigorous review process and selecting outstanding papers for presentation at the conference. We would also like to thank Jonathan Giffin, Andrew Myers, Sriram Rajamani, and V.N. Venkatakrishnan for accepting our invitation to deliver invited keynote talks at the conference. The effort made by the Tutorial Chair, Rakesh Verma, in selecting tutorial sessions on topics of contemporary interest in this field deserves special mention. We would also like to thank the Tutorial Speakers who kindly agreed to deliver their lectures.

We hope that you will find the proceedings of ICISS 2010 stimulating and a source of inspiration for future research.

December 2010

Sushil Jajodia
S.C. Sahasrabudhe

Message from the Technical Program Chairs

This volume contains the papers selected for presentation at the 6th International Conference on Information Systems Security (ICISS 2010) held during December 17–19, 2010 in Gandhinagar, India. ICISS is part of an effort started five years ago as an initiative to promote information security-related research in India. Held annually it now attracts strong participation from the international research community.

This year we received 51 papers from 19 countries all over the world. After a rigorous review process, the Program Committee selected 14 papers for presentation. Each paper was reviewed by at least three Program Committee members. All the Program Committee members discussed the reviews during a two-week on-line discussion phase. We would like to thank the authors of all the papers for submitting their quality research work to the conference. Our special thanks go to the Program Committee members and the external for sparing their time in carrying out the review process meticulously.

We were fortunate to have four eminent experts as invited keynote speakers. Their lectures provided fertile ground for stimulating discussions at the conference. As in previous years, the main conference was preceded by two days of tutorial presentations. We would like to thank the Tutorial Chair, Rakesh Verma, for arranging an excellent tutorial program. We would also like to thank the speakers who agreed to deliver tutorial lectures: Agostino Cortesi, Rop Gonggrijp, J. Alex Halderman, Alexander Malkis, Hari Prasad, Amitabh Saxena, and Poorvi Vora.

We would like to thank the General Chairs, Sushil Jajodia and S.C. Sahasrabudhe, members of the Steering Committee and previous PC Chair, Atul Prakash, on whom we frequently relied upon for advice throughout the year. We would also like to thank Drew Davidson for maintaining the conference website.

Finally, we would like to thank the conference publisher Springer for their co-operation. We hope that you will find the papers in this volume technically rewarding.

December 2010

Somesh Jha
Anish Mathuria

Conference Organization

Program Chairs

Somesh Jha   University of Wisconsin, USA
Anish Mathuria   DA-IICT, India

Program Committee

Claudio Agostino Ardagna   University of Milan, Italy
Bezawada Bruhadeshwar   IIIT-Hyderabad, India
Mihai Christodorescu   IBM T.J. Watson Research Center, USA
Cas Cremers   ETH Zurich, Switzerland
Naranker Dulay   Imperial College London, UK
Debin Gao   Singapore Management University, Singapore
Jon Giffin   Georgia Institute of Technology, USA
Sushil Jajodia   George Mason University, USA
Gunter Karjoth   IBM Zurich Research Laboratory, Switzerland
Zhenkai Liang   National University of Singapore, Singapore
Javier Lopez   University of Malaga, Spain
Keith Martin   Royal Holloway University of London, UK
Debdeep Mukhopadhyay   IIT-Kharagpur, India
Srijith K. Nair   British Telecom, UK
Karthik Pattabiraman   University of British Columbia, Canada
Gunther Pernul   University of Regensburg, Germany
Atul Prakash   University of Michigan Ann Arbor, USA
Kouichi Sakurai   Kyushu University, Japan
Nitesh Saxena   Polytechnic Institute of New York University,
                                  USA
R. Sekar   SUNY Stony Brook, USA
Shamik Sural   IIT-Kharagpur, India
S.P. Suresh   Chennai Mathematical Institute, India
Vipin Swarup   MITRE, USA
Patrick Traynor   Georgia Institute of Technology, USA
Venkat Venkatakrishnan   University of Illinois Chicago, USA
Rakesh Verma   University of Houston, USA
Poorvi Vora   George Washington University, USA
Guilin Wang   University of Birmingham, UK

General Chairs

Sushil Jajodia   George Mason University, USA
S.C. Sahasrabudhe   DA-IICT, India

Tutorial Chairs

Chandan Mazumdar   Jadavpur University, India
Rakesh Verma   University of Houston, USA

Publicity Chair

Claudio Agostino Ardagna   University of Milan, Italy

Finance Chair

Manik Lal Das   DA-IICT, India

Steering Committee

Sushil Jajodia (Chair)   George Mason University, USA
Aditya Bagchi   Indian Statistical Institute, India
Somesh Jha   University of Wisconsin, USA
Gargi Keeni   Tata Consultancy Services, India
A.K. Majumdar   IIT Kharagpur, India
Chandan Mazumdar   Jadavpur University, India
Atul Prakash   University of Michigan Ann Arbor, USA
Pierangela Samarati   University of Milan, Italy
R. Sekar   SUNY Stony Brook, USA
A.K. Kaushik   Ministry of Communications and IT, Govt. of
                           India
Gulshan Rai   Department of Information Technology, Govt.
                           of India

External Reviewers

A. Baskar
Abhijit Das
Adam Young
Andreas Reisser
Bailey Basile
Cheng-Kang Chu
Chester Rebeiro
Christian Broser
Christoph Fritsch
Chunhua Su
David Keppler
Isaac Agudo
Jingyu Hua
Jonathan Voris
Krishnaprasad Thirunarayan
Liang Zhao
Ludwig Fuchs
Mario Frank

Moritz Riesner
Oliver Gmelch
Pablo Najera
Qi Xie
Rajat Subhra Chakraborty
Rehana Yasmin
Rodrigo Roman
Ruben Rios
Sai Teja Peddinti
Shengdong Zhao
Shinsaku Kiyomoto
Stephanie Wehner
Steven Gianvecchio
Tzipora Halevi
Yanjiang Yang
Yizhi Ren
Yoshiaki Hori

Table of Contents

Access Control and Auditing

System Security

Analyzing Explicit Information Flow

Sriram K. Rajamani

Microsoft Research India
sriram@microsoft.com

Constraining information flow is fundamental to security: we do not want secret information to reach untrusted principals (confidentiality), and we do not want untrusted principals to corrupt trusted information (integrity).

Even if we ignore covert channels and implicit information flow, explicit information flow is still hard to analyze due the size and complexity of large systems. In this talk, we describe our experiences in building automatic analyses for finding explicit information flow vulnerabilities in large systems. In particular, we reflect on our experiences in building the following three analysis tools:

- In the NETRA project [3], we systematically analyze and detect explicit information-flow vulnerabilities in access-control configurations. Here, we dynamically generate a snapshot of access-control metadata, and perform static analysis on this snapshot to check for violations of specified policies. We use Datalog to represent configurations, OS mechanisms as well as information-flow policies uniformly, and use Datalog inference to detect policy violations.
- In the EON project [1], we extend Datalog with some carefully designed constructs that allow the introduction and transformation of new relations. For example, these constructs can model the creation of processes and objects, and the modification of their security labels at runtime. Then, we analyze information-flow properties of such systems can be analyzed by asking queries in this language.
- In the MERLIN project [2], we automatically infer specifications for explicit information flow in programs. We begin with a data propagation graph, which represents interprocedural flow of information in the program, and model information flow paths in the propagation graph using probabilistic constraints. We solve the resulting system of probabilistic constraints using factor graphs, which are a well-known structure for performing probabilistic inference.

We summarize our experiences, and reflect on the role of automated analyses in finding explicit information flow vulnerabilities, and making our systems secure with respect to explicit information flow. We describe what kinds of errors our tools are able to find, and tricks we had to do in order to reduce false positives, and make our tools usable. We present our views on directions for future research in this area. We also speculate on what it would take to design systems where explicit information flows are secure by design.

S. Jha and A. Maturia (Eds.): ICISS 2010, LNCS 6503, pp. 1–2, 2010.
© Springer-Verlag Berlin Heidelberg 2010

References

1. Chaudhuri, A., Naldurg, P., Rajamani, S.K., Ramalingam, G., Velaga, L.: Eon: modeling and analyzing dynamic access control systems with logic programs. In: Proceedings of the 15th ACM Conference on Computer and Communications Security, CCS 2008, pp. 381–390. ACM, New York (2008)
2. Livshits, B., Nori, A.V., Rajamani, S.K., Banerjee, A.: Merlin: specification inference for explicit information flow problems. Programming Languages Design and Implementation, PLDI 2009, Also appears in SIGPLAN Notices 44(6), 75–86 (2009)
3. Naldurg, P., Schwoon, S., Rajamani, S.K., Lambert, J.: Netra: seeing through access control. In: Proceedings of the Fourth ACM Workshop on Formal Methods in Security, FMSE 2006, pp. 55–66. ACM, New York (2006)

WebAppArmor: A Framework for Robust Prevention of Attacks on Web Applications

(Invited Paper)

V.N. Venkatakrishnan, Prithvi Bisht, Mike Ter Louw, Michelle Zhou,
Kalpana Gondi, and Karthik Thotta Ganesh

Department of Computer Science
University of Illinois at Chicago

Abstract. As the World Wide Web continues to evolve, the number of web-based attacks that target web applications is on the rise. Attacks such as Cross-site Scripting (XSS), SQL Injection and Cross-site Request Forgery (XSRF) are among the topmost threats on the Web, and defending against these attacks is a growing concern. In this paper, we describe WEBAPPARMOR, a framework that is aimed at preventing these attacks on existing (legacy) web applications. The main feature of this framework is that it offers a unified perspective to address these problems in the context of existing web applications. The framework incorporates techniques based on static and dynamic analysis, symbolic evaluation and execution monitoring to retrofit existing web applications to be resilient to these attacks.

1 Introduction

The number of World Wide Web users has risen to nearly 1.5 billion [58], a fifth of the worldís population. Development of innovative web based technologies has resulted in this explosive growth. Using the Web, end-users have benefited tremendously in numerous areas such as electronic commerce, health care and education. Due to the importance of these services, the web has attracted participation from a diverse populace.

In this scenario, the trend is progressing towards richer "Web 2.0" applications. *Exciting and interactive* user driven content such as blog, wiki entries and YouTube videos, are becoming the norm for web content rather than the exception, as evidenced by social networking sites such as Facebook. The growth of these sites has been fueled by highly attractive revenue models and business opportunities from advertising. As a result, we are moving away from a Web of static HTML pages to *responsive, feature rich* pages laden with content from several sources. With the rise in popularity of client-side scripting and AJAX, the web has been turned into a full fledged programming platform, enabling feature-rich applications to be implemented.

Unfortunately, this transition is becoming a source of serious security problems that target web applications, and consequently end-users. A recent survey by the security firm Symantec suggests that malicious content is increasingly being delivered by Web based attacks [16], such as Cross-site (XSS) Scripting, SQL Injection and Cross-site Request Forgery (XSRF). More recently, self-propagating worms such as Samy and Yammanner have spread by exploiting Cross-site Scripting vulnerabilities in web

S. Jha and A. Maturia (Eds.): ICISS 2010, LNCS 6503, pp. 3–26, 2010.
© Springer-Verlag Berlin Heidelberg 2010

applications hosting social networking sites and email services. Studies on the Samy MySpace worm report that it spread at rates much faster than previous Internet worms. The worm spread over active web sessions involving about 1,000,000 users in just under 20 hours! [23]. Researchers suggest that these worms can be further employed to create a distributed botnet without the need for any user involvement [21]. The recent SQL injection attack based Heartland data breach [7] resulted in information theft of approximately 130 millions credit / debit cards, thus victimizing members of the general public.

A fundamental reason for the success of these attacks is that the development of web security technology and standards has not kept up with the pace of adoption of these new web technologies. The increasing growth of the Web suggest that this adoption trend is perhaps irreversible. Since existing web application security and browser security models were designed and developed without anticipating these new applications, we need the techniques that *retrofit* security in existing applications.

Our focus is different from approaches to vulnerability analysis, say using static analysis, that are useful in debugging phases to help identify vulnerabilities, which a programmer must consider and patch. Our focus is on *automated prevention* techniques, which aim to automatically retrofit applications so that they are secured against web-based attacks. Our focus on prevention is guided by the following two pragmatic reasons: (i) prevention techniques are perhaps the only recourse for already deployed web applications that are vulnerable to these attacks (ii) automated techniques for prevention are the only solution to the challenge of scalability; manually changing applications is expensive, error-prone and time consuming, leading to exposure to these attacks for a longer window-of-time.

The thesis of our approach is that effective solutions for retrofitting web applications can be achieved by automatically extracting application intentions from their code. Deviations from these intentions can then be monitored to successfully prevent attacks.

The philosophy of discovering intent in order to stave attacks rests on the following two simple observations:

(a) web applications are written implicitly assuming benign inputs and encode its intentions to achieve a certain behavior on these inputs, and

(b) maliciously crafted inputs subvert the program into straying away from these intentions, leading to successful attacks.

If intentions were clearly formulated and expressed formally (say by the web application developer), these attacks can be prevented. However, clear intent is often absent, both in legacy and newly engineered software.

Since intentions are not clearly expressed in programs, our approach is to infer these intentions automatically from web application code. We then use discovered intentions to engineer effective automatic solutions that are integrated in a framework called WEBAPPARMOR that is aimed at retrofitting web applications.

In this paper, we survey the following key results developed through WEBAPPARMOR.

- **Symbolic Evaluation Techniques for Inferring Intended Behavior.** A web application's intended behavior (which we call its *model*) needs to be elicited in order to constrain its actual behavior during execution. We develop novel symbolic evaluation techniques that build models to precisely capture the intended behavior of a web application. Based on these models, we build clean and robust solutions [12,63] to the problems of SQL injection and Cross-site request forgery (XSRF).

- **Cross-site Scripting Defenses for Existing Browsers.** In Cross-site Scripting (XSS) attacks, output (HTML/JavaScript) of a web application server is interpreted by a client browser, which then becomes a staging point for these attacks. The problem is compounded by the difficulty that there are a plethora of browsers, each of which may interpret the web application's output in a different way. Hence, we develop browser-side enforcement techniques [51] that ensure that the web application's behavior on the client side conforms to the model. The key benefit of our approach is that it requires no changes to browser code base either in the form of patches or plugins, thus effective on all *existing browsers*.

- **Fine-grained Web Content Restrictions.** As the Web is increasingly becoming a platform for content aggregated from multiple sources, content from different origins (such as advertisements) are mixed and rendered in a browser. Existing browser security models have been developed without considering security issues in such integration. In this case, we cannot build models of third party content on the web application (server) side, as content is only aggregated on the client side browser. We therefore develop confinement techniques [50] on the browser side that will prevent attacks from malicious content by restricting their capabilities.

Along with these research contributions, WEBAPPARMOR also has resulted in a number of practical tools. Specifically, this research has resulted in the following tools: TAPS[12] for SQLIA prevention, X-PROTECT [63] for XSRF prevention, BLUEPRINT[51] for XSS prevention and ADJAIL[50] for fine-grained content restrictions.

The rest of this paper is organized as follows: we provide an overview of our framework in Section 2. We describe our approach to prevent SQL injection in Section 3 and XSRF attacks in Section 4. Techniques for preventing XSS attacks in our framework are described in Section 5. Finally, we describe an approach for applying fine-grained restrictions on advertisements Section 6. Section 7 provides a conclusion.

2 Overview

Figure 1 shows a typical Facebook profile page as seen by the end user. Notice that the content of this page has been aggregated from several sources: the user's own profile information, peer comments and third-party advertisements. We will use this page as the running example for the various problems tackled by WEBAPPARMOR.[1] Specifically, we investigate preventive solutions for the following problems (We will explain the attacks in detail in the following sections).

- A) **SQL injection.** As illustrated in Figure 1, malicious input can be entered by a user through input fields such as a search box, which may result in executing malicious queries in the database.

---

[1] We use Facebook as an illustrative example, we are not trying to suggest that Facebook itself suffers from these actual problems, even though it has been a subject of a large number of security problems [39].

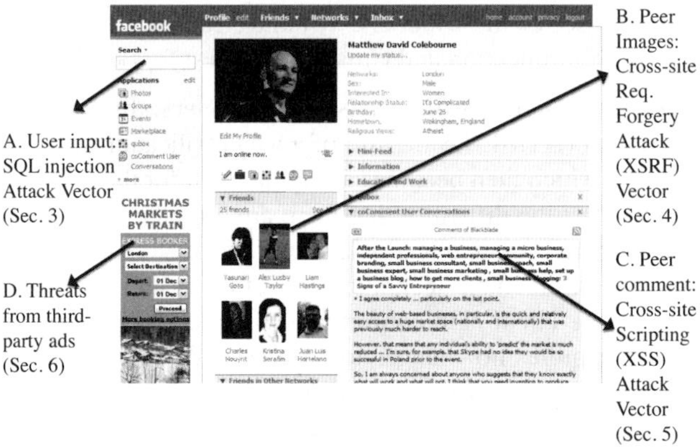

Fig. 1. A typical Facebook profile with content aggregated from multiple sources

- B) **Cross-site Request Forgery (XSRF).** This attack on web applications is staged with the help of a browser with an active session, by links (such as profile images) that result in server side operations, such as injecting malicious code.

- C) **Cross-site Scripting (XSS).** These attacks result from untrusted user inputs such as peer comments, and result in malicious script code execution on the web browser.

- D) **Web Advertisements.** Advertisements are third-party content that are mixed and rendered with site content and rendered in the browser, shown in Figure 1 D.). We provide facilities for web applications to enforce fine-grained controls on this content.

2.1   Methodology

WEBAPPARMOR infers the intended behaviors of web applications by analysis of these applications, and automatically transforms web applications to enforce this intended behavior to prevent attacks. Now the precise definition of "intended behavior" and "enforcement" of intended behaviors depend on the problem at hand. For instance, for cross-site scripting attacks, the intended behavior for an input request may be a web page that contains a precise description of regions of untrusted content. Enforcement will entail ensuring that contents in these untrusted regions do not lead to script execution.

The key idea in WEBAPPARMOR (see accompanying figure) is the introduction of *models* that assist the web application and the web browser in determining the web-application intended behavior corresponding to the original input request. Since the intended behavior will change based on the actual inputs received by the application, the generated models will also be tied to each run in the web application.

While these models can be created manually for each path in the application by the web application developer, the process can be tedious, error prone and potentially incomplete for large web applications. Hence, WEBAPPARMOR involves *model*

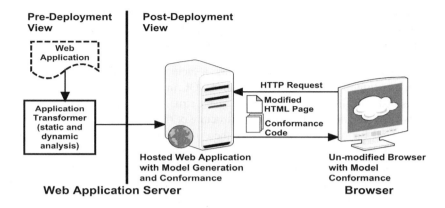

Web Application Server   **Browser**

generation techniques that automatically extract the model. We perform this extraction through a combination of static and dynamic analysis techniques, during the pre-deployment stage as shown in the pre-deployment view of the above figure.

Once a model is generated, WEBAPPARMOR ensures that the output of the web application conforms to the model, thereby preventing attacks. This step, *model conformance*, is to ensure that the output of the web application agrees with the model. The web application may itself be able to perform this step depending on the problem at hand. For instance, if the actual behavior results in a SQL query, the web application itself will enforce the intended query structure dictated by the model. This will be accomplished by transforming the web application to only issue a query that has the intended structure.

However, it is not possible for the server side of the web application to ensure sound model conformance in all cases. In the case of cross-site scripting attacks, it is the web browser that interprets the output of the web application, including any script content. It is not possible for the server to predict how the browser will interpret content, simply because there are a plethora of browsers, each of which interprets the web application's output in a different way (Section 5). WEBAPPARMOR therefore builds confinement techniques at the browser end to ensure model conformance. Therefore, for every web request, the browser receives any requested page accompanied by its model, along with (trusted) code that will assist the browser in enforcing this model. This is shown in the post-deployment view of the figure.

Web advertisements are third-party content that are integrated in the browser-side. We can neither expect nor trust third party sites to provide models, and therefore develop confinement techniques to enforce the web site's policy on advertisement content. An important point to note is that confinement code is written in JavaScript, and therefore can be supported by *existing browsers* without requiring any browser customization.

3   Preventing SQL Injection Attacks

In this section we present a technique to enforce models by construction to mitigate SQL Injection Attack (SQLIA). First, we leverage the insight gained by other researchers [49,15], that malicious inputs change the structure of SQL queries generated by the application. Therefore, it suffices to learn the query structure intended by the program to detect injection attacks. In specific, *parse tree structures of intended queries are the models that can aid in mitigation of SQLIA*. Second, to enforce the above model we transform programs to make use of PREPARE statements.

PREPARE statements. PREPARE statements, a facility provided by many database platforms, constitutes a robust defense against SQL injections. PREPARE statements are objects that contain pre-compiled SQL query structures (without data). PREPARE statements guarantee that data cannot alter structure of the pre-compiled SQL queries.

The key goal for our transformation is then to modify parts of the program that generate vulnerable queries to make use of PREPARE statements. Intuitively, such a transformation forces the application to generate model-complying code i.e., preserving structures of queries through PREPARE statements. Such a program transformation would ensure, without the overhead of additional monitoring, that attacks cannot be successful.

3.1   Problem Statement

Consider Figure 1 (a), which allows the user to search for a name. The following code snippet is used as a running example and handles this request at the server side: it applies a (filter) function (f) on the input ($u) and then combines it with constant strings to generate a query ($q). This query is then executed by a *SQL sink* (query execution statement) at line 6.

```
1. $u = input();
2. $q1 = "select * from X where uid LIKE '%";
3. $q2 = f($u); // f - filter function
4. $q3 = "%' order by Y";
5. $q = $q1.$q2.$q3;
6. sql.execute($q);
```

The running example is vulnerable to SQL injection if input $u can be injected with malicious content and the filter function f fails to eliminate it. For example, the user input ‹ ' OR 1=1 -- › provided as $u in the above example can list all users of the application. Typically, user inputs such as $u are expected to contribute as data literals in the queries and SQL injection attacks violate this expectation. The following is an equivalent PREPARE statement based program for the running example.

```
1. $q = "select...where uid LIKE ? order by Y";
2. $stmt = prepare($q);
3. $stmt.bindParam(0, "s", "%".f($u)."%");
4. $stmt.execute();
```

The question mark in the query string $q is a "place-holder" for the query argument %f($u)%. In the above example, providing the malicious input u = ' or 1=1 -- to the prepared query will not result in a successful attack as the actual query is parsed with these placeholders (prepare instruction generates PREPARE statement), and the actual binding to placeholders happens *after* the query structure is finalized (bindParam instruction). Therefore, the malicious content from $u cannot influence the structure of query.

The Transformation Problem. The desired changes to applications (especially large ones) are challenging and tedious to achieve through manual transformation. First,

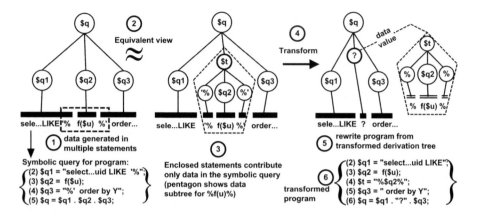

Fig. 2. TAPS SQL injection prevention: step (1) generates symbolic queries, steps (2-3) separate data reaching the queries, step (4) removes data from symbolic queries, and steps (5-6) generate the transformed program

depending on the control path a program may generate and execute different SQL queries at a sink. Such sinks need to be transformed such that each control path gets its corresponding PREPARE statement (intended model). Further, each such control flow may span multiple procedures and modules and thus requires inter-procedural analysis. Second, for each control flow query arguments must be extracted from the original program statements which requires tracking of all statements that may contribute to data arguments. In the running example, the query argument %f($u)% is generated at line 5, and three statements provide its value: f($u) from line 3, and enclosing character (%) from line 2 and 4, respectively.

3.2 Program Transformation for Model Enforcement

We first observe that the original program's instructions already contain the programmatic logic (in terms of string operations) to build the structure of its SQL queries. This leads to the crucial idea behind our approach, called TAPS [12]: *if we can precisely identify the program data variable that contributes a specific argument to a query, then replacing this variable with a safe placeholder string (?) will enable the program to programmatically compute the PREPARE statement at runtime.*

The problem therefore reduces to precisely identifying query arguments that are computed through program instructions. We solve this problem through symbolic execution. Intuitively, during any run, the SQL query generated by a program can be represented as a symbolic expression over a set of program inputs (and functions over those inputs) and program-generated string constants. For instance, by symbolically executing our running example program, the following symbolic query is obtained:

```
SELECT...WHERE uid LIKE '%f($u)%' ORDER by Y
```

Once we obtain the symbolic query, we analyze its parse structure to identify data arguments for the PREPARE statement. For our running example, we get the argument %f($u)%. Our final step is to traverse the program backwards to the program statements that generate these arguments, and modify them to generate placeholder (?) instead.

Now, we have changed a data variable of a program, such that the program can compute the body of the PREPARE statement at runtime.

In our running example, after replacing contributions of program statements that generated the query data argument %f($u)% with a placeholder (?), $q at line 5 contains the following PREPARE statement body at runtime:

```
SELECT...WHERE uid LIKE ? ORDER by Y, %$q2%
```

The corresponding query argument is the value %$q2%. Note that the query argument includes contributions from program constants (such as %) as well as user input (through $q2).

Approach overview. Figure 2 gives an overview of our approach for the running example. For each path in the web application that leads to a query, TAPS generates a derivation tree that represents the structure of the symbolic expression for that query. For our example, $q is the variable that holds the query, and step 1 of this figure shows the derivation tree rooted at $q that captures the query structure. The structure of this tree is analyzed to identify the contributions of user inputs and program constants to data arguments of the query, as shown in steps 2 and 3. In particular, we want to identify the subtree of this derivation tree that confines the string and numeric literals, which we call the *data subtree*. In step 4, we transform this derivation tree to introduce the place-holder value, and isolate the data arguments. This change corresponds to a change in the original program instructions and data values. In the final step 5, the rewritten program is regenerated. The transformed program programmatically computes the body of the PREPARE statement in variable $q and the associated argument in variable $t.

Conditional Statements. TAPS first individually transforms each control path that could compute a SQL query. To do so it creates program slices from System Dependency Graph. Once each individual path is transformed it then makes changes to the source code of the original program. One issue that arises while doing so is that of a *conflict*: when path P_1 and P_2 of a program share an instruction I that contributes to the data argument, and I may not undergo the same transformation in both paths. We detect such cases before making any changes to the program and avoid transformation of paths that may result in conflicts.

Loops. TAPS summarizes loop contributions using symbolic regular expressions. The goal is essentially to check if placeholder (?) can be introduced in partial SQL queries computed in loop bodies. Given the loop summary, we require that the loop contribution be present in a "repeatable" clause of the SQL grammar. To do so we require statements in the loop body to satisfy the following rules: (1) the statement is of the form $q \rightarrow x$ where x is a constant or an input OR (2) it is left recursive of the form $q \rightarrow qx$, where x itself is not recursive, i.e., resolves to a variable or a constant in each loop iteration. If these conditions holds, we introduce placeholders in the loop body. This strategy only covers a small, well defined family of loops. However, our evaluation suggests that it is quite acceptable in practice.

Limitations. TAPS requires developer intervention if either one of the following conditions hold: (i) program changes query strings containing placeholder (?) (ii) a well-formed SQL query cannot be constructed statically (iii) SQL query is malformed because of infeasible paths (iv) conflicts are detected along various paths (v) query is constructed in a loop that cannot be summarized.

Evaluation. We tested our prototype implementation on 9 open source applications (total 46900 Lines of Code). Out of the 227 analyzed sinks (a total of 803 control flows) we were able to transform 222 sinks (780 flows). The untransformed flows were contributed by: a) unhandled loops (18 flows) b) statically unavailable SQL queries (3 flows) and c) limitations of the SQL parser (2 flows). Our scheme successfully transformed 23 flows that computed queries in loops and satisfied the stipulated conditions. Our approach changed a small fraction of original lines of code as a result of this transformation (1.7%). We also assessed performance overhead on a microbench that manipulated varying sized query arguments. Over this stress test, we did not find any noticeable deviations in response times of the transformed and the original application.

Related work. Contemporary SQL injection defenses fall into two classes: (a) statically detect vulnerabilities [35,59] or (b) employ runtime monitoring to prevent attacks [14,15,49,60,41,25,44,11]. Static detection techniques do not offer prevention capabilities, and therefore require the involvement of a programmer. Prevention techniques forbid execution of a query that does not match the intended query's structure. Apart from performance overheads, these techniques make nontrivial changes to the program code and have motivated efforts to explore blackbox solutions[48].

In summary, our approach learns intended models (SQL query structures) and transforms the program to enforce this model by construction (through PREPARE statements). For a detailed treatment of the approach, we refer the reader to [12].

4   Cross Site Request Forgery (XSRF)

Background. Consider the Facebook running example. Say the user has successfully logged onto his / her Facebook account and the website has set a session cookie for authenticating subsequent requests. Say the web application embeds all peer images in the profile page of current user as shown in Figure 1 (B). Now consider the following URL:

```
<img src="http://myfacebook.com/s.php?action=edit&name=XSRF">
```

When the image tag is rendered on the user's browser, it generates an HTTP request back to the server with the URL specified by the *src* attribute. Since the destination of this request is the same domain, the client browser automatically sends the session cookie with the request (the browser sends cookies only with requests to the same domain). When the web application processes this request, it ends up defacing the user's profile title with an absurd value. This is the anatomy of a typical XSRF attack. Such a malicious URL can either be injected by an attacker on the Facebook web site or hosted by an attacker web site. Further, similar XSRF attacks can be launched via other HTML tags, e.g., <a>, <frame> , and <form> that can be automatically submitted via malicious JavaScript.

Related Work. XSRF attacks have received relatively less attention when compared to other web attacks. A common approach to defend XSRF attacks [29,30,62] is based on a secret token, which is a randomized number assigned to each session. A web request is considered to be intended only when it can provide both a valid session cookie and a valid secret token. For example, Jovanovic et al. [30] is a token-based defense that adopted a server side proxy based URL re-writing approach. Although effective, a major drawback is that a web proxy can not differentiate between application generated URLs from attacker injected URLs i.e., it would add secret tokens in, say an attacker injected XSRF URL as well, which would successfully satisfy the secret based checks. Another major drawback is that the secret token can be leaked at the client since the token is directly added to all URLs in HTML by the proxy. Once leaked, the token-based defense is no longer effective as the attacker can craft a malicious URL with the leaked token to pass the secret token check. Finally, the conventional wisdom to "disable JavaScript" to prevent attacks, does not apply to these attacks as XSRF URLs do not need to contain any scripts to be successful.

Approach Overview. The problem of XSRF is caused by a browser's inability to differentiate between the web application's generated (intended) and malicious (unintended) URLs, and web application's treatment of any request accompanied by a cookie as an intended request. We note that a browser does not have enough contextual information to make a distinction between unintended and intended requests, and resorts to include authenticated tokens such as cookies with all outgoing requests to a particular domain. It is the web application that is in a perfect position to determine all intended requests (i.e., URLs generated by it that do not involve untrusted content). This forms the basis of our defense in which a web application is transformed such that it can differentiate between intended and unintended requests through rewriting its intended URLs to make use of a secret token.

Our approach computes a model of intended URLs. Once computed, these intended URLs are augmented with a secret token to differentiate themselves from unintended URLs. A transformed web application then enforces conformance by requiring a correct token before complying with the client request. This prevents XSRF attacks as malicious requests will be unable to satisfy the conformance check. Further, the transformed web application transforms URLs present in HTML such that the secret token can not be leaked via URL sharing or several other means (to be discussed next) at the client.

Approach. The key idea to identify intended URLs that require the secret token is to identify the complementary set of URLs, i.e., URLs that do not require the secret token. Once they are determined, all remaining URLs in HTML are intended URLs. We categorize the complementary set of URLs into the following two types: (1) unintended URLs that are injected or influenced by user input, e.g., the malicious image URL given in the Facebook running example, and (2) intended public URLs that are side-effect free. Consider the following URL:

```
<a href="http://myfacebook.com/search.php?name=abc">Search</a>.
```

It allows any users to search for people, without requiring the web application to perform any private/sensitive operations. Adding the token to it is not only unnecessary but would also result in an unnecessary exposure of the token in URLs and hence increase chances of token leaks.

We identify URLs of the first type (injected) via standard information flow (taint) tracking techniques. The code that tracks the information flow is inserted in the web application code by our transformer in the pre-deployment phase, and then activated

```
1 | <script type="text/javascript"> ...
2 | function addToken(id) {
3 |   var st = ...;  // read token cookie to 'st'.
4 |   var elem = document.getElementById(id);
5 |   elem.href = elem.href + '?secretToken=' + st;    // add token
6 | } </script>
7 | <!-- An intended and private URL: transformed -->
8 | <a href="http://myfacebook.com/s.php?action=edit&name=user1"
9 |    id="alink1" onclick="addToken('alink1');"
10|    onmouseover="removeToken('alink1')">Edit</a>
```

Fig. 3. An example of a transformed HTML generated in an authenticated session (new code in bold)

in the post-deployment phase to separate the unintended URLs. To identify URLs of the second type (intended and public), we statically examine web application code in the pre-deployment phase as follows. Each application file's control flow is explored in an inter-procedural fashion. An application file that does not conduct an authentication check is identified as *public*. URLs that are handled by such files are public and hence will not be rewritten with the token.

Once the intended URLs in HTML are identified, we apply a novel technique to add the secret token to them. The key idea is to supply the secret token to URLs at the client on a *need* basis. It guarantees that the secret token never appears in HTML / JavaScript. Specifically, the transformed web application adds the conformance code written in JavaScript to the HTML, and then sends the transformed HTML to the un-modified browser. The JavaScript code, once invoked at the client, adds the secret token to the URLs. This scheme avoids unnecessarily supplying the token to all the intended URLs. Figure 3 shows an example of a transformed HTML containing a transformed URL. The token is added when the link is used. Note that the malicious injected image URL given in the Facebook example and the public search URL given above will not be transformed.

The motivation behind the above transformation is to prevent token leaks, e.g., through sharing of the URLs present in the client side code. This could happen in existing token-based XSRF defenses which transform the HTML by adding the secret token to all URLs. Our approach does not embed tokens directly in the client-side code but uses JavaScript to supply it at the client. The secret token is supplied to the client through the HTTP Set-Cookie header of the HTTP response when the authenticated session is established. Furthermore, we apply a technique to transform third-party URLs such that the token is not leaked through the HTTP REFERER header in requests to third-party servers.

Also, the web application code is transformed to perform model conformance checks for secret tokens before complying with the client request. As XSRF attacks aim to trigger the web application to perform private (i.e., sensitive) operations at the server, the code to check for validity of secret tokens will need to be inserted into the control flows that perform sensitive operations. We use the following observation to precisely place such checks: *sensitive operations can only be performed in authenticated sessions.* We thereby transform the web application in the pre-deployment phase by inserting the token checks to the code locations where authentication checks are performed. The sensitive operations are now protected by the secret token checks.

In comparison to checking the token on every request, a common method adopted by existing token-based defenses, our solution has two advantages: (1) it enables sharing public URLs among users and ensures the public resources' availability, as HTTP requests of public URLs are not checked for valid tokens, and (2) it avoids overprotecting the public resources accessed through public URLs.

Discussion. The presence of JavaScript poses additional problems for XSRF defense. XSRF URLs built by successful XSS attacks may get access to such hidden tokens. For instance, a script running in the page could read the token cookie. Our XSS defense (described in 5) is based on JavaScript rewriting of untrusted content and we combine the two defenses in our end-to-end framework. This combination will have a benefit that was not addressed in the prior work: to obtain robust XSRF prevention even in the presence of XSS attacks.

We also note that our solution does not prevent XSRF attacks in web applications that suffer from the *Authentication Bypass* problem. However, if the application is vulnerable to bypass, it can be exploited with a much simpler non-XSRF attack.

Evaluation. To evaluate the effectiveness and efficiency of our approach we implemented a tool, called X-PROTECT, and tested it on eight medium-sized *commercial* Java/JSP-based web applications. The tool transforms the web application in the pre-deployment phase and transforms URLs in HTML in the post-deployment phase. The experiments results indicate that X-PROTECT transformed applications effectively prevent XSRF attacks, as well as accept legitimate requests. Furthermore, the transformed applications prevent token leaks at the client side. X-PROTECT transformation led to a moderate increase in sizes of the class files which ranged from 22.2% - 24.5% and a moderate client-end response overhead which ranged from 7% - 22%..

5   Preventing Cross-Site Scripting Attacks

Background. We refer to Figure 1 (C). Consider the comments entered by peers to the Facebook profile. Say that the following code on the web application reproduces the comment from the variable u_comment.

```
out.println("<P>" +u_comment+"</P>");
```

Unfortunately, this code is vulnerable to XSS, as the comment field can contain scripting commands: e.g., <script>...stealCookie()...</script>. When such injected code executes in the client browser, it has full access to client-side content including sensitive client-side state such as cookies.

Removing unauthorized code. Similar to SQL injection, cross-site scripting is also a problem where untrusted "data" contributes to "code" (scripts). This raises the natural question of whether there is a clean way to isolate code from data and prevent

Table 1. Comparison of related work, listing advantages and disadvantages

Server Side Approaches	Advantages (A) Disadvantages (D)
Vulnerability Analysis Techniques [35,59,31,56,8]	**(A)** Can leverage on sound approaches for identifying vulnerable locations **(D)** Rely on filtering for defense
Unsafe data ("taint"-like) tracking [41,44,49,60,13]	**(D)** Output sanitized data to browser. Vulnerable to attacks exploiting browser flaws
Filtering [3,2,1]	**(A)** Ease of deployment **(D)** Hard to get filters right especially for free-form HTML. Need to anticipate browser behavior.
Browser-side impact mitigation [33,42]	**(A)** Savvy users can protect themselves **(D)** Do not protect against all XSS attacks (e.g. unauthorized bank transactions performed within the same origin, attacks on web page integrity)
Browser-server collaboration [28,47,53]	**(A)** Very precise, prevents all attacks **(D)** Does not work on shrink-wrapped browsers, requires *custom* browser changes, limits scalability; unsuitable from web-service provider perspective
BluePrint[51] Empowers web application to precisely enforce no-script policy	**(A)** Works for unmodified browsers **Challenge:** How to achieve desired attack prevention uniformly on all unmodified browsers? **(A)** Permit free-form HTML **Challenge:** To be permissive yet prevent unauthorized script execution?

cross-site scripting, similar to PREPARE statements for SQL injection. However, as shown in [13,36], the attack surface of this problem is much more varied and complex than that of SQL injection.

In prior work [36], we termed this the *Hypertext Isolation* problem and studied it in detail. Hypertext isolation is a *simple* facility that enables a web application to instruct a browser to mark certain portions of an HTML document as untrusted. If such facilities were available and supported by web browsers, cross-site scripting attacks can be prevented simply by disallowing script execution from these untrusted regions. For instance, "comment" sections in a blog, or "user reviews" of Amazon products are regions that contain untrusted content that could be ignored by a browser, thus offering a clean solution to XSS prevention.

In [36], we analyzed several possible proposals for addressing this problem, and compared them. We concluded that *there exists no satisfactory solution to the hypertext isolation problem that is supported by all of current browsers*. The draft version of upcoming HTML 5 standard [55] does not propose any hypertext isolation facility, even though XSS is a long recognized threat and several informal solutions have been suggested by concerned members of the web standards community. In the meantime, XSS has risen to become the top threat on the Internet.

Background. Recent research work in this area can be divided into two general approaches: (1) changing the web application to filter content to render safely in the browser (server side approach) or (2) changing the browser to render content safely (browser side approach). We show them visually in Table 1.

As shown in the figure, a majority of server side defenses rely on input filtering as the main line of defense. Reliance of filtering as the sole mechanism for preventing attacks is becoming problematic as applications allow users to input content-rich HTML such as blog and wiki entries. In this context, filtering faces a difficult challenge: allowing all safe HTML in user input, while blocking potentially harmful script input. Here, disallowing use of HTML control characters is not a practical solution, because every control character that can be used to introduce attack code also has a legitimate use in some safe, non-script context. For example, the < character needs to be present in links and text formatting, and the double-quote (") character needs to be present in generic text content. Both are legitimate user inputs and considered safe. Therefore, to safely accommodate user input that is allowed to contain HTML structure, filter functions have grown more sophisticated: instead of simply filtering control characters, they disallow suspicious character *sequences*. This is typically done by modeling such sequences through regular expressions. Yet, this technique is notoriously hard to get right, as any such regular expression must also incorporate browser behavior, as we show below.

A second issue that makes robust prevention of XSS attacks very challenging is the lack of agreement among various mainstream browsers in parsing HTML. As a consequence of this, a number of XSS attacks including Samy MySpace worm [46], have begun exploiting browser parsing "quirks", evading sanitization functions to launch successful XSS attacks. The reason for the presence of these quirks is partly due to the fact that browsers are built to forgive malformed HTML in web pages, in the interest of making web pages meaningful to end users even in the event of missing tags or broken links. However, this forgiving nature can be exploited to launch sophisticated XSS attacks. A large number of example input strings, employing quirks for various browsers that can launch successful XSS attacks, are documented at the *XSS Cheat Sheet* website [26]. The above two issues make filtering very challenging: *Constructing a sound filtering function that guarantees absence of script execution on all browsers, is an open research problem.*

Preventing attacks that exploit browser behavior purely from the server side is difficult due to the above two issues. Indeed, a browser is in the best possible position to anticipate such behavior, and precise prevention of XSS attacks can be achieved if client browsers could distinguish authorized from unauthorized scripts. This was the strategy used in BEEP [28], and this approach is fundamentally more sound than any of the filtering-based approaches discussed earlier. The biggest drawback of this approach is that it requires *custom* browser modifications, and therefore will not be supported by unmodified ("shrink-wrapped") browsers. Although the defense strategy proposed in BEEP is a noble long-term goal towards robust protection, the strategy leaves a large void in near-term protection. Web applications cannot presume all users will employ a customized browser. Agreement on standards and incorporating such standards in the normal browser revision cycle is a long, complicated process. Another objective is to derive a *browser-neutral* solution: one that works on currently-deployed, unmodified browsers. Summarizing our objectives:

> **Goal: Automated Prevention of Cross-Site Scripting Attacks.** The above discussion highlights the immediate need for a solution that:
>
> 1. *robustly protects* against XSS attacks, even in the presence of browser parsing quirks,
>
> 2. *supports* benign, structured HTML derived from untrusted user input, and is
>
> 3. *compatible* with existing browsers currently in use by today's web users.

Our Approach. Consider a web application that generates a web page to be rendered by web browser. The application accepts and processes user input that is embedded in the web page. The web application does not intend untrusted regions in the web page to contain scripts.

During the parsing process in the browser, this intention of web application may not be respected, as there is a threat that the browser may infer an unintended script, because untrusted characters are being examined by the browser's parsers (both HTML and JavaScript). Our goal is therefore to assist the web application to convey its intentions to browser (by supplying code for enforcing these intentions), and thereby enact a *precise no-script* policy over untrusted content.

Basic Idea. As noted earlier, there is no interface available in currently deployed web browsers for declaring the precise no-script policy to be enforced over untrusted page regions. Our objective is then to effectively create this interface using the low-level *Document Object Model* (DOM) primitives that are available on all browsers that support JavaScript. We first note that untrusted content needs to be parsed by the browser, and the decisions made in this process ultimately determine the scripts identified from this content. As noted above, we cannot entrust browsers with crucial parsing decisions on script identification. Our objective therefore is to enable a web application to effectively take control of parsing decisions. By systematically reasoning about the flow of untrusted HTML in a browser, we develop an approach that provides facilities for a web application to automatically enforce its intentions on the browser's interpretation process by supplying a "blueprint" - a parse tree of untrusted web content that is free of XSS attacks. Our approach is described in detail in [51].

Augmenting the web application. For the web application to become the decision-making authority over what content should be contained in an untrusted region, we first enable it to understand the syntactic structure (parse tree) of the region and remove any script elements from it. Our defense provides this ability to the server side application, by augmenting it with a lightweight standards compliant HTML parser along with a whitelist of static content types. The web application now needs to output this whitelisted content in a way that the JavaScript interpreter is never consulted on untrusted content.

As already mentioned, due to differences in parsing our parser may not share the actual browser's parsing view to arrive at the same syntax. To consider this, let us look at an example attack string from [26]:

```
<script src=http://de.xe/evil.js?<b>
```

This attack is successful on Firefox 2.0 and Netscape 8.1 (Gecko) browsers. It is unusual because it evades detection engines by employing (a) a script tag that is not terminated by > and (b) the absence of a matching close `</script>` tag. When untrusted content that contains the above text is given to some other parser on the server side, it will perhaps interpret all the above characters as text data, as it is not syntactically well-formed. However, if directly written to output and interpreted by Firefox or Netscape browsers, script content will result.

The crux of our approach is to take the model of this content (in the above case, a "text data" node), and convert it into actual web content on the target browser while taking away all parsing decisions from the target browser. In our approach, this is achieved by replacing the untrusted content with a simple script that invokes the Document Object Model (DOM) API to reconstruct the same parse structure as intended by the server. In the above example, the actual text will effectively be replaced by a call to `document.createTextNode()`.

In [51], we examine a browser's parsing process in detail to illustrate why the above approach works. In a typical browser, the HTML parser tokenizes all input and constructs the DOM. During this crucial process, script nodes are identified, and for any such nodes, the JavaScript interpreter is invoked. Our approach *avoids* the call to the JavaScript interpreter for untrusted content, essentially stripping this capability from the browser. Therefore, by construction, our approach never introduces any DOM nodes that trigger the JavaScript interpreter.

Essentially, our approach enables a web application to precisely program the browser to reproduce the safe approximation. Browser programming is performed using a very limited subset of the DOM API. We built a small lightweight JavaScript library that essentially reproduces all safe HTML without introducing script content. Calls to routines in this library are inserted by the web application in every location where untrusted output is generated for the browser.

Dual-use content types. The base whitelisting approach to content classification is sufficient to remove all script code from untrusted content. However, it eliminates some content types that are essential for practical reasons. It is hard to imagine web content without hyperlinks, but hyperlinks of the form `<a href="javascript:...">` can be used to execute malicious script code and thus need to be removed. Similarly, style rules are needed to express rich content. However, certain browsers (IE) will interpret script code if a style rule uses the form: `expression(...)`. Disallowing these two content types, URI and style rules, will significantly impact the expressiveness of untrusted content. Therefore our approach allows them, and we have developed techniques for transforming them into an equivalent form that still upholds the no-script policy of the web application. For further details, we refer the reader to [51].

Evaluation. Extensive experiments with BLUEPRINT demonstrate its strong resilience against subtle XSS attacks. At the time of testing, the growing XSS Cheat Sheet [4] contained 113 entries. Of these, we classified 94 entries as XSS attack examples, and the rest were non-XSS attacks. For each of the eight mainstream browsers (including Chrome, Opera, Safari, IE and Firefox), BLUEPRINT successfully defended all 94 XSS attacks, thus protecting these browsers from their own parsing quirks.

6 Preventing Confidentiality and Integrity Attacks from Untrusted Advertisements

Background. Another important problem that is faced by a vast majority of web sites is safe inclusion of third party advertisements. Business opportunities enabled through web based advertising have made advertisements an economic necessity in nearly every popular web site. However, the New York Times home page hijack [54] demonstrated the threat faced by every web application from rogue advertisements. We refer to the third-party advertisement shown in Figure 1 (D). It is displayed through third-party JavaScript that is enclosed in the HTML of the Facebook web page. The script has access to the DOM of the user's profile page, including sensitive client state such as cookies and private content such as user's personal images. A malicious ad script can therefore compromise the integrity and confidentiality of a user's profile page.

Main Issues. A mechanism that ensures web application security in the context of supporting ads needs to address the following additional issues: (1) be compatible with the current types of advertisements, (e.g., banner ads and inline ads) and (2) retain the same number of clicks and impressions which determines the revenue model of ads, and (3) allow for network targeting algorithms used by the ad network, and (4) preserve the user experience in interacting with ads to retain effectiveness in advertising.

Related Work. One solution is to eliminate scripts at the server, as done in cross-site scripting defenses. It, however, will eliminate the support for contextual targeting which is crucial for advertising revenues for web providers. It may also negatively impact the end-user experience due to the loss of client-side interactivity. Privads [24] and Adnostic [52] address this problem primarily from a end-user privacy perspective. There have been a number of works [18,17,34,37,38,20] in the area of JavaScript analysis that restrict content from ad networks to provide security protections. These works focus on limiting the JavaScript language features that untrusted scripts are allowed to use. Other approaches [45,61,32,22,40,19,43] have been pursued to transform untrusted JavaScript code to interpose runtime policy enforcement checks. Since these works are aimed at general JavaScript security, they are not specialized to the problem of securing ads for publishers, where the main issue is ensuring transparent interposition.

Approach Overview. We revisit the Facebook example. Let us say the publisher wishes to carry ads in Facebook application. To enable ads, the publisher embeds an ad network's JavaScript code within the HTML of the Facebook page. In the benign case, this JavaScript code scans the page displayed to find keywords for contextual targeting, then dynamically loads a relevant ad. For simplicity, we refer to the ad network's JavaScript and an advertiser's JavaScript (the latter loaded dynamically by the former) as *the ad script*.

The main idea behind our approach, called ADJAIL [50], is to confine the ad script to a hidden isolated environment (basically an invisible "iframe"). We then detect effects of the ad script that would normally be observable by the end user, had the script not been confined by the framework. These effects are replicated, subject to policy based constraints, outside the isolated environment for presentation to the user. Any user actions are then forwarded to the isolated environment to allow for a response by the ad script. Thus we facilitate a *controlled cycle* of interaction between the user and the advertisement, enabling dynamic ads while blocking several malicious behaviors in a manner transparent to users. In the rest of this section, we present the high level details of ADJAIL and sketch some of the basic research issues.

Ad confinement using shadow pages. In ADJAIL, the publisher wants to ensure ad script does not access the publisher's private data, as a basic policy. This private data may include any user session information (such as cookies), any private information (such as address book). Such data is normally accessible via the browser's document object model (DOM) script interfaces.

To enforce the publisher's policy, we leverage on browser enforcement of the *same-origin policy* (SOP) [57], an access control mechanism available in all major JavaScript-enabled browsers. Web browsers enforce the SOP to prevent mutually distrusting web sites from accessing each others JavaScript code and data. As a script instantiates code and data items, the browser places each item under the ownership of the script's *origin* principal. Whenever a script references code or data, both the script and item being accessed must be owned by the same origin, else access is denied.

To enforce the publisher's ad script policy, we begin by removing the ad script from the publisher's page. Next, we embed a hidden `<iframe>` element in the page. This `<iframe>` has a different origin URI, thus invoking the browser's SOP and thereby imposing a code and data isolation barrier between the contents of the `<iframe>` and enclosing page. Finally, we add the ad script to the page contained in the hidden `<iframe>`. We refer to the hidden `<iframe>` page as the *shadow page*, and the enclosing Facebook page as the *real page*. This transformation just described is depicted in the figure below:

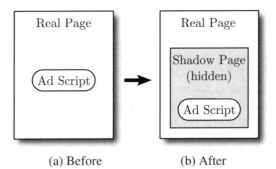

(a) Before   (b) After

In the process of rendering the real page, the browser will now render the shadow page, executing the ad script within. Our use of the SOP mechanism effectively relegates this ad script to an isolated execution environment. All access by ad script to script code or data in the real page will be blocked due to enforcement of the SOP. Furthermore, the ad script can not retrieve confidential data via DOM interfaces, as access to those API are denied by SOP. We can now say the publisher's basic policy is enforced if (1) all such ad scripts are relocated to the shadow page, and (2) the browser correctly enforces the SOP.

Controlled user interaction with ads. Consider an ad script that loads a product image, or *banner*. Normally the banner appears on the real page, but since the ad script runs in the shadow page, the banner is rendered on the shadow page instead. Without further steps, the user viewing the real page will never see this banner because the shadow page is hidden. In our approach, the user is able to interact with the shadow page ad by content mirroring and event forwarding, subject to policy based constraints in our framework, as discussed below.

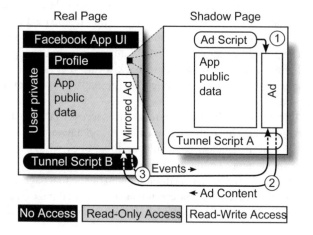

Fig. 4. Overview of ADJAIL integrated with a Facebook application. Ad script is given read-only access to public data on web pages for contextual targeting purposes. Ad script can write to designated area to right of public ad content. Confidential data such as user profile and address book are inaccessible to ad script.

A detailed view of the real page and shadow page that depicts mirroring of ad content in our framework is shown in Figure 4. We add a tunnel script (A) to the shadow page that monitors page changes made by the ad script (1), and conveys those changes (2) to the real page via inter-origin message conduits [9,27]. We add a complementary tunnel script (B) to the real page that receives a list of shadow page changes and replicates their effects on the real page. Thus when ad script creates a banner image on the shadow page, Tunnel Script A sends a description of the banner to Tunnel Script B, which then creates the banner on the real page for the end user to see.

Event forwarding. Ads sometimes respond in complex ways to user generated events such as mouse movement and clicks. To facilitate this interaction, ADJAIL captures relevant events on mirrored ad content and forwards these events (Figure 4 (3)) to the shadow page for processing. If the ad script responds to the mouse-move event by altering the banner or producing new ad content, these effects need to be replicated on the real page by our mirroring strategy outlined above.

Ad policies. All information flow between the real page and shadow page needs to be mediated by our policy enforcement mechanism. This mechanism enforces policy rules which are specified by the publisher as annotations in the real page HTML. For the Facebook example in Figure 4, the following is an example of an access control policy being specified:

```
1  <div id="ProfileBody" policy="allow-read-subtree: true;">
2      Public web app data text here...
3  </div>
4  <div id="advertisement" policy="allow-write-subtree: true;"></div>
```

Note that the policy is on the nodes in the DOM tree specified by their ids. The policy in line 1 allows the ad script read-only access to the public app data on the real page. Read-only access is enforced by initially populating the shadow page with content from the real page (ref. App public data in Figure 4). If ad script makes changes to read-only content, those changes must not be mirrored back to the real page. Any attempts to mirror those changes to the real page public data (perhaps by a compromised Tunnel Script A) are denied.

The policy in line 4 permits the ad script read-write access to the sidebar on the right of the public web app data. This is the region where the ad banner is to appear. When ad script creates content in the shadow page sidebar, this policy will allow our mirroring logic to reproduce that content on the real page sidebar.

Our policy enforcement mechanism is implemented on the real page as part of Tunnel Script B. As stated earlier, the ad script can not access the real page (including Tunnel Script B) due to SOP enforcement. Therefore ad script can not tamper with our policy enforcement mechanism.

Other Issues. To monitor policy nodes in the shadow page for changes, we need an effective way to realize these changes. One approach is to use mutation events [5], but this facility is not available across all browsers. We therefore use a simpler DOM interposition strategy for mirroring changes.

The two-way synchronization introduces a host of different issues related to event triggers and references. For example, advertisements often contain background images specified through CSS styles, and we need to enable this synchronization to preserve user experience. (A naive, second HTTP request to retrieve this background image may not preserve the number of impressions.) Similarly, inline ads pose a different set of challenges. These ads display a small (pop-up) box when the mouse is moved over the relevant text, usually underlined. The main issue here is to preserve the scroll position, geometry and layout when content is mirrored back to the real page. We refer to [50] for a discussion on these issues.

Evaluation. We implemented the ADJAIL prototype, including the policy language used to restrict ads, code to construct real and shadow pages, and code to facilitate interaction between the two pages. We then tested ADJAIL on six popular ad networks. The experimental results demonstrated that ADJAIL is compatible with these mainstream ad networks. We then performed a security evaluation that tested the prototype with many different attacks. ADJAIL was shown to be effective in preventing these threats. Our performance evaluation revealed that ADJAIL caused acceptable performance overheads.

7   Conclusion

In this paper, we surveyed the results developed in the WEBAPPARMOR framework. The various research efforts in this framework address some of the most serious threats faced by web applications today. While our framework offers robust protection against these well-known threats, there are other relatively less explored threats on web applications for which such prevention measures are challenging. One example is that of business logic vulnerabilities, and our ongoing work [10] extends WEBAPPARMOR towards the direction of automatically detecting and preventing these vulnerabilities.

Acknowledgments

We thank Prasad Sistla for his contributions to SQL injection research surveyed in this paper. Thanks are due to Megha Chauhan and Rohini Krishnamurti for their contributions and implementation support for this research. This work was partially supported by National Science Foundation grants CNS-0551660, ITR-0716498, CNS-0716584, CNS-0845894, and CNS-0917229, .

References

1. htmLawed: PHP Code to Purify & Filter HTML, http://www.bioinformatics.org/phplabware/internal_utilities/htmLawed/ (retrieved on October 10, 2010)

2. kses - PHP HTML/XHTML filter, http://sourceforge.net/projects/kses/ (retrieved on October 10, 2010)

3. PHP Input Filter, http://sourceforge.net/projects/phpinputfilter/ (retrieved on October 10, 2010)

4. XSS (Cross Site Scripting) Cheat Sheet. Esp: for filter evasion, http://ha.ckers.org/xss.html (retrieved on October 10, 2010)

5. DOM mutation events. W3C draft (November 2003)

6. 16th Annual Network & Distributed System Security Symposium, San Diego, California, USA (February 2009)

7. TJX Hacker Charged With Heartland, Hannaford Breaches (August 2009), http://www.wired.com/threatlevel/2009/08/tjx-hacker-charged-with-heartland (retrieved on October 10, 2010)

8. Balzarotti, D., Cova, M., Felmetsger, V., Jovanovic, N., Kirda, E., Kruegel, C., Vigna, G.: Saner: Composing Static and Dynamic Analysis to Validate Sanitization in Web Applications. In: Proceedings of the 29th IEEE Symposium on Security and Privacy, SP 2008, Oakland, California, USA (2008)

9. Barth, A., Jackson, C., Mitchell, J.C.: Securing Frame Communication in Browsers. In: Proceedings of the 17th Conference on Security Symposium, SS 2008, San Jose, California, USA (2008)

10. Bisht, P., Hinrichs, T., Skrupsky, N., Bobrowicz, R., Venkatakrishnan, V.N.: NoTamper: Automatic Blackbox Detection of Parameter Tampering Opportunities in Web Applications. In: Proceedings of the 17th ACM Conference on Computer and Communications Security, CCS 2010, Chicago, Illinois, USA (2010)

11. Bisht, P., Madhusudan, P., Venkatakrishnan, V.N.: CANDID: Dynamic Candidate Evaluations for Automatic Prevention of SQL Injection Attacks. ACM Trans. Inf. Syst. Secur. 13(2), 1–39 (2010)

12. Bisht, P., Prasad Sistla, A., Venkatakrishnan, V.N.: Automatically Preparing Safe SQL Queries. In: Proceedings of the 14th International Conference on Financial Cryptography and Data Security, FC 2010, Tenerife, Canary Islands, Spain (2010)

13. Bisht, P., Venkatakrishnan, V.N.: XSS-GUARD: Precise Dynamic Prevention of Cross-Site Scripting Attacks. In: Zamboni, D. (ed.) DIMVA 2008. LNCS, vol. 5137, pp. 23–43. Springer, Heidelberg (2008)

14. Boyd, S.W., Keromytis, A.D.: SQLrand: Preventing SQL Injection Attacks. In: Jakobsson, M., Yung, M., Zhou, J. (eds.) ACNS 2004. LNCS, vol. 3089, pp. 292–302. Springer, Heidelberg (2004)

15. Buehrer, G., Weide, B.W., Sivilotti, P.A.G.: Using Parse Tree Validation to Prevent SQL Injection Attacks. In: Proceedings of the 5th International Workshop on Software Engineering and Middleware, SEM 2005, Lisbon, Portugal (2005)

16. Symantec Corporation. Symantec internet security threat report. Technical report, Symantec Corporation (March 2008)

17. Crockford, D.: ADsafe, http://www.adsafe.org/ (retrieved on October 10, 2010)

18. Facebook Developers. Facebook JavaScript,
http://wiki.developers.facebook.com/index.php/FBJS
(retrieved on October 10, 2010)

19. Felt, A., Hooimeijer, P., Evans, D., Weimer, W.: Talking to Strangers Without Taking Their Candy: Isolating Proxied Content. In: Proceedings of the 1st Workshop on Social Network Systems, SNS 2008, Glasgow, Scotland (2008)

20. Finifter, M., Weinberger, J., Barth, A.: Preventing Capability Leaks in Secure JavaScript Subsets. In: Proceedings of the 17th Network and Distributed System Security Symposium, NDSS 2010, San Diego, California, USA (2010)

21. Fisher, D.: Hackers broaden reach of cross-site scripting attacks (March 2007),
ComputerWeekly.com

22. Caja, G.: A source-to-source translator for securing JavaScript-based web content, http://code.google.com/p/google-caja/ (retrieved on October 10, 2010)

23. Grossman, J.: Cross site scripting worms and viruses. Technical report, WhiteHat Security Inc. (June 2007)

24. Guha, S., Cheng, B., Reznichenko, A., Haddadi, H., Francis, P.: Privad: Rearchitecting online advertising for privacy. Technical Report MPI-SWS-2009-004, Max Planck Institute for Software Systems, Kaiserslautern-Saarbruecken, Germany (October 2009)

25. Halfond, W.G.J., Orso, A., Manolios, P.: Using Positive Tainting and Syntax-aware Evaluation to Counter SQL Injection Attacks. In: Proceedings of the 14th ACM SIGSOFT International Symposium on Foundations of Software Engineering, FSE 2006, Portland, Oregon, USA (2006)

26. Hansen, R.: XSS cheat sheet, http://ha.ckers.org/xss.html (retrieved on October 10, 2010)

27. Jackson, C., Wang, H.J.: Subspace: Secure cross-domain communication for web mashups. In: Proceedings of the 16th International Conference on World Wide Web, WWW 2007, Banff, Alberta, Canada (2007)

28. Jim, T., Swamy, N., Hicks, M.: Defeating Script Injection Attacks with Browser-enforced Embedded Policies. In: Proceedings of the 16th International Conference on World Wide Web, WWW 2007, Banff, Alberta, Canada (2007)

29. Johns, M., Winter, J.: RequestRodeo: Client Side Protection against Session Riding. In: Proceedings of the OWASP Europe 2006 Conference, OWASP-APPSEC 2006, Leuven, Belgium (2006)

30. Jovanovic, N., Kirda, E., Kruegel, C.: Preventing Cross Site Request Forgery Attacks. In: Proceedings of the 2nd IEEE Communications Society International Conference on Security and Privacy in Communication Networks, SecureComm 2006, Baltimore, Maryland, USA (2006)

31. Jovanovic, N., Kruegel, C., Kirda, E.: Pixy: A Static Analysis Tool for Detecting Web Application Vulnerabilities (Short Paper). In: Proceedings of the 2006 IEEE Symposium on Security and Privacy, SP 2006, Oakland, California, USA (2006)
32. Kikuchi, H., Yu, D., Chander, A., Inamura, H., Serikov, I.: JavaScript Instrumentation in Practice. In: Ramalingam, G. (ed.) APLAS 2008. LNCS, vol. 5356, pp. 326–341. Springer, Heidelberg (2008)
33. Kirda, E., Kruegel, C., Vigna, G., Jovanovic, N.: Noxes: A Client-side Solution for Mitigating Cross-site Scripting Attacks. In: Proceedings of the 21st ACM Symposium on Applied Computing, SAC 2006, Dijon, France (2006)
34. Benjamin Livshits, V., Guarnieri, S.: Gatekeeper: Mostly Static Enforcement of Security and Reliability Policies for JavaScript Code. In: Proceedings of the 18th USENIX Security Symposium, SS 2009, Montreal, Canada (2009)
35. Benjamin Livshits, V., Lam, M.S.: Finding Security Vulnerabilities in Java Applications with Static Analysis. In: Proceedings of the 14th USENIX Security Symposium, SS 2005, Baltimore, Maryland, USA (2005)
36. Louw, M.T., Bisht, P., Venkatakrishnan, V.N.: Analysis of Hypertext Markup Isolation Techniques for XSS Prevention. In: Workshop on Web 2.0 Security and Privacy (W2SP), W2SP 2008, Oakland, California, USA (2008)
37. Maffeis, S., Mitchell, J.C., Taly, A.: Language-Based Isolation of Untrusted JavaScript. In: Proceedings of the 22nd IEEE Computer Security Foundations Symposium, CSF 2009, Port Jefferson, New York, USA (2009)
38. Maffeis, S., Mitchell, J.C., Taly, A.: Run-Time Enforcement of Secure JavaScript Subsets. In: Web 2.0 Security and Privacy, W2SP 2009, Oakland, California, USA (2009)
39. McFeters, N.: Multiple facebook vulnerabilities reported on full-disclosure. Zero-Day Vulnerabilities blog (July 2008)
40. Microsoft Live Labs. Web Sandbox, http://websandbox.livelabs.com (retrieved on October 10, 2010)
41. Nguyen-Tuong, A., Guarnieri, S., Greene, D., Shirley, J., Evans, D.: Automatically Hardening Web Applications using Precise Tainting. In: Proceedings of the 20th IFIP Conference on Information Security, SEC 2005, Makuhari-Messe, Chiba, Japan (2005)
42. Vogt, P., Nentwich, F., Jovanovic, N., Kirda, E., Kruegel, C., Vigna, G.: Cross-Site Scripting Prevention with Dynamic Data Tainting and Static Analysis. In: Proceedings of the 14th Annual Network & Distributed System Security Symposium, NDSS 2007, San Diego, CA, USA (2007)
43. Phung, P.H., Sands, D., Chudnov, A.: Lightweight self-protecting JavaScript. In: Proceedings of the 4th ACM Symposium on Information, Computer and Communications Security, ASIACCS 2009, Novotel Rockford Darling Harbour, Sydney, Australia (2009)
44. Pietraszek, T., Berghe, C.V.: Defending Against Injection Attacks through Context-Sensitive String Evaluation. In: Valdes, A., Zamboni, D. (eds.) RAID 2005. LNCS, vol. 3858, pp. 124–145. Springer, Heidelberg (2006)
45. Reis, C., Dunagan, J., Wang, H.J., Dubrovsky, O., Esmeir, S.: BrowserShield: Vulnerability-driven filtering of dynamic HTML. In: Proceedings of the 7th USENIX Symposium on Operating Systems Design and Implementation, OSDI 2006, Seattle, Washington, USA (2006)
46. Samy. I'm popular. Description of the MySpace worm by the author, including a technical exaplanation (2005), http://namb.la/popular (retrieved on October 10, 2010)
47. Saxena, P., Song, D., Nadji, Y.: Document Structure Integrity: A Robust Basis for Cross-site Scripting Defense. In: Proceedings of 16th Annual Network & Distributed System Security Symposium, NDSS 2009, San Diego, California, USA (2009)
48. Sekar, R.: An Efficient Black-box Technique for Defeating Web Application Attacks. In: Proceedings of the 16th Annual Network and Distributed System Security Symposium, NDSS 2009, San Diego, California, USA (2009)

49. Su, Z., Wassermann, G.: The Essence of Command Injection Attacks in Web Applications. In: Proceedings of the 33rd Symposium on Principles of Programming Languages, POPL 2006, Charleston, South Carolina, USA (2006)
50. Louw, M.T., Ganesh, K.T., Venkatakrishnan, V.N.: AdJail: Practical Enforcement of Confidentiality and Integrity Policies on Web Advertisements. In: Proceedings of the 19th USENIX Security Symposium, SS 2010, Washington, DC, USA (2010)
51. Louw, M.T., Venkatakrishnan, V.N.: Blueprint: Robust Prevention of Cross-site Scripting Attacks for Existing Browsers. In: Proceedings of the 30th IEEE Symposium on Security and Privacy, SP 2009, Oakland, California, USA (2009)
52. Toubiana, V., Narayanan, A., Boneh, D., Nissenbaum, H., Barocas, S.: Adnostic: Privacy Preserving Targeted Advertising. Technical report
53. Van Gundy, M., Chen, H.: Noncespaces: Using Randomization to Enforce Information Flow Tracking and Thwart Cross-site Scripting Attacks. In: Proceedings of the 16th Annual Network & Distributed System Security Symposium, NDSS 2009, San Diego, California, USA (2009)
54. Vance, A.: Times Web Ads Show Security Breach. NY Times (September 2009) (retrieved on October 10, 2010)
55. World Wide Web Consortium (W3C). HTML 5: A vocabulary and associated APIs for HTML and XHTML (working draft) (January 2008), http://www.w3.org/TR/2008/WD-html5-20080122/
56. Wassermann, G., Su, Z.: Static Detection of Cross-site Scripting Vulnerabilities. In: Proceedings of the 30th International Conference on Software Engineering, ICSE 2008, Leipzig, Germany (2008)
57. Wikipedia contributors. Same origin policy (February 2008), http://en.wikipedia.org/w/index.php?title=Same_origin_policy&oldid=190222964
58. World Internet Usage Statistics. Internet bulletin (March 2008), http://www.internetworldstats.com/stats.htm
59. Xie, Y., Aiken, A.: Static Detection of Security Vulnerabilities in Scripting Languages. In: Proceedings of the 15th USENIX Security Symposium, SS 2006, Vancouver, BC, Canada (2006)
60. Xu, W., Bhatkar, S., Sekar, R.: Taint-Enhanced Policy Enforcement: A Practical Approach to Defeat a Wide Range of Attacks. In: Proceedings of the 15th USENIX Security Symposium, SS 2006, Vancouver, BC, Canada (2006)
61. Yu, D., Chander, A., Islam, N., Serikov, I.: JavaScript instrumentation for browser security. In: Proceedings of the 34th Annual ACM Symposium on Principles of Programming Languages, POPL 2007, Nice, France (2007)
62. Zeller, W., Felten, E.W.: Cross-site request forgeries: Exploitation and prevention. Technical report, Princeton University (Fall 2008)
63. Zhou, M., Bisht, P., Venkatakrishnan, V.N.: Strengthening XSRF Defenses for Legacy Web Applications Using White-box Analysis and Transformation. In: 6th International Conference on Information Systems Security, ICISS 2010 (December 2010) (to appear)

Toward Securely Programming the Internet

Andrew C. Myers

Department of Computer Science, Cornell University, Ithaca NY 14853, USA
andru@cs.cornell.edu
http://www.cs.cornell.edu/andru

Abstract. Computation and persistent storage are rapidly moving into the distributed domain. Yet we are offered very weak security and privacy assurance, especially as complex information systems share information across trust boundaries. A fundamental problem is that these systems are contructed at too low a level of abstraction. Higher-level abstractions are needed for building complex distributed information systems securely and composably.

Fabric [1] is a new decentralized platform that embodies this approach. Heterogeneous, mutually distrusting network nodes can securely share both information and computation. Its high-level programming language makes distribution and persistence largely transparent to programmers. However, its Java-like object model is extended to label data resources with explicit confidentiality and integrity policies. Exposing these policies to programmers and to the underlying run-time system enables programmers to reason about security, and enables the system to enforce them through a combination of compile-time and run-time mechanisms. Optimistic, nested transactions ensure consistency across all objects and nodes. A peer-to-peer dissemination layer helps to increase availability and to balance load. Results from applications built using Fabric suggest that Fabric has a clean, concise programming model, offers good performance, and enforces security.

Reference

1. Liu, J., George, M.D., Vikram, K., Qi, X., Waye, L., Myers, A.C.: Fabric: a platform for secure distributed computation and storage. In: Proc. 22nd ACM Symp. on Operating System Principles (SOSP), pp. 321–334 (October 2009)

S. Jha and A. Maturia (Eds.): ICISS 2010, LNCS 6503, p. 27, 2010.
© Springer-Verlag Berlin Heidelberg 2010

Attribution of Malicious Behavior

Jonathon Giffin and Abhinav Srivastava

School of Computer Science
Georgia Institute of Technology
Atlanta, Georgia, United States
{giffin,abhinav}@cc.gatech.edu

Abstract. Internet-connected computer systems face ongoing software attacks. Existing defensive solutions, such as intrusion detection systems, rely on the ability to identify malicious software (malware) in order to prevent its installation. This approach remains imperfect, resulting in widespread, persistent malware infections, malicious execution, and transmission of undesirable Internet traffic. Over the past several years, we have begun to develop solutions that help computer systems automatically recover from unknown malicious software infections by identifying and disabling the software. Our work departs from previous malware analysis because it employs strict post-infection analysis matching real-world environments: it assumes that security monitoring does not exist during the critical malware installation time and identifies potentially malicious software infecting a system given only observations of the infected system's execution. This paper reports on our progress attributing undesirable network behavior to malicious code and highlights upcoming research challenges we expect to face as we begin to automatically excise that code from infected systems.

1 Introduction

Worldwide computer systems continue to execute malicious software that degrades the systems' performance delivered to their legitimate users, consumes network capacity by generating high volumes of unwanted traffic, and damages the usability of network services and email for other computer users connected to the Internet. Prevention systems designed to disallow the installation of malicious software have failed to prevent its proliferation. The problem now shifts to that of managing and controlling the infections. Network-based detectors can effectively identify machines participating in the ongoing attacks by monitoring the traffic to and from the systems. Detection alone, however, does not improve the operation of the Internet or the health of other machines connected to the network, and it does not reduce the production of unwanted network traffic and load. We require remediation and repair of the individual machines infected with the malicious software participating in global attack networks.

Remediation is inherently a local problem. Just as the original installation of the malicious software was on a victim host, a principled response to the software must also be at the host. Local remediation disables unknown malicious

S. Jha and A. Maturia (Eds.): ICISS 2010, LNCS 6503, pp. 28–47, 2010.
© Springer-Verlag Berlin Heidelberg 2010

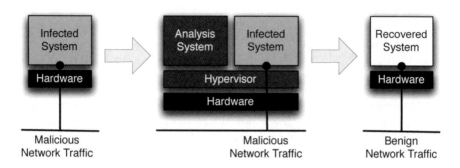

Fig. 1. Overview of attack attribution and system recovery

software on infected systems while retaining benign system functionality and data, which excludes the trivial solution of a complete system reset and reinstall. This constraint allows recovery in environments that are not professionally managed; for example, an Internet service provider (ISP) could provide such a recovery service to their clients. Correcting the underlying malicious software infection rather than suppressing the externally visible symptoms of the infection has clear benefit. Remediation will diminish email spam traffic, diminish junk data in the Internet, reduce the volume of lost personal information, and reduce wasted execution on systems.

Over the past several years we have been developing technologies leading towards local, automated recovery from attacks. Our ultimate goal, not yet reached, is to reclaim infected systems, reduce unwanted computational load on the systems, and reduce garbage traffic on networks by disabling or disrupting an attack's functionality. We leverage the effectiveness of network-based infected machine identification to establish a ground truth for an infection: whatever on the system is sending or receiving the malicious traffic identified by the network system participating in an infection. Once existing network-based detection systems flag a system as infected, our techniques then identify software components on the system that comprise the malicious software installation. Online monitoring of the infected system's execution allows our analysis to attribute the undesirable network traffic to the software components comprising the infection (Fig. 1). We use virtualization technology to create both a protected domain for our software and an unprotected domain that hoists the infected system into a virtual machine. Our attribution analysis is similar to forensic analysis, but it focuses on identifying unknown attacks rather than on preserving information for legal use.

This paper reports on our significant progress addressing the preliminary problems of remediation: attributing observed malicious behaviors to malicious software components installed on infected systems. We have created complex cross-domain monitoring systems—*VMwall*, *Pyrenée*, and *Gateway*—that track the execution of an infected system from a safe, isolated virtual machine. We identify sophisticated attacks that install malicious kernel modules or drivers and alter the normal execution of benign processes via code injection and thread injection. We create a new, uncircumventable monitoring interface within a kernel's address space allowing our attack attribution analysis software to trace the execution of untrusted kernel drivers.

Numerous challenges will arise in the next steps: successful remediation of Internet-scale attacks given the attribution information computed using the techniques described in this paper. In the closing sections of this paper, we consider three challenges. (1) Attacks that add unsafe plugins into benign software like a web browser must have their components correctly identified, otherwise remediation will produce an erroneous result. (2) We must track malicious data to and from the network through operating system, library, application, and plugin software. (3) The recovered system should be robust against future reinfection by the same attack, even though we may have no knowledge of the attack's entry point into the system or of the actual nature of the attack itself beyond its network functionality. As we pursue solutions to those research challenges in coming years, we hope to advance understanding of malware behavior, improve virtual machine based analysis, and infer unobserved historical activity from current behavior.

2   Overview

Our final goal is to design strategies and systems to recover computer systems infected with persistent malicious software. *Persistent malware* has fundamental characteristics: it executes continuously, often as a background process of which the computer system's user is unaware, and it restarts its execution upon system reboot. Persistent malware encompasses many of the attacks comprising today's malware pandemic, including bots, worms, and spyware. Persistence is a basic property of the software, as each installation represents a resource that provides the human attacker with computational power, network connectivity, and confidential data. As a resource, each system has monetary value to the attacker, and the attacker retains her wealth by maintaining her installed malware. System recovery from infection targets the malicious software's need to remain persistent.

The complete infection analysis and recovery system is comprised of numerous components. To date, we have implemented three components related to the attribution of observed malicious network behaviors to undesirable, unknown software on an infected system. Section 3 presents an overview of *VMwall*, a technology that maps malicious network flows to processes responsible for sending or receiving data in those flows. When malware includes kernel-mode components, traditional execution monitors are incapable of tracking code execution behaviors, so we developed *Gateway* to facilitate execution tracing of in-kernel modules or drivers (Sect. 4). Processes at the end of a malicious flow may be benign applications subverted by malware via a variety of code injection attacks. *Pyrenée*, described in Sect. 5, identifies these parasitic behaviors. We expect these components to be suitable to commodity computer systems that regularly become infected with malware, and we work in both Windows and Linux environments.

Attack analysis and attribution commences after network-based detection systems identify some visible symptom of the infection. The owner or administrator of the victim system will then reboot into a external bootable medium containing the complete analysis and recovery system. The system boots into a virtual machine environment [3] that executes a hypervisor on the native hardware and two virtual machines (VMs) atop the hypervisor (Fig. 1). One machine, the *security domain*, executes with full system privilege and contains the attack attribution logic. Once initialized, the security domain then boots the original, infected system as a second, unprivileged virtual machine. Since the privileged VM booted first, its analyzer is able to monitor the complete boot-time and run-time operation of the infected system, though it has no clean-state reference system available for comparison.

The attack analyzer monitors and logs the execution behavior of the infected system. Any operation visible outside of the operating system may be captured by the analyzer. For example, system calls issued by applications executing in the unprivileged VM can be intentionally redirected through the privileged domain for logging [41]. All network activity in the infected system passes through a virtual network interface that is, in reality, instrumentable software executing in the privileged domain. The set of events generated by the unprivileged domain and observable at the forensic analyzer provide a coarse view of the domain's execution activity.

Presumably, the persistent malware installed in the infected system restarts its execution shortly after the unprivileged domain is booted. As the malware again sends and receives malicious network traffic, the network-based detector will see evidence of the infection. The detector then informs the infection analysis system which specific network flows triggered detection. The analyzer must then identify the software components in the infected system responsible for the malicious traffic: this is the actual attribution of responsibility for the observed undesirable behaviors.

Infection remediation, not yet implemented in our prototype, then attempts to restore normal execution properties of the unprivileged domain. Our plan is for it to automatically generate a candidate recovered system by disabling the functionality of each component in the set produced by the attribution analysis. Automatic hypothesis testing then allows the remediator to verify the correctness of the recovery. It will reboot the unprivileged domain into the candidate system. The attack analyzer can again monitor the system's execution; when normal system functionality remains present but network-based detectors find no malicious network traffic, then the candidate system was a correct restoration. Recovery failures propagate backward and force the remediator to produce a new candidate. The cycle continues until reaching correctness.

3   Process Attribution

Many persistent attacks that consume or produce unwanted Internet traffic execute as standalone applications on the machines that they have infected. For

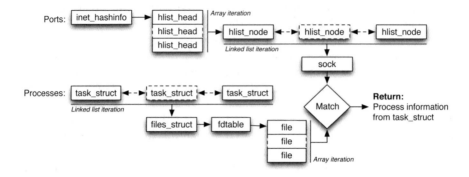

Fig. 2. Data structure traversal to correlate network flows to process endpoints in Linux

example, bots participating in a botnet are often processes that execute as daemons or network server software. Our attack analysis and remediation system identifies the malicious application as part of the infection. In the absence of malicious kernel components that alter kernel information, the analyzer makes use of kernel data when correlating malicious traffic to malicious software.

A *network attribution sensor* called *VMwall* maps network-level packet information to host-level process identities [55]. Given a network sensor (NIDS) alert for some suspicious traffic flow, the network attribution sensor determines which process is the local endpoint of that flow in the untrusted VM. This process may be malicious, or it may be a benign process altered by a parasitic malware infection (discussed in Sect. 5).

VMwall identifies the process that is the endpoint of a flow by parsing and interpreting kernel data structures. As VMwall executes in a different virtual protection domain, its kernel state inspection will build upon the principles of virtual machine introspection: the extraction of state information from the memory state of a separate virtual machine. Figure 2 shows an example of state inspection for the Linux 2.6 kernel. By traversing the data structures corresponding to executing processes and to sockets bound to connections, the analyzer is able to identify the specific process communicating using the malicious network data. State inspection is surprisingly efficient and appears to be a promising approach: our measurements show overheads of just several hundred microseconds per flow or connection establishment.

Correlation of network traffic to processes in common real-world infection analysis scenarios is less straightforward than Fig. 2 might suggest. Traversing kernel data structures requires knowledge of the kernel's data layout. Many attacks occur against versions of the Windows operating system, and virtual machine introspection is then complicated by the closed nature of commercial kernels. We make use of debug symbol information available for Windows kernels to provide the initial hooks into their data structures, and we apply reverse engineering to determine how to parse the kernel data needed to perform correlation.

3.1   Virtualization-Based Security

Our design makes use of virtual machine technology to provide isolation between malicious code and our security software. We use Xen [3], an open source hypervisor that runs directly on the physical hardware of a computer. The virtual machines running atop Xen are of two types: unprivileged domains, called domU or guest domains, and a single fully-privileged domain, called dom0. We run normal, possibly vulnerable software in domU and deploy VMwall network attribution sensor in the isolated dom0.

The strong isolation provided by a hypervisor between dom0 and the guest domains complicates the ability to correlate network flows with software executing in a guest domain. Yet, dom0 has complete access to the entire state of the guest operating systems running in untrusted virtual machines. *Virtual machine introspection* (VMI) [17] is a technique by which dom0 can determine execution properties of guest VMs by monitoring their runtime state, generally through direct memory inspection. VMI allows security software to remain protected from direct attack by malicious software executing in a guest VM while still able to observe critical system state.

XenAccess [71] is a dom0 userspace introspection library for Xen developed by researchers at the Georgia Institute of Technology. VMwall uses XenAccess APIs to map raw memory pages of domU's kernel inside dom0. It then builds higher-level memory abstractions, such as aggregate structures and linked data types, from the contents of raw memory pages by using the known coding semantics of the guest operating system's kernel.

VMwall uses virtual machine introspection to attribute observed network packets to responsible processes. It receives introspection requests from the network intrusion detection system containing network information such as source port, source IP address, destination port, destination IP address, and protocol. It first uses the packet's source (or destination) IP address to identify the VM that is sending (or receiving) the packet. When it finds the VM, it then tries to find the process that is bound to the source (or destination) port.

3.2   Parsing Kernel Data Structures

One of the principle challenges in successful use of VMI is correctly comprehending the contents of raw domU memory. To identify processes using the network, VMwall must parse high-level kernel data structures from the raw memory pages provided by XenAccess. Process and network information is not available in a single data structure but instead is scattered over many data structures. VMwall works in steps by first identifying the domU kernel data structures that store IP address and port information. Then, it identifies the process handling this network connection by iterating over the list of running processes and checking each process to see if it is bound to the port. When it finds the process bound to the port, it extracts the process' identifier, its name, and the full path to its executable.

This provides VMwall with sufficient information to traverse kernel data structures. VMwall uses known field offsets to extract the virtual addresses of pointer field members from the mapped memory pages. It then maps domU memory pages by specifying the extracted virtual addresses. This process is performed recursively until VMwall traverses the data structures necessary to extract the process name corresponding to the source or destination port of a network communication. Figure 2 shows the list of the kernel data structures traversed by the user agent to correlate a TCP packet and process information. First, it tries to obtain a reference to the socket bound to the port number specified in the packet. After acquiring this reference, it iterates over the list of processes to find the process owning the socket. Finding the correct process completes the attribution of network behaviors to processes.

4   Kernel-Space Monitoring

The view of malicious software comprised of a single user-space application, as taken in Sect. 3, is overly simplistic. More generally, malware may contain kernel-mode software such as Linux kernel modules and Windows filter drivers. Indeed, the expectation that malicious code will execute within the kernel is a primary motivator for the attack attribution system's isolation in a separate virtual machine. Kernel-mode malware complicates attack component analysis. Straightforward correlation of malicious network traffic with a process sending or receiving that traffic will identify a benign process as the endpoint—as an example, connections with no receiving process often appear to be owned by the init process. This situation is troubling, as we may unknowingly include benign software as part of the attack.

Malicious kernel-level activity is already happening. For example, srizbi implements a full spam client with command-and-control in a single kernel-mode driver [32,63], and the lvtes keylogger is just a kernel-mode driver intercepting users' keystrokes [8]. These *full kernel malware* [34] instances evade software execution monitors that track process' behavior at the system call interface: they invoke kernel functionality with function calls from a driver rather than with system calls from a process. In order to observe the behavior of kernel-mode malware and correctly attribute malicious activity, security software instead must additionally monitor the function-call interface between drivers and the core kernel.

Our solution improves the view of the execution monitor so that it can identify kernel components participating in an infection. In upcoming work [57], we will present a kernel driver behavioral monitor called *Gateway* that interposes on all kernel APIs invoked by untrusted drivers, passes information regarding their invocations asynchronously to a higher-level security monitor, and ensures complete mediation so that malicious drivers cannot escape observation. Gateway's monitoring provides an analysis foundation for kernel-mode malware components in the same way that system call monitoring allows malicious processes to be traced. In fact, our Pyrenée component, discussed next, builds on the monitoring facilities provided by Gateway in order to track certain on-host malicious activity.

5   Identifying Process Manipulation

Malware instances exhibit complex behaviors designed to prevent discovery or analysis by defensive utilities. Malicious software often subverts the normal execution of benign processes by modifying their in-memory code image via various injection attacks. For example, the Conficker worm injects undesirable dynamically linked libraries (DLLs) into legitimate software [65]. In another example, the Storm worm injects code into a user-space network process from a malicious kernel driver to initiate a DDoS attack from the infected computers [45]. These manipulative *parasitic* actions help malware execute behaviors—such as spam generation, denial-of-service attacks, and propagation—without themselves raising suspicion. When analyzing a misbehaving system to identify and eradicate malware, it is important both to terminate maliciously-acting but benign processes and to find other software that may have induced the malicious activity.

We augment our network attribution sensor (VMwall, Sect. 3) with automatic identification of evasive parasitic behaviors via a *host attribution sensor* called *Pyrenée* [56]. When paired with VMwall, Pyrenée correlates network-level events with host-level activities, so it applies exclusively to attacks that send or receive detectably-suspicious traffic. However, the additional inclusion of Pyrenée allows us to effectively detect parasitic behavior occurring both from user and kernel malware.

A process can suffer from parasitic behaviors either from another process or an untrusted kernel driver. To counter that, the host-attribution sensor monitors the execution of both user-level processes and untrusted kernel drivers. Pyrenée monitors system calls and their parameters invoked by processes to detect the process-to-process parasitic behavior. To detect untrusted drivers' parasitic DLL and thread injection behaviors,we contain untrusted drivers in an isolated address space from the kernel. This design provides Pyrenée with the ability to monitor kernel APIs invoked by untrusted drivers and enables it to detect parasitic behaviors originating from the untrusted drivers.

5.1   Parasitic Malware Behaviors

Parasitic malware alters the execution behavior of existing benign processes as a way to evade detection. These malware often abuse both Windows user and kernel API functions to induce parasitic behaviors. We consider a malware parasitic if it injects either executable code or threads into other running processes. The parasitic behaviors can originate either from a malicious user-level process or a malicious kernel driver. Table 1 lists the different cases in which malware can induce parasitic behavior.

User-level parasitism occurs when a malicious user process injects a DLL or raw code along with a thread into a running benign process as explained in Cases 1A and 1B. To detect a process-to-process parasitic behavior, Pyrenée continuously monitors the runtime behavior of all processes executing within the victim VM by intercepting their system calls [21,16]. On Windows systems, note that we monitor the *native API*, or the transfers from userspace to kernel space,

Table 1. Different parasitic behavior occurring from user- or kernel-level

Number	Source	Target	Description
1A	Process	Process	DLL and thread injection
1B	Process	Process	Raw code and thread injection
2A	Kernel driver	Process	DLL and thread alteration
2B	Kernel driver	Process	Raw code and thread alteration
2C	Kernel driver	Process	Kernel thread injection

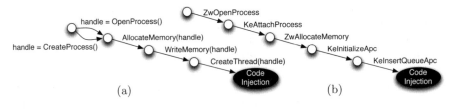

(a)   (b)

Fig. 3. Runtime parasitic behavioral models for Windows. (a) Process-to-process injection. (b) Driver-to-process injection.

rather than the userspace API. High-level API monitors are insecure and may be bypassed by knowledgeable attackers, but native API monitoring offers complete mediation for user-level processes. Pyrenée uses an automaton description of malware parasitism to determine when DLL or thread injection occurs. The automaton (Fig. 3a) characterizes the series of system calls that occur during an injection.

Kernel-level parasitism occurs when a malicious kernel driver injects either a DLL or raw code followed by the alteration of an existing targeted process' thread (Cases 2A and 2B). A kernel-level malicious driver can also create a new thread owned by any process as explained in Case 2C. To detect kernel-to-process parasitic behavior, the host attribution sensor monitors all kernel APIs invoked by untrusted drivers. However, there is no monitoring interface inside the kernel for drivers similar to the system-call interface provided to user applications. To solve this problem, Pyrenée builds on top of the in-kernel monitoring API provided by Gateway.

Due to the isolated address space created by Gateway, Pyrenée intercepts all kernel APIs invoked by untrusted drivers. As with user-level parasitic behaviors, the sensor uses an automaton to characterize the parasitic behavior originating from malicious drivers. In our current prototype, we create an automaton based on the kernel asynchronous procedure call based code injection (Fig. 3b).

5.2   Component Aggregation

The three components—VMwall, Gateway, and Pyrenée—act cohesively as a unit to attribute observed malicious network behaviors to responsible processes (Fig. 4). A network intrusion detection system identifies inbound or outbound network traffic of suspicion; we use off-the-shelf network intrusion detection

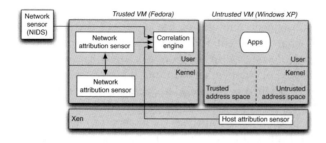

Fig. 4. Architecture for attack attribution in the possible presence of parasitic malware behavior

systems (NIDS) like BotHunter [26], Snort, or Bro. The VMwall network attribution sensor and the Pyrenée host attribution sensor are software programs executing in the isolated high-privilege dom0 virtual machine and Xen hypervisor, respectively. Pyrenée relies on the domU kernel space monitoring functionality provided by Gateway to identify kernel-to-user parasitic behaviors. A correlation engine, also running in the trusted dom0, then aggregates data from both network attribution and host attribution to determine the malicious software present in the victim.

6 Related Developments

Our work attributing observations of malicious behaviors to the software responsible for those actions bridges many aspects of software security. Here, we list other research developments in forensic analysis, malware analysis, information flow tracking, virtual machine based protections, and attack recovery.

6.1 Post-Mortem Forensic Analysis of Attacks

Several projects have produced forensic analysis systems designed to determine how an installed attack initially entered the system. ReVirt [13] allowed an analyst to study the execution of an intrusion in order to gain comprehension of the malicious software's behavior. The system logged fine-grained, system-wide execution properties that would allow replay of the period of execution during which installation of malicious software occurred; logging must begin while the system is in a clean state so that installation behavior may be recorded. BackTracker [35] automated the ReVirt analysis. Starting from evidence of an intrusion, such as a malicious file, BackTracker identified files and processes that could have affected the detection point. Working backward through log information, the system determined the attack's entry point into the system. As with ReVirt, BackTracker required continuous, pervasive log information beginning with a clean system; these logs totaled over 1 GB of data per system per day.

Systems reliant upon event logs must ensure that log information is free from tampering. Forensix [23] monitored all actions on a system in a manner similar to ReVirt and BackTracker, but it used offsite storage for log security. As with BackTracker, subsequent analysis of the database then revealed how attacks operated. Goel et al. [24] created dependency rules among files, processes, and sockets based on information in the Forensix logs to characterize data flows in a manner similar to our dependency graph. These rules then propagated data from a manually specified set of unsafe processes to files in the file system. By reverting the file system to an earlier, clean state and replaying all non-malicious events recorded in the log, the authors could then rebuild the clean file system.

Elsaesser and Tanner [14] developed an analysis system that did not require extensive logging. Given a description of the victim system, a list of its vulnerabilities, the unauthorized access gained by an attacker, and templates of possible exploits, they suggested possible ways that the attack could have occurred. Although this system dispensed with event logging, it instead required predefined specifications of system vulnerabilities and exploits. This is an unusual requirement: it suggested that users and administrators were aware of the vulnerabilities in their software and the types of exploits against those vulnerabilities, but chose not to patch the flaws. Instead, they retained the vulnerability information for use only after an attack occurred.

Some systems include human input to better guide the discovery of the root cause of an attack. Stallard and Levitt [58] encoded common manual forensic analysis procedures as expert rules amenable to automation. Gladyshev and Patel [22] modeled a complete computer system as a finite state machine describing the possible ways in which the system may execute, and they then exhaustively explored all paths in the state machine to find those that reach an unsafe state. Stephenson [59] determined underlying root causes of attacks using extensive manual work, including interviews with users and administrators, log analysis, and operational policy analysis.

Forensic analysis used for legal purposes often centers around collecting and analyzing dumps of main memory [7, 36, 48, 52, 53, 54, 61] or file system images [5]. Memory analyzers knowledgeable of system-wide memory layout have better ability to determine attack state than analyzers that treat memory as an unstructured byte array. Researchers have considered the ability to make use of predefined specifications of kernel data structures [6, 11, 67] on both Linux and Windows victim systems. Although previous forensic analysis of memory operated offline on dump files, the analyses are similar to our online virtual machine introspection.

6.2 Malicious Code Analysis

Where forensic analysis attempts to identify malware based on observed behaviors, malware analysis instead uses a malware instance to determine its likely behaviors. Malware analysis today primarily uses runtime monitoring to discover behaviors due to the reverse engineering protections employed by malware to defeat static analysis. Virtual machines provide convenient testing platforms on which analysts can safely execute malware and log its activity [50,2]. By starting with the virtual machine in a known clean state, then all changes induced during execution of the malware can be attributed to the malware itself, an analysis approach called baselining [43].

Baselining is ultimately not a workable general solution in our environment. We expect that realistic deployments of infection recovery systems will not have a clean reference system available for comparison. We must discover components of an installed attack and its alterations to the file system based only on the infected system itself. For specific uses, baselining may be able to provide evidence of an infection's behavior. For example, an attack that alters or overwrites a system library file leaves the altered file on the system. Subsequent analysis could compare all known system libraries against a database of known legitimate versions of each library; any file not matching a known version may have been damaged by the attack.

Other malware understanding tools [70] have also been built upon virtualization technology. Dinaburg et al. [10] developed an analysis system that, among other functionality, traced the execution of system calls in a manner similar to Pyrenée. Martignoni et al. [40] proposed a system that built a model of high-level malware behavior based upon observations of low-level system calls; like that system, Pyrenée uses a high-level characterization of DLL and thread injection identified via low-level system-call monitoring. Our current system does not employ the performance-costly taint analysis used by Martignoni, though as we pursue solutions to additional open remediation problems, fine-grained taint analysis may be unavoidable.

6.3   Information Flow Analysis

Plausible solutions to open research problems centered around identification of malicious sub-components of processes will likely leverage information flow analysis. Panorama [73] used a software program's information access and processing behavior to identify malware. The research observed that a fundamental property of privacy-breaching malware, such as spyware, key loggers, sniffers, backdoors, and rootkits, was their suspicious use of confidential data. The system detected malware with that trait by executing suspect software in a clean environment, providing test inputs to the environment meant to represent secret data, and monitoring the software's execution to see if it spied on the data. In a similar way, BotSwat [60] used coarse information flow analysis to detect bots based on their command-response behavior. The system used taint analysis to determine if data input from the network to a suspect program is passed as an argument to a subsequent system call. Panorama and BotSwat are malware analysis systems used as detectors of privacy violating software and command-response malware.

Other uses of taint analysis have arisen. TaintBochs [9] augmented the Bochs emulator with taint analysis to determine the length of time that confidential data remained in memory. Jiang et al. [27,28] used taint analysis to detect worms propagating in real time. That system, which must execute before the worm infection begins, identified attacks that self-propagate by exploiting vulnerabilities in network service software. Newsome and Song [44] developed TaintCheck, a system that can detect exploits against software flaws and, with the aid of the exploit instance, can then create an intrusion detection signature that prevents further use of the exploit.

6.4   Virtual-Machine Based Protections

With the burgeoning availability of hardware supported virtualization [12], many security solutions are employing virtual machines as part of their design [49, 17, 69, 18, 4, 38, 31, 51, 20, 69, 19, 68, 13]. Pyrenée requires the ability to observe behaviors occurring in the victim system's virtual machine. Recent research [30, 29] developed execution monitors for software executing in separate virtual machines. Other work [41] adapted traditional process tracing at the system call interface to the virtual machine environment by ensuring that security software in the protected domain remains able to follow the stream of system calls invoked by applications in the insecure system.

While the system call interface provides a good view of system-level activity in the victim, we require the ability to perform more detailed execution tracing. Payne et al. [47] pioneered a new technique that allowed security software to insert hook operations into the victim system while benefiting from protections against removal by any malicious code executing in the victim. This design allowed arbitrary instrumentation in the victim and opens the fine-grained visibility needed for our analysis.

Gateway uses virtualization to create isolated memory regions on an infected host, separating a kernel from untrusted drivers in the same address space. Other isolation solutions built on foundations other than virtual machines. Nooks [62] confined drivers to a separate address space using hardware page protection. Its goal was fault isolation; a malicious driver could easily bypass its protection. Vx32 [15] and NaCl [72] isolated applications' extensions in sandboxed environments to protect the applications' code and data from malicious extensions, and they used segmentation and programming language techniques to prevent extensions from breaking out of the sandbox.

6.5   Infection Recovery

Recovery proposals exist in other contexts. Ammann et al. [1] restored damaged portions of databases after malicious transactions have been committed. Although this appears to be a different problem domain, the lessons of the work have relevance to operating system infection recovery. The Microsoft Windows Vista operating system provided transactional file system operations with semantics similar to database transactions [46]. A defensive system similar to that of Ammann et al. could conceivably be used to recover a file system damaged by the installation of malicious software. Likewise, Tripathy and Panda [66] recovered data deleted from databases by maintaining a log of operations performed against the database. Grizzard et al. [25] restored a kernel's system call dispatch table after it became overwritten by kernel-mode rootkit. Szor [64] studied possible responses to virus attacks, including termination of virus processes.

Our infection analysis ultimately modifies the system to disable components of a persistent attack. Other attack recovery strategies have been proposed.

The Microsoft Windows Malicious Software Removal Tool [42] is a commercially deployed system that removes specific instances of malicious software preprogrammed into the utility. Although the widespread use of the tool provides the opportunity for great impact upon installed malicious software, the limitation to a small number of known instances diminishes its usefulness. Other commercial anti-virus and anti-spyware systems have the same drawbacks. Consider that the high number of infected systems in the Internet today exists in spite of these commercial tools; clearly alternative infection remediation technologies are needed.

7   Next Steps: From Attribution to Remediation

This paper has summarized our currently completed work attributing observed network behaviors to the responsible malicious code installed on an infected system. Looking forward, we are reaching a point in the project where we will transition from analysis to action. As we begin to develop remediation strategies, we anticipate new challenges to arise. We conclude the paper with a presentation of three research areas where we expect to find difficulty.

7.1   Identification of Malicious Application Components

Complexities of user-space applications complicate the identification of malicious software participating in a network attack. Common applications, most notably web browsers, feature plugin- or addon-based architectures that allow for arbitrary code inclusion at application runtime. An otherwise benign application may exhibit malicious behavior if it loads an unsafe plugin or addon during its execution, a property common to browser-based spyware. Other attacks may overwrite benign system libraries with trojaned versions containing malicious functionality. Applications using such libraries may then generate malicious behaviors when invoking altered library functions. However, the attack remains in the library and not in the application. When observing execution at the granularity of processes, included code appears to be indistinct from the core application. Such a granularity will prevent our system from separating the actual attack code from the benign application, and there is no injection action for Pyrenée to identify. It is likely that we must analyze software at finer granularity.

Analysis and instrumentation of executable software combined with runtime virtual machine introspection (VMI) may provide the fine-grained visibility. Instrumentation added to the application will reveal precisely what code is loaded during actual use of the software. When alerted to the presence of attack traffic by a network-based detector, the attribution software can then use *application-level VMI* to peer into the runtime state of the process to determine what component generated or will use the network data. When the component is a library loaded by the application during its execution, then only the plugin need be included as a component of the infection.

7.2 Disabling of Suspect Code

Once the attribution system identifies the components of a malware infection, then an *infection remediator* can begin *automated hypothesis testing* to restore legitimate operation of the system. The remediator produces a hypothesis, that is, the expectation that a set of components, when disabled, will prevent malicious execution while permitting benign execution. It tests the hypothesis by deactivating the components and restarting the unprivileged virtual machine. Once the system boots into the candidate recovered system, we again monitor the system's execution. We verify that symptoms of the attack disappear: the NIDS should no longer generate alerts from the network traffic inbound to and outbound from the candidate. We verify that legitimate functionality remains: applications should execute without error. If the hypothesis test succeeds, then the remediator makes the alteration permanent. If the test fails, then it must revise the hypothesis based on the type of failure. For example, the malware may regenerate itself from a file on disk not originally included as part of the infection.

7.3 Reinfection Prevention

Recovery from an attack disables a particular installed instance of the attack. The underlying flaw that permitted the attack to gain a foothold on the system likely remains. A subsequent reinfection may occur if it is possible for the system to return to the same malicious state as in the original instance. We would like system recovery to prevent reinfection by producing a repaired system not susceptible to the same attack. This has a medical analogue: exposure to an attack instance inoculates the system to further attempted attacks. If successful, this provides a step towards self-healing systems, assisted, of course, by the network-based detection of the original infection.

However, reinfection prevention is not straightforward. Our assumption that recovery begins after a system has become infected by the attack implies that the recovery software has no visibility over the events causing the attack to enter the system. There are a myriad of possibilities; for example, a network service program could have a programming flaw, any document processing application could erroneously handle local files received as email attachments, an email reader itself could be flawed, and so on. Previous research into self-healing software [37,33,39] focused on automated repairs to specific types of programming flaws, commonly buffer overflows. With no knowledge of the attack's point-of-entry, we cannot apply those prior solutions to this new problem. While BackTracker [35] determined the entry point of attacks, it required fine-grained system logging operating before and during the installation of the attack; this does not coincide with our design requirements. To further complicate reinfection prevention, the attack may establish itself on a system through non-technical means. It may entice the human user of the system into executing the malicious installation program via social engineering practices. Solutions to such environments may require always-active monitoring of a sort similar to that of currently deployed commercial anti-virus utilities.

8   Conclusions

We are considerably better at detecting Internet-scale malware infections then we are at preventing their installation. Victim systems hosting malicious software reveal themselves as they participate in subsequent malicious behavior. Network-based detection systems can identify infected machines participating in organized activity by detecting the symptoms of the attack, the communication fundamental to organizing a collection of systems into a single network, or the propagation of malicious software from system-to-system. Network-based detection can determine which systems are infected, but it cannot heal the systems or the Internet traffic. In response to this need, we developed three components that when aggregated, permit attribution of malicious network traffic identified by a NIDS back to responsible processes on infected systems. This technology provides the foundation for subsequent development of automated remediation for unknown attacks of unknown origin.

Acknowledgements

This material is based upon work supported by National Science Foundation contract number CNS-0845309. Any opinions, findings, and conclusions or recommendations expressed in this material are those of the authors and do not reflect the views of the NSF or the U.S. Government.

References

1. Ammann, P., Jajodia, S., Liu, P.: Recovery from malicious transactions. IEEE Transactions on Knowledge and Data Engineering 14(5) (September/October 2002)
2. Bailey, M., Oberheide, J., Andersen, J., Mao, Z.M., Jahanian, F., Nazario, J.: Automated classification and analysis of internet malware. In: Kruegel, C., Lippmann, R., Clark, A. (eds.) RAID 2007. LNCS, vol. 4637, pp. 178–197. Springer, Heidelberg (2007)
3. Barham, P., Dragovic, B., Fraser, K., Hand, S., Harris, T., Ho, A., Neugebauer, R., Pratt, I., Warfield, A.: Xen and the art of virtualization. In: ACM Symposium on Operating System Principles (SOSP), Bolton Landing, NY (October 2003)
4. Borders, K., Zhao, X., Prakash, A.: Siren: Catching evasive malware. In: IEEE Symposium on Security and Privacy, Oakland, California (May 2005)
5. Brumley, D., Song, D.: Privtrans: Automatically partitioning programs for privilege separation. In: USENIX Security, San Diego, California (August 2004)
6. Burdach, M.: Digital forensics of the physical memory. Whitepaper, Secure Network Systems, LLC (March 2005)
7. Carrier, B., Grand, J.: Hardware-based memory aquisition procedure for digital investigations. Journal of Digital Investigations 1(1) (2004)
8. Chakrabarti, A.: An introduction to Linux kernel backdoors, http://www.infosecwriters.com/hhworld/hh9/lvtes.txt (last accessed August 05, 2010)

9. Chow, J., Pfaff, B., Garfinkel, T., Christopher, K., Rosenblum, M.: Understanding data lifetime via whole system simulation. In: 13th USENIX Security Symposium, San Diego, California (August 2004)
10. Dinaburg, A., Royal, P., Sharif, M., Lee, W.: Ether: Malware analysis via hardware virtualization extensions. In: ACM Symposium on Computer and Communications Security (CCS), Alexandria, Virginia (October 2008)
11. Dolan-Gavitt, B.: The VAD tree: A process-eye view of physical memory. In: Digital Forensic Research Workshop (DFRWS), Pittsburgh, Pennsylvania (August 2007)
12. Dong, Y., Li, S., Mallick, A., Nakajima, J., Tian, K., Xu, X., Yang, F., Yu, W.: Extending Xen* with Intel Virtualization Technology. Intel Technology Journal 10(3) (August 2006)
13. Dunlap, G.W., King, S.T., Cinar, S., Basrai, M.A., Chen, P.M.: ReVirt: Enabling intrusion analysis through virtual-machine logging and replay. In: Operating Systems Design and Implementation (OSDI), Boston, Massachusetts (December 2002)
14. Elsaesser, C., Tanner, M.C.: Automated diagnosis for computer forensics. Tech. rep., The MITRE Corporation (September 2001)
15. Ford, B., Cox, R.: Vx32: Lightweight user-level sandboxing on the x86. In: USENIX Annual Technical Conference (ATC), Boston, Massachusetts (June 2008)
16. Forrest, S., Hofmeyr, S.A., Somayaji, A., Longstaff, T.A.: A sense of self for UNIX processes. In: IEEE Symposium on Security and Privacy, Oakland, California (May 1996)
17. Garfinkel, T., Rosenblum, M.: A virtual machine introspection based architecture for intrusion detection. In: Network and Distributed System Security Symposium (NDSS), San Diego, California (February 2003)
18. Garfinkel, T., Rosenblum, M., Boneh, D.: Flexible OS support and applications for trusted computing. In: 9th Hot Topics in Operating Systems (HOTOS), Lihue, Hawaii (May 2003)
19. Garfinkel, T., Rosenblum, M., Boneh, D.: Flexible OS support and applications for trusted computing. In: 9th Hot Topics in Operating Systems (HOTOS), Lihue, Hawaii (May 2003)
20. Garnkel, T., Pfaff, B., Chow, J., Rosenblum, M., Boneh, D.: Terra: A virtual machine-based platform for trusted computing. In: ACM Symposium on Operating Systems Principles (SOSP), Bolton Landing, New York (October 2003)
21. Giffin, J., Jha, S., Miller, B.: Detecting manipulated remote call streams. In: 11th USENIX Security Symposium, San Francisco, California (August 2002)
22. Gladyshev, P., Patel, A.: Finite state machine approach to digital event reconstruction. Digital Investigation Journal 1(2) (May 2004)
23. Goel, A., Feng, W.-c., Maier, D., Feng, W.-c., Walpole, J.: Forensix: A robust, high-performance reconstruction system. In: 2nd International Workshop on Security in Distributed Computing Systems (SDCS), Columbus, Ohio (June 2005)
24. Goel, A., Po, K., Farhadi, K., Li, Z., de Lara, E.: The Taser intrusion recovery system. In: 20th ACM Symposium on Operating System Principles (SOSP), Brighton, United Kingdom (October 2005)
25. Grizzard, J., Levine, J., Owen, H.: Re-establishing trust in compromised systems: Recovering from rootkits that trojan the system call table. In: Samarati, P., Ryan, P.Y.A., Gollmann, D., Molva, R. (eds.) ESORICS 2004. LNCS, vol. 3193, pp. 369–384. Springer, Heidelberg (2004)
26. Gu, G., Porras, P., Yegneswaran, V., Fong, M., Lee, W.: BotHunter: Detecting malware infection through IDS-driven dialog correlation. In: 16th USENIX Security Symposium, Boston, Massachusetts (August 2007)

27. Jiang, X., Buchholz, F., Walters, A., Xu, D., Wang, Y., Spafford, E.H.: Tracing worm break-in and contaminations via process coloring: A provenance-preserving approach. IEEE Transactions on Parallel and Distributed Systems 19(7) (July 2008)
28. Jiang, X., Walters, A., Buchholz, F., Xu, D., Wang, Y., Spafford, E.: Provenance-aware tracing of worm break-in and contaminations: A process coloring approach. In: 26th IEEE International Conference on Distributed Computing Systems (ICDCS), Lisboa, Portugal (July 2006)
29. Jiang, X., Wang, X.: Out-of-the-box monitoring of VM-based high-interaction honeypots. In: Kruegel, C., Lippmann, R., Clark, A. (eds.) RAID 2007. LNCS, vol. 4637, pp. 198–218. Springer, Heidelberg (2007)
30. Jiang, X., Wang, X., Xu, D.: Stealthy malware detection through VMM-based 'out-of-the-box' semantic view. In: ACM Symposium on Computer and Communications Security (CCS), Alexandria, Virginia (November 2007)
31. Jones, S.T., Arpaci-Dusseau, A.C., Arpaci-Dusseau, R.H.: VMM-based hidden process detection and identification using Lycosid. In: ACM Workshop on Virtual Execution Environments (VEE), Seattle, Washington (March 2008)
32. Kasslin, K.: Evolution of kernel-mode malware, http://igloo.engineeringforfun.com/malwares/ Kimmo_Kasslin_Evolution_of_kernel_mode_malware_v2.pdf (last accessed August 05, 2010)
33. Keromytis, A.D.: Characterizing self-healing software systems. In: 4th International Conference on Mathematical Methods, Models and Architectures for Computer Networks Security (MMM-ACNS), St. Petersburg, Russia (September 2007)
34. Kasslin, K.: Kernel malware: The attack from within, http://www.f-secure.com/weblog/archives/ kasslin_AVAR2006_KernelMalware_paper.pdf (last accessed August 05, 2010)
35. King, S.T., Chen, P.M.: Backtracking intrusions. In: ACM Symposium on Operating System Principles (SOSP), Bolton Landing, New York (October 2003)
36. Kornblum, J.: Using every part of the buffalo in Windows memory analysis. Digital Investigation Journal (January 2007)
37. Liang, Z., Sekar, R., DuVarney, D.C.: Automatic synthesis of filters to discard buffer overflow attacks: A step towards realizing self-healing systems. In: USENIX Annual Technical Conference (ATC), Anaheim, California (April 2005)
38. Litty, L., Lagar-Cavilla, H.A., Lie, D.: Hypervisor support for identifying covertly executing binaries. In: USENIX Security Symposium, San Jose, California (August 2008)
39. Locasto, M.E., Sidiroglou, S., Keromytis, A.D.: Software self-healing using collaborative application communities. In: Network and Distributed Systems Security Symposium (NDSS), San Diego, California (February 2006)
40. Martignoni, L., Stinson, E., Fredrikson, M., Jha, S., Mitchell, J.C.: A layered architecture for detecting malicious behaviors. In: Lippmann, R., Kirda, E., Trachtenberg, A. (eds.) RAID 2008. LNCS, vol. 5230, pp. 78–97. Springer, Heidelberg (2008)
41. Meng, J., Lu, X., Dong, G.: A novel method for secure logging system call. In: IEEE International Symposium on Communications and Information Technology, Beijing, China (October 2005)
42. Microsoft: The Microsoft Windows malicious software removal tool, revision 49.0 (July 2008), http://support.microsoft.com/?kbid=890830

43. Monroe, K., Bailey, D.: System baselining—a forensic perspective, verion 1.3 (September 2006), http://ftimes.sourceforge.net/Files/Papers/baselining.pdf
44. Newsome, J., Song, D.: Dynamic taint analysis for automatic detection, analysis, and signature generation of exploits on commodity software. In: Network and Distributed System Security Symposium (NDSS), San Diego, California (February 2005)
45. OffensiveComputing: Storm Worm Process Injection from the Windows Kernel, http://www.offensivecomputing.net/?q=node/661 (last accessed April 15, 2010)
46. Olson, J.: NTFS: Enhance your apps with file system transactions. MSDN Magazine (July 2007), http://msdn.microsoft.com/en-us/magazine/cc163388.aspx
47. Payne, B.D., Carbone, M., Sharif, M., Lee, W.: Lares: An architecture for secure active monitoring using virtualization. In: IEEE Symposium on Security and Privacy, Oakland, California (May 2008)
48. Petroni, N., Walters, A., Fraser, T., Arbaugh, W.: FATKit: A framework for the extraction and analysis of digital forensic data from volatile system memory. Digital Investigation Journal 3(4) (December 2006)
49. Petroni Jr., N.L., Hicks, M.: Automated detection of persistent kernel control-flow attacks. In: ACM Symposium on Computer and Communications Security (CCS), Alexandria, Virginia (November 2007)
50. Rajab, M.A., Zarfoss, J., Monrose, F., Terzis, A.: A multifaceted approach to understanding the botnet phenomenon. In: Internet Measurement Conference (IMC), Rio de Janeiro, Brazil (October 2006)
51. Riley, R., Jiang, X., Xu, D.: Guest-transparent prevention of kernel rootkits with VMM-based memory shadowing. In: Lippmann, R., Kirda, E., Trachtenberg, A. (eds.) RAID 2008. LNCS, vol. 5230, pp. 1–20. Springer, Heidelberg (2008)
52. Ruff, N.: Windows memory forensics. Journal in Computer Virology 4(2) (May 2008)
53. Schultz, J.S.: Offline Forensic Analysis Of Microsoft Windows XP Physical Memory. Master's thesis, Naval Postgraduate School (September 2006)
54. Schuster, A.: Searching for processes and threads in Microsoft Windows memory dumps. In: Digital Forensic Research Workshop, DFRWS (2006)
55. Srivastava, A., Giffin, J.: Tamper-resistant, application-aware blocking of malicious network connections. In: Lippmann, R., Kirda, E., Trachtenberg, A. (eds.) RAID 2008. LNCS, vol. 5230, pp. 39–58. Springer, Heidelberg (2008)
56. Srivastava, A., Giffin, J.: Automatic discovery of parasitic malware. In: Jha, S., Sommer, R., Kreibich, C. (eds.) RAID 2010. LNCS, vol. 6307, pp. 97–117. Springer, Heidelberg (2010)
57. Srivastava, A., Giffin, J.: Efficient monitoring of untrusted kernel-mode execution. In: Network and Distributed System Security Symposium (NDSS), San Diego, California (February 2011)
58. Stallard, T., Levitt, K.: Automated analysis for digital forensic science: Semantic integrity checking. In: Omondi, A.R., Sedukhin, S.G. (eds.) ACSAC 2003. LNCS, vol. 2823. Springer, Heidelberg (2003)
59. Stephenson, P.: Modeling of post-incident root cause analysis. International Journal of Digital Evidence 2(2) (Fall 2003)
60. Stinson, E., Mitchell, J.C.: Characterizing bots' remote control behavior. In: 4th International Conference on Detection of Intrusions & Malware, and Vulnerability Assessment (DIMVA), Lucerne, Switzerland (July 2007)
61. Stover, S., Dickerson, M.: Using memory dumps in digital forensics. Login 30(6) (December 2005)

62. Swift, M.M., Bershad, B.N., Levy, H.M.: Improving the reliability of commodity operating systems. In: ACM Symposium on Operating System Principles (SOSP), Bolton Landing, New York (October 2003)
63. Symantec: Spam from the kernel: Full-kernel malware installed by mpack, http://www.symantec.com/connect/blogs/ spam-kernel-full-kernel-malware-installed-mpack (last accessed August 05, 2010)
64. Szor, P.: Memory scanning under NT. In: 9th International Virus Bulletin Conference, Vancouver, British Columbia (October 1999)
65. ThreatExpert: Conficker/downadup: Memory injection model, http://blog.threatexpert.com/2009/01/ confickerdownadup-memory-injection.html (last accessed April 15, 2010)
66. Tripathy, S., Panda, B.: Post-intrusion recovery using data dependency approach. In: IEEE Workshop on Information Assurance and Security, West Point, New York (June 2001)
67. Urrea, J.M.: An Analysis of Linux RAM Forensics. Master's thesis, Naval Postgraduate School (March 2006)
68. Wang, Z., Jiang, X., Cui, W., Ning, P.: Countering kernel rootkits with lightweight hook protection. In: ACM Symposium on Computer and Communications Security (CCS), Chicago, Illinois (November 2009)
69. Whitaker, A., Cox, R.S., Shaw, M., Gribble, S.D.: Constructing services with interposable virtual hardware. In: Symposium on Networked Systems Design and Implementation (NSDI), San Francisco, California (March 2004)
70. Willems, C., Holz, T., Freiling, F.: Toward automated dynamic malware analysis using cwsandbox. IEEE Security & Privacy 5(2) (March 2007)
71. XenAccess Project: XenAccess Library, http://xenaccess.sourceforge.net/ (last accessed April 4, 2008)
72. Yee, B., Sehr, D., Dardyk, G., Chen, B., Muth, R., Ormandy, T., Okasaka, S., Narula, N., Fullagar, N.: Native client: A sandbox for portable, untrusted x86 native code. In: IEEE Symposium on Security and Privacy, Oakland, California (May 2009)
73. Yin, H., Song, D., Egele, M., Kruegel, C., Kirda, E.: Panorama: Capturing system-wide information flow for malware detection and analysis. In: ACM Conference on Computer and Communications Security (CCS), Arlington, Virginia (October 2007)

Unifying Facets of Information Integrity

Arnar Birgisson, Alejandro Russo, and Andrei Sabelfeld

Chalmers University of Technology, 412 96 Gothenburg, Sweden

Abstract. Information integrity is a vital security property in a variety of applications. However, there is more than one facet to integrity: interpretations of
integrity in different contexts include *integrity via information flow*, where the
key is that trusted output is independent from untrusted input, and *integrity via
invariance*, where the key is preservation of an invariant. Furthermore, integrity
via invariance is itself multi-faceted. For example, the literature features formalizations of invariance as predicate preservation (*predicate invariance*), which is
not directly compatible with invariance of memory values (*value invariance*).
This paper offers a unified framework for integrity policies that include all of the
facets above. Despite the different nature of these facets, we show that a straightforward enforcement mechanism adapted from the literature is readily available
for enforcing all of the integrity facets at once.

1 Introduction

Information integrity is a vital security property in a variety of applications. However,
there is clearly more than one facet to integrity. Indeed, security textbooks [40, 25]
agree that it is hard to pin down the essence of integrity, and surveys [33, 45, 42] and
tutorials [26] identify a range of integrity flavors.

Integrity in the area of information flow often means that trusted output is independent from untrusted input [10]. This is dual to the classical models of confidentiality [9, 30, 17, 24], where public output is required to be independent from secret input.
Integrity in the area of access control [45] is concerned with improper/unauthorized data
modification. The focus is on preventing data modification operations, when no modification rights are granted to a given principal. Integrity in the context of fault-tolerant
systems is concerned with preservation of actual data. For example, a desired property
for a file transfer protocol on a lossy channel is that the integrity of a transmitted file is
preserved, i.e., the information at both ends of communication must be identical (which
can be enforced by detecting and repairing possible file corruption). Integrity in the
context of databases often means preservation of some important invariants, such as
consistency of data and uniqueness of database keys.

The list of different interpretations of integrity can be continued, including rather
general notions as integrity as *expectation of data quality* and integrity as guarantee of
accurate data and *meaningful data* [45, 40].

Sabelfeld and Myers [42] observe that integrity has an important difference from
confidentiality: a computing system can damage integrity without any external interaction, simply by computing data incorrectly. Thus, strong enforcement of integrity
requires proving program correctness.

S. Jha and A. Maturia (Eds.): ICISS 2010, LNCS 6503, pp. 48–65, 2010.
© Springer-Verlag Berlin Heidelberg 2010

Seeking to clarify the area of integrity policies, Li et al. [31] suggest a classification for data integrity policies into *information-flow*, *data invariant*, and *program correctness* policies. In a similar spirit, Guttman [26] identifies *causality* and *invariance* policies as two major types of data integrity policies.

With the classification by Li et al. [31] as a point of departure, we present a general framework for the different facets of integrity that include information-flow, invariance, and correctness aspects. Furthermore, we argue that integrity via invariance is itself multi-faceted. For example, the literature (cf. [31]) features formalizations of invariance as predicate preservation (*predicate invariance*), which is not directly compatible with invariance of memory values (*value invariance*).

This paper offers a unified framework for integrity policies that include all of the facets above. A key feature of the framework is generalized invariants that can represent a range of properties from program correctness to predicate and value invariance. Our formalization shows that program correctness (which was previously identified as a separate type of integrity [31]) in fact subsumes invariance-based integrity.

Figure 1 illustrates the policy set inclusion. We comment on the characteristic policy examples that correspond to points in the diagram (the formal definitions of these policies are postponed to Section 2). Notation x and x' denotes the values of the corresponding variable before and after program execution. An example of a value invariance policy is $x = x'$, i.e., the value of the variable stays unchanged. An example of a predicate invariance policy is $x > 0 \Rightarrow x' > 0$, i.e., if the variable is positive initially, it must stay positive at the end of execution. Value invariance is inherently about the relation of some expression before

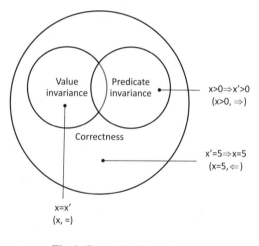

Fig. 1. Generalized invariance

and after the execution. On the other hand, predicate invariance is inherently about preservation of some predicate on the current memory. As we explain in detail in Section 2, these policies are not directly compatible because (i) in order to mimic value invariance (as in $x = x'$) by predicate invariance, the final memory needs to explicitly include the initial memory, and (ii) in order to mimic predicate invariance (as in $x > 0 \Rightarrow x' > 0$) by value invariance, the predicate to be preserved needs to be encoded, if at all possible, into expression equality.

Further, there are properties beyond invariance that are integrity properties. For example, $x' = 5 \Rightarrow x = 5$ is a property that assures that if the final value of the variable is 5, then it has not been modified compared to its initial value. This corresponds to a general class of properties, called *program correctness* properties. Thanks to its generality, program correctness can model all of the integrity flavors, including meaningfulness and consistency. In fact, any program property can be represented as long as it can be described by a generalized predicate that has access to initial and final memories. (As we remark in Section 8, an extension of the framework to handle intermediate states appears natural.)

Note that the goal of the paper is not to achieve as much expressiveness as possible. Indeed, a wide range of formalisms exists for reasoning about program correctness from Hoare logic [29] to refinement types [23], and a large body of work in-between [37]. Furthermore, logic-based mechanisms have been explored for reasoning about confidentiality [18, 8, 2, 6]. Instead, we aim at a treatment of integrity that allows us to express the different flavors in a uniform and convenient fashion that is directly connected to enforcement.

Indeed, despite the different nature of the integrity facets, we show that a straightforward enforcement mechanism adapted from the literature is readily available for enforcing all of the integrity facets at once. This mechanism, as proposed by Askarov and Sabelfeld [5], is originally for enforcing an information release (or *declassification*) policy of *delimited release* [43]. It guarantees that the values of declassification expressions (called *escape hatches*) have not changed compared to their initial values by performing a dynamic check at declassification time. We observe that the dual of this mechanism allows tracking both safe *endorsement* (i.e., intentional increase in trust to a given expression), and it is readily available to track correctness and therefore invariance properties. Indeed, the latter facets of integrity can be straightforwardly guaranteed by checking immediately before termination whether the desired correctness/invariance property is satisfied and terminating normally only in the case of positive outcome.

The possibility of easily deploying Askarov and Sabelfeld's enforcement [5] for a wide range of integrity policies (for which the enforcement was not originally designed) is a one of the greatest benefits of our approach. It liberates us from the necessity of designing a multi-dimensional enforcement framework of complexity similar to the policy framework.

A summary on the tightness of integration offered by our approach follows. We achieve tight integration on the enforcement side: a single enforcement mechanism is suitable to support all facets of integrity, including those that it has not been designed to support. On the policy side, the integration between information flow and correctness facets is not tight as these facets are inherently distinct. Nevertheless, within the correctness facet, we achieve tight integration of various flavors of invariants into our generalized invariant framework.

In the rest of the paper, we present a generalized definition for integrity as invariance (Section 2), recap a standard definition of integrity as information flow (Section 3), show how to enforce all facets of integrity with a single enforcement mechanism (Section 4), discuss endorsement (Section 5), extensions and practical aspects (Section 6), related work (Section 7), and offer some concluding remarks (Section 8).

To clarify the scope of this paper, we note that the focus is on *information integrity* (or data integrity), i.e., the integrity of data (in contrast to *system integrity* that addresses the integrity of the processing software and hardware units). Hence, integrity refers to information integrity throughout the paper.

2   Integrity via Invariance

Before we launch into formal definitions of the concepts described above, we need some preliminaries. In particular, we must define what it means for a program to terminate. We use the term *memories* for mappings from variables to values. We work with semantics given as a small-step transition system with configurations of some form C, where the transition system defines transitions of the forms

$$C \longrightarrow C \quad \text{and} \quad C \longrightarrow m$$

where m is a memory. A transition of the second kind represents the terminating transition. If such a transition is contained in a trace, then it will always be the last one given that there are only transitions of the above forms. An example of a configuration is the tuple $\langle c, m \rangle$ where c is a syntactic term (*command* or *program*) and m is a *memory*.

Definition 1 (Termination). *We say that configuration C_0 terminates in a memory m, written $C_0 \downarrow m$ if and only if there exists a trace*

$$C_0 \rightarrow C_1 \rightarrow \ldots \rightarrow C_n \rightarrow m$$

(according to some particular semantics which is usually clear from the context.) If no such trace exists, we write $C_0 \not\downarrow$.

Note that $C_0 \not\downarrow$ covers both the cases when programs diverge, i.e., they have an infinite execution trace, or when they get stuck before reaching a terminal state.

2.1   Value Invariance

A value invariant states that the value of an expression should not change by executing a program. We define value invariants to be expressions which are required to evaluate to the same value only in the initial and the final memory of a terminating program. We write $m(e)$ to denote the value of an expression e with respect to a memory m.

Definition 2 (Value invariant). *Let e be an expression. We say that a program c satisfies the value invariant e if and only if*

$$\forall m . \quad \langle c, m \rangle \downarrow m' \quad \Longrightarrow \quad m(e) = m'(e).$$

A simple example of a value invariant would be the expression x, corresponding to $x = x'$ in Figure 1. This value invariant states that the variable x is not modified by running the program. Note that it may be modified *during* the execution of the program, as long as its original value is restored in the end. Another simple example is the expression $x + y$, which allows x and y to change, as long as their changes are balanced so that their sum stays constant.

On the other hand, there are some interesting "invariants" which we cannot describe by value invariants. This includes, for example, the invariant $x > 42$, which in some ways resembles a pair of a pre- and a postcondition. Treating this boolean expression as a value invariant requires that if the expression is false in the initial memory, it must also be false in the final memory. However, by our intuition, starting from a memory where the expression is false, we would like the program to be valid no matter the final value of the expression. This leads us to another notion of invariance from the literature.

2.2   Predicate Invariance

Predicate invariance [31] resembles very much pre- and postconditions from Hoare logic [29, 37]. A predicate invariant consists of a boolean predicate on memories that programs must preserve.

Definition 3 (Predicate invariant). *For a predicate φ on memories, a program c satisfies the predicate invariant φ if and only if*

$$\forall m . \qquad \langle c, m \rangle \downarrow m' \quad \Longrightarrow \quad \varphi(m) \Rightarrow \varphi(m').$$

Predicate invariants allow us to easily describe invariants such as $x > 0$ (see Figure 1) with the intuitive semantics described above. The intuitive idea described by Li et. al. is that φ can be used to describe when a memory has a *good* property, where it is desirable that programs preserve that property in the final memory.

However, there are also important examples of invariants which are not captured by predicate invariance. For example, the simple value invariant x, i.e., a given variable maintains it value, cannot be modeled as a predicate invariant without passing the initial value of the variable to the final memory. Thus, the two types of invariants are incompatible. In the next section we define a new notion of invariance which unifies the two.

2.3   Generalized Invariance

We can observe that both of the above notions of invariance quantify over all initial memories, which for deterministic languages corresponds to quantifying over all runs of a particular program. If we treat (terminating) programs purely as a transformation on memories, then a possible general notion of invariance is simply a predicate on the initial and final memories. A given program satisfies such an invariant if all pairs of initial and final memories that it relates satisfy the predicate. Obviously, this captures the two notions of invariance above.

We provide a particularly convenient policy language that is equivalent in expressiveness to a general predicate on initial and final memory. The goal is that an invariant can be easily specified by the programmer and enforced by, e.g., a runtime monitor. Thus, we specify invariants by two expressions, one to be evaluated in initial memory and one in final memory, along with a binary predicate on those values. As we will see in Section 5, this is a particularly beneficial way to specify invariants because of smooth integration with *endorsement*.

Definition 4 (Generalized invariant). *A generalized invariant is a triple (e_1, e_2, P), where e_1, and e_2 are expressions, and P is a binary predicate on values. A program c satisfies such an invariant if and only if*

$$\forall m . \qquad \langle c, m \rangle \downarrow m' \quad \Longrightarrow \quad P\big(m(e_1), m'(e_2)\big)$$

We can explore the expressiveness of this notion of invariance. We can immediately observe that it captures the previously defined notions of invariance. Any value invariant e is represented by the generalized invariant $(e, e, =)$. Similarly, any predicate invariant φ is represented by $(\varphi, \varphi, \Rightarrow)$. These observations are depicted in Figure 2.

Generalized invariants can also describe more general notions of correctness. Our example of $x' = 5 \Rightarrow x = 5$ from Section 1 can be described by $(x = 5, x = 5, \Leftarrow)$. If we want to make sure a certain variable increases by running a program, we can write $(x, x, <)$.

Generalized invariance	e_1	e_2	P
Value invariance	e	e	$=$
Predicate invariance	φ	φ	$\Rightarrow$

Fig. 2. Kinds of invariance

It may not be clear why we would call such a condition as the last one an *invariant*, as it appears to state that something *has to* change. However, the property $m(x) < m'(x)$ must hold for all initial and final memories m and m', if we are to say that the program in question satisfies it. In other words, the property predicate by itself is an invariant for all runs of a program.

Another important facet of integrity is that we do not want untrusted inputs to have any influence on trusted outputs. This facet cannot be described by generalized invariants [34, 46], and is the topic of the next section.

3   Integrity via Information Flow

Information-flow integrity policies restrict how untrustworthy data flows inside programs. These policies seek to prevent corrupting critical information. For example, the (untrusted) data input of an in-flight entertainment system must not affect the auto-pilot control system (critical component), but the auto-pilot control system might be allowed to display information in the in-flight entertainment systems, such as estimated time of arrival. For simplicity, we only consider two integrity levels: H_i (high integrity) for trustworthy and L_i (low integrity) for untrustworthy data. A common baseline policy for information flow is the *noninterference* policy [17, 24]. This policy states that trustworthy data cannot be affected by untrustworthy values (written as $L_i \not\sqsubseteq H_i$). However, there is no risk for untrusted data to be affected by trusted data. In this case, we indicate $H_i \sqsubseteq L_i$. The integrity levels H_i and L_i form a two-point security lattice [19] that indicates how information can flow inside programs.

As before, we write $\langle c, m \rangle \downarrow m'$ for a terminating execution of program c under the initial memory m and final memory m'. We assume that every variable in memory is assigned an integrity level. Memories m_1 and m_2 are *high-integrity equivalent*, written $m_1 =_{H_i} m_2$, if they agree on high integrity values. The following definition captures the noninterference security policy.

Definition 5 (Noninterference). *A program c satisfies noninterference if for any memories m_1 and m_2 such that $\langle c, m_1 \rangle \downarrow m_1'$, and $\langle c, m_2 \rangle \downarrow m_2'$, then*

$$m_1 =_{H_i} m_2 \quad \Longrightarrow \quad m_1' =_{H_i} m_2'.$$

The definition above ignores nonterminating executions of programs. This kind of definition is known as *termination-insensitive* noninterference [47, 42, 1]. In some cases, attackers can still affect the termination behavior of the program. However, we ignore the termination channel because its bandwidth is negligible [1] in our setting.

$$n \in \mathbb{Z}, \quad x \in Vars, \quad op \in \{+, -, \dots\}$$

$$e ::= n \mid x \mid e \, op \, e$$

$$c ::= \mathtt{skip} \mid x := e \mid c; c \mid \mathtt{if} \ e \ \mathtt{then} \ c \ \mathtt{else} \ c \mid \mathtt{while} \ e \ \mathtt{do} \ c$$

Fig. 3. Syntax

SKIP

$$\langle \mathtt{skip}, m \rangle \xrightarrow{nop} \langle \varepsilon, m \rangle$$

ASSIGN

$$\langle x := e, m \rangle \xrightarrow{a(x,e)} \langle \varepsilon, m[x \mapsto m(e)] \rangle$$

SEQ1 $\dfrac{\langle c_1, m \rangle \xrightarrow{\beta} \langle c_1', m' \rangle \quad c_1' \neq \varepsilon}{\langle c_1; c_2, m \rangle \xrightarrow{\beta} \langle c_1'; c_2, m' \rangle}$

SEQ2 $\dfrac{\langle c_1, m \rangle \xrightarrow{\beta} \langle \varepsilon, m' \rangle}{\langle c_1; c_2, m \rangle \xrightarrow{\beta} \langle c_2, m' \rangle}$

IF1 $\dfrac{m(e) \neq 0}{\langle \mathtt{if} \ e \ \mathtt{then} \ c_1 \ \mathtt{else} \ c_2, m \rangle \xrightarrow{b(e)} \langle c_1; end, m \rangle}$

IF2 $\dfrac{m(e) = 0}{\langle \mathtt{if} \ e \ \mathtt{then} \ c_1 \ \mathtt{else} \ c_2, m \rangle \xrightarrow{b(e)} \langle c_2; end, m \rangle}$

WHILE1

$$\dfrac{m(e) \neq 0}{\langle \mathtt{while} \ e \ \mathtt{do} \ c, m \rangle \xrightarrow{b(e)} \langle c; end; \mathtt{while} \ e \ \mathtt{do} \ c, m \rangle}$$

WHILE2

$$\dfrac{m(e) = 0}{\langle \mathtt{while} \ e \ \mathtt{do} \ c, m \rangle \xrightarrow{b(e)} \langle end, m \rangle}$$

END

$$\langle end, m \rangle \xrightarrow{f} \langle \varepsilon, m \rangle$$

TERM$_c$

$$\langle \varepsilon, m \rangle \xrightarrow{term(m)} m$$

Fig. 4. Command semantics

Information-flow integrity can be seen as the dual to confidentiality. To illustrate this connection, we assume confidentiality levels L_c and H_c for public and secret information, respectively. Observe that the integrity requirements $L_i \not\sqsubseteq H_i$ and $H_i \sqsubseteq L_i$ are the duals to the ones $L_c \sqsubseteq H_c$ and $H_c \not\sqsubseteq L_c$, which indicate that secret information cannot be leaked to public recipients. This confidentiality policy underlies the original definitions of noninterference [17, 24]. Due to this duality, the techniques developed for confidentiality can also be used to guarantee information-flow integrity. In the next section, we extend a runtime monitor for enforcing information-flow confidentiality to enforce both information-flow and invariance integrity.

4 Enforcement

To illustrate the idea behind enforcement, we consider a simple imperative language with the syntax and semantics given in Figures 3 and 4, respectively. The syntax and semantic rules are mostly standard [48] except for minor extensions. We include a pseudo-term end that indicates leaving the scope of an if or a while. This term generates a transition described by the rule END. The rule TERM_c is also nonstandard and, together with the empty term ε, it guarantees that a terminating run of any program ends with a transition generated by this rule. Transitions in the semantics are labeled with an event β. The purpose of labeled events as well as rules END and TERM_c is communication with the runtime monitor, which is described next.

We present an extension to the dynamic monitor found in [5] in order to enforce both information-flow integrity and generalized invariants.

Figure 5 gives the monitor semantics. The monitor is a separate transition system whose transitions are labeled with the same kind of events β as the command transitions. This is used to synchronize the two executions. Furthermore, the monitor may block progress of the program, in case the program can do a transition with a certain event but the monitor is not able to match it.

$$\text{NOP} \frac{}{\langle i, st, \mathcal{I}\rangle \xrightarrow{nop} \langle i, st, \mathcal{I}\rangle}$$

$$\text{FLOW} \frac{lev(e) \sqsubseteq \Gamma(x) \qquad lev(st) \sqsubseteq \Gamma(x)}{\langle i, st, \mathcal{I}\rangle \xrightarrow{a(x,e)} \langle i, st, \mathcal{I}\rangle}$$

$$\text{BRANCH} \frac{}{\langle i, st, \mathcal{I}\rangle \xrightarrow{b(e)} \langle i, lev(e): st, \mathcal{I}\rangle}$$

$$\text{FINISH} \frac{}{\langle i, hd: st, \mathcal{I}\rangle \xrightarrow{f} \langle i, st, \mathcal{I}\rangle}$$

The monitor enforces information-flow integrity with the rules FLOW, BRANCH and FINISH, in the same way as [5]. The first rule allows direct assignments of an expression e to a variable x, indicated by the event $a(x,e)$,

$$\text{TERM}_m \frac{\forall(e_1, e_2, P) \in \mathcal{I} : P(i(e_1), m(e_2))}{\langle i, st, \mathcal{I}\rangle \xrightarrow{term(m)} \langle i, st, \mathcal{I}\rangle}$$

Fig. 5. Monitor semantics

only if e has the same or higher integrity than x (Γ maps variables to their integrity levels.) The rule also ensures that the minimum level $lev(st)$ on the *context stack st* is at least as high as x's level. This is to prevent *implicit flows* [20], i.e., flows via control flow. The stack contains the levels of expressions affecting control flow. It is maintained by the rules BRANCH and FINISH, which synchronize with the program entering or leaving an if or while block, as indicated by the events $b(e)$ and f, respectively.

The rule TERM_m synchronizes with program termination and enforces the invariance integrity policy. The monitor carries in its state a set of generalized invariants, as well as a snapshot of the initial memory, and uses these to ensure all the invariants are satisfied by the execution. If not, this rule blocks the program from terminating.

Before proving the desired properties of our monitor we should make a small note about its practicality. While it is certainly infeasible to store a snapshot of the initial memory of a program, this is only a feature of our theoretical model. In practice the only additional state required to enforce a set of invariants $\mathcal{I}$, are the values of the first expression of each one, as evaluated in initial memory. A monitor needs only evaluate these expressions at the start, store their values and then at the end evaluate the second expression as well as the predicate of each invariant. Since we expect the set of invariants to be relatively small given their expressiveness, the overhead of adding invariant enforcement is small compared to the information flow enforcement overhead of the original monitor from [5]. Controlling the complexity of the expressions and predicates of course remains the responsibility of the policy writer.

In the rest of the section, we will talk about *monitored programs* which refers to a program which is run in lockstep with a monitor. For convenience, we represent monitored programs with a monitor combination operator $\sharp$, whose semantics is defined with the following two rules, where C_c is the configuration of program semantics, and C_m is that of the monitor semantics.

$$\frac{C_c \xrightarrow{\beta} C'_c \quad C_m \xrightarrow{\beta} C'_m}{C_c \sharp C_m \longrightarrow C'_c \sharp C'_m} \qquad \frac{C_c \xrightarrow{\beta} m \quad C_m \xrightarrow{\beta} C'_m}{C_c \sharp C_m \longrightarrow m} \tag{1}$$

Note that $\sharp$ is a meta-operator, it works on configurations rather than syntactic terms.

We can immediately state and prove one useful property of such monitored processes. If an unmonitored program does not terminate, then adding a monitor can not make it terminate. This is obvious from the right rule above, a terminating transition of the unmonitored program is a premise for proving a terminating transition of the monitored one. Nevertheless it is useful to state this explicitly as a lemma.

Lemma 1 (Failstop correctness). *For any monitored program* $C_c \sharp C_m$, *we have*

$$C_c \sharp C_m \downarrow m \quad \Longrightarrow \quad C_c \downarrow m.$$

Proof. If the monitored program terminates, there is a terminating trace with transitions proved by the rules (1). By taking the left premise of each transition proof, it is straightforward to construct a terminating trace for the unmonitored program $\langle c, m \rangle$.

Since the terminating transition must be due to the right rule, it is obvious that both traces terminate in the same memory. $\qquad\square$

Throughout the paper, we assume finite sets of generalized invariants $\mathcal{I}$. Given a set of generalized invariants $\mathcal{I}$, we can now prove that the monitor presented in Figure 5 is sound, in the way that a monitored program that terminates satisfies all invariants of $\mathcal{I}$ and satisfies noninterference. An important ingredient to this is that all invariants are decidable. We assume evaluation of their expressions is decidable, but we also require that checking each invariant's predicate is decidable as well.

Theorem 1 (Soundness). *Let c be a command and* $\mathcal{I}$ *a set of (generalized) invariants with decidable predicates. Then, for all memories m it holds that*

$$\langle c, m \rangle \sharp \langle m, [], \mathcal{I} \rangle \downarrow m' \quad \Longrightarrow \quad \forall (e_1, e_2, P) \in \mathcal{I} : P(m(e_1), m'(e_2)),$$

i.e., the monitored program satisfies all of the invariants in $\mathcal{I}$. *Furthermore, if* m_1 *and* m_2 *are high-integrity equivalent memories, and* $\langle c, m_i \rangle \sharp \langle m_i, [], \mathcal{I} \rangle \downarrow m'_i$, *with* $i \in \{1, 2\}$, *then* m'_1 *is high-integrity equivalent to* m'_2, *i.e., the monitored program satisfies noninterference.*

Proof. We note that $\mathcal{I}$ stays unchanged by the monitor. Since $\langle c, m \rangle$ terminates in m', there exists a trace

$$\langle c, m \rangle \sharp \langle m, [], \mathcal{I} \rangle \longrightarrow \cdots \longrightarrow C'_c \sharp C'_m \longrightarrow m'$$

The last rule of a monitored execution can only be the right rule of (1), which in turn means the rule used to prove the left premise is TERM_c and that $C'_c = \langle \varepsilon, m' \rangle$. Consequently, the last transition of this trace must have the following proof tree:

$$\cfrac{\text{TERM}_c \; \cfrac{}{\langle \varepsilon, m' \rangle \overset{term(m')}{\longrightarrow} m'} \qquad \text{TERM}_m \; \cfrac{\forall (e_1, e_2, P) \in \mathcal{I} : P(m(e_1), m'(e_2))}{\langle m, st, \mathcal{I} \rangle \overset{term(m')}{\longrightarrow} \langle m, st, \mathcal{I} \rangle}}{\langle \varepsilon, m' \rangle \sharp \langle m, st, \mathcal{I} \rangle \longrightarrow m'}$$

The only premise in this proof must thus hold, which concludes the proof of the invariance part.

For proof of the noninterference part we refer to [5]. □

It is a natural question to ask also if the monitor is complete. Informally, we would formulate this in the following way: If a program satisfies a set of invariants to begin with, a monitored version will not diverge unless the program does also. The presented monitor enforces both information flow integrity as well as invariant integrity. The monitor is not complete in enforcing noninterference. For example, the program $h := l; h := 0$, where h and l are high- and low-integrity variables, respectively, is blocked by the monitor although it satisfies noninterference. However, we can prove that if the information-flow integrity is set aside, then the monitor is complete in enforcing invariance integrity.

We will use the following fact (that is straightforward to prove): If all variables used in a program have the same integrity level, then no execution of the monitored version $\langle c, m \rangle \sharp \langle m, [], \mathcal{I} \rangle$ (where $\mathcal{I}$ is arbitrary) will get stuck due to the rule FLOW being disabled. This is obvious since the premises of the rule are always true if all integrity levels are equal. We can now state and prove the completeness of the monitor with respect to invariant integrity policies.

Theorem 2 (Completeness of invariance enforcement). *Let c be a command, m some memory, and $\mathcal{I}$ a set of generalized invariants with decidable predicates. Assume all variables used in c have the same integrity level. Then, if the (unmonitored) program $\langle c, m \rangle$ satisfies the invariants in $\mathcal{I}$, i.e.,*

$$\langle c, m \rangle \downarrow m' \quad \Longrightarrow \quad \forall (e_1, e_2, P) \in \mathcal{I} : P(m(e_1), m'(e_2)),$$

then the program either diverges by itself or the monitored version also terminates (in some memory):

$$\langle c, m \rangle \not\downarrow \quad \vee \quad \langle c, m \rangle \sharp \langle m, [], \mathcal{I} \rangle \downarrow m''.$$

Proof. If the premise holds because $\langle c, m \rangle$ does not terminate, then the conclusion holds trivially. In the other case, when $\langle c, m \rangle \downarrow m'$ and

$$\forall (e_1, e_2, P) \in \mathcal{I} : P(m(e_1), m'(e_2)), \tag{2}$$

then we consider the terminating trace

$$\langle c, m \rangle = \langle c_0, m_0 \rangle \longrightarrow \dots \longrightarrow \langle c_n, m_n \rangle \longrightarrow m'. \tag{3}$$

From the command semantics we can see that the last transition is due to rule TERM_c.

Now consider the monitored version $\langle c, m \rangle \sharp \langle m, [], \mathcal{I} \rangle$. If this does not terminate, it must be because the monitor blocks the execution at some point. This can only happen if rules FLOW or TERM$_m$ are disabled. However, the rule FLOW is never disabled since there is no violation of information-flow integrity, and so the monitor can only block due to the termination rule being disabled. This would mean that the monitored program gets stuck just before the last transition of (3), since this is the only transition that can potentially synchronize with TERM$_m$. This means $m_n = m'$ and thus we are already in final memory at this point. Since TERM$_m$ is disabled, its premise is false. However being in final memory, its premise is exactly (2), which we assumed true. Thus, the monitored program must terminate.   □

The completeness theorem states that our monitor will never stop an otherwise terminating and correct program. In other words, the monitor does not raise false alarms.

However, completeness alone is not enough, since the monitor could potentially terminate in a different final memory than the original, correct program does. Of course, this is not desirable, so we follow with a proof that our monitor is *transparent*, i.e., it does not alter the semantics of correct programs.

Theorem 3 (Transparency of invariance enforcement). *Let c be a command, m a memory, and $\mathcal{I}$ a set of generalized invariants with decidable predicates. We assume that all variables in c have the same integrity level. If the (unmonitored) program satisfies the invariants in $\mathcal{I}$, formally*

$$\langle c, m \rangle \downarrow m' \quad \Longrightarrow \quad \forall (e_1, e_2, P) \in \mathcal{I} : P(m(e_1), m'(e_2)),$$

then, the following implications hold:

$$\langle c, m \rangle \downarrow m' \quad \Longrightarrow \quad \langle c, m \rangle \sharp \langle m, [], \mathcal{I} \rangle \downarrow m', \quad and$$
$$\langle c, m \rangle \nmid \quad \Longrightarrow \quad \langle c, m \rangle \sharp \langle m, [], \mathcal{I} \rangle \nmid$$

Proof. First, assume that $\langle c, m \rangle \downarrow m'$. By the completeness theorem above, the monitored version terminates in some memory m''. To see that $m' = m''$, observe the last transition of the monitored trace. This transition is due to the right rule of (1) whose first premise can only be met by the last transition of (3) from the last proof. By the definition of that rule, the conclusion indeed "returns" the same memory m'. This proves the first implication. The second implication is a simple contrapositive of Lemma 1. □

5   Endorsement

When dealing with confidentiality, it is sometimes necessary to intentionally release, or *declassify*, some confidential information [44]. Analogously for integrity, it is sometimes necessary to boost the integrity of some piece of untrustworthy data to trustworthy. For example, the integrity of user-provided data can be raised after the data is sanitized. Dually to declassification, *endorsement* converts low integrity into high integrity data.

This section introduces a security condition and an enforcement mechanism for endorsement that can be seen as the dual of *delimited release* [43, 5]. We include the

$$\frac{}{\langle x := \texttt{endorse}(e), m\rangle \stackrel{end(x,e,m)}{\longrightarrow} \langle \varepsilon, m[x \mapsto m(e)]\rangle} \qquad \frac{i(e) = m(e) \quad lev(st) \sqsubseteq \Gamma(x)}{\langle i, st, \mathcal{I}\rangle \stackrel{end(x,e,m)}{\longrightarrow} \langle i, st, \mathcal{I}\rangle}$$

Fig. 6. Rules for endorsement

command $x := \texttt{endorse}(e)$ in our language for boosting the integrity of expression e from low to high. The semantic rule, depicted in Figure 6, simply performs the assignment and triggers the event $end(x, e, m)$ for communication with the monitor.

The security condition, dubbed *delimited endorsement*, captures what it means to be secure for programs involving endorsements.

Definition 6 (Delimited endorsement). *Consider a program c containing exactly n endorsement commands $x_1 := \texttt{endorse}(e_1), \ldots, x_n := \texttt{endorse}(e_n)$, where expressions $e_1, \ldots, e_n$ are called escape hatches. Command c is secure if for all memories m_1 and m_2 such that $m_1 =_{H_i} m_2$, $\forall i.m_1(e_i) =_{H_i} m_2(e_i)$, $\langle c, m_1\rangle \downarrow m'_1$, and $\langle c, m_2\rangle \downarrow m'_2$, we have $m'_1 =_{H_i} m'_2$.*

Intuitively, delimited endorsement establishes that a program is secure if whenever two high-integrity equivalent memories are indistinguishable by escape hatches, then they must also be indistinguishable by the program itself: terminating runs of the program in these memories leads to high-integrity equivalent final states. One way to enforce this condition is by checking whether the value of any escape-hatch expression at the time of endorsement is the same as it was at the beginning of computation. This brings us to the enforcement.

The monitor rule for endorsement is also given in Figure 6. It checks that the endorsed value $m(e)$ of expression e in memory m is indeed the same in the initial and current memory ($i(e) = m(e)$). This restriction avoids laundering, i.e., abusing the endorsement mechanisms to endorse other data than the one indicated by $x := \texttt{endorse}(e)$ [43, 5]. Similar as for regular assignments, restriction $lev(st) \sqsubseteq x$ is used to avoid implicit flows.

The mechanisms to enforce invariants in Figure 5 can be easily reused for enforcing endorsement. Observe that $i(e) = m(e)$ can be interpreted as a particular kind of invariant $P(i(e), m(e'))$, where P is the equality predicate $=$, and expressions e and e' are the same.

The following theorem establishes the formal guarantees obtained by the enforcement rules.

Theorem 4. *For any program c, the monitored execution of c (with the initial configuration $\langle c, m\rangle \sharp \langle m, [], \mathcal{I}\rangle$ for memory m) satisfies delimited endorsement.*

Proof. It follows by an adaptation of Askarov and Sabelfeld's proof [5] for delimited release. The failstop property of the monitor allows for a straightforward adaption of the proof: the invariant-checking part is largely orthogonal since all the monitor can do is to block the execution, in which case the high-integrity equivalence does not need to be tracked.   □

As it was for the information-flow part of the monitor in Section 4, the delimited endorsement monitor is incomplete in the information-flow part for the same reason.

6   Extensions and Practical Aspects

The enforcement mechanisms presented in Section 4 and 5 can be naturally extended to support I/O operations and a form of access control. We briefly outline the principles behind such extensions and discuss practical aspects.

6.1   I/O

Programs often require to take inputs as well as produce outputs during execution. Defining and tracking delimited release in the presence of communication primitives is described in [5]. When considering inputs, the restriction $i(e) = m(e)$ needs to be revised because it does not allow to declassify (endorse in our case) variables that have been updated by inputs.

Askarov and Sabelfeld [5] remark that inputs may introduce fresh data into programs and, therefore, they distinguish them from regular updates. They propose a monitor that allows to declassify information when the value being declassified $(m(e))$ matches the value of the expression in a memory that records most recent inputs. If no inputs where performed for a given variable e, the value considered for that variable is the one found in the initial memory. In a similar fashion, it is possible to modularly extend the rules in Figures 5 and 6 to consider a *context level input* label ct, which records if there has been an input in a high context, and update memory i in the monitor's state every time that an input is produced. The extended monitor then disallows endorsement if the input context label ct has low integrity. This is necessary because inputs, unlike branch/loop guards, are not lexically-bounded in their impact. The update of memory i on every input allows the monitor to have a memory where each variable's value refers either to its last input or its value at the initial memory (i.e., no inputs are performed for that variable).

In the presence of outputs, checking invariants at the end of program execution needs to be revised. Data invariants could refer to outputs produced by programs, e.g., every credit-card number sent to a server must be formed by 16 digits. To express this, it is sufficient to apply rule TERM$_c$ at every output produced by the program. In principle, it is possible to allow programmers to indicate what invariants must be checked at what outputs.

When considering inputs and outputs, the security condition for declassification in [5] is based on the attacker's knowledge [21, 4, 6]. With this in mind, it is possible to use the same semantics techniques to handle endorsement in presence of communication primitives. In fact, the dual of the attacker knowledge in [5] can be interpreted as the attacker capabilities to control or affect computations regarding high integrity data [3].

6.2   Access Control

As mentioned in Section 1, integrity in the area of access control [45] focuses on preventing data modification operations when no modification access is granted to a given principal. Policies of the kind "resource R cannot be written by principal P" cannot be naturally enforced by noninterference. The main reason is the degree of freedom that noninterference allows regarding entities at the same security level. Noninterference only restricts how information flows among different security levels. To illustrate this, assume an information-flow enforcement mechanism is in place. Whatever security level variable R is assigned to, it is still possible to read its content, concatenated with itself, and save it back to R. Observe that these operations only manipulate data at security level R. In contrast, our monitor can be easily adapted to enforce that no write operation is invoked on R by P or, more generally, no changes are performed on resource R by just establishing, through an invariant, that the content of R is the same at the beginning and at the end of the program. Moreover, if considering endorsement as given in Figure 6, it is possible to enforce no changes on R by endorsing it at the end of the program. Direct enforcement of no unauthorized write operations is of course also possible when the monitor has access to the entire trace.

6.3 Practical Aspects

Preliminary results from a Haskell-based library for integrity [22] suggest light implementation overhead to enforce integrity policies in presence of I/O and access control requirements. Diserholt [22] shows how to build a secure password administrator that preserves confidentiality of passwords as well as several facets of integrity policies, e.g., password must be difficult to guess (integrity via invariance), certain operations should not write the contents of some files (access control), and user input cannot determine the utilized hash function (integrity via information flow). We argue that it is not difficult to reformulate the concrete case study in [22] using our approach and obtain similar results.

7   Related Work

Being one of the most fundamental security properties, integrity is subject to a vast area of research. We refer to security textbooks [40, 25] that discuss assorted flavors of integrity, and integrity surveys [33, 45] and tutorials [26] that develop integrity classifications. Section 1 also contains pointers to various interpretations of integrity in various disciplines.

To the best of our knowledge, our framework is the first to unify information integrity for programs. As mentioned previously, our departure point is the classification by Li et al. [31]. Our contribution compared to this classification is a more general model of invariants (Li et al. only discuss predicate invariants), a more general model of information flow (Li et al. do not consider endorsement), and a unified view, where we show that program correctness subsumes invariance policies. In addition, we also offer a unified enforcement mechanism that guarantees all aspects of integrity at once.

Information-flow integrity dates back to Biba's integrity model [10], which dualizes Bell and LaPadula's model [9, 30] for mandatory access control. The Clark-Wilson integrity model [15] is a classical model that focuses on separation of duties and transactions.

Although information integrity for programs has been unexplored compared to confidentiality, it has recently received increasing attention. Languages such as Perl, PHP, and Ruby offer dynamic integrity checks that are based on *tainting*, a runtime mechanism for tracking explicit flows.

Ørbæk and Palsberg [38, 39] define instrumented information-flow semantics for integrity in λ-calculus. The semantics is based on integrity label manipulation. An unsoundness related to the impact of flow sensitivity on information flow has been recently uncovered [41].

Heintze and Riecke [28] consider integrity as dual to confidentiality in their study of information flow for a language based on λ-calculus. Li and Zdancewic unify confidentiality and integrity policies [32] in the context of information downgrading.

A line of work on robust declassification [49, 35, 3] is based on an interplay between confidentiality and integrity, where information release (of high confidentiality data) is allowed only if it cannot be manipulated by the attacker (through attacker-controlled low integrity data) to release additional information. The Java-based Jif tool [36], as well as its web-based extensions [14, 13], implement robustness policies.

Sabelfeld and Sands [44] introduce dimensions of declassification, with the main focus on declassification of confidentiality levels. They informally discuss the dual of dimensions of declassification: dimensions of endorsement.

We draw on delimited release [43] when it comes to enforcement of integrity policies. Although delimited release is a confidentiality property, its enforcement includes information-flow aspects and is capable of enforcing generalized invariants. This paper builds on a runtime mechanism for delimited release by Askarov and Sabelfeld [5]. A static static alternative to tracking delimited release has been explored by Sabelfeld and Myers [43].

Boudol and Kolundzija [11] combine programming constructs for expressing access-control and declassification policies. Access control is represented at language level, with explicit granting, restricting, and testing access rights. Information-flow policies and access control have been also integrated at language level by Banerjee and Naumann [7], although without considering declassification.

Haack et al. [27] explore reasoning about explicit flows in program logic. They arrive at two kinds of integrity notions: *flow-based* and *format-based*. The former is an information-flow policy, and the latter is concerned with proper formatting (they give an example policy such as "a phone number field should only contain numbers"). This latter type of integrity is subsumed by generalized invariance.

Cheney et al. [12] investigate semantic foundations for *data provenance* in databases. Provenance is concerned with tracking the origin of information, and so Cheney et al. model it as a dependency analysis.

Diserholt [22] proposes a library that handles confidentiality and integrity policies in Haskell. Besides handling confidentiality, the library is also able to combine information-flow integrity, predicate invariants, and some means for access control. Similarly to this paper, their work is inspired by the classification of integrity policies in [31].

Clarkson and Schneider [16] propose contamination and suppression as quantitative definitions of integrity. The former is dual to quantitative information leakage, whereas the later measures how much information is lost from outputs. The study of suppression includes program suppression due to malicious influence and implementation errors as well as channel suppression due to information loss about inputs to a noisy channel.

8 Conclusions

We have presented a uniform framework for information integrity. The framework incorporates a range of integrity aspects from information-flow integrity to program correctness. The framework integrates different types of integrity as invariance. We show that some of the invariant-based policies are not compatible with each other (cf. value vs. predicate invariance). Nevertheless, they are naturally represented in our framework as program correctness properties. Endorsement policies naturally extend information-flow policies and also fit into the framework.

Despite being general, our integrity framework is realizable. A single enforcement mechanism [5] (for tracking delimited information release) turns out to be an excellent match for enforcement of integrity. It supports both information-flow integrity, including extensions with endorsement policies, as well as correctness properties, including the various flavors of invariance. This mechanism is scalable to handling communication primitives.

Future work is focused on the directions outlined in Section 6. We explore both formal aspects of policies in the presence of communication and access control and practical aspects of enforcement, with inlining transformation and library-based enforcement as our main goals. Another direction of work is an extension of the framework to represent trace properties, i.e., properties of sequences of intermediate states. We expect the extension of the framework and monitor rather straightforward: generalized invariants can just as well refer to the full traces, and enforcement corresponds to enforcing *safety* [46] properties.

It is important to support our results with practical findings from case studies. Preliminary results from a Haskell-based library for integrity [22] suggest light implementation overhead.

Acknowledgments. Thanks are due to Michael Clarkson for useful comments. This work was funded by the European Community under the WebSand project and the Swedish research agencies SSF and VR. Arnar Birgisson is a recipient of the Google Europe Fellowship in Computer Security, and this research is supported in part by this Google Fellowship.

References

[1] Askarov, A., Hunt, S., Sabelfeld, A., Sands, D.: Termination-insensitive noninterference leaks more than just a bit. In: Jajodia, S., Lopez, J. (eds.) ESORICS 2008. LNCS, vol. 5283, pp. 333–348. Springer, Heidelberg (2008)

[2] Amtoft, T., Bandhakavi, S., Banerjee, A.: A logic for information flow in object-oriented programs. In: Proc. ACM Symp. on Principles of Programming Languages, pp. 91–102 (2006)

[3] Askarov, A., Myers, A.C.: A semantic framework for declassification and endorsement. In: Gordon, A.D. (ed.) Programming Languages and Systems. LNCS, vol. 6012, pp. 64–84. Springer, Heidelberg (2010)

[4] Askarov, A., Sabelfeld, A.: Gradual release: Unifying declassification, encryption and key release policies. In: Proc. IEEE Symp. on Security and Privacy, pp. 207–221 (May 2007)

[5] Askarov, A., Sabelfeld, A.: Tight enforcement of information-release policies for dynamic languages. In: Proc. IEEE Computer Security Foundations Symposium (July 2009)

[6] Banerjee, A., Naumann, D., Rosenberg, S.: Expressive declassification policies and modular static enforcement. In: Proc. IEEE Symp. on Security and Privacy (May 2008)

[7] Banerjee, A., Naumann, D.A.: Stack-based access control and secure information flow. Journal of Functional Programming 15(2), 131–177 (2005)

[8] Barthe, G., D'Argenio, P., Rezk, T.: Secure information flow by self-composition. In: Proc. IEEE Computer Security Foundations Workshop, pp. 100–114 (June 2004)

[9] Bell, D.E., LaPadula, L.J.: Secure computer systems: Mathematical foundations. Technical Report MTR-2547, Vol. 1, MITRE Corp., Bedford, MA (1973)

[10] Biba, K.J.: Integrity considerations for secure computer systems. Technical Report ESD-TR-76-372, USAF Electronic Systems Division, Bedford, MA (Also available through National Technical Information Service, Springfield Va., NTIS AD-A039324) (April 1977)

[11] Boudol, G., Kolundzija, M.: Access-control and declassification. In: Proc. Mathematical Methods, Models, and Architectures for Computer Networks Security. Communications in Computer and Information Science, vol. 1, pp. 85–98. Springer, Heidelberg (2007)

[12] Cheney, J., Ahmed, A., Acar, U.: Provenance as dependency analysis. In: Arenas, M. (ed.) DBPL 2007. LNCS, vol. 4797, pp. 138–152. Springer, Heidelberg (2007)

[13] Chong, S., Liu, J., Myers, A.C., Qi, X., Vikram, K., Zheng, L., Zheng, X.: Secure web applications via automatic partitioning. In: Proc. ACM Symp. on Operating System Principles, pp. 31–44 (October 2007)

[14] Chong, S., Vikram, K., Myers, A.C.: Sif: Enforcing confidentiality and integrity in web applications. In: Proc. USENIX Security Symposium, pp. 1–16 (August 2007)

[15] Clark, D.D., Wilson, D.R.: A comparison of commercial and military computer security policies. In: Proc. IEEE Symp. on Security and Privacy, pp. 184–193 (May 1987)

[16] Clarkson, M., Schneider, F.B.: Quantification of integrity. In: Proc. IEEE Computer Security Foundations Symposium (July 2010)

[17] Cohen, E.S.: Information transmission in sequential programs. In: DeMillo, R.A., Dobkin, D.P., Jones, A.K., Lipton, R.J. (eds.) Foundations of Secure Computation, pp. 297–335. Academic Press, London (1978)

[18] Darvas, A., Hähnle, R., Sands, D.: A theorem proving approach to analysis of secure information flow. In: Proc. Workshop on Issues in the Theory of Security (April 2003)

[19] Denning, D.E.: A lattice model of secure information flow. Comm. of the ACM 19(5), 236–243 (1976)

[20] Denning, D.E., Denning, P.J.: Certification of programs for secure information flow. Comm. of the ACM 20(7), 504–513 (1977)

[21] Dima, C., Enea, C., Gramatovici, R.: Nondeterministic noninterference and deducible information flow. Technical Report 2006-01, University of Paris 12, LACL (2006)

[22] Diserholt, A.: Providing integrity policies as a library in Haskell. Master Thesis, Chalmers University of Technology, Gothenburg (March 2010), http://www.cse.chalmers.se/~russo/albert.htm

[23] Freeman, T., Pfenning, F.: Refinement types for ml. In: Proc. ACM SIGPLAN Conference on Programming Language Design and Implementation, pp. 268–277 (1991)

[24] Goguen, J.A., Meseguer, J.: Security policies and security models. In: Proc. IEEE Symp. on Security and Privacy, pp. 11–20 (April 1982)

[25] Gollmann, D.: Computer Security, 2nd edn. Wiley, Chichester (2006)

[26] Guttman, J.: Invited tutorial: Integrity. Presentation at the Dagstuhl Seminar on Mobility, Ubiquity and Security (February 2007), http://www.dagstuhl.de/07091/, Slides at, http://web.cs.wpi.edu/~guttman/

[27] Haack, C., Poll, E., Schubert, A.: Explicit information flow properties in JML. In: Proc. WISSEC (2008)

[28] Heintze, N., Riecke, J.G.: The SLam calculus: programming with secrecy and integrity. In: Proc. ACM Symp. on Principles of Programming Languages, pp. 365–377 (January 1998)

[29] Hoare, C.A.R.: An axiomatic basis for computer programming. Comm. of the ACM 12(10), 576–580 (1969)

[30] LaPadula, L.J., Bell, D.E.: Secure computer systems: A mathematical model. Technical Report MTR-2547, Vol. 2, MITRE Corp., Bedford, MA (1973); Reprinted in J. of Computer Security 4(2-3), pp. 239–263 (1996)

[31] Li, P., Mao, Y., Zdancewic, S.: Information integrity policies. In: Workshop on Formal Aspects in Security and Trust, FAST 2003 (2003)

[32] Li, P., Zdancewic, S.: Unifying confidentiality and integrity in downgrading policies. In: Workshop on Foundations of Computer Security, pp. 45–54 (June 2005)

[33] Mayfield, T., Roskos, J.E., Welke, S.R., Boone, J.M., McDonald, C.W.: Integrity in automated information systems. Technical Report P-2316, Institute for Defense Analyses (1991)

[34] McLean, J.: A general theory of composition for trace sets closed under selective interleaving functions. In: Proc. IEEE Symp. on Security and Privacy, pp. 79–93 (May 1994)

[35] Myers, A.C., Sabelfeld, A., Zdancewic, S.: Enforcing robust declassification and qualified robustness. J. Computer Security 14(2), 157–196 (2006)

[36] Myers, A.C., Zheng, L., Zdancewic, S., Chong, S., Nystrom, N.: Jif: Java information flow. Software release (July 2001), http://www.cs.cornell.edu/jif

[37] Naumann, D.: Theory for software verification. Draft (January 2009), http://www.cs.stevens.edu/~naumann/pub/theoryverif.pdf

[38] Ørbæk, P.: Can you trust your data? In: Mosses, P.D., Nielsen, M. (eds.) CAAP 1995, FASE 1995, and TAPSOFT 1995. LNCS, vol. 915, pp. 575–590. Springer, Heidelberg (1995)

[39] Ørbæk, P., Palsberg, J.: Trust in the λ-calculus. J. Functional Programming 7(6), 557–591 (1997)

[40] Pfleeger, C.P., Pfleeger, S.L.: Security in Computing, 4th edn. Prentice Hall, Englewood Cliffs (2006)

[41] Russo, A., Sabelfeld, A.: Dynamic vs. static flow-sensitive security analysis. In: Proc. IEEE Computer Security Foundations Symposium (July 2010)

[42] Sabelfeld, A., Myers, A.C.: Language-based information-flow security. IEEE J. Selected Areas in Communications 21(1), 5–19 (2003)

[43] Sabelfeld, A., Myers, A.C.: A model for delimited information release. In: Futatsugi, K., Mizoguchi, F., Yonezaki, N. (eds.) ISSS 2003. LNCS, vol. 3233, pp. 174–191. Springer, Heidelberg (2004)

[44] Sabelfeld, A., Sands, D.: Declassification: Dimensions and principles. J. Computer Security 17(5), 517–548 (2009)

[45] Sandhu, R.S.: On five definitions of data integrity. In: Proceedings of the IFIP WG11.3 Working Conference on Database Security VII, pp. 257–267 (1994)

[46] Schneider, F.B.: Enforceable security policies. ACM Transactions on Information and System Security 3(1), 30–50 (2000)

[47] Volpano, D., Smith, G., Irvine, C.: A sound type system for secure flow analysis. J. Computer Security 4(3), 167–187 (1996)

[48] Winskel, G.: The Formal Semantics of Programming Languages: An Introduction. MIT Press, Cambridge (1993)

[49] Zdancewic, S., Myers, A.C.: Robust declassification. In: Proc. IEEE Computer Security Foundations Workshop, pp. 15–23 (June 2001)

Determining the Integrity of Application Binaries on Unsecure Legacy Machines Using Software Based Remote Attestation

Raghunathan Srinivasan[1], Partha Dasgupta[1],
Tushar Gohad[2], and Amiya Bhattacharya[1]

[1] Arizona State University, Tempe AZ 85281, USA
{raghus,partha,amiya}@asu.edu
[2] MontaVista Software, LLC
tusharsg@gmail.com

Abstract. Integrity of computing platforms is paramount. A platform is as secure as the applications executing on it. All applications are created with some inherent vulnerability or loophole. Attackers can analyze the presence of flaws in a particular binary and exploit them. Traditional virus scanners are also binaries which can be attacked by malware. This paper implements a method known as Remote Attestation entirely in software to attest the integrity of a process using a trusted external server. The trusted external server issues a challenge to the client machine which responds to the challenge. The response determines the integrity of the application.

Keywords: remote attestation; integrity measurement; code injection.

1   Introduction

An untrusted computing platform poses many risks for its user (Alice). Execution of a security sensitive program ($\mathcal{P}$) can be tampered in many ways by an attacker (Mallory). Mallory can modify the binary image of $\mathcal{P}$ on the secondary storage media, Mallory can modify its executing in-core image, or Mallory can execute another program $\mathcal{P}'$ which mimics $\mathcal{P}$'s behavior. These changes can be made so that the untrusted platform reveals some secrets about Alice to Mallory. These attacks occur as Alice may execute many unverified or unsecure applications on the platform along with $\mathcal{P}$. It is estimated that on average programs can contain between 6 - 16 bugs per 1000 lines of code (LOC) in an application binary [1]. It is estimated that fault density in Operating System (OS) kernels can range from 2 - 75 per 1000 LOC [8]. In addition an OS consists of many device drivers, which have error rates much higher than kernel code [2], hence it can be concluded that it is difficult to eliminate all vulnerabilities from a system.

All copies of an application are identical; this gives Mallory the opportunity to analyze the presence and locations of flaws in the application, and develop means to exploit these flaws. Operating Systems offer little or no fault isolation;

S. Jha and A. Maturia (Eds.): ICISS 2010, LNCS 6503, pp. 66–80, 2010.
© Springer-Verlag Berlin Heidelberg 2010

this can lead to a malware rapidly obtaining control of a computing platform [17]. Detection of malicious logic is known to be difficult [3] and smart malware can render detection schemes ineffective; this is due to the fact that traditional detection mechanisms operate off application binaries which can be disabled or patched to escape detection [15]. Consequentially a user (Alice) has to request integrity measurement of the platform from an external agent, or an entity that operates beyond the bounds of the operating system.

Hardware and virtualization based attestation schemes have been researched intensively. Hardware based schemes involve taking integrity measurements by using the Trusted Platform Module (TPM) chip provided by the Trusted Computing Group [16], [11], [6], or with the use of a secure coprocessor that can be placed on the PCI slot [17], [9]. Virtualization schemes involve the hypervisor or a Domain 0 trusted OS obtaining integrity measurements on an untrusted guest OS [5], [10]. Hardware schemes have significant drawbacks: they require specialized hardware, cannot be re-programmed easily, are difficult to manage, and have the stigma of Digital Rights Management (DRM) attached to them. Virtualization requires greater resources than a system that operates on only one native OS. Software based solutions to measure the integrity of a platform involve the use of a set of techniques known as Remote Attestation, which can allow a remote agent to determine whether a particular application executing on a platform has been tampered. These set of techniques can be extended to determine the integrity of all applications on the platform.

In this paper a software based solution is implemented to measure the integrity of an application using a trusted external server (Trent). Trent issues a challenge to the client application $\mathcal{P}$. The response provided by $\mathcal{P}$ allows Trent to determine whether its integrity is compromised. The challenge should have inherent characteristics that prevent Mallory from forging any section of the results generated. A software protocol allows Mallory to perform various attacks. If the challenge is not significantly different for every attestation instance, Mallory can construct a replay of a response from a previous instance of the attestation. If the challenge is not complicated enough, Mallory can compute the response without executing the requested challenge and send the results to Trent. In addition, Mallory may bounce the challenge to another machine which contains a clean copy of the program to obtain results of the challenge. Mallory may also execute the challenge in a sandbox to determine its results.

To mitigate these situations Trent generates a new instance of attestation code $\mathcal{C}$ which is sent to Alice for execution. $\mathcal{C}$ is binary code which is injected by the application $\mathcal{P}$ on itself, in addition, $\mathcal{C}$ does not require the system library support as it executes any required system call by executing software interrupts. This prevents any user level malware from tampering with the results of integrity measurements, the kernel should not be compromised for this process to work. It may be argued that since the kernel is not compromised, it can be used to perform the entire attestation. This scenario would require that the OS keep track of every possible vendor's binaries, which can be a difficult task. The attestation is performed by an external agent to free up such complex requirements at

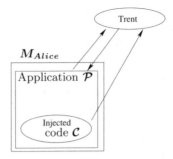

Fig. 1. Overview of Remote Attestation

the OS end. Injection of code on a client machine (M_{Alice}) to obtain integrity measurements is a novel aspect of the solution provided in this work. This reduces the window of opportunity that Mallory may have to analyze operations being performed on M_{Alice}.

The operations performed by C in each attestation instance are changed to prevent Mallory from performing a *replay* attack. There are many operations performed during attestation that make determining the response difficult for Mallory without executing C. In addition, C measures some machine and process identifiers which are determined through the system interrupt interface to make forging of results difficult. C has inherent programming constraints which ensure that if C executes, it sends the results back to Trent.

Fig. 1 provides an overview of remote attestation. Trent is a trusted entity who has knowledge of the structure of a clean copy of the process (P) to be verified. Trent has to be a trusted server, as Alice executes code received from Trent. Trent provides executable code (C) to Alice which is injected on P. C takes overlapping MD5 hashes and overlapping arithmetic checksums on sub-regions of P and returns the results to Trent. This prototype determines the integrity of a binary executing at (M_{Alice}). This protocol is robust against user mode viruses that can modify system libraries, but not against rootkits. The remote attestation implemented as part of this work is more robust and works under harder constraints moredifficult than those implemented in previous works *Pioneer* [13], *Genuinity*, [7].

The remainder of this work is organized as follows, section describes the related work for integrity measurement, section 3 describes the threat model and attack scenarios and their fixes in detail, section 4 describes the design of the software based remote attestation, section 5 presents the implementation details, section 6 describes work that is proposed as an extension of completing the remote attestation, and section 7 concludes the paper.

2   Related Work

Integrity measurement involves checking if the program code executing within a process, or multiple processes, is legitimate or has been tampered. It has been implemented using hardware, virtual machine monitors, and software based detection schemes. Some hardware based schemes operate off the TPM chip provided by the Trusted Computing Group [16], [11], [6], while others use a hardware coprocessor which can be placed into the PCI slot of the platform [17], [9]. The schemes using the TPM chip involve the kernel or an application executing on the client obtaining integrity measurements, and providing it to the TPM, the TPM signs the values with its private key and may forward it to an external agent for verification. The coprocessor based schemes read measurements on the machine without any assistance from the OS or the CPU on the platform, and compare measurements to previously stored values.

Terra uses a trusted virtual machine monitor (TVMM) and partitions the hardware platform into multiple virtual machines that are isolated from one another [5]. Hardware dependent isolation and virtualization are used by Terra to isolate the TVMM from the other VMs. Terra relies on the underlying TPM to take some measurements and hence is unsuitable for legacy systems. In *Pioneer* [13], the integrity measurement is done without the help of hardware modules or a VMM. The verification code for the application resides on the client machine. The verifier (server) sends a random number (nonce) as a challenge to the client machine. The response to the challenge determines if the verification code has been tampered or not. The verification code then performs attestation on some entity within the machine and transfers control to it. This forms a dynamic root of trust in the client machine. *Pioneer* assumes that the challenge cannot be redirected to another machine on a network, however, in many real world scenarios a malicious program can attempt to redirect challenges to another machine which has a clean copy of the attestation code. *Pioneer* incorporates the values of Program Counter and Data Pointer, in its checksum procedure; both the registers hold virtual memory addresses. An adversary can load another copy of the client code to be executed in a sandbox like environment and provide it the challenge. This way an adversary can obtain results of the computation that the challenge produces and return it to the verifier. *Pioneer* also assumes that the server knows the exact hardware configuration of the client for performing a timing analysis; this places a restriction on the client to not upgrade or change hardware components.

Genuinity [7] implements a remote attestation system in which the client kernel initializes the attestation for a program. It receives executable code and maps it into the execution environment as directed by the trusted authority. The executable code performs various checks on the client program, returns the results to a verified location in the kernel on the remote machine, which returns the results back to the server. The server checks if the results are in accordance with the checks performed, if so the client is verified. This protocol requires operating system (OS) support on the remote machine for many operations including loading the attestation code into the correct area in memory, obtaining hardware values such as TLB. It also requires the client OS to disable interrupts in order to have confidence that the attestation code actually executed. However, if a client OS is corrupted then it may choose to not disable interrupts in which case various meta-information about the process incorporated into the checksum will not be correct. Another problem with this scheme is that the results are communicated to the server by the kernel and not the downloaded code. This may allow a malicious OS to analyze and modify certain values that the code computes. In *TEAS* [4], the authors propose a remote attestation scheme in which the verifier generates program code to be executed by the client machine. Randomized code is incorporated in the attestation code to make analysis difficult for the attacker. The analysis provided by them proves that it is very unlikely that an attacker can clearly determine the actions performed by the verification code; however implementation is not described as part of TEAS and certain implementation details often determine the effectiveness of a particular solution.

SWATT [12] implements remote attestation scheme for embedded devices where the attestation code resides on the node to be attested. The code contains a pseudorandom number generator (PRG) which receives a seed from the verifier. The attestation code includes memory areas which correspond to the random numbers generated by PRG as part of the measurement to be returned to the verifier. The obtained measurements are passed through a keyed MAC function, the key for the instance of MAC operation is provided by the verifier. The problem with this scheme is that if an adversary obtains the seed and the key to the MAC function, the integrity measurements can be spoofed as the attacker would have access to the MAC function and the PRG code. Remote Attestation for Wireless Sensors has also been implemented by sending executable code to the sensor node. The node executes the code which returns measurements to the Base station [14]. This method appears similar to the one presented in this work, however, in this paper we provide remote attestation for a x86 based computer which has many nuances like protected code sections while sensor nodes do not. Injecting executable code into the process running on a x86 based computer is a harder task than injecting executable code in a sensor node. In addition, this paper also attempts to detect impersonation of a client machine by a machine controlled by an attacker which is not covered in the above work.

In this paper remote attestation is implemented by downloading new (randomized and obfuscated) attestation code for every instance of the operation. Executing attestation code that is recently downloaded from an external machine makes it difficult for the attacker to fake any results that are produced by the attestation code. This is because Mallory has no prior knowledge of the structure or content of the code, as a result of which the attacker has no knowledge of the operations performed by the downloaded code. This means that to launch a successful attack, Mallory would have to perform an 'impromptu' analysis of the operations performed and report the forged results to Trent within a specific time frame. This can be considered difficult to achieve.

3   Threat Model and Attack Scenarios

Alice executes a security sensitive application $\mathcal{P}$. Alice wants to know whether $\mathcal{P}$ has been tampered in any way prior to entering sensitive information in it.

Alice contacts Trent (who is a Trusted external agent) to attest $\mathcal{P}$. In order to determine the integrity of $\mathcal{P}$, Trent needs to obtain measurements from M_{Alice}. To achieve this, Trent provides executable code $\mathcal{C}$ to Alice to execute, Alice in turn injects the code on the application $\mathcal{P}$ to be attested. It is assumed that Trent has prior knowledge of the binary image of $\mathcal{P}$. This is a reasonable assumption as Trent can take these measurements locally on a known pristine copy of $\mathcal{P}$ even if Trent was not the vendor who generated $\mathcal{P}$. $\mathcal{C}$ performs certain checks on M_{Alice} to determine whether $\mathcal{P}$ has been tampered. It must be noted that denial of service based attacks, or process termination attacks which do not allow $\mathcal{C}$ to measure and communicate results to Trent will also be flagged as a tampered system at Trent's end.

3.1   Threat Model and Assumptions

It is assumed that Mallory may have installed a backdoor at M_{Alice} which can inform Mallory that an attestation process has been initiated. The backdoor may divert the challenge to another machine inside Mallory's control which can provide the response for the challenge. The backdoor can also utilize dis-assembly tools to determine the operations performed by the challenge. In addition the backdoor may attempt to execute the challenge inside a sandbox to determine the results of the response.

Since Trent is a trusted server, it is assumed that Alice will execute the code provided by Trent. Trent may be the vendor of the binary or a commercial provider of remote attestation service for many binaries. It is also assumed that Alice has a digital signature scheme, which can identified that the executable code was generated by Trent. The attestation code determines the IP address of the client which serves as its machine identifier, due to this it is assumed that Alice is not executing the programs behind a NAT. $\mathcal{C}$ executes OS calls by utilizing software interrupts, due to this it is assumed that the OS on M_{Alice} is not compromised by a *rootkit*. The presence of a *rootkit* would require the use of a VMM or a hardware based checker to determine integrity. It can also be noted that there are many software interrupts in the Linux operating system, due to which it can be assumed that a user level malware will find it difficult to intercept the operations of software interrupts.

It is assumed that $\mathcal{P}$ is not self-modifying code. Any integrity measurement technique cannot obtain measurements on self modifying code as the state of the code section changes with time and execution. Moreover, on computing platforms based on the Intel x86 architecture, the code section is 'write protected' by default, which reduces the scenario of self modifying code existing in common applications.

3.2   Fixing Attack Scenarios

Trent has to prevent Mallory from performing attacks that can compromise the attestation protocol. To achieve this, Trent must incorporate a degree of randomness and obfuscation in the system, so that it is difficult for Mallory to gain any knowledge about the computed response. Trent randomizes the operations performed by the attestation routine, inserts operations that are not executed, and inserts operations that do not impact the calculation of the response. Trent also checks the state of the open network connections on M_{Alice} to determine whether there are multiple copies of $\mathcal{P}$ executing on M_{Alice}. If Mallory executes a clean copy of $\mathcal{P}$ to perform the challenge-response sequence with the server, $\mathcal{P}$ would open a network port to communicate with Trent. In such scenarios $\mathcal{C}$ would observe two ports with the remote connection to Trent, and would flag it as an error. It can be argued that Mallory may force both versions of $\mathcal{P}$ to share the network port. However such sharing would not occur normally on a clean copy of $\mathcal{P}$, or without the explicit intervention of the OS. For the latter to happen, the OS must be corrupted by a *rootkit*, a scenario that is not considered in this work. To determine whether $\mathcal{C}$ was replayed to another machine, Trent obtains machine identifiers of M_{Alice}. As a last step Trent utilizes the technique of self-modifying code where some instructions in the challenge are modified post compilation, a separate section is placed in the challenge which fixes these instructions back to their original value during runtime.

4   Performing Remote Attestation

Fig. 2 shows the detailed steps in performing Remote Attestation. Alice makes a verification request and Trent sends a challenge which is the attestation routine. As part of the response Alice has to inject $\mathcal{C}$ at a specified location and execute it. $\mathcal{C}$ determines the machine identifier, socket and port state on the machine, process identifiers, arithmetic checksum on the code section of $\mathcal{P}$, and MD5 hash of the code section of $\mathcal{P}$. It must be noted that these measurements need not be performed in order, for randomization purposes they can be moved around.

4.1   Injection of Code on $\mathcal{P}$

The attestation code $\mathcal{C}$ is injected by $\mathcal{P}$ on itself. This allows $\mathcal{C}$ to execute within the process space of $\mathcal{P}$. This way $\mathcal{C}$ can utilize all descriptors of $\mathcal{P}$ on M_{Alice} without creating new descriptors. The advantage of this is that $\mathcal{C}$ cannot be executed in a sandbox easily and $\mathcal{C}$ can determine whether more than one set of descriptors are present for $\mathcal{P}$.

Implementation. At the client side $\mathcal{P}$ makes a connection request to Trent. Trent responds by providing the size of attestation routine $\mathcal{C}$ followed by the actual executable code to determine the integrity of $\mathcal{P}$. Trent also sends the information on the location inside $\mathcal{P}$ where $\mathcal{C}$ should be placed. $\mathcal{P}$ receives the code and prepares the area for injection by executing the OS call *mprotect* on the area. Once injection is complete, $\mathcal{P}$ creates a function pointer which points to the address of the location and calls $\mathcal{C}$ using the pointer.

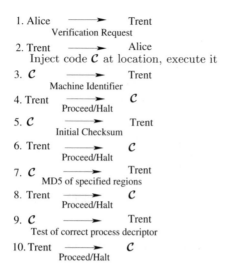

Fig. 2. Detailed steps in Remote Attestation process

4.2   Communication with Trent

The attestation routine does not have any calls to system libraries. This is because libraries may get compromised by an attacker to return incorrect results. In addition, the references to libraries are present at different location in every machine. It is easier to generate interrupts to execute the required functionality instead of placing the correct references to libraries in C. Moreover, a call to a system library may expose the functionality of the code to Mallory. Communication with Trent is achieved by executing the software interrupt with the interrupt number for the OS call *socketcall.*

Implementation. Communication to Trent is achieved by utilizing the socket connection that $\mathcal{P}$ created for an attestation request. All messages are sent to Trent using the *socketcall* system call. ASM code for a network send using *socketcall* is shown in Fig. 3. The routine allocates space on the stack for the parameter, followed by placing the parameters on the stack. The system call number for *socketcall* is 102, which is moved into the A register. The call number for a send in *socketcall* is 9, this value is moved to the B register, the location of the parameters are then moved to the C register and the system call is executed using the interrupt instruction (INT 80). Once the interrupt returns the stack is restored to the original value and the result is obtained in the A register. The functions provided inside *socketcall* is present in the Linux source code in the file $< include/linux/net.h >$.

4.3   Determining Machine Identifiers

To determine that $\mathcal{C}$ was not re-directed to another machine, Trent obtains the machine identifier on which $\mathcal{C}$ executes. Trent had received the request for

```
_asm_ (
        "sub    $16,%%esp\n"
        "movl   %%ebx,(%%esp)\n"
        "movl   %%ecx,4(%%esp)\n"
        "movl   %%edx,8(%%esp)\n"
        "movl   $0,12(%%esp)\n"
        "movl   $102,%%eax\n"
        "movl   $9,%%ebx\n"
        "movl   %%esp,%%ecx\n"
        "int    $0x80\n"
        "add    $16,%%esp\n"
        : "=a" (res)
        :"b" (send_sock), "c" (p_MD5Buf), "d" (len)
        );
```

Fig. 3. *send* routine through *socketcall* in ASM

attestation from Alice, hence has access to the machine IP address from which the request came. $\mathcal{C}$ obtains the IP address of the platform on which it is executing and communicates the result to Trent. Trent compares the two values to determine if the platform in which $\mathcal{C}$ is obtaining results is the same as the platform from which the request came. It can be argued that IP addresses are dynamic; however there is little possibility that any machine will change its IP address in the small time window between Alice requesting a challenge, to measurements being provided to Trent. M_{Alice} is not behind a NAT; hence Trent observes the IP address of M_{Alice} and $\mathcal{C}$ reports the same address. It can be argued that Mallory may have redirected the challenge to another machine ($M_{Mallory}$), and changed the address of the network interface on $M_{Mallory}$ to match that of M_{Alice}, but as M_{Alice} is not behind a NAT it would be difficult for Mallory to provide the address to another machine on an external network and achieve successful communication.

Implementation. $\mathcal{C}$ determines the IP address of M_{Alice} using system interrupts. The interrupt ensures that the address present on the network interface is correctly reported to Trent. This involves loading the stack with the correct operands for the system call, placing the system call number in the A register and the other registers and executing the interrupt instruction. Reading the IP address involves creating a socket on the network interface and obtaining the address from the socket by means another system call *ioctl*. The obtained address is in the form of an integer which is converted to the standard A.B.C.D representation.

4.4   Determining MD5 and Arithmetic Checksum

To determine whether the code section of $\mathcal{P}$ has been tampered, $\mathcal{C}$ computes an MD5 hash on the code section of $\mathcal{P}$. It is possible that since the code section of the binary is available, Mallory may compute the MD5 hash of every possible boundary region prior to Trent sending a challenge. To prevent this attack, Trent defines sub-regions in the binary and also defines overlaps on the sub-regions before measuring the MD5 hash of the overlapping regions. Overlapping checksums ensure that if by accident the sub-regions are defined identically in two different versions of C, the overlap provides a second set of randomization and ensures that the results of computation produced by C are different. This also ensures that some random sections of P are present more than once in the checksum making it more difficult for Mallory to hide any modifications to such regions.

To increase the complexity of the attestation procedure, Trent changes the MD5 measurement to a two phase protocol. MD5 code cannot be randomized, only changes that can be made in it are the changes to the overlapping sub-regions To prevent possible attacks on this protocol, Trent also obtains an arithmetic checksum of the code section of P. The checksum is taken on overlapping sub-regions as described above. The sub-regions defined for the arithmetic checksum are different from the sub-regions defined for obtaining the MD5 hash.

Implementation. The sub-regions on the MD5 hash are defined by Trent in the un-compiled code of the attestation routine using constants. Prior to compilation, Trent runs a pre-processor which generates random numbers to change these constants. The checksum operations are randomized by creating a basic arithmetic operation for a memory location and modifying the basic arithmetic operation to create alternate operations. This provides a pool of operations that can be performed on each memory location. During code generation, one operation is randomly selected for each memory location and placed in the attestation routine. This changes the arithmetic operations performed for every attestation request. The results of these operations are stored temporarily on the stack. Trent changes the pointers on the stack for all the local variables inside C for every instance.Trent places many instructions that never execute and inserts some operations that are performed on M_{Alice}, but not included as part of the results sent back to Trent. Trent also places a time limit (T) within which the response for these computations must be received. The addition of these operations is aimed at making analysis of operations difficult for Mallory within the time frame.

4.5 Determining Process Identifiers

To determine that the attestation routine was not bounced to execute inside a second copy of P, Trent obtains the state of the machine by comparing the open descriptors on M_{Alice} against a known state of a clean machine. Trent knows that in a clean machine there must be only one set of file descriptors that are used by P. If there are multiple copies of the descriptors used by P, then an error is reported to Trent. C identifies descriptors that match the known descriptors used by P and determines the process utilizing these descriptors in the system. If the process utilizing these descriptors are the same as the process inside which C executes then an OK state is sent to Trent.

Implementation. $\mathcal{C}$ obtains the pid of the process ($\mathcal{P}_0$) under which it is executing using the system interrupt for *getpid*. It locates all the remote connections established to Trent from M_{Alice}. This is done by reading the contents of the '/proc/net/tcp' file. The file has a structure shown in Fig. 4. This file has some more fields which are omitted from the figure. Once all the connections are identified, $\mathcal{C}$ utilizes the *inode* of each of the socket descriptor to locate any process utilizing it. This is done by scanning the '/proc/< *pid* >/fd' folder for all the running processes on M_{Alice}. In the situation that $\mathcal{P}$ is not corrupted, there should be only one process id ($\mathcal{P}_0$) utilizing the identified inode. If it encounters more than one such process, then it sends an error message back to Trent.

sl	local_address	rem_address	st	tx_queue	rx_queue	tr	tm->when	retrnsmt	uid	timeout	inode
0:	0100007F:1F40	00000000:0000	0A	00000000:00000000		00:00000000	00000000	0	0		5456
1:	00000000:C3A9	00000000:0000	0A	00000000:00000000		00:00000000	00000000	0	0		4533
2:	00000000:006F	00000000:0000	0A	00000000:00000000		00:00000000	00000000	0	0		4473
3:	0100007F:0277	00000000:0000	0A	00000000:00000000		00:00000000	00000000	0	0		5690
4:	0100007F:0019	00000000:0000	0A	00000000:00000000		00:00000000	00000000	0	0		5358
5:	0100007F:743A	00000000:0000	0A	00000000:00000000		00:00000000	00000000	0	0		5411

Fig. 4. Contents of /proc/net/tcp file

4.6   Generation of Attestation Code

To prevent Mallory from analyzing operations performed by $\mathcal{C}$, Trent places some obfuscations and randomizations inside the generated code. In addition, a time threshold (T) is created, if $\mathcal{C}$ does not respond back in a stipulated period of time (allowing for network delays), Trent informs Alice of a possible compromise. To prevent Mallory from performing any dis-assembly based analysis on $\mathcal{C}$, Trent can also choose to remove some instructions in $\mathcal{C}$ while sending the code to M_{Alice}. A code restore section is placed inside $\mathcal{C}$ such that during execution this section changes the modified instructions to the correct values. This makes it difficult for Mallory to determine the exact contents of $\mathcal{C}$ without executing it.

Implementation. Trent generates $\mathcal{C}$ for every instance of verification request. The source code of $\mathcal{C}$ is divided into four blocks, independent of each other. Trent assigns randomly generated sequence numbers to the four blocks and places them accordingly inside $\mathcal{C}$ source code. $\mathcal{C}$ allocates space on the local stack to store computational values. Instead of utilizing fixed locations on the stack, Trent replaces all variables inside $\mathcal{C}$ with pointers to locations on the stack. To allocate space on the stack Trent declares a large array of type char of size N, which has enough space to hold contents of all the other variables simultaneously. Trent executes a pre-processor which assigns locations to the pointers. Trent may also choose to change the instructions inside the executable code such that they cause analysis tools to produce incorrect results. $\mathcal{C}$ contains a section ($\mathcal{C}_{restore}$) which changes these modified instructions back to their original contents when it executes. $\mathcal{C}_{restore}$ contains the offset from the current location and the value to be

Table 1. Average code generation time at server end

Machine	Test generation time (ms)	Compilation time (ms)	Total time (ms)
Pentium 4	12.3	320	332
Quad Core	5.2	100	105

placed inside the offset. Trent places information to correct the modified instructions inside $\mathcal{C}_{restore}$. $\mathcal{C}_{restore}$ is executed prior to executing other instructions inside $\mathcal{C}$ and $\mathcal{C}_{restore}$ corrects the values inside the modified instructions.

5   Results

The remote attestation scheme was implemented on Ubuntu 8.04 (Linux 32 bit) operating system using the gcc compiler; the application $\mathcal{P}$ and attestation code $\mathcal{C}$ were written in the C language. The time threshold (T) is an important parameter in this implementation. The value of T must take into account network delays. Network delays between cities in IP networks are of the order of a few milliseconds [18]. Measuring the overall time required for one instance of Remote Attestation and adding a few seconds to the execution time can suffice for the value of T. The performance of the system was measured by executing the integrity checks on the source code for VLC media player interface [19]. Some sections of the program were removed for compilation purposes. The performance of the system was measured on two pairs of systems. One pair of machines were legacy machines executing on an Intel Pentium 4 processor with 1 GB of ram, and the second pair of machines were Intel Core 2 Quad machine with 3 GB of ram. The tests measured were the time taken to generate code including compile time, time taken by the server to do a local integrity check on a clean copy of the binary and time taken by the client to perform the integrity measurement and send a response back to the server. The time taken for compiling the freshly generated code is reported in Table 1. As expected, the Pentium 4 machine has slightly lower performance than a platform with 4 Intel Core 2 processors.

The integrity measurement code $\mathcal{C}$ was executed locally on the server and sent to the client for injection and execution. The time taken on the server to execute is the time the code will take to generate integrity measurement on the client as both machines were kept with the same configuration in each case. These times are reported in Table 2. As the code takes only in the order of milliseconds to execute on the client platform, the value for T can be set in the order of a few seconds to allow for network delays.

It can be observed from Table 1 that it takes an order of a few hundred milliseconds for the server to generate code, while from Table 2, it can be observed that the integrity measurement is very light weight and returns results in the order of a few milliseconds. Due to this, the code generation process can be viewed as a huge overhead. However, the server need not generate new code for every instance of a client connection. It can generate the measurement code

Table 2. Time to compute measurements

Machine	Server side execution time (ms)	Client side execution time (ms)
Pentium 4	0.6	22
Quad Core	0.4	16

periodically every second and ship out the same integrity measurement code to all clients connecting within that second. This can alleviate the workload on the server.

6   Extended Verified Code Execution

Once Remote Attestation determines the integrity of a program, the server begins communication and sharing of sensitive data with the client program. However, Mallory may choose to wait till the attestation process is completed, then substitute the client program $\mathcal{P}$ with a corrupted program $\mathcal{P}_c$. To prevent Mallory from achieving this, Trent has to obtain some guarantee that the process that was attested earlier is the same process performing the rest of the communication. Trent cannot make any persistent changes to the binary as Mallory would detect these changes under the current threat model. Trent has to change the flow of execution from normal in the client process such that the sequence of events reported will allow Trent to determine whether the previously attested process is executing.

As discussed before, Trent knows the layout of the program $\mathcal{P}$. At the end of Remote Attestation, Trent sends a new group of messages to $\mathcal{C}$. The message contains some code executable code $\mathcal{F}_1$ that Trent instructs $\mathcal{C}$ to place at a particular location in $\mathcal{P}$. Trent also instructs $\mathcal{C}$ to modify a future function call

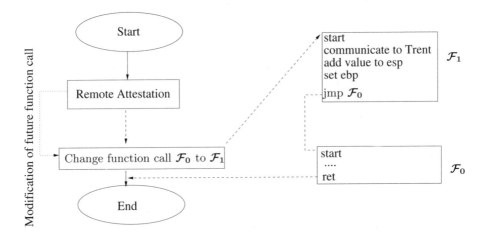

Fig. 5. Change of flow of execution

$\mathcal{F}_0$ in $\mathcal{P}$ such that instead of calling $\mathcal{F}_0$, $\mathcal{P}$ calls $\mathcal{F}_1$. $\mathcal{F}_1$ communicates back to Trent, this way Trent knows that the copy of $\mathcal{P}$ which was attested in the previous step is still executing. At the end of its execution, $\mathcal{F}_1$ undoes all its stack operation and jumps to the address where $\mathcal{F}_0$ is located. This would constitute extended verified code execution and can be seen in Fig. 5. This work can be pursued as a future work of remote attestation.

7   Conclusion and Future Work

This paper implements a method for implementing *Remote Attestation* entirely in software. A number of other schemes in literature that address the problem of program integrity checking were presented as related work. This work reduces the window of opportunity for the attacker Mallory to provide fake results to the trusted authority Trent by implementing various forms of obfuscation and providing new executable code for every run. This scheme was implemented on Intel x86 architecture using Linux and its performance was measured. This paper also presented future work to be pursued to detect compromises that occur after the completion of remote attestation.

Acknowledgements. This material is based upon work supported in part by the National Science Foundation under Grant No. CNS-1011931. Any opinions, findings, and conclusions or recommendations expressed in this material are those of the author(s) and do not necessarily reflect the views of the NSF.

References

1. Basili, V., Perricone, B.: Software errors and complexity: an empirical investigation0. Communications of the ACM 27(1), 52 (1984)
2. Chou, A., Yang, J., Chelf, B., Hallem, S., Engler, D.: An empirical study of operating systems errors. In: Proceedings of the Eighteenth ACM Symposium on Operating Systems Principles, pp. 73–88. ACM, New York (2001)
3. Cohen, F.: Operating system protection through program evolution* 1. Computers & Security 12(6), 565–584 (1993)
4. Garay, J., Huelsbergen, L.: Software integrity protection using timed executable agents. In: Proceedings of the 2006 ACM Symposium on Information, Computer and Communications Security, pp. 189–200. ACM, New York (2006)
5. Garfinkel, T., Pfaff, B., Chow, J., Rosenblum, M., Boneh, D.: Terra: A virtual machine-based platform for trusted computing. ACM SIGOPS Operating Systems Review 37(5), 206 (2003)
6. Goldman, K., Perez, R., Sailer, R.: Linking remote attestation to secure tunnel endpoints. In: Proceedings of the First ACM Workshop on Scalable Trusted Computing, p. 24. ACM, New York (2006)
7. Kennell, R., Jamieson, L.: Establishing the genuinity of remote computer systems. In: Proceedings of the 12th USENIX Security Symposium. pp. 295–308 (2003)
8. Ostrand, T., Weyuker, E.: The distribution of faults in a large industrial software system. In: Proceedings of the 2002 ACM SIGSOFT International Symposium on Software Testing and Analysis, p. 64. ACM, New York (2002)

9. Petroni Jr., N., Fraser, T., Molina, J., Arbaugh, W.: Copilot-a coprocessor-based kernel runtime integrity monitor. In: Proceedings of the 13th Conference on USENIX Security Symposium, vol. 13, p. 13. USENIX Association (2004)

10. Sahita, R., Savagaonkar, U., Dewan, P., Durham, D.: Mitigating the Lying-Endpoint Problem in Virtualized Network Access Frameworks. In: Clemm, A., Granville, L.Z., Stadler, R. (eds.) DSOM 2007. LNCS, vol. 4785, pp. 135–146. Springer, Heidelberg (2007)

11. Sailer, R., Zhang, X., Jaeger, T., Van Doorn, L.: Design and implementation of a TCG-based integrity measurement architecture. In: Proceedings of the 13th USENIX Security Symposium, pp. 223–238 (2004)

12. Seshadri, A., Perrig, A., Van Doorn, L., Khosla, P.: Swatt: Software-based attestation for embedded devices. In: Proceedings of 2004 IEEE Symposium on Security and Privacy, pp. 272–282. IEEE, Los Alamitos (2004)

13. Seshadri, A., Luk, M., Shi, E., Perrig, A., van Doorn, L., Khosla, P.: Pioneer: verifying code integrity and enforcing untampered code execution on legacy systems. ACM SIGOPS Operating Systems Review 39(5), 1–16 (2005)

14. Shaneck, M., Mahadevan, K., Kher, V., Kim, Y.: Remote software-based attestation for wireless sensors. In: Molva, R., Tsudik, G., Westhoff, D. (eds.) ESAS 2005. LNCS, vol. 3813, pp. 27–41. Springer, Heidelberg (2005)

15. Srinivasan, R., Dasgupta, P.: Towards more effective virus detectors. Communications of the Computer Society of India 31(5), 21–23 (2007)

16. Stumpf, F., Tafreschi, O., Röder, P., Eckert, C.: A robust integrity reporting protocol for remote attestation. In: Second Workshop on Advances in Trusted Computing, WATC 2006 Fall, Citeseer (2006)

17. Wang, L., Dasgupta, P.: Coprocessor-based hierarchical trust management for software integrity and digital identity protection. Journal of Computer Security 16(3), 311–339 (2008)

18. Web-link: Global ip network latency, http://ipnetwork.bgtmo.ip.att.net/pws/network_delay.html (retrieved on January 17, 2010)

19. Web-link: Vlc media player source code ftp repository, http://download.videolan.org/pub/videolan/vlc/ (retrieved on February 24, 2010)

Stamp-It: A Method for Enhancing the Universal Verifiability of E2E Voting Systems

Mridul Nandi[1], Stefan Popoveniuc[2], and Poorvi L. Vora[3]

[1] Department of Computer Science, C.R. Rao AIMSCS Institute
mridul.nandi@gmail.com
[2] KT Consulting
poste@gwu.edu
[3] Department of Computer Science, The George Washington University
poorvi@gwu.edu

Abstract. Existing proposals for end-to-end independently-verifiable (E2E) voting systems require that voters check the presence of a "receipt" on a secure bulletin board. The tally is then computed from all the receipts. Anyone can determine that the computation is correct— that is, the computation of the tally from the receipts is universally-verifiable. The fraud detection probability depends on the number of voters checking their receipts and the number of votes modified. This paper proposes an enhancement, *Stamp-It*, that does not require voters to check published receipts. It allows anyone to determine whether the tally is correctly computed, with probability independent of the number of voters who checked their receipt, extending the universal verifiability of the process. It does not require any additional computations to be performed during the election, and is hence very well-suited for use with the paper-ballot-based E2E systems. Finally, as an add-on, the enhancement does not degrade the original scheme.

1 Introduction

A large number of recent cryptographic voting system proposals [4,7,6,8,2,1,5] enable voters to audit an election outcome without requiring that they trust the voting system or election officials. This paper describes an enhancement that increases the robustness of the verifiability guarantees of the systems.

The general approach of the end-to-end independently verifiable (E2E) voting system proposals is to give each voter a receipt containing an encryption of the vote he or she cast. Through encryption audits, voters may determine that, with high probability, the encryption is correct. The voting system posts all the receipts on a public bulletin board, and each voter can check that his or her receipt is correctly posted. If the receipt is incorrectly posted, or if is not posted at all, the voter can bring his or her receipt as proof of malfeasance. It is assumed that a large enough number of voters do check the correct posting of their receipts, and that the voting system cannot accurately predict which voters will not check their receipts. All the receipts are collectively transformed into a

S. Jha and A. Maturia (Eds.): ICISS 2010, LNCS 6503, pp. 81–95, 2010.
© Springer-Verlag Berlin Heidelberg 2010

tally in a manner that (a) allows the general public to check that the tally is indeed derived from the set of receipts while (b) protecting the confidentiality of the ballot. Thus, the presence and correct representation of votes on the public bulletin board is *voter-verifiable*. The correctness of the tally computation—given the correctness of the encrypted votes on the secure bulletin board—is *universally verifiable*.

1.1   Limitations of Current Systems

Note that the ability to verify tally computation is meaningless if the public bulletin board does not contain correct receipts. Hence, the ability to detect fraud requires that (a) a large enough number of voters check their receipts, (b) the voting system cannot predict which voters will not check their receipts, and (c) the set of receipts checked by the voters is the same as the set of receipts used to produce the final tally. These requirements may not always be met. For example, while 30% of the voters checked their receipts in the student election at Université Catholique de Louvain [1], under 4% checked in the 2009 Takoma Park, MD municipal election [3]. Further, individual voters might provide a number of hints to the voting system to indicate whether they are likely to check receipts; for example, paper receipts might be discarded in on site trash cans. Finally, if the bulletin board can distinguish between a voter and an auditor, voters and auditors can be provided different sets of receipts. This may not be difficult, because the voter typically asks for a single ballot and provides its serial number, while an auditor need only ask for the entire set of receipts.

Voters may not be interested in performing any extra steps other than casting the ballot. This should not mean, however, that the election is not verified. Currently, candidates and non-voting observers—some of whom may not be physically present—are left with no means of assessing the validity of an election outcome if voters do not to check their receipts.

1.2   Stamp-It

In this paper, we propose an enhancement, *Stamp-It*, that allows anyone to check that all the receipts have been correctly posted. It assumes that at least one of several election associates does not collude with the voting system, and the integrity adversary is computationally bounded. Stamp-It is an add-on: it does not degrade the voter-verifiability and universal verifiability properties of the original E2E proposals, allowing those properties to hold without requiring that the election associates be trusted, and without requiring that the adversary be computationally bounded. Additionally, for those voting systems that provide computational privacy, Stamp-It does not degrade this property.

The additional functionality of Stamp-It comes about from its use of verification codes, generated by election associates who are trusted to not all collude with the voting system (which may wish to present an incorrect tally without being caught). The verification codes behave as signatures, by the election associates, on the receipts. When used with paper ballot systems, Stamp-It can be implemented using invisible ink so that the associates are not required to be online during the election, when the codes are provided to voters.

After the election, the voting system posts the verification codes along with the receipts on the bulletin board. Election associates are not required to participate when verification codes and receipts are checked, because associates also provide self-opening commitments to the codes. Anyone can check the self-opening commitments to determine that the codes are associated with the receipts, and, hence, that the receipts are correctly posted. Thus, voters need not later check that the receipt is correctly posted; they may, however, perform this task if they wish to.

From the voter's perspective, the process of obtaining the receipt does not change for electronic-ballot systems. For paper-ballot systems, however, the process gets slightly more complicated with the use of Stamp-It. With respect to the adversarial model, access to the complete ballot before the election affects both the privacy and the integrity guarantees (it affects only the (computational) privacy guarantees of other paper-based protocols). The enhancement does not address the issues of stuffing ballot boxes with additional ballots or of election officials spoiling paper ballots by marking additional votes if these are not addressed by the original system. Finally, when used with a paper-ballot system Stamp-It assumes certain properties of invisible ink (such as those made by the Scantegrity II system, used by the City of Takoma Park for the municipal election of November 2009). In particular, it assumes that the symbols printed with the invisible ink are not visible unless explicitly exposed.

Section 2 presents related work. Section 3 presents an informal description of the voting ceremony and section 4 a formal description of the front end of the system. Section 5 presents the security analysis (universal verifiability and the add-on property) of the enhancement. Section 6 addresses different types of attacks, and modifications that allow for the satisfaction of other properties. Section 7 presents conclusions.

2   Related Work

In this section we provide a brief review of E2E voting systems, and alternate solutions to the problem of receipt checking.

2.1   E2E Voting Systems

The general approach of the end-to-end independently verifiable (E2E) voting systems is to give each voter a receipt containing an encryption of the vote he or she cast. A voter may choose to challenge the encryption [2]; the voting system responds with a proof that it did encrypt the correct vote. For example, the voting machine may reveal the random numbers used for an asymmetric-key encryption. For another example, it might open a commitment made by it before the election, to the substitution cipher used for the particular ballot. If it cannot prove it correctly encrypted the vote cast by the voter, the voter knows it has been cheating. The vote-encryption phase of a cryptographic voting protocol is

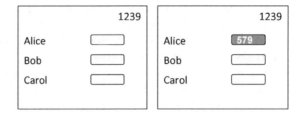

Fig. 1. Unmarked and Marked Scantegrity Ballots

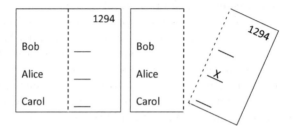

Fig. 2. Unmarked and marked Prêt à Voter Ballots Showing Receipt

thus an interactive phase: the voter provides the voting system with a choice, the system responds with an encryption of the choice, the voter then communicates whether to cast the encrypted vote or to audit it, and the system responds by casting the vote or providing a proof respectively.

In paper-ballot E2E systems the ballots are designed so as to enable the interaction of the vote-encryption phase without the presence of a computer. Voters are able to encrypt their votes by simply filling out a paper ballot. For example, the Scantegrity ballot looks like a regular optical scan ballot. Printed in invisible ink in the ovals are *confirmation codes* corresponding to the encryption of that choice. When a voter marks an oval, he obtains the encryption of that choice in the form of the confirmation code, see Figure 1. He notes the encryption along with the serial number of the ballot. To audit the encryption the voter fills up all ovals and checks the confirmation codes against the commitments (to the correspondence between confirmation numbers and candidates) provided by the voting system before the election and opened after the election (thus the result of the audit is known after the election). (The voting system opens commitments for only uncast and unspoiled ballots).

In another example, the Prêt à Voter voting system presents the voter with a permuted list of candidates. The position of the voter's mark is an encryption of the vote, and, with the ballot serial number, forms the receipt. (See Figure 2.) A ballot is audited by challenging the system to open commitments corresponding to that ballot, revealing the ordering of the candidates and checking it against that printed.

If an encryption fails an audit; that is, an incorrect vote is encrypted, this is easily proven because the voter's choice is noted on the paper ballot. Electronic ballot systems are considerably weaker from this perspective. If, on being challenged, the voting system reveals a proof of encryption of an incorrect vote, the voter has no way of proving that it is indeed incorrect because he has no record of what he communicated. A paper ballot behaves as a write-once tape recording the protocol interaction between the voter and the voting system and provides proof of the nature of the interaction during an audit. Such a proof cannot be provided by electronic ballots when the encrypting computer is not trusted. (This problem is addressed through the use of procedures for electronic ballot systems).

2.2   Other Approaches to the Problem of Receipt Checking

There are simple approaches to the problem of receipt checking that are not completely satisfactory. We note a few here.

A set of election associates who are trusted to not all collude with the voting system are assigned to the task of checking receipts. Multiple copies of receipts may be made at the polling booth and handed one each to the associates, who then check the receipts online. This trivial solution, however, requires election associates to do all their work after the election, and is hence vulnerable to denial-of-service style attacks. Further, it requires election associates to be present at the poll site, or requires a secure chain of custody on the receipts (the problem of maintaining a secure chain of custody of voted ballots is exactly the kind of issue end-to-end verifiable voting systems seek to address). Stamp-It also uses election associates, but does not require them to be involved after the election.

If it is possible to perform computations at the time of voting, receipt values can be electronically signed by the election associates and the signatures posted on the secure bulletin board with the receipts. Anyone can then check the signatures and verify the presence of receipts on the board without voters checking their own receipts. This, however, requires all election associates to be online during the election, and requires that it be possible for voters to check digital signatures in the polling booth or just outside it. Stamp-It provides similar properties to this approach when used with electronic ballots.

In a manner similar to that used by VoteBox [10] to prevent ballot stuffing, the receipt value can contain, in addition to the encrypted vote, a hash of several previous receipt values. The checking of a single receipt corresponds to the checking of all receipts before it in the chain[1]. In order for this approach to be successful, voters should have a means of verifying the hash values on their receipts while in the polling booth, or, practically speaking, just outside.

When Stamp-It is used with paper-ballot systems, it has properties similar to those of the second solution above. Additionally, Stamp-It does not require any

---

[1] None of the authors were present at EVT/WOTE 2009 rump session, but their understanding is that this approach was proposed by Josh Benaloh at that time.

computations to be performed at the time of voting, and allows for an interactive protocol between the voter and each election associate even though the associates do not need to be online during the election.

3   Informal Description of Stamp-It

3.1   Actors

For each election, we assume the following actors: voters, election officials, election associates, designated printing auditors, public auditors, a public bulletin board. Stamp-It makes the following assumptions about the actors: The election officials do not collude with the voters or the election associates or the designated printing auditors. The election associates do not collude with the printing auditors. The bulletin board is secure and append-only.

3.2   The Modified Paper Ballot

While the use of Stamp-It is not very complicated when ballots are electronic, when used with paper ballots the paper ballots need to be modified. We exemplify its use with a Prêt à Voter [6] ballot combined with Scantegrity II [5] confirmation numbers. However, other ballot styles can be used, e.g. PunchScan [8]. Electronic ballot styles can also be used if the set of possible (unsigned) receipts is small.

Stamp-It uses a counterfoil for the ballot style of the corresponding end-to-end system. A sample ballot is presented in Figure 3(a) and the corresponding Stamp-It counterfoil is presented in Figure 3(b). The Scantegrity II confirmation numbers shown on the ballot are printed in invisible ink, which is developed when the voter applies a rubber stamp dabbed with developing ink. The voter then sees the confirmation number for the candidate she marked and for no other candidate. Care must be taken to ensure that the rubber stamp has enough ink on it so that the number is exposed.

The Stamp-It counterfoil has a series of verification numbers underneath each candidate, encoded in 2D barcodes also printed in invisible ink—see Figure 3(c). In order to facilitate the exposure of the barcodes corresponding to the chosen candidate, the ballot is printed on "carbon" paper—the ink on the back of the ballot also reacts with the invisible ink, developing it and making it visible. The election authority gets to see the Stamp-It verification barcodes exposed for each ballot, and no other verification barcodes printed on the counterfoil. It is required to publish the exposed barcodes on a public bulletin board along with the Scantegrity confirmation code. The ballot, as the voter sees it, is presented in Figure 4(a). The Stamp-It counterfoil, as the election authority sees it, is presented in Figure 4(b).

3.3   Voting Ceremony as the Voter Sees It

To vote, the voter dabs the rubber stamp into the ink pad, finds his or her favorite candidate and marks the entire rectangle in which the candidate is printed. As in Scantegrity II, a confirmation number will appear next to the marked candidate.

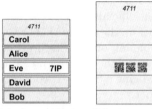

4711	
Carol	BX7
Alice	988
Eve	7IP
David	JR8
Bob	FFM

(a) A Prêt à Voter ballot with Scantegrity II confirmation codes printed in invisible ink

(b) A Stamp-It counterfoil, 2D-barcodes printed in invisible ink

(c) A larger view of the 2D-barcode

Fig. 3. The ballot is stacked on top of the Stamp-It counterfoil

4711	
Carol	
Alice	
Eve	7IP
David	
Bob	

(a) A marked ballot, as the voter sees it

(b) A marked Stamp-It counterfoil, as the election authority sees it

Fig. 4. Marked ballot and Stamp-It counterfoil

The voter then casts her ballot into an optical scan machine or a ballot box, and turns her counterfoil over to an election official. If the voter wishes, she may write down the confirmation number along with the serial number of her ballot. She may later check that these are correctly posted on a public bulletin board, as in Scantegrity II. However, even if no voter does this, Stamp-It provides a secondary mechanism which ensures, given the assumptions mentioned earlier, that the election officials correctly post all the necessary information for the checking of the tally.

Except for the random order of candidates, the voter's experience is largely the same as in currently-used optical scan systems, if he or she does not keep receipts. Additionally, the voter need not do anything after leaving the polling place. If the voter chooses to keep a receipt, the voter's experience is similar to that with Scantegrity (except for the random ordering of candidates).

3.4   What Actually Happens during the Voting Ceremony

The main idea behind Stamp-It is that the election officials only get to see the Stamp-It verification codes for the positions marked by the voters. Thus they can only publish on the public bulletin board these Stamp-It verification codes. Anyone can check, through checking verification code commitments, that the verification code does correspond to the posted position (the Prêt à Voter receipt). While the voter may check that the public bulletin board contains correct receipts, this is no longer necessary.

We describe the steps which are introduced by the use of the Stamp-It counterfoil as an enhancement to an end-to-end verifiable system:

1. Each designated Stamp-It election associate publishes commitments which tie a verification code to a position and a ballot (e.g. designated Stamp-It associate 3, ballot 4711, position 2, verification code 77484888277735910). The verification code is long enough so that it cannot be easily guessed and someone with knowledge of a valid confirmation number would be able to check the commitment without the need for any additional information.
2. The Stamp-It counterfoils are printed collectively by the election associates and given to the election officials as close to the election as possible (this might be as late as just before the election). The verification codes are printed as 2D barcodes in invisible ink on the Stamp-It counterfoils.
3. The election officials prepare the end-to-end setup, and assemble two-page ballots, the bottom page being a Stamp-It counterfoil and the top page being printed on "carbon" paper.
4. Before the election, each designated printing auditor is allowed to choose a number of random ballots (and corresponding counterfoils) and check that the printing on them is according to the commitments.
5. In the process of voting, the voter reveals the Stamp-It verification codes for the position she marks.
6. The ballot is deposited in the ballot box, while the Stamp-It counterfoil is scanned and the revealed Stamp-It verification codes and positions are immediately published by the election officials on the public bulletin board.
7. The Stamp-It counterfoil is shredded.
8. At the end of election day, the election officials produce a public report containing the serial numbers of the voted ballots (and thus used Stamp-It counterfoils). The report is signed and checked by public observers and candidate representatives present at the polling place.
9. The positions that were marked represent the encoded votes (Prêt à Voter receipts) which serve as input to a publicly-verifiable tallying scheme. As these positions are tied to the Stamp-It verification codes through the commitments posted by the election associates, anyone can check their correctness, along with the correctness of the reported tally.

4   Formal Description of Stamp-It

In this section we describe formally the Stamp-It ballot and the protocol. We also provide an analysis of the protocol.

4.1 Formal Description

Convention: Each of a set of c candidates is associated with a member of the set $\mathbb{Z}_c$ based on its rank in an alphabetically-ordered list. (Note that the algebraic structure of $\mathbb{Z}_c$ plays no role here). For example, Alice, Bob and Carol are assigned to be 0, 1 and 2 respectively when they are the only three candidates. One may include "no choice" as one candidate, which will always be last in the list.

In addition to the election officials, c' independent election associates participate in the voting protocol. Designated print auditors audit the printed ballots and Stamp-It counterfoils. Independently, voters may also optionally audit these.

Publishing public parameters. Before the election, election officials (EOs) make the following parameters public.

1. The number of ballots, N.
2. Specifications (including public keys if any) of cryptographic algorithms such as commitment schemes, digital signature schemes, hash functions etc. used in the protocol.
3. Two code spaces $\mathcal{C}$ (of small size, e.g. set of all strings of three alpha-numeric characters) and $\mathcal{C}'$ (large enough that an exhaustive search is infeasible, e.g. the set of all strings of twenty hexadecimal characters).

Publishing commitments. Election officials (EOs) and the c' election associates make the following commitments and publish them.

1. The ith election associate generates independent random verification codes $C'_{S,i}(p)$ from the code space $\mathcal{C}'$, $1 \leqslant S \leqslant N$, $p \in \mathbb{Z}_c$. All associates publish the hash-outputs of the codes for a pre-selected secure[2] hash function H.
2. For each serial number S, EOs secretly generate random confirmation codes $C_S(p), 0 \leqslant p < c$ and a shuffle or permutation π_S over $\mathbb{Z}_c$. The EOs publish commitments to all confirmation codes and the candidate shuffles π_S. The EOs also publish any other commitments that might be required for the computation of the tally from the confirmation codes (this would depend on the back-end used). Finally, the EOs publish commitments to the entire set of confirmation codes used per ballot, arranged in ascending order.

All the commitments are signed. Commitments to verification codes are self-opening commitments, so that election associates are not required to participate after the election, and are not required for the opening of the commitments to verification codes. Commitments to confirmation codes are not self-opening. This is because we attempt to retain as much as possible of the original Scantegrity design as possible; Scantegrity confirmation codes are short so as to be easy to remember, and commitments to the short codes cannot be self-opening and pre-image secure.

---

[2] The hash function H restricted on $\mathcal{C}'$ is preimage resistant.

Definition 1. Ballot and Stamp-It Counterfoil *A ballot paper associated with serial number S consists of a permutation π_S on $\mathbb{Z}_c$ (candidate shuffle) and a tuple of random codes $\langle C_S(p)\rangle_{p\in\mathbb{Z}_c}$, where $C_S(p) \in \mathcal{C}$. For each position $p \in \mathbb{Z}_c$, $\pi_S(p)$ and $C_S(p)$ denote a candidate and the corresponding confirmation code respectively. Each ballot is associated with a Stamp-It counterfoil printed by a set of c' election associates. The Stamp-It counterfoil associated with serial number S is the tuple of randomly-generated verification codes $\langle C'_{S,i}(p)\rangle_{i,p}$ where $1 \leqslant i \leqslant c'$, $0 \leqslant p < c$ and $C'_{S,i}(p) \in \mathcal{C}'$.*

We describe how a voter votes for a candidate $x \in \mathbb{Z}_c$ on a ballot with serial number S. The verification codes are printed in invisible ink on the Stamp-It counterfoil. That is, verification are not available to the EO before the election.

1. Voter finds $p \in \mathbb{Z}_c$ such that $\pi_S(p) = v$, the candidate of his or her choice. (p is the position of the vote v on the ballot with serial number S)
2. Voter obtains the pth verification codes $C'_{S,i}(p)$, $1 \leqslant i \leqslant c'$ of each election associate from the Stamp-It counterfoil. He also obtains the confirmation code $C_S(p)$ from the ballot.
3. Voter gives the obtained verification codes $C'_S(p) := C'_{S,1}(p)\|\ldots\|C'_{S,c'}(p)$ along with (S, p) to the EO and destroys the Stamp-It counterfoil so that EOs cannot obtain any verification codes that were not exposed.

Step 2 above is implemented by using invisible ink as described in Section 3. When polls close, EOs publish $(S, p, C'_S(p))$ for each cast ballot with serial number S. Knowing π_S, EOs can compute the vote for the serial number S. The back-end would eventually provide a proof that the final result is correctly computed from the all positions p_S.

4.2 Stamp-It as an Enhancement

The following generalization of Stamp-It may be used to enhance other voting protocols. Let $\mathcal{P}$ be a paper-based E2E voting protocol. (The generalization of Stamp-It for an electronic voting protocol is straightforward, where online election associates sign, or provide self-opening commitments to, the voter's receipt.) Let $E : \mathcal{V} \times \mathcal{K} \to \mathcal{E}$ be the encryption algorithm used by the voting protocol, where K, $\mathcal{V}$ and $\mathcal{E}$ denote the key-space, the set of all votes and the set of encrypted votes, respectively. Let $K_1, \ldots, K_N$ be the encryption keys for the encryption algorithm; K_i corresponding to ballot serial number i. The encryption keys are usually implicitly present in the paper-based ballots; see, for example, [9] for a description how several E2E system ballots are of this form. Consider a voting protocol which publishes the encrypted votes where the subset $\mathcal{E}' = E(\mathcal{V}, K_S) \subset |\mathcal{E}|$ corresponding to a ballot S is small (a small multiple of the number of options in a race).

The Stamp-It counterfoil associated with serial number S is the tuple of randomly-generated verification codes $\langle C'_{S,i}(e)\rangle_{i,e}$ where $1 \leqslant i \leqslant c'$, $e \in \mathcal{E}'$ and $C'_{S,i}(e) \in \mathcal{C}'$. The tuple is constructed by c' election associates before the election. (It is assumed that the associates do not all collude with the voting system to change the election outcome). The associates also commit to the verification codes they generate before the election. For example, the commitments could be based on hash functions. During the casting phase, the voter obtains encrypted vote e corresponding to his vote v and ballot number S. In the enhanced protocol, the voter provides the values of $C'_{S,i}(e)$ for all i to the election official. In addition to all other information required to be posted on the secure bulletin board for $\mathcal{P}$, the election officials also provide these values. Anyone can verify that the supplied verification codes are correct with respect to the commitments posted before the election. When the commitments are simply hashes of the verification codes, the EA need not reveal any additional information after the election.

5   Security Analysis of Stamp-It

5.1   Universal Verifiability Analysis

We assume that the number of ballots cast is exactly the number of receipts on the bulletin board. This may be ensured through a simple procedure, see section 6.

The voter-verifiability property of the enhanced system is clearly no different from that of the original system. As long as voters check confirmation codes uniformly at random, the voter-0verifiability property of the original system holds.

Now we demonstrate that universal verifiability is extended; that is, that anyone can check the correctness of the tally even if voters do not check the bulletin board for receipts. (Voters do perform some verification at the time of voting, however. For example, by casting the vote they verify that the encrypted value was obtained by following the process of casting a vote). For simplicity we assume that the hash function is a random oracle. One may obtain a similar result for a pre-image resistant hash function. We choose $\mathcal{C}'$ large enough such that $N/|\mathcal{C}'| = \delta$ is negligible. The following result holds even if not a single voter checks his or her confirmation code.

Theorem 1. (Universal Verifiability) *If (a) at least one of the c' election associates does not collude with the EOs; (b) $H : \mathcal{C}' \rightarrow \{0,1\}^{hSize}$ is a random oracle; and (c) EOs do not have access to the invisible codes on the Stamp-It counterfoils, then the probability of an undetected mismatch between true cast positions and corresponding published positions is approximately $q \times c \times \delta$ where $\delta = \frac{N}{|\mathcal{C}'|}$ and q is the number of random oracle queries made by the EOs.*

Proof. We have a total of c verification codes per election associate for each of the N ballots, resulting in a total of $M = c \times N$ verification codes whose values are committed to by each election associate. In order for an undetected mismatch between true cast positions and corresponding published positions, the EOs must successfully replace a true verification code, corresponding to a true cast position, with a valid verification code for an uncast but published position, for all election associates. Suppose all but one of the election associates colludes with the EOs and makes available their printed verification numbers for all positions on all ballots. Then the EOs must guess correctly a valid verification code for the non-colluding associate, for at least one of the ballots. If the EOs make a query to H, the probability that this query corresponds to one of the verification codes is $c \times \delta$. If the EOs make q queries, the probability that one corresponds to a verification code is approximately $q \times c \times \delta$ for q small compared to $(c \times \delta)^{-1}$. (As H is a random oracle, each queried hash value is independent of any other, and of the verification codes). $\hspace{2cm}$ □

5.2   The Stamp-It Enhancement as an Add-on That Does Not Degrade the Security of the Original Scheme

Now we show that the enhancement is simply an add-on that does not degrade the original protocol. In particular, all the security notions present in $\mathcal{P}$ are present in the enhancement. Because we have already demonstrated the verifiability properties of the enhancement, we now provide a short sketch of the fact that the privacy/incoercibility properties of the original scheme are also retained. In order to do so, we show that, given the appropriately-defined inputs, the information obtained from an enhanced protocol can be simulated by an adversary from the information obtained from the original protocol. We assume that the physical process of constructing the ballot does not reveal information about the position of candidates on the receipt layer.

Given a ballot-based voting protocol $\mathcal{P}$, let $\mathcal{P}'$ be the enhanced voting protocol. Let $\mathbf{Cor}'$ be the set of corrupted players in the enhanced protocol $\mathcal{P}'$ and $\mathbf{Cor} = \mathbf{Cor}' \setminus \mathbf{EA}$ the corresponding set of corrupted players in the original protocol $\mathcal{P}$, where $\mathbf{EA}$ is the set of election associates. That is, $\mathbf{Cor}$ and $\mathbf{Cor}'$ are identical except for the possible presence of one or more election associates in the latter. We represent the election associates forming the difference between the two sets by $\mathbf{Cor}_{\mathrm{EA}} = \mathbf{Cor}' \cap \mathbf{EA}$. Let $(x, \mathsf{view}(\mathbf{Cor}))$ and $(x', \mathsf{view}(\mathbf{Cor}'))$ denote the pair of input and view of the corrupted players in $\mathcal{P}$ and $\mathcal{P}'$ respectively. Note that x is a sub-tuple of x' since $\mathbf{Cor} \subseteq \mathbf{Cor}'$.

To prove that $\mathcal{P}'$ is an add-on over $\mathcal{P}$ we need to show that for any corrupted players $\mathbf{Cor}'$ and their inputs x' the view $\mathsf{v}' = \mathsf{view}(\mathbf{Cor}')$ can be efficiently simulated from $\mathsf{v} = \mathsf{view}(\mathbf{Cor})$ and x'. In other words, the view of the corrupted players in the enhanced protocol can be simulated from their inputs and the view of the corresponding corrupted players in the original protocol.

We write $\mathsf{v}' = \mathsf{v} \| \mathsf{v}_{\mathrm{enh}}$ where $\mathsf{v}_{\mathrm{enh}}$ is the additional part of the view due to the enhancement, and is as follows:

- When there is no corrupted election associate, $\mathsf{v}_{\mathrm{enh}}$ consists of the tuple of all published verification codes $\langle C_{S,i}(e_S) \rangle_{S \in \mathcal{S}, i}$ and hash values of all verification codes (i.e. commitments to all verification codes generated by election associates) where $1 \leqslant i \leqslant c'$, S varies over all cast serial numbers and e_S is the encrypted vote corresponding to the ballot number S, i.e. $e_S = E(v_S, K_S)$ where v_S and K_S are the vote and the keys used in the ballot with serial number S.

 – When one or more election associates are corrupted, in addition to the above, their verification codes are included as part of their input as well.

We now provide a sketch of the proof that $\langle C_{S,i}(e_S)\rangle_{S\in S,i}$ and the hash values of all verification codes can be simulated from v and x'. Since the inputs of the election associates contain their verification codes, we need to simulate (1) $C_{S,i}(e_S)$ for $i \notin \mathbf{Cor}_{\mathrm{EA}}$ and cast ballot serial number S, (2) hash values $\mathrm{Hash}(C_{S,i}(e))$ for all $e \in \mathcal{E}'$, and all serial numbers S. Since $C_{S,i}(e)$'s are generated independently and uniformly (also independently of the keys K_S), $C_{S,i}(E(v_S, K_S))$ is also independent of $E(v_S, K_S)$ for any choice of the vote v_S. Thus $C_{S,i}(e_S)$ are statistically independent of v, which contains $E(v_S, K_S)$ and can be simulated. Similarly, because all codes are independently generated, the simulator can generate all verification codes and output the hashes of these for (2). Thus we have sketched the following useful result for our enhancement Stamp-It.

Theorem 2. *The view of corrupted players in the enhanced protocol can be simulated from their inputs and the view of the corresponding corrupted players in the original scheme.*

6   Discussion

In this section we provide reasoning for some of the choices we made while designing the protocol, and briefly present the alternatives and how they might change system properties. We do not discuss the properties that may have already been discussed by others; for example, the properties of invisible ink.

We first describe a potential threat to the system that leads to a violation of one of the assumptions of Theorem 1, and ways to address it. The assumption that EOs do not have access to printed invisible ink codes on the counterfoil may not always be valid. In particular, it might be possible to read the invisible codes using hyper-spectral equipment, either before or after the election. In order to prevent EOs from replacing one set of verification codes with another, we require that voted serial numbers are committed to at the end of the election, in the presence of election observers and candidate representatives[3], and that voted counterfoils are shredded. We also require that counterfoils are provided as close to election day as possible, and are stored in tamperproof containers. (Note that it is much easier to ensure secure storage of ballots over a single night than it is for the weeks over which ballots are stored for manual audits). One may require additionally that all voted or non-voted counterfoils be returned to election associates, so they may check that these are not tampered with.

We now provide our reasoning for the use of self-opening commitments. With the use of self-opening commitments, election associates are not required to participate after the election as they need not be involved in the opening of the commitments and the checking of the published positions. This requires, however, that the verification codes be long enough so that even a small fraction

---

[3] This is also a requirement for other paper-ballot-based end-to-end systems, such as Scantegrity.

of the space of all verification codes cannot be tested by trial and error by EOs attempting to change the recorded position of the vote, and the corresponding verification code. It also implies that a computationally unbounded adversary (such as an unbounded EO) can correctly and efficiently guess verification codes and replace these (as well as the corresponding positions and hence the votes) with ones of its choice. If no voters check confirmation codes, this change will not be detected. If election associates could be involved after the election to open commitments, it would be possible to use unconditionally hiding commitments and to thus prevent the unbounded adversary from successfully guessing codes in the absence of voters checking confirmation codes. Note that, if a large enough number of voters checks confirmation codes, an unbounded EO would not be able to change verification codes without being detected, because voters would detect a change in confirmation codes.

7   Conclusions

We have presented an enhancement to end-to-end verifiable systems that provides universal verifiability for the end-to-end process (and not just of tally computation) if (a) a set of election associates will perform certain simple tasks before the election, and can be trusted to not all collude with the voting system (or election officials) to change the tally and (b) the integrity adversary is computationally bounded. When these assumptions are not satisfied, the verifiability properties of the original end-to-end system (voter-verifiability of cast vote representation and universal verifiability of the tally when the adversary is computationally unbounded) still hold. Further, if the original scheme provides computational privacy, the add-on preserves this property. The enhancement is simple and allows for election verification in the absence of voter-verification, without putting much of a burden on election associates. Because associates are not required to perform any tasks after the election, the election is not vulnerable to a denial of service attack by the associates. For this reason, and because it does not require computations to be performed at the time of voting, it is more robust than other simpler proposals.

Acknowledgements

A large part of this research was performed while Mridul Nandi was at The George Washington University. He would like to acknowledge the support of NSF Award No 0937267. Poorvi L. Vora would like to acknowledge the support of NSF Award Number 0831149.

References

1. Adida, B., deMarneffe, O., Pereira, O., Quisquater, J.-J.: Electing a university president using open-audit voting: Analysis of real-world use of helios. In: IAVoSS Workshop On Trustworthy Elections (WOTE 2009), Montreal, Canada (August 2009)

2. Benaloh, J.: Simple verifiable elections. In: Proceedings of the USENIX/Accurate Electronic Voting Technology Workshop 2006 on Electronic Voting Technology Workshop, EVT 2006, p. 5. USENIX Association, Berkeley (2006)
3. Carback, R., Chaum, D., Clark, J., Conway, J., Essex, A., Herrnson, P.S., Mayberry, T., Popoveniuc, S., Rivest, R.L., Shen, E., Sherman, A.T., Vora, P.L.: Scantegrity II Municipal Election at Takoma Park: The First E2E Binding Governmental Election with Ballot Privacy. In: Proceedings of the 19th USENIX Security Symposium (August 2010)
4. Chaum, D.: Secret-ballot receipts: True voter-verifiable elections. IEEE Security and Privacy, 38–47 (January/February 2004)
5. Chaum, D., Carback, R., Clark, J., Essex, A., Popoveniuc, S., Rivest, R.L., Ryan, P.Y.A., Shen, E., Sherman, A.T.: Scantegrity II: End-to-end verifiability for optical scan election systems using invisible ink confirmation codes. In: Proceedings of the USENIX/Accurate Electronic Voting Technology Workshop, EVT 2007. USENIX Association (2008)
6. Chaum, D., Ryan, P.Y.A., Schneider, S.: A practical voter-verifiable election scheme. In: di Vimercati, S.d.C., Syverson, P.F., Gollmann, D. (eds.) ESORICS 2005. LNCS, vol. 3679, pp. 118–139. Springer, Heidelberg (2005)
7. Andrew Neff, C.: Practical high certainty intent verification for encrypted votes (2004), http://citeseerx.ist.psu.edu/viewdoc/download?doi=10.1.1.134.1006&rep=rep1&type=pdf
8. Popoveniuc, S., Hosp, B.: An introduction to PunchScan. In: IAVoSS Workshop On Trustworthy Elections (WOTE 2006), Robinson College, Cambridge UK (June 2006)
9. Popoveniuc, S., Vora, P.: A framework for secure electronic voting. In: IAVoSS Workshop On Trustworthy Elections (WOTE 2008), Katholieke Universiteit, Leuven, Belgium (July 2008)
10. Sandler, D., Derr, K., Wallach, D.S.: Votebox: a tamper-evident, verifiable electronic voting system. In: Proceedings of the 17th USENIX Security Symposium, SS 2008, pp. 349–364. USENIX Association, Berkeley (2008)

Strengthening XSRF Defenses for Legacy Web Applications Using Whitebox Analysis and Transformation

Michelle Zhou, Prithvi Bisht, and V.N. Venkatakrishnan

Department of Computer Science
University of Illinois at Chicago
{yzhou,pbisht,venkat}@cs.uic.edu

Abstract. Cross Site Request Forgery (XSRF) is regarded as one of the major threats on the Web. In this paper, we propose an approach that automatically retrofits the source code of legacy web applications with a widely-used defense approach for this attack. Our approach addresses a number of shortcomings in prior blackbox solutions for automatic XSRF protection. Our approach has been implemented in a tool called X-PROTECT that was used to retrofit several commercial Java-based web applications. Our experimental results demonstrate that the X-PROTECT approach is both effective and efficient in practice.

Keywords: Cross Site Request Forgery, Attack Prevention, Whitebox Analysis.

1 Introduction

Cross Site Request Forgery (XSRF) is web-based attack that is often referred to as a "sleeping giant" [1] among web-based threats. There have been many high-profile XSRF vulnerabilities that have gained attention in the recent past, including attacks [19] on popular websites such as the New York Times and YouTube.

An XSRF attack is typically staged when a victim user who is logged on to a vulnerable website visits an attacker controlled Web-page (We present an example of this attack in Section 2.). In this scenario, the attacker controlled content forces the victim user's browser to initiate unintended requests to the vulnerable website. The user's browser, which acts as an accomplice for the attacker in this case, issues these unintended requests with the user's credentials (e.g., session identifiers), resulting in unauthorized actions (such as initiating purchases or transactions).

The problem of preventing XSRF attacks is effectively the problem of determining if a given incoming HTTP request was *originally intended* by the web application. If this can be done successfully, the web application can filter unintended requests and thereby prevent these attacks. Since the web browser attaches session credentials with every request (whether intended or not), session identifiers cannot serve as a basis for making this distinction.

Documents from another origin (such as untrusted web pages visited by the user's browser) are a frequent source of unintended requests. A web application server can determine the origin of any request by looking at the REFERER header of the HTTP request, which specifies the Uniform Resource Identifier (URI) of the document from which the request was initiated. Unfortunately, the REFERER header is optional in the

S. Jha and A. Maturia (Eds.): ICISS 2010, LNCS 6503, pp. 96–110, 2010.
© Springer-Verlag Berlin Heidelberg 2010

HTTP specification, and is often suppressed by enterprise firewalls due to confidentiality and privacy concerns [7]. The ORIGIN header [7] was proposed to address the above shortcomings of the REFERER header. While the adoption of the ORIGIN header by browser vendors is expanding, support for it is still not available in several mainstream browsers.

The lack of browser support for XSRF protection has led web applications to rely mostly on server-side solutions, of which the secret token defense is the most well adopted one. In this approach, a server-generated secret token (distinct from the session credentials) is appended as an additional parameter to all the URIs intended by the server. Subsequently, whenever an HTTP request is received, the presence of the secret token enables the server to determine if this request was originally intended.

As the secret-token defense requires no special support from browsers, it is a very widely deployed defense approach. This paper considers the problem of automatically transforming an existing (or legacy) web application with the secret token defense to filter out requests that mount XSRF attacks. Automatic solutions require little or no human intervention in contrast to manual solutions that require extensive programmer involvement. As they tend to drastically reduce development time, web applications using such automated mechanisms can be patched and re-deployed relatively quickly, without leading to prolonged exposure to attacks that is typical of the manual patching process.

The novel direction pursued by our approach involves whitebox analysis and transformation of the web application. In contrast to blackbox mechanisms [11,12] that employ secret token protection, a whitebox approach is very precise in identifying the intended requests of a web application. This enables the web application to guard all its sensitive resources from XSRF requests, while freely allowing access to non-sensitive requests (e.g., public URIs), without over-protecting the application.

The rest of the paper is organized as follows. Section 2 presents an overview of XSRF attacks and discusses issues in the existing secret-token-based XSRF defenses. Section 3 presents an overview of our approach. The next two sections Section 4 and Section 5 provide details of transformations done to safeguard applications. Section 6 presents our experimental evaluation on open-source web applications. Section 7 gives an overview of the existing literature and we conclude in Section 8.

2   Background

Assumptions. This paper assumes that the web application uses an appropriate Cross-site Scripting (XSS) defense. In absence of XSS protection, it is very hard to prevent XSRF attacks, as malicious script content can initiate HTTP requests to launch XSRF attacks. Furthermore, we do not address the *login XSRF* attack [7] in which a victim is ushered into an attacker controlled session. We also assume that the application does not suffer from *Authentication Bypass problem* i.e., a sensitive operations can *only* be performed in an authenticated session (if the application is vulnerable to bypass, it can be exploited with a much simpler non-XSRF attack). Finally, we assume that the network traffic is encrypted to protect against active network attackers as described in [7].

```
 1| if (checkSecurity(session)) {
 2|   String sAction = getParam(request,"action");
 3|   if (sAction == "delete") {
 4|     String sSQL = "delete from items where id="
 5|                    + getParam(request, "id");
 6|     db_executeSQL(sSQL);
 7|   }
 8|   ..//list books to be deleted,generate URL_0
 9|   out.write("<a href=\"Books.jsp?
10|     action=delete&id=1\">Delete</a>\n"); ..
11| }
12| String comments = db_readComments(); ..
13| out.write("<a href=\"Search.jsp\">
14|     Search Books</a>\n");      //generate URL_1
15| out.write("<a href=\"http://www.a.com\">
16|     External Link</a>\n");     //generate URL_2
17| out.write(comments);//show reviews,has URL_3
```

Fig. 1. Bookstore web page   **Fig. 2.** Books.jsp handles requests and generates HTML

2.1   Running Example

To illustrate XSRF attacks, let us consider a simplified online Bookstore application [3] shown in Figure 1. The web page is rendered in an authenticated session and
contains four hyperlinks (underlined font): the first three are application generated to
allow a user to delete a book, search books, or visit an external website, and the last link
is embedded in a malicious review comment submitted by another user. Figure 2 shows
a code snippet of the application that handles the request and generates this page. The
code first authenticates HTTP request by checking validity of the session associated
with the request (Line 1). If valid, it constructs a delete query based on parameters
action and id and generates URLs to delete other books (Lines 2–10). All statements
that contributed URLs in the response are annotated as URL_0 – URL_3, respectively.

Suppose this application is hosted at a domain http://www.mybooks.com and a
user (after authenticating at this domain) visits another web page controlled by an attacker. Further, assume that the visited malicious page embeds the following image tag:
<img src="http://www.mybooks.com/Book.jsp?action=delete&id=1">.
The presence of the <img> tag automatically induces the browser to make the HTTP
GET request. Furthermore, the browser follows the *Same Origin Policy* (SOP) and sends
the session cookie of mybooks.com along with the HTTP request. On the server side,
this request passes the session check and causes deletion of the book with id 1, successfully completing an XSRF attack. This deletion operation was successful despite
the fact that it was neither requested by the user, nor did the server provide a trusted
link that was intended to initiate such a deletion operation. This is a typical example of an XSRF attack. XSRF attacks are typically launched through <img> and similar
HTML elements that point to resources on the web through URLs e.g., <a>, <iframe>,
<form>.

A defense for XSRF attacks therefore requires additional measures to distinguish
between server-intended requests and attacker-initiated requests as described next.

2.2   Existing Secret-Token-Based Defenses and Limitations

The most well known technique to prevent XSRF attacks augments the sessions with an additional *XSRF secret token*. Besides the session cookie, a random secret token is associated with each session. A web request is considered as an intended request only if it has both: a valid session cookie and a valid XSRF secret token. Unlike a session cookie, which is attached by a browser to *any* request to the same domain (whether the request was made by a link generated by the server or not), the secret token approach, if correctly implemented in an application, enables the server to identify if the request originated from a link generated by the server.

A number of existing research efforts, such as CSRFGuard [2], RequestRodeo [11], NoForge [12], and Zeller et al. [19] have developed techniques for XSRF prevention using the token-based defense as the basis. In this, [2,11,12] are implemented as black-box proxies and perform two key operations: (a) intercept all HTTP requests and validate the token before forwarding requests to the web application, and (b) intercept HTTP responses and add the token by re-writing all URLs in responses. NoForge [12], a server-side blackbox proxy, maps each session to a unique token. RequestRodeo [11], a client-side blackbox proxy, maps each HTTP response URL to a unique token. Zeller et al. [19] recommend a whitebox approach to store tokens at the client side as cookies. While these solutions have identified several issues in addressing XSRF protection in legacy applications, they still fall short of providing a satisfactory treatment of XSRF protection as they fail to address one or more of the following four issues, as summarized in Table 1.

1. *Unsharable public URLs* We refer to all resources of a web application that can be accessed without authentication as *public* resources and URLs pointing to such parts as *public URLs*. A blackbox defense re-writes all URLs in HTML responses to also contain a token corresponding to the session of a particular user. It makes each re-written URL valid only in a given user's session. Such URLs cannot be shared (say in email or chat messages) even though they point to public resources of the web application. In the running example, assume that the Search functionality is public then the corresponding URL_1 is a public URL. A blackbox defense would re-write this URL to contain $user_1$'s token. When $user_2$ tries to use this URL, the application rejects it as it does not provide the token corresponding to the session of $user_2$.

2. *Coarse-grained XSRF protection* Another flip-side of the issue 1 discussed above is *coarse-grained protection*. After a web session is established, *all* HTTP requests are intercepted by the blackbox proxies to validate the token. In the running example Search is a public functionality and a blackbox proxy would still validate presence of a valid token to grant access to it. Such coarse-grained protection may affect the availability of public resources. In contrast, *fine-grained* protection, in which secret token checks are performed only on private requests, will provide the necessary availability for public resources, with the additional security protection for private resources.

3. *Same-domain XSRF attacks* Such attacks aim to bypass token-based defenses by tricking the defense mechanism to add valid secret tokens to malicious URLs. In

Table 1. Compare token-based XSRF defenses. A '✓' denotes the approach has the property.

Approaches	Share Public URLs (1)	Fine-grained XSRF Protection (2)	Prevent Same-domain XSRFs (3)	Prevent Client Leaks (4)	Automated Approach
NoForge [12]					✓
RequestRodeo [11]	✓				✓
Zeller & Felten [19]	✓	✓			
X-Protect	✓	✓	✓	✓	✓

Figure 1, the HTML of the page contains two URLs to delete a book: URL_0 (intended) and URL_3 (injected along with review comments). A blackbox defense that re-writes HTML pages cannot distinguish such injected URLs from intended URLs. Consequently, in re-write step, a valid XSRF token is added to the malicious URL_3 as well which then successfully bypasses the token-based defense.

4. *Client-side secret token leaks* By re-writing URLs to contain tokens, all blackbox approaches embed tokens directly in the client side code. The presence of XSRF token in the client side code then opens up different ways in which it can be leaked e.g., sharing URLs or HTML source code. Once leaked, they render the token-based defense ineffective e.g., attacker can craft an XSRF attack URL with the victim's token. In the running example, token would be leaked if (a) any of URL_0–URL_3 is shared with another user or (b) URL_2 is accessed.

Table 1 summarizes the existing token-based defenses and our approach X-PROTECT. Columns two through five indicate if the above issues 1 through 4 are addressed in each of these approaches. Column six indicates if each of these defenses is an automatic solution. As summarized by this table, the approach presented in this paper addresses all of the above issues in blackbox mechanisms. It does so by adopting a whitebox (source-code-based) approach to analyzing the web application. An overview and the high level principles behind our approach appear in the following section.

3   Approach Overview

This section provides overview of our approach which aims to strengthen known token-based XSRF defenses. We specifically aim to (a) avoid over-protecting resources and (b) prevent the secret token leak / misuse.

Figure 3 shows our approach that consists of two stages: offline and online, in safeguarding the application. In the offline stage, the web application source code is transformed which is then subsequently deployed. During the online stage, this deployed application selectively validates XSRF token for HTTP requests. An HTTP request can access sensitive (non-public) resources only if token validation succeeds. Further, the application transforms the HTML and delivers it to an unmodified browser that assists in XSRF prevention and token protection. In the rest of this section, we provide an overview of activities performed in each stage and the key principles behind our approach.

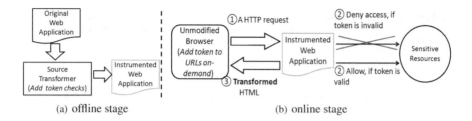

(a) offline stage   (b) online stage

Fig. 3. Overview of X-PROTECT

1. Offline adding token checks via source code transformation. X-PROTECT follows a whitebox approach that automatically adds token checks to the application's source code such that each request that triggers sensitive operations, undergoes token validation. The key challenge in this stage lies in identifying source code locations to add such checks and we address it by leveraging a novel insight about authentication checks done by web applications. Further, this stage adds code to control lifetime of the token (initialization/deletion), and perform information flow (taint) tracking that guides the online token supply as described in the next stage (Section 4).

2. Online server-side HTML transformation and client-side token attachment. The checks added in the offline phase demand the presence of a valid token at runtime for HTTP requests that trigger sensitive operations. The goal of this online phase is to precisely add tokens only to those URLs that require secret tokens. The key challenge here is in limiting exposure of the token in the client side code and avoiding its misuse. We present a novel approach to address this challenge through server-side HTML transformation and client-side on-demand token attachment. First, with the help of information flow tracking, we only transform application generated URLs in HTML responses thus avoiding misuse of token. Second, the transformation ensures that the secret token is supplied to URLs on *need basis* at the client thus minimizing exposure of the token in the client side code. (Section 5)

Our solution has the following three properties:

$\mathcal{P}_1$: secret tokens are only added to legitimate requests

$\mathcal{P}_2$: secret tokens are never present in the HTML / JavaScript

$\mathcal{P}_3$: secret tokens are only checked when necessary

We wish to note that using a pure blackbox approach neither $\mathcal{P}_1$ nor $\mathcal{P}_3$ can be satisfied. Since the extent of untrusted content is not known to a black-box approach, they end up violating $\mathcal{P}_1$ by adding secret tokens to injected third-party/same-domain URLs. Since the paths in the web application code that lead to sensitive operations are not available to a blackbox approach, they can only check secret token on every request, thereby violating $\mathcal{P}_3$. These observations guided our choice of a whitebox analysis of the server side code.

Another important property that we aim for is $\mathcal{P}_2$. As discussed before, blackbox approaches embed secret tokens in the HTML directly that can then be a source of leak.

```
1|  if(validSecretToken()) {
2|      stat.executeUpdate(sSQL);
3|  } else {
4|      .. redirect to login page
5|  }
```

```
1|  if (checkSecurity(session)
2|      && validSecretToken()) {
3|      lines 2-10 in running example
4|  }
5|  ..
```

Fig. 4. An intuitive approach: Insert the token check before each sensitive operation

Fig. 5. Our solution: Insert the token check along with each authentication check

In our approach, this property is held by adding JavaScript functions to the HTML at the server, and invoking them at the client when a URL is used. The following two sections elaborate how our approach satisfies the above three properties.

4   Server-Side Code Transformation

The offline transformation of web application adds XSRF secret validation checks at appropriate places. The key challenge is in precisely placing these checks such that they do not *overprotect* and thus reduce application's availability or *underprotect* and fail to thwart XSRF attacks.

As a vulnerable web application fails to sufficiently protect sensitive operations, an intuitive XSRF defense is to *protect each sensitive operation by validating the token immediately before the sensitive operation*. Figure 4 illustrates validation of XSRF token before deletion of a book record in our running example (line 6 in Figure 2). Although precise, this solution requires detailed specification of sensitive operations of an application. Unfortunately, each application has its own notion of sensitive operations e.g., a read operation may be sensitive/public based on database tables it accesses. A manual specification of sensitive operations for large applications may require application-specific domain knowledge and sometimes be tedious and error-prone.

To avoid the aforementioned complexities, we analyzed placement of sensitive operations in web applications and found that web applications typically execute sensitive operations in the context of an authenticated user. This analysis led to the following observation that our secret check placement relies on: *sensitive operations can only be performed in authenticated sessions*. This observation is not satisfied by web applications that suffer from the Authentication Bypass problem which is out of this work's scope.

Locations for placing secret checks. In general, checks for authenticated sessions can either be explicit or implicit. On the one hand, checks take the form of conditionals to validate authentication tokens supplied with HTTP requests against server side state. On the other hand, checks can be implicit and often use authentication tokens in operations that fail if the client is not authenticated. For example, in a session-cookie-based authentication, the server-side session object may contain a flag to identify authenticated sessions by fetching the session object corresponding to the session cookie (explicit check). This can also be enforced implicitly by storing the flag in a database table and querying the database with the session cookie.

Our solution strengthens these authentication checks by identifying them and additionally validating the XSRF secret token at the same program location. Intuitively, a code block guarded by the authentication check may contain operations that are intended to be performed only in an authenticated session. These operations are also the typical target of XSRF attacks. By requiring that such checks also validate the secret token, our XSRF token placement precisely strengthens these vulnerable blocks of code in the web application. As shown in Figure 5, the explicit authentication check is now strengthened by additional check of XSRF token (in bold).

Transformation to add the secret token check. X-PROTECT requires a per-application configuration file to identify operations that check, set and reset authentication status. Given this information, X-PROTECT performs a DEF-USE analysis of the source code. By finding the invocations of authentication status getter method, X-PROTECT locates program variables which are initialized with the authentication status, i.e., DEF locations. It then locates all the program statements that use such variables, i.e., USE locations. These variables if used in conditional statements, represent program statements that validate authentication status explicitly. X-PROTECT then augments their conditional expressions by adding a condition to validate the secret token.

An approach to locate conditional statements may miss implicit checks. In implicit use, authenticated tokens often uniquely identify authenticated users e.g., a field in the database table may be set for authenticated session ids. To strengthen such implicit checks, X-PROTECT identifies all DEF locations that are not used in conditionals before being used at one or more USE locations. Intuitively, these locations represent program statements that read authentication status but may not use it explicitly in conditionals. For such DEF locations, code is added to validate the secret before call to getter method of the authentication status. The idea is to forbid an implicit use of authenticated status without supplying the correct XSRF secret token. For DEF locations that may be used explicitly or implicitly, X-PROTECT guards the DEF location with secret token validation as well as augments the conditional expressions in explicit use with the secret token check.

This transformation guarantees satisfaction of principle $\mathcal{P}_3$ presented in §3. In comparison to black-box approaches it does not suffer from over-protection (issues 1 and 2 described in §2), as the instrumented web application would not validate the secret token for public requests. Moreover, the solution has two advantages over the intuitive solution outlined in the beginning: First, it does not require complete specification of sensitive operations. We only require specification of the authentication operation, a much smaller task than enumerating all the sensitive operations of an application. Second, the program code executed on authentication failure is reused to cover token validation failure as well, thereby avoiding need for any additional code.

Insert the code to initialize/reset the token. Clearly, we only need the XSRF token at all program locations where authentication status is available. An intuitive approach is then to mirror the lifecycle of authentication status to initialize/reset the XSRF token. In specific, all setter invocations for the authentication status that do not use default value (unauthenticated) are identified. X-PROTECT then inserts code to initialize the secret token value at all such locations. The remaining invocations of the setter method are statements that reset authentication status and direct the source transformer to insert code to reset the secret token as well.

Apart from the above program changes, X-PROTECT also augments the web application code to track the flow of data from untrusted sources to HTML pages. As taint tracking techniques are fairly standard in current security literature (e.g., [17]), we do not elaborate it further. This tracking allows identification of application generated (trusted) parts of the web page which then enables precise transformation of the HTML code as described in the next section.

5   HTML Transformation

5.1   Identifying URLs to Retrofit

Based on their targets, all URLs in HTML responses fall into one of the following two categories: *same-domain URLs* that target the same application and *other-domain URLs* that target third party web applications. It is straightforward for any XSRF defense to distinguish between these two types of URLs. However, as mentioned in §2, we note that same-domain URLs can also come from untrusted sources and should not be augmented with secret tokens as it would permit same-domain XSRF attacks. The taint tracking conducted by the instrumented application identifies parts of response HTML that were contributed by untrusted sources and enables X-PROTECT to identify application generated URLs.

Once we have the mechanism to identify web application generated URLs, a simple approach would add tokens to all trusted same-domain URLs. However, this would result in an unnecessary exposure of tokens in URLs and hence increase chances of token leaks. In specific, we observe that all public URLs created by the application do not need the secret token, and employ the following process to identify public URLs: For each web application file F, X-PROTECT statically traverses the control flow graph of F's entry function and all invoked functions in an inter-procedural fashion. If in any path an authentication check is found, all URLs targeting file F are deemed private. Otherwise all URLs targeting file F are deemed public. URLs not targeting any application file, e.g., `<img src="image/img.gif">`, are deemed public too.

5.2   Supplying Token at the Client Side

X-PROTECT transforms trusted same-domain private URLs by using JavaScript. For HTML tags that embed URLs, X-PROTECT identifies event functions that are invoked when such URLs are actually used and updates them to embed token in the URL at runtime. As presence of token in HTML/JavaScript can lead to leaks, X-PROTECT supplies the token as a cookie, similar to [19]. Subsequently, JavaScript code reads the token from cookie and adds it to the URL of the tag. To limit the exposure of URLs with token values, X-PROTECT employs a similar JavaScript-based solution to remove the token when the URL value is used in operations other than HTTP request generation.

Figure 6 (X-PROTECT added code in bold) shows transformed HTML for the running example that supplies token through `onclick` event handler and `removeToken()` removes it for other user interactions e.g., `mouseover` event. Table 2 summarizes handling of the other tags. In our experience, this strategy has worked well for GET as well as POST requests (e.g., target URL of `form` tags is retrofitted before form submission).

```
 1 | <script type="text/javascript"> ...
 2 | function addToken(id) {
 3 |   var st = ...;  // read token cookie to 'st'.
 4 |   var elem = document.getElementById(id);
 5 |   elem.href = elem.href + '?secretToken=' + st;   // add token
 6 | } </script>
 7 | <!-- URL₀: intended private, transformed -->
 8 | <a href="Books.jsp?action=delete&id=1"
 9 |   id="alink1" onclick="addToken('alink1');"
10 |   onmouseover="removeToken('alink1')">Delete</a>
11 |
12 | <a href="Search.jsp">Search Books</a> <!-- URL₁: public, unchanged. -->
13 |
14 | <!-- URL₂: third-party URL, transformed. -->
15 | <a href="Referer.jsp?url=http://www.a.com">External Link</a>
16 |
17 | <!-- URL₃: untrusted, unchanged -->
18 | <a href="Books.jsp?action=delete&id=1">Delete</a>
```

Fig. 6. An example of the transformed HTML in an authenticated session

Table 2. Intended private same-domain URL transformation (new code in bold)

HTML Tags	URL Example	Transformed Format
<form>	<form action= "A.jsp"> ...</form>	<form action="A.jsp" **id="form1" onsubmit="addTokenToForm('form1');">** <input type="hidden" name="secretToken" value=""/> ...</form>
<frame> <iframe> <img> <script>	<frame src="B.jsp"> ... </frame>	<frame **id="f1"** src=""> </frame> **<script type="text/javascript"><!-- var st = readCookie('SecretToken'); document.getElementById('f1').src='B.jsp?secretToken='+st; //--></script>**

The secret token is supplied by adding the HTTP Set-Cookie header in responses from web pages that initialize / reset secret token (Section 4). Each same-domain private request to the application contains the token as a cookie as well as an input parameter. The token validation passes at the instrumented application only when these two token values match. The token cookie is secure from malicious client-side scripts since we assume earlier that a XSS defense is in place. If the application intends to use the HttpOnly flag to prevent cookies from being accessed by JavaScript, the token can be directly appended to those URLs that require it. However, this may lead to token leaks as described earlier.

Prevent token leaks through REFERER headers of third-party URLs. When the token appears in the URL of a web page, visiting a third-party URL in the page can leak the token through the REFERER header. Although client side solutions exist to control the content of the REFERER header e.g., [18], they rely on per-client configuration. We hence employ a server-side solution that aims to alter the REFERER header contents by using redirection. Each third-party URL is re-directed through a web page that does not perform any sensitive operations. Hence, the token is not added to URL of the web

Table 3. Third-party URL transformation (new code in bold). Other tags are not transformed.

HTML Tags	Third-party URL Example	Transformed Format	HTML Generated by Transformed URL
\<a\> \<frame\> \<iframe\>	\<a href= "http://www.a.com"\> External link \</a\>	\<a href="**Referer.jsp?url=** http://www.a.com"\> External link \</a\>	\<html\>\<head\>\<meta http-equiv="Refresh" content="0; URL= http:// www.a.com"\>\</head\>\</html\>
\<img\>	\<img src= "http://www.a.com /img.gif"\>	**\<iframe src= "imgFrm/iframe1.html" ...\> \</iframe\>**	\<html\>\<body\>\<img src= "http://www.a.com/img.gif"\> \</body\>\</html\>

page. Table 3 summarizes these transformations e.g., \<a\> is re-written with the help of HTTP Meta Refresh tag and \<img\> is embedded within a \<iframe\>. The REFERER header of external \<a\> is either empty or set to the transformed URL, depending on different browsers. The REFERER header of external image is set to the iframe address.

The above transformation enforces principles $\mathcal{P}_1$ and $\mathcal{P}_2$ described in Section 3. Further, the HTML responses do not contain the token, which is set as a cookie. Being only dependent on JavaScript, our approach is browser and platform agnostic.

5.3 Discussion

As X-PROTECT removes the REFERER header, it may not be directly applicable to applications that rely on REFERER header for origin checks or preventing *deep linking*. Such applications could use X-PROTECT by using other means to determine the request origin e.g., ORIGIN header [7]. In addition, our solution and all other XSRF solutions cannot protect token leaks due to *CSS history attack* [16], which essentially finds the token through the use of the "visited links" feature and brute-force.

6 Evaluation

We implemented a prototype tool to evaluate X-PROTECT on Java/JSP-based applications. The source code transformer uses Soot framework [4]. The HTML transformer is written on top of the Firefox HTML parser.

Web applications. We chose eight *commercial* web applications listed in Table 4 from http://www.gotocode.com. They were medium in size and varied from 8K to 27K Lines of Bytecode (LOBC). The first six applications have also been used in previous research efforts in their experiments on SQL injection defense [6,10].

Test suite. For each of the selected applications, we created a set of test cases that covered all JSP files. These test cases explored all control paths in these applications by sending public/private HTTP requests with/without valid secret tokens in pre- and post-authentication sessions. The test cases were enriched by exploits found in a senior-level undergraduate security course. Further, we verified that the test cases contained reflected as well as same-domain XSRF attacks. None of these selected applications deployed any XSRF prevention measures.

Table 4. (a) XSRF defense effectiveness results. (b) HTML transformation results.

Web App. Name	(a) **XSRF Defense Effectiveness**			(b) **HTML Transformation**		
	Benign Requests/ FPs	Hostile Requests /Caught	Pub. Req. w. Invalid Token/Accepted	Num. of 3rd-Party URLs	Num. of App-gen. Private URLs	% Transformed URLs
	(1)	(2)	(3)	(1)	(2)	(3)
Classifieds	56/0	14/14	8/8	85	341	25.1%
Bookstore	65/0	24/24	9/9	63	944	44.7%
Portal	46/0	22/22	10/10	106	977	38.6%
Empldir	15/0	8/8	3/3	12	161	44.9%
Events	23/0	8/8	5/5	13	146	37.7%
BugTracker	40/0	17/17	4/4	33	344	42.3%
TaskManager	42/0	15/15	6/6	30	475	36.3%
YellowPages	30/0	12/12	4/4	65	255	58.4%

Experiment setup. Our experimental setup consisted of two servers (2GB RAM, 2 GHz dual core processor) and one client (1GB RAM, 2 GHz dual core processor) connected over an Ethernet network. Both servers were setup to contain same LAMP (Linux Apache MySQL PHP) configuration. We deployed all original applications on one server and all instrumented applications on the other. We then used `wget` command and `Perl` scripts to automatically send HTTP requests and compare HTTP responses from the instrumented and corresponding original applications. Similar responses for a hostile request were counted as a failure to prevent XSRF attack (ignoring transformed HTML changes).

Effectiveness in attack prevention. Table 4(a) summarizes results of effectiveness testing. Column one lists the total number of benign requests issued and number of requests accepted by the instrumented applications. The benign requests include public requests without valid secret tokens issued in pre- and post-authentication sessions and private requests with valid secret tokens. Column two lists the number of hostile requests issued in post-authentication session and number of attacks defended by the instrumented applications. Each hostile request represents a valid reflected or same-domain XSRF attack on the original application. Column three lists the number of public requests with invalid secret tokens issued in post-authentication sessions and the number of requests accepted by the instrumented applications.

The results of these experiments indicate that X-PROTECT transformed applications effectively prevent both reflected and same-domain XSRF attacks (addressing issue 3 in §2.2). Furthermore, the transformed applications accept all public requests with invalid secret tokens and thereby allow sharing of public URLs (addressing §2.2 issue 1) without token validation (addressing §2.2 issue 2). X-PROTECT transformation led to a moderate increase in sizes of the class files which ranged from 22.2% - 24.5%.

HTML transformation. Table 4(b) summarizes the HTML transformation data collected from HTML responses generated by the instrumented applications in authenticated sessions. Column one shows the number of third-party URLs present in HTML responses to benign requests with valid tokens. They were all transformed to prevent

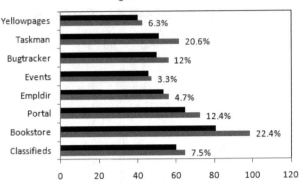

Fig. 7. Client end response time (in ms)

token leaks through the REFERER header. Column two shows the number of application generated private URLs present in HTML responses to benign or hostile requests. All of them were transformed to get the tokens at runtime. Column three shows the percentage of transformed URLs in all HTML responses.

This experiment indicates that X-PROTECT transformed applications prevent the token leaks (addressing issue 4). Only 25.1% - 58.4% of URLs present in HTML responses were transformed. These varying percentages were mainly attributed to varying number of public same-domain image URLs that were not transformed. YellowPages application's high percentage of transformed URLs was attributed to the fact that only 7.8% of its URLs pointed to public same-domain images. In comparison, Bookstore application had 24.5% such URLs.

We also verified the transformed HTML by loading it on different browsers: FireFox 3.0, Internet Explorer 8.0, and Opera 10.0, and then manually verifying that they rendered identically to the HTML response from the original applications. All legitimate URLs on these pages worked as intended.

Performance overhead. We used JMeter [5] to measure the average browser end response times of HTTP requests to the original and the transformed applications in authenticated sessions. We then computed averages for 100 sample runs for each test. As shown in Figure 7 the performance overheads ranged from 7% - 22%. These moderate overheads were mainly attributed to the taint tracking instrumentation and HTML transformation code. As all machines in our setup were on the same Ethernet, responses did not incur significant network delays, reflecting worst-case scenarios. For real world settings that have higher network delays, performance overhead of X-PROTECT may be significantly lower.

Discussion. X-PROTECT was able to defend all XSRF attacks on the web applications in the test suite. This ability crucially relies on a correct and complete specification of the per-application configuration file to identify parts of the program that make use of authentication status. For evaluated applications, this configuration file was trivial and often consisted of a getter and a setter method names along with their arguments.

However, for more complex applications, care must be taken to correctly list getters/ setters as well as include all such methods that are used for the same purpose. Incorrect specification may lead to missed augmentation of authentication checks and subsequently may adversely affect the effectiveness.

7 Related Work

Token-based XSRF defenses have been discussed in the background section, and this section discusses the non token-based defenses. BEAP [14] is a browser-based mechanism to defend against XSRF attacks. It infers user intended requests and strips the authentication information, e.g., `Cookie` header, from any requests that may not reflect the user's intention. The approach is attractive as it does not change existing web applications. [7] introduces the concept of login-XSRF attack that ushers a victim into an attacker controlled session. It proposes use of the `ORIGIN` header in HTTP requests to defend against XSRF attacks. However, [14] and [7] cannot prevent same-domain XSRF attacks.

A few other recent papers [9,15] discuss prevention of XSRF attacks by curbing the unlimited network access of pages on the client. However, these techniques require extensive changes to web applications as well as browsers. [13] presents a client-side policy framework to monitor all outgoing web requests and enforces a cross-domain policy provided by the server. In comparison, our approach does not require the server or client to provide the policies. Swaddler [8], an anomaly-based approach, detects a set of web attacks including XSRF attacks that violate the normal workflow of a web application. However, attacks that do not violate the normal workflow would be successful.

We also analyzed three most popular application development frameworks, namely `Apache Struts`, `ASP .Net` and `Ruby on Rails` and their support for XSRF prevention. These frameworks require a developer to tag the locations in the source code that must embed a secret token and locations that must validate them. Once tagged, these frameworks automatically generate necessary code to embed and validate secrets. Unfortunately, these defenses are not applicable to legacy applications and restrict the defenses to `POST` requests only.

8 Conclusion

XSRF is regarded as one of the major dormant threats to web applications. This paper analyzed state of the art XSRF defenses and their limitations. We presented an approach that retrofits the web application code to mitigate XSRF attacks. By performing a whitebox analysis, it strengthens XSRF defense offered by the existing approaches and addresses their limitations. Through our prototype implementation, we evaluated proposed approach on several open source applications and were able to defend all attacks with moderate performance overheads.

Acknowledgments

We thank the anonymous reviewers for their helpful and thorough feedback on drafts. This work was partially supported by National Science Foundation grants CNS-0551660, ITR-0716498, CNS-0716584, CNS-0845894, and CNS-0917229.

References

1. http://www.darkreading.com/security/app-security/
   showArticle.jhtml?articleID=208804131
2. http://www.owasp.org/index.php/Category:OWASP_CSRFGuard_
   Project
3. Open source web applications, http://www.gotocode.com
4. Soot: A Java Optimization Framework, http://www.sable.mcgill.ca/soot/
5. Apache. The JMeter Project, http://jakarta.apache.org/jmeter
6. Bandhakavi, S., Bisht, P., Madhusudan, P., Venkatakrishnan, V.N.: Candid: Preventing sql injection attacks using dynamic candidate evaluations. In: Proceedings of the 14th ACM Conference on Computer and Communications Security, CCS 2007, pp. 12–24. ACM, New York (2007)
7. Barth, A., Jackson, C., Mitchell, J.C.: Robust defenses for cross-site request forgery. In: Proceedings of the 15th ACM Conference on Computer and Communications Security, CCS 2008, pp. 75–88. ACM, New York (2008)
8. Cova, M., Balzarotti, D., Felmetsger, V., Vigna, G.: Swaddler: An approach for the anomaly-based detection of state violations in web applications. In: Kruegel, C., Lippmann, R., Clark, A. (eds.) RAID 2007. LNCS, vol. 4637, pp. 63–86. Springer, Heidelberg (2007)
9. Crites, S., Hsu, F., Chen, H.: OMash: Enabling secure web mashups via object abstractions. In: Proceedings of the 15th ACM Conference on Computer and Communications Security, CCS 2008, pp. 99–108. ACM, New York (2008)
10. Halfond, W.G.J., Orso, A.: Amnesia: Analysis and monitoring for neutralizing sql-injection attacks. In: Proceedings of the 20th IEEE/ACM International Conference on Automated Software Engineering, ASE 2005, pp. 175–183. ACM, New York (2005)
11. Johns, M., Winter, J.: Requestrodeo: Client side protection against session riding. In: Piessens, F. (ed.) Proceedings of the OWASP Europe 2006 Conference, Refereed Papers Track, Report CW448, pp. 5–17. Departement Computerwetenschappen, Katholieke Universiteit Leuven (May 2006)
12. Jovanovic, N., Kirda, E., Kruegel, C.: Preventing cross site request forgery attacks. In: Proceedings of the Second IEEE Conference on Security and Privacy in Communications Networks (SecureComm), pp. 1–10 (2006)
13. Maes, W., Heyman, T., Desmet, L., Joosen, W.: Browser protection against cross-site request forgery. In: Proceedings of the First ACM Workshop on Secure Execution of Untrusted Code, SecuCode 2009, pp. 3–10. ACM, New York (2009)
14. Mao, Z., Li, N., Molloy, I.: Defeating cross-site request forgery attacks with browser-enforced authenticity protection. In: Dingledine, R., Golle, P. (eds.) FC 2009. LNCS, vol. 5628, pp. 238–255. Springer, Heidelberg (2009)
15. Oda, T., Wurster, G., van Oorschot, P.C., Somayaji, A.: Soma: Mutual approval for included content in web pages. In: Proceedings of the 15th ACM Conference on Computer and Communications Security, CCS 2008, pp. 89–98. ACM, New York (2008)
16. SecureThoughts.com. Hacking CSRF Tokens using CSS History Hack (2009),
    http://securethoughts.com/2009/07/
    hacking-csrf-tokens-using-css-history-hack
17. Xu, W., Bhatkar, S., Sekar, R.: Taint-enhanced policy enforcement: A practical approach to defeat a wide range of attacks. In: USENIX Security Symposium (2006)
18. Zalewski, M.: Refcontrol : Add-ons for Firefox,
    https://addons.mozilla.org/en-US/firefox/addon/953
19. Zeller, W., Felten, E.W.: Cross-site request forgeries: Exploitation and prevention. Technical report, Princeton University (Fall 2008)

Coverage Criteria for Automatic Security Testing of Web Applications

Thanh Binh Dao[1] and Etsuya Shibayama[2]

[1] Dept. of Mathematical and Computing Sciences, Tokyo Institute of Technology,
2-12-1 O-okayama Meguro Tokyo Japan
dao3@is.titech.ac.jp
[2] Information Technology Center, The University of Tokyo,
2-11-16 Yayoi Bunkyo-ku Tokyo Japan
etsuya@ecc.u-tokyo.ac.jp

Abstract. In security testing of web applications, the selection of coverage criteria for adequacy evaluation of test cases is based on the trade off between test cost and vulnerability detection effectiveness. Coverage criteria used in traditional software testing such as branch coverage and statement coverage are commonly used but they are not originally defined for security testing purpose. In this paper, we present an overview of the limitations of those common coverage criteria and propose wrapper coverage, vulnerability-aware sink coverage and vulnerability-aware wrapper coverage as other options that are more appropriate for security testing. We conduct an experiment of security testing of real-world web applications to evaluate the usefulness and discuss about the usage of these proposed coverage criteria.

Keywords: automatic security testing, web application, coverage criteria.

1 Introduction

In security testing of web applications, the selection of coverage criteria for adequacy evaluation of test cases is based on the trade off between test cost and vulnerability detection effectiveness. Coverage criteria such as branch coverage and statement coverage used in traditional software testing [17] are also applied for security testing in many researches [16, 12]. Branch coverage-based methods try to generate test cases to execute as many program branches as possible. While high effectiveness of vulnerability detection can be achieved, the security test tends to be time-consuming because they try many test cases that are unrelated to any vulnerability. Statement coverage, on the hand, focuses on the execution of each statement in the program. It requires any statement to be executed at least once by test cases. When using statement coverage in security testing, security sensitive sinks such as database query function *mysql_query* become the targets of coverage measurement. In many real web applications, the function mysql_query is wrapped by wrapper functions and called indirectly

S. Jha and A. Maturia (Eds.): ICISS 2010, LNCS 6503, pp. 111–124, 2010.
© Springer-Verlag Berlin Heidelberg 2010

through these wrappers. Therefore, the coverage of function call statement of *mysql_query* may reach 100% quickly and the security test stops while the coverage of wrapper calls is still low. Because wrapper calls lead to the execution of *mysql_query* in different program paths, vulnerabilities existing in the execution of unexecuted wrapper calls will be missed. Therefore, statement coverage is not appropriate to use in the security testing of web applications for effective vulnerability detection.

Another problem with these common coverage criteria is that they are not originally defined for security testing purpose. They consider only the execution of statements or branches regardless of whether vulnerabilities have been found by those execution. Thus, these coverage results may not be good metrics for adequacy evaluation of test cases of security testing.

To address these problems, we propose new coverage criteria: *wrapper coverage vulnerability-aware wrapper coverage* and *vulnerability-aware sink coverage* which are more appropriate for evaluating the adequacy of test cases of security testing. These criteria In web applications where security sinks are indirectly used through wrapper functions, developers should use wrapper coverage instead of sink coverage. The vulnerability-aware consideration while introduces more test cases, it helps improve the vulnerability detection effectiveness of sink coverage and wrapper coverage. These coverage criteria are not proposed as the complete substitution of traditional criteria but rather as other options when vulnerability detection of security testing is required to be effective in a reasonable testing time.

To evaluate the effectiveness of our proposed coverage criteria, we conducted an experiment in which we used the tool Volcano developed in our previous work [8]. Volcano is a white-box automatic security testing tool for finding SQL Injection vulnerabilities in web applications. We modified Volcano so that it is able to generate test cases based on the traditional coverage criteria and the proposed criteria.

This paper makes the following contributions:

- We present the problems of common coverage criteria in security testing of web applications.
- We propose and define new types of coverage criteria to deal with those problems.
- We show the effectiveness of the proposed coverage criteria through experiment results.

In this paper, section 2 describes web application vulnerabilities with SQL Injection vulnerability in detail and existing security testing techniques. Section 3 discusses the problems of traditional coverage criteria when using in security testing. The proposed criteria for dealing with those problems are presented in section 4. Section 5 and 6 describe the experimental result and discussion. Section 7 talks about the related work and finally section 8 concludes this paper.

2   Background

2.1   Web Application Vulnerabilities

Many web application vulnerabilities have been well documented and the mitigation methods have also been introduced [1]. The most common cause of those
vulnerabilities is the insufficient input validation. Any data originated from outside of the program code, for example input data provided by user through a
web form, should always be considered malicious and must be sanitized before
use. SQL Injection, Remote code execution or Cross-site Scripting are the very
common vulnerabilities of that type [3]. Below is a brief introduction to SQL Injection vulnerability though the security testing method presented in this paper
is not limited to it.

SQL injection vulnerability allows an attacker to illegally manipulate database
by injecting malicious SQL codes into the values of input parameters of http
requests sent to the victim web site.

```
1: <?php
2: $result = mysql_query("SELECT {*} FROM users WHERE
       username='" . $_GET['username'] . "' AND usertype='user'");
3: show_result($result);
4: ?>
```

Fig. 1. An example of a program written in PHP which contains SQL Injection vulnerability

Figure 1 shows a program that uses the database query function *mysql_query*
to get user information corresponding to the user specified by the GET input parameter *username* and then print the result to the client browser. A normal http
request with the input parameter *username* looks like "http://example.com/
index.php?username=bob". The dynamically created database query at line 2
is "SELECT * FROM users WHERE username='bob' AND usertype='user'".

This program is vulnerable to SQL Injection attacks because *mysql_query*
uses the input value of *username* without sanitizing malicious codes.
A malicious code can be a string that contains SQL symbols or keywords. If an attacker send a request with SQL code ('alice'–') injected "http://example.com/index.php?username=alice'–", the query becomes
"SELECT * FROM users WHERE username='alice'--' AND usertype='user'".
In this query, the quote character encloses previous quote, and the symbol "--"
comments out the subsequent text. The program will illegally get and show
secret information of user *alice* instead of *bob*.

To protect from SQL Injection in this case, the program must escape all
SQL symbols and keywords in user-provided input value before using to create
the database queries. As another countermeasure, developers can use prepared
statement instead of using function *mysql_query* [2]. However, while there are

many ways to protect program from vulnerabilities, many developers are still lack of skill to use them to write secure code so that we can still find many vulnerability reports today [19].

2.2 Automatic Security Testing

Security testing methods for web applications can be classified into black-box testing and white-box testing.

Black-box testing is a method that executes the test without knowing anything about the internal structure and operation of the web applications under test. Generally, it sends attack requests with malicious codes injected to the web site and then searches the response html pages for signatures such as error messages to detect vulnerabilities [10, 4, 5, 6]. Black-box testing is fast and useful especially when the source code of the web application program is not available. However, one of the limitation is that the test result cannot show exactly where the vulnerabilities are in the program code. Furthermore, without knowing anything about the source code, black-box testing may not be able to create effective test cases and may miss many vulnerabilities.

On the other hand, white-box testing, also known as structural testing, is based on analysis the internal structure and operation of the web application. Static analysis is one of the techniques widely used [7, 11, 18]. Based on well understanding of the program code, although extra time is required for code analysis, they can create useful test cases to find vulnerabilities and can achieve better results than black-box testing.

In previous work, we have created a tool called Volcano, a white-box style automatic security testing tool to find SQL Injection vulnerabilities in web applications written in PHP language [8]. Security testing by Volcano is separated into two steps described below.

- Step 1: Volcano firstly acts as black-box testing that uses initially provided http requests to generate test cases for the target web application. New test cases is created from static links and web forms found in the response html pages. Attack requests are created by injecting prepared SQL attack codes into the value field of input parameters. Step 1 finishes when no more new links or forms are found.
- Step 2: Volcano utilized input data generation techniques [9] to create test cases in order to execute branches which are not executed by previous test cases. The purpose is to increase branch coverage hoping that by exploring more branches the test will find more vulnerabilities. In addition to the algorithm of generating input data for executing character string predicate [9], a similar algorithm is also applied for numerical comparison predicates.

Volcano uses taint tracking technique to track taint information of input data and detect vulnerabilities by finding the tainted SQL symbols and keywords in dynamically generated SQL queries of the web application under test [20]. The experiment results of security testing to find vulnerabilities in existing web applications showed the effectiveness of Volcano.

3   Limitation of Traditional Coverage Criteria in Security Testing

In this section, we discuss the limitation of traditional coverage criteria when using in security testing.

```
1: <?php
2: function query($sql) {
3:    mysql_query($sql);
4: }
5:
6: if ($_GET['mode'] == "news" && isset($_GET['newsid'])) {  // (1)
7:    $content = query("SELECT * FROM news WHERE newsid="
                   . $_GET['newsid']);
8:    /* code to show content here */
9: } else {
10:    $sql = "SELECT * FROM articles";
11:    if (! empty($_GET['articleid'])) {     // (2)
12:      $sql .= " WHERE articleid=" . $_GET['articleid'];
13:    }
14:    $content = query($sql);
15:    /* code to show content here */
16: }
17:
18: $counter = query("SELECT * FROM access_counter");
19: /* code to show counter here */
20: ?>
```

Fig. 2. An example of a web application written in PHP language

Figure 2 shows an example of a web application written in PHP language. The program defines function *query* at line 2 to wrap the function *mysql_query* which is called at line 3. In real web applications, the wrapper of *mysql_query* is commonly used, especially when development in oriented object programming style. The wrapper may contain code for input sanitization or manipulation of query result. The program starts to execute from line 6. If the value of input parameter $_GET['mode'] is "news", the program will create and execute an SQL query at line 7 to get news content corresponding to the *newsid* from database server. Otherwise, an SQL query $sql is created at line 10. This query string is extended at line 12 to specify condition of the field *articleid* if its value received from GET method is not empty. The program finally get the information of web access status from the database at line 18 and display to client web browser.

At line 7, because $_GET['newsid'] is used directly, the program is vulnerable to SQL Injection attacks at this point. If line 12 is executed, the program is also vulnerable here because $_GET['articleid'] is used without sanitization. The dynamically generated malicious SQL queries are finally passed through wrapper *query* to the function *mysql_query* and then sent to database server. In this program, even though *mysql_query* is called only at line 3, it is actually executed by the wrapper calls *query* at line 7 and line 14. The query in line 18 does not contain any input data so it is safe with SQL Injection attacks.

To find both two vulnerabilities in this program, a security test must generate test cases to execute both branches of the predicate (1) at line 6, and also to test the TRUE branch of predicate (2) at line 11.

Consider the situation when a security test finished some test cases, and assume that only the FALSE branch of predicate (1) from line 9 and the FALSE branch of predicate (2) were executed by these test cases. This is the case when the web application is requested once by an http request that does not contain parameters *mode* and *articleid*. So no vulnerability was found at this step. We will see how the security test generates further test cases when test case generation is based on branch coverage and sink coverage criteria.

3.1 Branch Coverage-Based Security Testing

Branch coverage criterion requires each branch in the program to be executed at least once by test cases. Thus, branch coverage-based security test will try to generate new test cases so that the TRUE branch of predicate (1) and the TRUE branch of predicate (2) will be executed. In the program in Figure 2, to do that, new test cases c an be created by setting the values of input parameters properly. With the test cases in which the malicious SQL codes are injected into the value of $_GET['newsid'] or $_GET['articleid'], the security test can detect all two vulnerabilities when executing the queries created at line 7 and line 12.

In general, branch coverage criterion is a good option for exhaustive testing of web applications. Branch coverage-based method is able to cover many executions of the program, thus has more chance to find vulnerabilities However, when there are many branches that are not related to vulnerabilities, generating test cases for executing these branches only increase test cost without finding any more vulnerabilities.

3.2 Sink Coverage-Based Security Testing

Sink coverage criterion requires all calls to security sinks to be executed at least once during the test. The program in Figure 2 executes the wrapper *query* at line 18, and thus execute the sink *mysql_query* at line 3 in the operation of any request. Hence, the coverage of the sink *mysql_query* reaches 100% right after the first test case. So sink coverage-based security testing stops generating test cases for executing the TRUE branch of predicate (1) and predicate (2). As the result, no vulnerability will be found.

Sink coverage is one of the most simplest coverage criteria that make the test stop quickly, but the effectiveness of vulnerability detection is often low.

3.3 Problem Summary and Our Approach

The space of test cases of branch coverage-based methods is too large, but with statement coverage, it is too confined. In this research, we propose wrapper coverage, an intermediate criterion that is more suitable for security testing. We also propose the consideration of "vulnerability-aware" to improve the effectiveness of sink coverage and wrapper coverage in security testing.

4   Proposed Coverage Criteria

4.1   Wrapper Coverage

Definition. A wrapper is a function that contains call(s) to security sensitive sinks in its execution. If function f1 calls function f2 and f2 calls a security sink, both f1 and f2 are wrappers of the security sink.

A call to a wrapper of a security sensitive sink is covered if it is executed at least once by a test case.

Wrapper coverage measures the percentage of covered wrapper calls out of the total number of wrapper calls existing in the program.

With this definition, both wrapper coverage and sink coverage consider only the execution status, not the vulnerability detection result.

Wrapper Coverage-based Security Testing. Wrapper coverage criterion requires the security testing method to create test cases for executing wrappers as many as possible. Test cases for executing a branch should be created if the target branch block contains calls to the wrappers of security sensitive sinks.

When testing the program in Figure 2, test case for executing the TRUE branch of predicate (1) will be created because it contains a call to wrapper *query*. The test case in which input parameter $_GET['newsid'] is injected with malicious SQL codes can reveal the vulnerability here.

However, because the TRUE branch of predicate (2) does not contain any calls to wrappers or sinks, no test case will be generated to execute this branch. Thus, even though wrapper coverage-based security testing can find vulnerability at execution of line 7, which cannot be found by sink coverage-based method, it is still unable find vulnerability when executing line 14. To address this problem, we consider the concept of *vulnerability-aware* as described in the next part.

4.2   Vulnerability-Aware Wrapper Coverage

While a branch does not contain calls to sinks or wrappers, it may contain operations that affect the revealing of vulnerabilities in the subsequent code executed after the execution of this branch block. For example, the TRUE branch of predicate (2) contains assignment of variable $sql so that the execution of wrapper *query* at line 14 becomes dangerous. Thus, simply ignoring branches that do not contain wrappers and sinks may reduce the effectiveness of vulnerability detection. We propose vulnerability-aware wrapper coverage criterion that takes into account the vulnerability detection result of previous test cases when deciding to generate new test cases for executing a branch.

In a test case, if the execution of a security sensitive sink results in the success of an attack, all of the preceding calls of its wrappers are also consider vulnerable. For example, in the program in Figure 2, if in an SQL Injection test case, the program executes the TRUE branch of predicate (1), then execution of function *mysql_query* at line 3 and also the execution of wrapper *query* at line 7 are considered vulnerable.

Definition. A call to a wrapper of a security sensitive sink is covered if it is executed at least once and is detected as vulnerable by a test case.

Vulnerability-aware wrapper coverage measures the percentage of covered vulnerable wrappers out of the total number of wrapper calls existing in the program.

Vulnerability-Aware Wrapper Coverage-based Security Testing. Test cases for executing a branch should be created if the target branch block contains calls to wrappers or security sensitive sinks, or if the subsequent code, which is executed after the execution of the target branch block, contains calls to wrappers or security sensitive sinks which have not been detected to be vulnerable by previous test cases.

With vulnerability-aware wrapper coverage, we can see that because the subsequent code of the TRUE branch of predicate (2) contains call to the wrapper *query* at line 14, the security test will generate test cases to execute this branch. As the result, it will find vulnerability when executing *query* at line 14. The program in Figure 2 is a very typical case for showing the difference between vulnerability-aware wrapper coverage and wrapper coverage.

4.3   Vulnerability-Aware Sink Coverage

We also consider vulnerability-aware concept for sink coverage in order to make the security testing more effective to find vulnerabilities.

Definition. A call to a security sensitive sink is covered if it is executed at least once and is detected to be vulnerable by a previous test case.

Vulnerability-aware sink coverage measures the percentage of covered vulnerable sink calls out of the total number of sink calls existing in the program.

Vulnerability-Aware Sink Coverage-based Security Testing. Test cases for executing a branch should be created if the target branch block contains calls to security sensitive sinks or if the subsequent code of the target branch block contains calls to security sensitive sinks which have not been detected to be vulnerable by previous test cases.

Considering the situation discussed in section 3, we can see that although *mysql_query* is executed in the first test case, it is still not detected to be vulnerable. Thus while the sink coverage of *mysql_query* reaches 100%, vulnerability-aware sink coverage is 0%. The security test will generate next test cases to execute the TRUE branch of predicate (1). If it is successful, the vulnerability at execution of *mysql_query* at line 3 is detected. The security test will stop generating test cases for executing the TRUE branch of predicate (2) and finish with one vulnerability found.

Table 1. Test subjects: five PHP web applications that are vulnerable to SQL Injection vulnerabilities

Web Application	Description	Lines of Code	No. of Conditions	No. of Sinks	No. of Wrapper Declaration	Calls
jobhut	Job board site	2278	94	1	18	79
mycrocms	CMS site	4256	380	9	60	223
pastelcms	CMS site	4929	279	1	17	162
easymoblog	Blog site	9996	768	86	23	143
phpaaCMS	CMS site	13434	368	4	29	114

5 Experiment

In this section, we present the experiment to evaluate the cost-effectiveness of security testing which uses the proposed coverage and traditional coverage criteria to guide the generation of test cases.

5.1 Experiment Setup

We randomly selected five PHP web applications which are reported in the Cyber Security Bulletins of US-Cert to be vulnerable to SQL Injection vulnerabilities. The detail information is shown in the Table 1.

There is one security sensitive sink used in these web applications, it is the database query function *mysql_query*. In the Table 1, "No. of Conditions" indicates the number of conditional statements in the program. "No. of Sinks" is the number of function calls to *mysql_query* in the program. "Declaration" is the number of function declarations of the wrappers of *mysql_query* and "Calls" is the number of calls to these wrappers in the program. In these web applications, **easymoblog** uses security sensitive sink *mysql_query* directly in many places while other web applications mainly use wrappers.

The Apache web server version 2.2, MySQL database server version 5.0 and the security testing tool Volcano (written in Java) are installed in the desktop PC with CPU Intel i7 2.85MHz, 3GB RAM, Ubuntu Linux OS. Volcano is modified so that its test case generation algorithm can switch between five types of coverage criteria: branch coverage, sink coverage, wrapper coverage, vulnerability-aware sink coverage and vulnerability-aware wrapper coverage.

Volcano uses one SQL attack code "1' or 1=1 –" to inject into the value of input parameters of http requests. Vulnerabilities are counted by the number of different vulnerable SQL query patterns at each call site of security sink "mysql_query". Two queries have same pattern if they have the same query structure and the same set of parameters, regardless of the value of these parameters. For example, two queries "SELECT * FROM users WHERE user='bob'" and "SELECT * FROM users WHERE user='alice'" have same pattern, while "SELECT * FROM users WHERE user='bob'" and "SELECT * FROM users WHERE user='1' or 1=1 –'" are different (the latter contains SQL keyword 'or'). By using this counting method, we assume that the queries with different patterns are created from different execution paths of the program, so they must be shown as different vulnerabilities.

5.2   Experiment Result

The experiment result is shown in Table 2. In this table and the following discussion, BC denotes Branch Coverage, SC is Sink Coverage, VASC is Vulnerability-Aware Sink Coverage, WC is Wrapper Coverage and VAWC is Vulnerability-Aware Wrapper Coverage. "Time" shows the execution time in second. "TCase" is the number of test cases. Column "Vuln" shows the total number of vulnerabilities detected by Volcano. Column "ExC" reports the total conditional statements executed during the test. "T&F" shows the number of conditional statements whose both True and False branches were executed by test cases. Column "Sink" and "Wrapper" respectively show the numbers of executed security sensitive sinks and wrappers. Note that the "Final Result" contains the result of "Step 1".

As shown in Table 2, for all web applications, BC-based method cost the most time because it created and executed more test cases than the methods of other coverage types. The test cases created by SC, VASC, WC, VAWC based methods were the subset of the test cases created by BC-based method. For comparison, the result of sink coverage and wrapper coverage are computed and shown in this table.

Except `mycrocms` and `easymoblog`, the security test of other web applications executed all security sensitive sink calls at step 1. So after that, SC-based method did not generate any more test cases and finished. The results of vulnerabilities found in `jobhut` and `phpaaCMS` clearly show the difference of effectiveness between BC and SC. Simply ignoring the branches that do not contain sink calls led to missing many vulnerabilities.

VASC-based method also stopped after the step 1 in the cases of `jobhut` and `pastelcms`. It is because execution of security sensitive sink $mysql\_query$ has already been detected to be vulnerable by previous test cases. For the web application `mycrocms`, `easymoblog` and `phpaaCMS`, VASC-based method generated other test cases in step 2 and found more vulnerabilities than SC-based method (except `phpaaCMS`).

WC-based method detected more vulnerabilities than SC-based method in all web applications. All of these web applications use wrappers in many place of the program instead of the security sensitive sink $mysql\_query$. Even though, `easymoblog` uses $mysql\_query$ directly in many places, a large number of wrapper calls are also used and this made the difference of vulnerability detection effectiveness between SC and WC-based security testing.

The experiment result shows that, the effectiveness of vulnerability detection of VAWC-based method is as good as BC-based method. All vulnerabilities detected by BC were detected by VAWC. The execution of VAWC-based method is a little bit faster than BC-based method in the case of `easymoblog` and `phpaaCMS` and about two times faster in the case of `mycrocms` and `pastelcms`. It indicates that, comparing to branch coverage, VAWC is also a good coverage criterion

Table 2. The experiment result of security testing of five real-world web applications

jobhut		Time	TCase	Vuln	Ex.B	T&F	Sink	Wrapper
Step 1		20	105	12	63 (67%)	24	1 (100%)	43 (54%)
	BC	152	386	19	79 (84%)	51	1 (100%)	48 (60%)
Final	SC	33	105	12	63 (67%)	24	1 (100%)	43 (54%)
Result	VASC	33	105	12	63 (67%)	24	1 (100%)	43 (54%)
	WC	52	166	14	75 (79%)	34	1 (100%)	45 (56%)
	VAWC	111	307	19	79 (84%)	41	1 (100%)	48 (60%)

mycrocms		Time	TCase	Vuln	ExC	T&F	Sink	Wrapper
Step 1		142	89	8	208 (54%)	47	6 (66%)	84 (39%)
	BC	6908	932	9	229 (60%)	86	7 (77%)	93 (43%)
Final	SC	544	89	8	208 (54%)	47	6 (66%)	84 (39%)
Result	VASC	2201	301	9	225 (59%)	80	7 (77%)	90 (41%)
	WC	1577	244	9	219 (57%)	74	6 (66%)	87 (40%)
	VAWC	3036	408	9	225 (59%)	81	7 (77%)	92 (42%)

pastelcms		Time	TCase	Vuln	ExC	T&F	Sink	Wrapper
Step 1		12	16	1	57 (20%)	3	1 (100%)	25 (15%)
	BC	207	130	3	60 (21%)	18	1 (100%)	31 (19%)
Final	SC	30	16	1	57 (20%)	3	1 (100%)	25 (15%)
Result	VASC	30	16	1	57 (20%)	3	1 (100%)	25 (15%)
	WC	54	41	2	58 (20%)	5	1 (100%)	27 (16%)
	VAWC	106	81	3	59 (21%)	13	1 (100%)	30 (18%)

easymoblog		Time	TCase	Vuln	ExC	T&F	Sink	Wrapper
Step 1		161	129	7	148 (19%)	25	28 (32%)	40 (27%)
	BC	3510	639	8	156 (20%)	31	31 (36%)	43 (30%)
Final	SC	2085	283	7	154 (20%)	28	31 (36%)	43 (30%)
Result	VASC	3316	581	8	154 (20%)	30	31 (36%)	43 (30%)
	WC	2090	283	8	154 (20%)	28	31 (36%)	43 (30%)
	VAWC	3301	581	8	154 (20%)	30	31 (36%)	43 (30%)

phpaaCMS		Time	TCase	Vuln	ExC	T&F	Sink	Wrapper
Step 1		50	255	17	103 (27%)	25	4 (100%)	72 (63%)
	BC	209	639	31	117 (31%)	54	4 (100%)	99 (86%)
Final	SC	83	255	17	103 (27%)	25	4 (100%)	72 (63%)
Result	VASC	97	287	17	103 (27%)	27	4 (100%)	72 (63%)
	WC	132	475	29	110 (29%)	44	4 (100%)	92 (80%)
	VAWC	174	564	31	117 (31%)	53	4 (100%)	99 (86%)

that gives high effectiveness of vulnerability detection while it helps reduce the number of test cases and thus the execution time.

The result of wrapper coverage varied depending on the selected coverage types. VAWC almost gave the same coverage result as BC in all tests and higher than SC, WC and VASC (except for easymoblog). In the case of mycrocms, the wrapper coverage of VASC is higher than both SC and WC based methods. However, for other web applications, the wrapper coverage by WC is equal or higher than by SC and VASC.

6   Discussion

The selection of coverage criteria is depended on the requirements of the security testing and the characteristics of the web application program.

If the time for test is limited or the test must be repeated in a short time, sink coverage criterion can be used. This criterion provides good vulnerability detection effectiveness when the web application program directly uses sinks instead of wrappers. If higher vulnerability detection effectiveness is required, wrapper coverage or vulnerability-aware sink coverage should be considered.

Wrapper coverage-based method costs more time than vulnerability-aware sink coverage when the web application program mainly uses wrappers (e.g. jobhut, pastelcms, phpaaCMS). On the other hand, if the program uses sinks directly (e.g. mycrocms, easymoblog), vulnerability-aware sink coverage-based method costs more time. However, for all cases, wrapper coverage-based method always provides better vulnerability detection effectiveness.

If reasonable time and high effectiveness is required, vulnerability-aware wrapper coverage is the best choice. However, when developers have time (e.g nightly test) or want to do the test in which the effectiveness of vulnerability detection is more concerned (e.g acceptance test), branch coverage is a good selection.

There may exist the case that vulnerability-aware wrapper coverage can not find vulnerabilities which can be detected by branch coverage-based method. For example, when there are many if-conditions which do not contain wrappers or sinks, if wrappers in subsequent code have already detected to be vulnerable after some test cases, the vulnerability-aware wrapper coverage-based method will stop without further examining the unexecuted branches. However, if there are vulnerabilities related to the operation of these unexecuted branches, vulnerability-aware wrapper coverage-based method may miss them. We did not find any similar case in our experiment.

In real security testing process, if the specification of the target web application are unknown, sink coverage can be selected as the first try to quickly get the rough result about the use of sinks and wrappers. This information can also be achieved by doing some simple searches on the web application program. After knowing these information, appropriate coverage criterion can be selected by following the above guidance to get better vulnerability detection result with regard to the execution time.

The experiment result shows that, the result of wrapper coverage and the number of detected vulnerabilities are approximately in linear relationship. Therefore, wrapper coverage can be used as a good metric to show the effectiveness of the security test. A security test with higher wrapper coverage may find more vulnerabilities than the lower one.

7   Related Work

Ben Smith [12] addressed the limitation of statement coverage and introduces target statement coverage (which is the same as sink coverage) and input variable coverage. Input variable coverage measures the percentage of input variables tested at least once by the test cases out of total number of input variables found in any target statement in the web application program. Although input variables are very meaningful in security testing for input validation, the coverage is not vulnerability-aware and the relationship between input variable coverage and vulnerabilities has not been shown. Our proposed wrapper coverage can be used as a good index to show the effectiveness of the security test.

Some coverage criteria are proposed for adequacy evaluation of testing of database interaction in applications[13, 14, 15]. There are two types of criteria, those that focus on data-flow and those that focus on the structure of the SQL queries sent to the database. Data interaction points, in the case of security testing, are similar to security sinks in that they are defined as any statement in the application code where SQL queries are issued to the relational database management system [13]. Defining the coverage criteria based on the data-flow and the structure of SQL queries could be good coverage criteria, but the analysis tends to be complicated.

8   Conclusion

In this paper, we presented the problems of traditional coverage criteria such as branch coverage and statement coverage when using for automatic security testing to evaluate the adequacy of automatically generated test cases. To address these problems, we proposed wrapper coverage, vulnerability-aware wrapper coverage, and vulnerability-aware sink coverage criteria as other options. The experiment result shows that these coverage criteria can be used as intermediate criteria with regard to the trade off between test cost and vulnerability detection effectiveness. We also discussed about the selection of appropriate coverage criteria for security testing of web applications.

References

[1] The Open Web Application Security Project: Vulnerability Category, http://www.owasp.org/index.php/Category:Vulnerability
[2] The Open Web Application Security Project: SQL Injection Prevention Cheat Sheet, http://www.owasp.org/index.php/SQL_Injection_Prevention_Cheat_Sheet
[3] Symantec Corporation: Five common Web application vulnerabilities, http://www.symantec.com/connect/articles/five-common-web-application-vulnerabilities
[4] Chinotec Technologies Company: Paros, http://www.parosproxy.org
[5] Acunetix. Acunetix Web Vulnerability Scanner (2008), http://www.acunetix.com/
[6] Hewlett-Packard Development Company. HP WebInspect software
[7] Jovanovic, N., Kruegel, C., Kirda, E.: Pixy: A Static Analysis Tool for Detecting Web Application Vulnerabilities (Short Paper). In: Proceedings of the 2006 IEEE Symposium on Security and Privacy, SP, pp. 258–263. IEEE Computer Society, Washinton (2006)

[8] Dao, T.-B., Shibayama, E.: Idea: Automatic Security Testing for Web Applications. In: Massacci, F., Redwine Jr., S.T., Zannone, N. (eds.) ESSoS 2009. LNCS, vol. 5429. Springer, Heidelberg (2009)

[9] Zhao, R., Lyu, M.R.: Character String Predicate Based Automatic Software Test Data Generation. In: Proceedings of the Third International Conference on Quality Software (QSIC 2003), p. 255. IEEE Computer Society, Washington (2003)

[10] Huang, Y., Huang, S., Lin, T., Tsai, C.: Web application security assessment by fault injection and behavior monitoring. In: Proceedings of the 12th International Conference on World Wide Web, WWW 2003, Budapest, Hungary, May 20-24, pp. 148–159. ACM, New York (2003)

[11] Livshits, V.B., Lam, M.S.: Finding security vulnerabilities in java applications with static analysis. In: Proceedings of the 14th Conference on USENIX Security Symposium, Baltimore, MD, July 31-August 05, vol. 14, p. 18. USENIX Association, Berkeley (2005)

[12] Smith, B., Shin, Y., Williams, L.: Proposing SQL statement coverage metrics. In: Proceedings of the Fourth International Workshop on Software Engineering For Secure Systems, SESS 2008, Leipzig, Germany, May 17-18, pp. 49–56. ACM, New York (2008)

[13] Halfond, W.G., Orso, A.: Command-Form Coverage for Testing Database Applications. In: Proceedings of the 21st IEEE/ACM International Conference on Automated Software Engineering, September 18-22, pp. 69–80. IEEE Computer Society, Washington (2006)

[14] Surez-Cabal, M.J., Tuya, J.: Using an SQL coverage measurement for testing database applications. In: Proceedings of the 12th ACM SIGSOFT Twelfth International Symposium on Foundations of Software Engineering, SIGSOFT 2004/FSE-12, Newport Beach, CA, USA, October 31-November 06, pp. 253–262. ACM, New York (2004)

[15] Kapfhammer, G.M., Soffa, M.L.: A family of test adequacy criteria for database-driven applications. In: Proceedings of the 9th European Software Engineering Conference Held Jointly with 11th ACM SIGSOFT International Symposium on Foundations of Software Engineering, ESEC/FSE-11, Helsinki, Finland, September 01-05, pp. 98–107. ACM, New York (2003)

[16] Kieyzun, A., Guo, P.J., Jayaraman, K., Ernst, M.D.: Automatic creation of SQL Injection and cross-site scripting attacks. In: Proceedings of the 31st International Conference on Software Engineering, May 16-24, pp. 199–209. IEEE Computer Society, Washington (2009)

[17] Zhu, H., Hall, P.A., May, J.H.: Software unit test coverage and adequacy. ACM Comput. Surv. 29(4), 366–427 (1997)

[18] Balzarotti, D., Cova, M., Felmetsger, V., Jovanov, N., Kirda, E., Kruegel, C., Vigna, G.: Saner: Composing Static and Dynamic Analysis to Validate Sanitization in Web Applications. In: IEEE Security and Privacy Symposium (2008)

[19] Cyber Security Bulletins, US-Cert, http://www.us-cert.gov/cas/bulletins/

[20] Nguyen-Tuong, A., Guarnieri, S., Greene, D., Shirley, J., Evans, D.: Automatically hardening web applications using precise tainting. In: Twentieth IFIP International Information Security Conference, SEC 2005 (2005)

A Practical Generic Privacy Language

Moritz Y. Becker[1], Alexander Malkis[2], and Laurent Bussard[3]

[1] Microsoft Research
[2] IMDEA Software
[3] EMIC

Abstract. We present a declarative language with a formal semantics for specifying both users' privacy preferences and services' privacy policies. Expressiveness and applicability are maximized by keeping the vocabulary and semantics of service behaviours abstract. A privacy-compliant data-handling protocol for a network of communicating principals is described.

1 Introduction

Privacy policy languages allow online services to specify and publish their privacy policies in a machine-readable way. The process of deciding, based on such a policy and the user's privacy preferences, whether or not to disclose user's personal data to the service can thus be automated. But, despite a growing need for privacy-aware technologies [21,1], adoption of privacy policy languages has been slow. This is due mainly to cultural and economical reasons [6], but existing privacy languages also suffer from *technical* limitations. Above all, due to their limited expressiveness and scope, they cannot express many natural language policies [24]. The problem is that policies are highly heterogeneous, spread out horizontally (coming from a wide variety of application domains with varying vocabulary and requirements) and vertically (expressed across all abstraction layers: legislation, organizational and business requirements, application requirements, low-level access control).

Academic research in this area has focused on developing more expressive privacy languages and logics directly specifying temporal service behaviours [2,4,22]. These efforts do not adequately address the problem of limited scope, and are not likely to be widely deployed in the real world for the following reasons.

Firstly, inherently informal interactions still cannot be expressed in these languages (e.g. "[...] we will tell our affiliates to limit their marketing to you [...]", from Citibank's privacy notice). Secondly, it is often unnecessary to precisely specify the meaning of a service behaviour. For instance, it is often sufficient to view "delete data within 7 days" as an atomic entity with some intuitive meaning, without specifying what "delete" or "within" precisely mean and entail. In such cases, precise temporal behaviour specifications are an unnecessary overhead, and force policy authors to think and work at too low a level of abstraction. Thirdly, some amount of ambiguity is often even *desirable* from the point of view of businesses and their legal departments. The precise behaviour semantics of these languages leaves no wiggle room, thus deterring the adoption.

Observing these shortcomings of existing privacy languages, we arrive at the following desirable design goals for a privacy language.

S. Jha and A. Maturia (Eds.): ICISS 2010, LNCS 6503, pp. 125–139, 2010.
© Springer-Verlag Berlin Heidelberg 2010

1. A privacy language should be generic in the ontology of service behaviours and hide the semantics of these behaviours by abstraction, in order to support the widest range of policies, both in a horizontal and vertical sense.
2. It should uniformly deal with both sides of disclosure of PII (personally identifiable information), namely user preferences and service policies, and enable satisfaction checking between the two.
3. It should support, and distinguish between, both permissions and obligations over service behaviours, in both user preferences and service policies.
4. As usability, and readability in particular [21], is a critical aspect in any practical policy language, its syntax should be reasonably human-readable.
5. The language built on top of the abstract behaviours should be expressive enough to be widely applicable. In particular, it should support parameterized behaviours, hierarchical data types, recursive relations, and arbitrary constraints.
6. It should support credential-based delegation of authority, which is crucial for modern decentralised and distributed architectures [13].

This paper presents a generic privacy policy language, S4P, designed with these goals in mind. Statements in S4P are meta-statements about abstract parameterised service behaviours. The service behaviours in S4P can be left abstract, which should be sufficient in most cases, or be instantiated to any required level of detail, using any of the many existing specification techniques including temporal logic, obligation languages, transition systems, or even concrete pieces of code. Concrete behaviour ontologies and semantics can be plugged into the language in a modular fashion according to need. The language is also agnostic about how and whether services enforce their policies. This is in line with the implicit trust model which requires users to trust services to adhere to their own policies, and is independent of whether enforcement is established informally via audit trails, by dynamic monitoring, or static analysis.

Despite its high abstractness, S4P encapsulates notions specific to privacy and data-handling. Apart from language design, we present:

– A proof-theoretic semantics that formalizes which queries are true in a policy or a preference, and, based on this notion, an algorithm to decide when a policy *satisfies* a user's preference (Section 3). This answers the question: "should the user agree to disclose her data?"
– A model-theoretic semantics that formalizes the intuitive meaning of policies and preferences in terms of abstract service behaviours and traces (Section 5). We also show that the satisfaction checking algorithm is sound with respect to the semantics. This answers the question: "what does it mean for a service to comply with its own policy, or with a user's preference?"
– A protocol that regulates communication of user data in a network of users and services (Section 6). This answers the question: "how can S4P enable safe communication in a network of collaborating agents?" The protocol ensures a useful safety property, despite the language's abstractness.

A small case study of a real-world privacy policy is presented in Section 4. Our implementation of S4P is briefly described in Section 7. The paper concludes with a discussion of S4P with regards to the six design goals from above (Section 8). A technical report contains a formalization of the protocol and full proofs [9].

2   Related Work

P3P [15] is a language for presenting a website's privacy notice in a structured, machine-readable way. User preferences cannot be expressed in P3P, so ad hoc mechanisms (e.g. the Privacy Tab Slider in Internet Explorer 6 or the syntactic pattern matching language APPEL [16]) for managing preferences and checking them against policies are required. The downside of this approach is that the exact correspondence between preferences and P3P policies is unclear, both syntactically and semantically. Policies can only express what a website *may* do and cannot express positive promises (e.g. "we will notify you if [...]"). Its vocabulary is fixed and web-centric, which limits its expressiveness further [18]. P3P does not satisfy any of the six design goals in Section 1.

DAMP [5] is a formal framework that links an internal privacy policy of an enterprise with its published policy. DAMP's main complexity stems from supporting hierarchical data types using modal operators. S4P supports hierarchical types via constraints (discussed in [7]). Like S4P, DAMP does not fix the vocabulary of actions and data types, and keeps the semantics of actions abstract. As such, it satisfies design goal 1 from Section 1, but not the other goals; for instance, DAMP cannot differentiate between promises and permissions.

Ardagna *et al.* [2] propose a unified language for expressing services' *access control policies*, users' *release policies*, and services' *data-handling policies*. The language does not support first-class obligations that are independent of access control rules [14], and a user's release policy (corresponding to "preference" in our terminology) cannot express requirements on the service's privacy promises. The language commits to a predefined vocabulary and lacks a model semantics.

Barth *et al.* [4] use linear temporal logic to specify positive and negative temporal constraints on the global trace of a network of principals exchanging user data. Satisfaction between preferences and policies is equivalent to checking entailment between two formulas. Hence for data sending actions, their logic satisfies our design goals 2 and 3 (but not the others). Behaviours other than sending data are not supported (particularly, no non-monotonic actions such as deletion), and extensions would be non-trivial as the effects of behaviours on the state are modelled explicitly.

EPAL [3] is a language for specifying and enforcing organizations' internal rules for accessing user data; essentially, it is an access control language (comparable to XACML [23]) with a privacy-centric vocabulary. It does not satisfactorily deal with specifying user preferences and matching them against policies.

3   S4P

Preliminaries. A phrase of syntax is *ground* iff no variables occur in it, and *closed* if no *free* variables (i.e., in the scope of a quantifier) occur in it.

The phrases in S4P are built from a first-order function-less signature Σ with constant symbols **Const** and some set of predicates **Pred**. As usual, an atom a is a predicate symbol applied to an expression tuple of the right arity. The predicate symbols are domain-specific, and we often write atoms in infix notation, e.g. Alice is a NicePerson.

In order to abstractly represent PII-relevant service behaviours, we assume a further set of predicate symbols **BehSymb**. Atoms constructed from predicates in **BehSymb** are called *behaviour atoms*. These are also usually written in infix notation and may include atoms such as ⟨delete Email within 1 yr⟩ and ⟨allow x to control access to FriendsInfo⟩.

Further, we assume a domain-specific first-order constraint language whose relation symbols are disjoint from **Pred**, but which shares variables and constants with Σ. A *constraint* is any formula from this constraint language. The only further requirement on the constraint language is the existence of a computable ground validity relation $\models$, i.e., we can test if a ground constraint is true (written $\models c$). The constraint language may, e.g., include arithmetics, regular expressions and constraints that depend on environmental data (e.g. time).

Assertions. An *assertion* α is of the form ⟨E says f_0 if $f_1, \ldots, f_n$ where c⟩, where E is a constant from **Const**, the f_i are *facts* (defined below), and c is a *constraint* on variables occurring in the assertion. In an assertion α = ⟨e says f if $f_1, \ldots, f_n$ where c⟩, the keyword "if" is omitted when $n = 0$; likewise, "where c" is omitted when $c =$ true.

Henceforth, we keep to the following conventions: x, y denote variables, E, U, S constants from **Const**, e denotes an expression (i.e., either a variable or a constant), c a constraint, a an atom, b a behaviour atom, B a ground behaviour atom, $\mathcal{B}$ a set of ground behaviour atoms, f a fact, F a ground fact, α an assertion, and $\mathcal{A}$ a set of assertions. We use θ for variable substitutions, and γ for ground total variable substitutions (mapping every variable to a constant).

Facts and queries. We can now define the syntax of *facts* f and *queries* q:

$$f ::= a \mid e \text{ can say } f \mid e \text{ may } b \mid e \text{ will } b$$
$$q ::= e \text{ says } f? \mid c? \mid \neg q \mid q_1 \wedge q_2 \mid q_1 \vee q_2 \mid \exists x(q)$$

Facts with can say are used to express *delegation of authority* and have a special query evaluation semantics, as defined in the proof system below. Facts involving may and will are not treated specially for query evaluation, but are essential for the privacy-related model semantics in Section 5.

For example, (2)–(18) in Fig. 1 are assertions, and (1) and (19) are queries.

Atomic query evaluation. A query is evaluated in the context of a set of assertions; a closed query evaluates to either true or false. Our query evaluation semantics is a simplified variant of the one from SecPAL [8]. We first define a two-rule proof system that generates ground judgements of the form $\mathcal{A} \vdash E$ says F:

$$\frac{\langle E \text{ says } f \text{ if } f_1, \ldots, f_n \text{ where } c \rangle \in \mathcal{A} \quad \models \gamma(c) \quad \text{For all } i \in \{1, \ldots, n\} : \mathcal{A} \vdash E \text{ says } \gamma(f_i)}{\mathcal{A} \vdash E \text{ says } \gamma(f)} \qquad \frac{\mathcal{A} \vdash E_1 \text{ says } E_2 \text{ can say } F \quad \mathcal{A} \vdash E_2 \text{ says } F}{\mathcal{A} \vdash E_1 \text{ says } F}$$

The first rule is derived from the standard modus ponens rule, and the second rule defines delegation of authority using can say.

For example, assertions (2), (3), (4), and (10) in Fig. 1 support the derivation of ⟨Alice says MS complies with COPPA?⟩: From (3) and (4) we get that Alice says that

TRUSTe is a member of COPPASchemes, which with (2) implies that TRUSTe can say who complies with COPPA. Combine it with (10).

Compound query evaluation. The relation $\vdash$ so far only deals with the case where the query is of the basic form $\langle e$ says $f?\rangle$. We extend it to all closed queries by interpreting compound queries as formulas in first-order logic. Formally, let $\mathcal{A}$ be a set of assertions and q be a closed query, $\mathcal{M}_{assr} = \{\alpha \mid \mathcal{A} \vdash \alpha\}$ and $\mathcal{M}_{constr} = \{c \mid \models c\}$. Then $\mathcal{A} \vdash q$ iff $\mathcal{M}_{assr} \cup \mathcal{M}_{constr} \models q$ in first-order logic.

User-service pair. In an *encounter* between a user and a service, the service requests a PII from the user, and the user may agree or disagree to the disclosure. Since the essential parameters of an encounter are the user and the service, it is useful to view these two parameters as a single pair:

A *user-service pair* $\tau = (U, S)$ is a pair of constants denoting the *user* (name) U (the PII owner) and the *service* (name) S (the requester and potential recipient of the PII) during an encounter.

Assertions may contain placeholders $\langle \mathsf{Usr} \rangle$ and $\langle \mathsf{Svc} \rangle$ which get dynamically instantiated during an encounter by U and S, respectively. That way, the same privacy preference can be used for encounters with multiple services, and the same privacy policy can be used for encounters with multiple users.

Will- and may-queries. Two particular classes of queries will serve in defining policy and preference later. In the following, let $\tau = (U, S)$ be a user-service pair.

- A τ-will-*query* q_w is a query in which no subquery of the form $\langle S$ says S will $b?\rangle$ occurs in the scope of a negation sign $(\neg)$.
- A τ-may-*query* q_m is a query in which no subquery of the form $\langle U$ says S may $b?\rangle$ occurs in a disjunction or in the scope of an existential quantifier or of a negation sign.

The definition above syntactically restricts the queries occurring in a policy or a preference to those that have an intuitive meaning in terms of an upper or a lower bound on behaviours. Disjunction and existential quantification are allowed and have an obvious meaning within a will-query, e.g.

$$\exists t \, (S \text{ says } S \text{ will delete } \mathtt{Email} \text{ within } t? \wedge t \leq 2\mathtt{yr}?).$$

A may-query, however, represents an upper bound on a service's behaviour, and disjunction does not make much sense in this context. If a service wanted to state that it may possibly use the user's email address for contact *or* for marketing (or possibly not at all), it would specify a *conjunctive* query:

$$U \text{ says } S \text{ may use } \mathtt{Email} \text{ for Contact?} \wedge U \text{ says } S \text{ may use } \mathtt{Email} \text{ for Marketing?}$$

If this query is successful in the context of U's preference, the service is permitted to use the email address for contact, marketing, both, or to not use it at all.

Policies and preferences. Now we define the syntax of preferences and policies:

- A τ-*preference* Π_{pr} is a pair $(\mathcal{A}_{pr}, q_w)$ where $\mathcal{A}_{pr}$ is a set of assertions and q_w a closed τ-will-query.

– A τ-*policy* Π_{pl} is a pair $(\mathcal{A}_{pl}, q_m)$ where $\mathcal{A}_{pl}$ is a set of assertions and q_m a closed τ-may-query.

Intuitively, the will-query q_w of the preference specifies a *lower bound* on the behaviours of the service. It expresses *obligations*, i.e., the behaviours that the service must exhibit. The assertions $\mathcal{A}_{pr}$ specify an *upper bound* on the behaviours, i.e., the *permissions*, and typically involve the modal verb may.

The may-query q_m of a policy expresses a *upper bound* on service's behaviours. The query advertises all *possible* relevant behaviours of the service. The service uses q_m to ask for permission for all behaviours that it might possibly exhibit. The assertions $\mathcal{A}_{pl}$ specify a *lower bound* on the behaviours, and typically involve the modal verb will. The service *promises* to exhibit the mentioned behaviours.

This intuition is formalized by a trace semantics in Section 5.

Satisfaction. Should a user agree to the disclosure of her PII? This depends on whether the service's policy *satisfies* her preference. Checking satisfaction consists of two steps. First, every behaviour declared as *possible* in the policy must be *permitted* by the preference. Thus, it is checked that the upper bound specified in the policy is contained in the upper bound specified in the preference. Intuitively, a service must ask for permission upfront for anything that it might do with a user's PII. Second, every behaviour declared as *obligatory* in the preference must be *promised* by the policy. Thus, it is checked that the lower bound specified in the preference is contained in the lower bound specified in the policy. Intuitively, a user asks the service to promise the obligatory behaviours.

Since these dualities are reflected in the language syntax, checking if a service policy satisfies a user preference becomes straightforward in S4P. We just need to check if the may-query in the policy and the will-query in the preference are both satisfied. In general, queries are not satisfied by a single assertion but by a set of assertions. This is because assertions may have conditions that depend on other assertions, and authority over asserted facts may be delegated to other principals. Hence the queries are evaluated against the union of the assertions in the policy *and* the preference.

Definition 1. *A τ-policy $\Pi_{pl} = (\mathcal{A}_{pl}, q_m)$ satisfies a τ-preference $\Pi_{pr} = (\mathcal{A}_{pr}, q_w)$ iff $\mathcal{A}_{pl} \cup \mathcal{A}_{pr} \vdash q_m \wedge q_w$.*

For example, if $\tau = (\texttt{Alice}, \texttt{MS})$, the τ-policy on the right in Fig. 1 satisfies the τ-preference on the left, because both queries (1) and (19) are derivable from assertions (2)–(18). We will look at this example more closely in the next section.

Complexity. The computational complexity of policy evaluation is usually given in terms of parameterized *data complexity*, where the size of the rules (assertions with conditions) is fixed, and the parameter is the number of facts (assertions without conditions). The data complexity of S4P is polynomial in general and linear for ground policies and preferences; this follows from complexity results on logic programming [20].

4   Case Study

Now we discuss an example to illustrate some of the concepts above and S4P's intended usage. In the following, the numbers in parentheses refer to Fig. 1.

(1) ⟨Svc⟩ says ⟨Svc⟩ will allow Alice to Edit ParentalControls?
∧ Alice says ⟨Svc⟩ complies with COPPA?

(2) Alice says x can say y complies with COPPA if
x is member of COPPASchemes.

(3) Alice says FTC can say
x is member of COPPASchemes.

(4) FTC says TRUSTe is member of COPPASchemes.

(5) ⟨Usr⟩ says ⟨Svc⟩ may use Cookies for x if
⟨Svc⟩ will revoke Cookies within t
where t ≤ 5yr.

(6) ⟨Usr⟩ says ⟨Svc⟩ can say ⟨Svc⟩ will
revoke Cookies within t.

(7) Alice says ⟨Svc⟩ may
allow Alice to action object.

(8) Alice says ⟨Svc⟩ may revoke Cookies within t.

(9) Alice says Alice is using software
MSNClient version 9.5.

(10) TRUSTe says MS complies with COPPA.

(11) MS says MS will allow ⟨Usr⟩ to Edit ParentalControls if
⟨Usr⟩ is member of *msntype*,
msntype supports parental controls,
⟨Usr⟩ is using software MSNClient version v
where v ≤ 9.5.

(12) MS says MSNPremium supports parental controls.

(13) MS says MNSPlus supports parental controls.

(14) MS says MSN9DialUp supports parental controls.

(15) MS says MSN can say x is member of g
where g ∈ {MSN,MSNPremium,MSNPlus,MSN9Dialup}

(16) MSN says Alice is member of MSNPremium.

(17) MS says ⟨Usr⟩ can say ⟨Usr⟩ is using software
MSNClient version v.

(18) MS says MS will revoke Cookies within 2yr.

(19) ⟨Usr⟩ says MS may use Cookies for AdTracking? ∧
⟨Usr⟩ says MS may revoke Cookies within 2yr? ∧
⟨Usr⟩ says MS may allow ⟨Usr⟩ to Edit ParentalControls?

Fig. 1. Alice's privacy preference (left), Microsoft privacy policy (right)

Alice's privacy preference. Where does Alice's preference (1–9) come from? There are several possibilities. First of all, she is offered to select among a small number of default preferences for specific application domains. Preferences could be customized using application- or browser-specific user interfaces that do not offer the full expressiveness and flexibility of S4P, but let the user extend or define exceptions to the predefined preferences. User agents can also download default preferences provided by trusted third parties for specific application domains. This case emphasizes the need for a trust delegation mechanism in the language.

Alice cares about online child protection, so her privacy preference contains will-query (1). According to this will-query, Alice requires web services she interacts with to allow her to edit parental control settings. Furthermore, she requires services to comply with the Federal Trade Commission (FTC) Children's Online Privacy Protection Act (COPPA). Of course, Alice does not exactly know which businesses comply with COPPA, so she delegates authority over COPPA compliance to privacy seal programs that certify COPPA compliance, using a "can say" assertion (2). But she does not know the entire list of such programs either, so she delegates authority over such schemes to the FTC (3). She also has a statement from the FTC saying that TRUSTe is such a scheme (4).

Alice's may-assertions allow any service to use cookies for any purpose as long as the service promises that the cookies expire within five years (5,6). Assertions (7,8) are default statements allowing service behaviours that Alice is asking for.

In our scenario, Alice uses MSN Client to access content from MSN, and has an assertion (9) stating the version of the client software (she may also have additional assertions stating other environment variables).

Microsoft's privacy policy. The English statements in *italics* are taken verbatim from Microsoft's Online Privacy Statement[1].

Microsoft is a member of the TRUSTe Privacy Program. This means that Microsoft complies with a number of privacy standards including, in particular, COPPA (10). *If you have an MSN Premium, MSN Plus, or MSN 9 Dial-Up account, and use MSN*

---

[1] Retrieved from http://privacy.microsoft.com/en-gb/fullnotice.mspx on 16/09/2010.

Client software version 9.5 or below, you can choose to set up MSN Parental Controls for the other users of that account (11–14). The various types of MSN membership are delegated to MSN, using can say (15).

MSN knows that Alice has a MSNPremium account (16). In our implementation, such assertions can be created on the fly during evaluation using interfaces to databases and directory services such as SQL Server and Active Directory.

Microsoft believes a user's claim about the version of her client (17).

When we display online advertisements to you, we will place a [sic] *one or more persistent cookies on your computer in order to recognize your computer each time we display an ad to you* (19). *The cookies we use for advertising have an expiry date of no more than 2 years* (18).

The may-query (19) explicitly mentions all behaviours for this encounter.

Satisfaction evaluation. Does the policy satisfy Alice's preference? Satisfaction is checked by evaluating Alice's will-query and the service's may-query against the union of the assertions in both preference and policy. The will-query (1) first checks whether the service allows Alice to edit parental control settings. The answer is yes according to assertion (11), because Alice is a member of MSN Premium according to MSN (16) which has been delegated authority over MSN Premium memberships (15). Furthermore, MSN Premium accounts support parental controls according to (12), and Alice is using a version of MSN client that supports parental controls (9) and is trusted on that fact (17).

The second part of (1) checks compliance with COPPA. This is established via a delegation from Alice to TRUSTe using (2) and (10). The condition in (2) is satisfied by another delegation chain, from Alice to FTC, using (3) and (4).

The may-query (19) consists of three conjuncts. The first one is satisfied by Alice's assertion (5) which in turn depends on (6) and Microsoft's will-assertion (18). The remaining two conjuncts are satisfied by Alice's may-assertions (7,8).

Hence Alice's preference is satisfied by the policy, so her user agent is willing to disclose her PII to the website.

5   Trace Semantics

Def. 1 induces an algorithm, based on query evaluation, for checking if a policy satisfies a preference, but it does not show that the algorithm is *correct*. As yet, no definition of "correct" exists. This section formalizes a notion of correctness and proves correctness of the satisfaction checking procedure.

Behaviour function and traces. Policies and preferences bound services' behaviours. We are interested in whether a particular run, or *trace*, of a service *complies* with a policy or a preference. Since we care only about PII-relevant behaviours exhibited by a trace, we keep the notion of trace as abstract as possible. We assume a set whose elements are called *traces*, as well as an *abstract behaviour function* **Beh** which maps each trace to a set of ground behaviour atoms. In order to maximize generality of our language, we make no further assumptions on **Beh**. Intuitively, a trace t exhibits exactly the behaviours in **Beh**(t). (Conversely, a ground behaviour atom can be seen as a trace property.)

Definition 2. *A trace t complies with a set of traces T iff $t \in T$. A set of traces T_1 is at least as strict as a set of traces T_2 iff $T_1 \subseteq T_2$.*

5.1 Trace Semantics of Policies

To specify the trace semantics of a policy, we need two auxiliary relations.

Promised obligations. Let $\tau = (U, S)$, let $\mathcal{A}$, $\mathcal{A}_{pl}$ be sets of assertions, and $\mathcal{B}$ a set of ground behaviour atoms. The relation $\mathcal{B} \models^{wa}_{\tau, \mathcal{A}} \mathcal{A}_{pl}$ holds if the behaviours in $\mathcal{B}$ include all behaviours promised by will-assertions in $\mathcal{A}_{pl}$ in the context of foreign assertions $\mathcal{A}$ (later, $\mathcal{A}$ will come from the user preference):

$$\mathcal{B} \models^{wa}_{\tau, \mathcal{A}} \mathcal{A}_{pl} \quad \text{iff} \quad \mathcal{B} \supseteq \{ B \mid \mathcal{A} \cup \mathcal{A}_{pl} \vdash S \text{ says } S \text{ will } B \}.$$

Queried permissions. Let $\tau = (U, S)$, $\mathcal{A}$ be a set of assertions, $\mathcal{B}$ a set of ground behaviour atoms, and q_m a τ-may-query. The relation $\mathcal{B} \models^{mq}_{\tau, \mathcal{A}} q_m$ holds if all behaviours in $\mathcal{B}$ are contained in the behaviours that *may* be exhibited, as specified by q_m, in the context of $\mathcal{A}$ (later, $\mathcal{A}$ will come from both the policy and the preference). The relation is defined as the smallest relation satisfying:

$\mathcal{B} \models^{mq}_{\tau, \mathcal{A}} U$ says S may B?, if $\mathcal{B} \subseteq \{B\}$;
$\mathcal{B} \models^{mq}_{\tau, \mathcal{A}} q_1 \wedge q_2$, if $\exists\ \mathcal{B}_1, \mathcal{B}_2$ such that $\mathcal{B} = \mathcal{B}_1 \cup \mathcal{B}_2$, $\mathcal{B}_1 \models^{mq}_{\tau, \mathcal{A}} q_1$ and $\mathcal{B}_2 \models^{mq}_{\tau, \mathcal{A}} q_2$;
$\emptyset \models^{mq}_{\tau, \mathcal{A}} q$, if $\mathcal{A} \vdash q$ and no subquery of the form $\langle U$ says S may $B? \rangle$ occurs in q.

Trace semantics of a policy. The following definition formalizes the intuitive meaning of a policy: a policy characterizes all those traces that respect both the lower and upper bounds on behaviours (as expressed by the will-assertions and the may-query, respectively, in the context of an additional set of assertions $\mathcal{A}$).

Definition 3. *Let $\tau = (U, S)$, $\Pi_{pl} = (\mathcal{A}_{pl}, q_m)$ be a τ-policy, and $\mathcal{A}$ a set of assertions. Then $\llbracket \Pi_{pl} \rrbracket^{pl}_{\tau, \mathcal{A}}$ denotes the set of all traces t such that*

$$\mathbf{Beh}(t) \models^{wa}_{\tau, \mathcal{A}} \mathcal{A}_{pl} \quad and \quad \mathbf{Beh}(t) \models^{mq}_{\tau, \mathcal{A}_{pl} \cup \mathcal{A}} q_m.$$

Example. Let $\tau = (\texttt{Alice}, \texttt{MS})$ and Π_{pl} consists of (10–19) from Fig. 1. Let $B_1 = \langle$allow `Alice` to `Edit` `ParentalControls`$\rangle$, $B_2 = \langle$revoke `Cookies` within `2yr`$\rangle$, and $B_3 = \langle$use `Cookies` for `AdTracking`$\rangle$. Let $\mathcal{A}$ consist of (2–9). Then $\llbracket \Pi_{pl} \rrbracket^{pl}_{\tau, \mathcal{A}}$ denotes the set of all traces t such that

$$\{B_1, B_2\} \subseteq \mathbf{Beh}(t) \subseteq \{B_1, B_2, B_3\},$$

which corresponds with the intention of the privacy policy described in Section 4.

5.2 Trace Semantics of Preferences

We specify the trace semantics of a preference by two other auxiliary relations.

Permissions. Let $\tau = (U, S)$, let $\mathcal{A}$, $\mathcal{A}_{pr}$ be sets of assertions, and $\mathcal{B}$ a set of ground behaviour atoms. The relation $\mathcal{B} \models^{ma}_{\tau, \mathcal{A}} \mathcal{A}_{pr}$ holds if all behaviours in $\mathcal{B}$ are contained in the set of behaviours permitted by the may-assertions in $\mathcal{A}_{pr}$ in the context of foreign assertions $\mathcal{A}$ (later, $\mathcal{A}$ will come from the service policy):

$$\mathcal{B} \models^{ma}_{\tau, \mathcal{A}} \mathcal{A}_{pr} \quad \text{iff} \quad \mathcal{B} \subseteq \{B \mid \mathcal{A} \cup \mathcal{A}_{pr} \vdash U \text{ says } S \text{ may } B\}.$$

Obligations. Let $\tau = (U, S)$, $\mathcal{A}$ be a set of assertions, $\mathcal{B}$ a set of ground behaviour atoms, and q_w a τ-will-query. The relation $\mathcal{B} \models^{wq}_{\tau, \mathcal{A}} q_w$ holds if the behaviours in $\mathcal{B}$ include all behaviours specified as required by q_w, in the context of $\mathcal{A}$ (later, $\mathcal{A}$ will come from both the service policy and the user preference). The relation is defined as the smallest relation satisfying the following:

$$\mathcal{B} \models^{wq}_{\tau, \mathcal{A}} S \text{ says } S \text{ will } B?, \quad \text{if } \mathcal{B} \supseteq \{B\};$$
$$\mathcal{B} \models^{wq}_{\tau, \mathcal{A}} q_1 \wedge q_2, \quad \text{if } \mathcal{B} \models^{wq}_{\tau, \mathcal{A}} q_1 \text{ and } \mathcal{B} \models^{wq}_{\tau, \mathcal{A}} q_2;$$
$$\mathcal{B} \models^{wq}_{\tau, \mathcal{A}} q_1 \vee q_2, \quad \text{if } \mathcal{B} \models^{wq}_{\tau, \mathcal{A}} q_1 \text{ or } \mathcal{B} \models^{wq}_{\tau, \mathcal{A}} q_2;$$
$$\mathcal{B} \models^{wq}_{\tau, \mathcal{A}} \exists x(q), \quad \text{if there is } E \in \textbf{Const} \text{ such that } \mathcal{B} \models^{wq}_{\tau, \mathcal{A}} q[E/x];$$
$$\mathcal{B} \models^{wq}_{\tau, \mathcal{A}} q, \quad \text{if } \mathcal{A} \vdash q \text{ and no subquery of the form } \langle S \text{ says } S \text{ will } B? \rangle \text{ occurs in } q.$$

Trace semantics of preferences. The following definition formalizes the trace semantics of a preference in the context of a set of assertions.

Definition 4. *For a user-service pair $\tau = (U, S)$, a τ-preference $\Pi_{pr} = (\mathcal{A}_{pr}, q_w)$, and a set $\mathcal{A}$ of assertions, $[\![\Pi_{pr}]\!]^{pr}_{\tau, \mathcal{A}}$ is the set of all traces t for which*

$$\textbf{Beh}(t) \models^{ma}_{\tau, \mathcal{A}} \mathcal{A}_{pr} \quad \text{and} \quad \textbf{Beh}(t) \models^{wq}_{\tau, \mathcal{A}_{pr} \cup \mathcal{A}} q_w.$$

Example. Let $\tau = (\texttt{Alice}, \texttt{MS})$ and Π_{pr} consists of (1–9) from Fig. 1. Let $\mathcal{A}$ consist of (10–18), $B_1 = \langle \text{allow Alice to Edit ParentalControls} \rangle$, and

$$\mathcal{B} = \{\text{allow Alice to } x\, y, \text{revoke Cookies within } x, \text{use Cookies for } x \mid x, y \in \textbf{Const}\}.$$

Then $[\![\Pi_{pr}]\!]^{pr}_{\tau, \mathcal{A}}$ denotes the set of all traces t such that

$$\{B_1\} \subseteq \textbf{Beh}(t) \subseteq \mathcal{B},$$

which corresponds with the intention of Alice's preference from Section 4.

5.3   Satisfaction and Compliance

Now we link up proof-theoretic satisfaction with model-theoretic compliance. Assuming that a service trace complies with the service's own policy, the theorem tells us that successfully evaluating all queries is indeed sufficient for guaranteeing that the service's trace also complies with the preference.

Theorem 1. *Let $\Pi_{pl} = (\mathcal{A}_{pl}, q_m)$ be a τ-policy and $\Pi_{pr} = (\mathcal{A}_{pr}, q_w)$ a τ-preference. If a trace t complies with $[\![\Pi_{pl}]\!]^{pl}_{\tau, \mathcal{A}_{pr}}$ and Π_{pl} satisfies Π_{pr}, then t complies with $[\![\Pi_{pr}]\!]^{pr}_{\tau, \mathcal{A}_{pl}}.$*

This theorem is completely independent of any concrete instantiation of traces, of the behaviours, and of the **Beh** mapping. The essential correctness property for *S4P* holds *despite* its abstractness. (Of course, if behaviour-specific properties are to be proved, then **Beh** needs to be filled with some structure.)

6   Safe Data Handling

In this section we describe a protocol for PII disclosure in a network of users and services that use S4P to express their preferences and policies, respectively. The protocol also regulates transitive communication of PIIs to third parties and evolution of privacy policies. The protocol guarantees privacy of users' PIIs.

User-service encounter. If a service S wishes to collect a PII from a user U, then the following steps are performed (here, $\tau = (U, S)$):

1. U and S decide on a τ-preference Π_{pr} and a τ-policy Π_{pl}, respectively, to be used for this encounter. These may be fixed or result from negotiation.
2. If Π_{pl} satisfies Π_{pr}, then U sends PII to S, otherwise the protocol is aborted. The trust model dictates who checks satisfaction: U (as the main stakeholder), S (wishing to keep parts of its policy secret), or a trusted third party. Available computational resources may also influence the decision.
3. S keeps a copy of Π_{pl} and Π_{pr} together with the PII.

Transitive service-service encounter. In most scenarios, disclosing a PII P to a third party S' represents a privacy-relevant behaviour, which should be denoted by a behavioural atom $\langle \text{send } P \text{ to } S' \rangle$ (e.g. $\langle \text{send Email to eMarketing} \rangle$) which the **Beh** mapping should keep track of.

A service S may thus only disclose a PII to a third party S' if

1. The policy of S allows the disclosure, and
2. The policy of S' complies with U's preference. Again, the trust model dictates the place to check satisfaction, e.g. at S (not requiring to trust S' on checking), at S' (who might have more resources), or at a trusted third party.

Policy evolution. A service may wish to alter its policy even after having collected the PII. For example, a service may want to disclose the PII to a previously unknown third party, even though the behaviour corresponding to the disclosure action was not declared in the may-assertions in the service's policy. Or it may wish *not* to delete PII despite having promised it in the will-query.

Strictly speaking, both cases represent compliance violations of the service's own original policy. Sometimes such violations should be permitted as long as the new behaviours still comply with the user's original preference. In this scheme, the service would need to alter its policy in such a way that the new behaviours comply with the new policy. It then has to check if the new policy still satisfies the preference. If so, the service may start complying with the new policy, otherwise it must continue complying with the original policy. This scheme guarantees that the service still complies with the user's preference.

Privacy guarantee. Assuming users and services follow the protocol and that all services comply with their own policies, the following safety property holds.

- If a service S possesses U's PII P, either U has sent P earlier to S directly,
- or else S obtained P via a third-party exchange from some service $\tilde{S}$ which possessed P at that time, and the user's preference says that $\tilde{S}$ may send P to S.
- In either case, the trace of S complies with the user's preference.

A formalization of the protocol and of the safety property is found in [9].

7   Implementation

Our prototype implementation focuses on three phases: evaluating policies and preferences, enforcing policies (including disclosure), and verifying trace compliance.

Evaluating policies and preferences. During an encounter, the service discloses its interface, i.e., the type of the required PII, and the associated privacy policy. The privacy policy is evaluated against the privacy preference as described in Section 3. When one or more PII have the required type and a suitable preference, the user is given a choice in a privacy-aware identity selection protocol. If the satisfaction check fails, the user can stop or modify her preferences.

We found that for typical policies, our implementation of satisfaction checking completes within a few milliseconds, even in the context of 10^6 atomic assertions.

Enforcing policies. Services store collected PIIs and keep track of associated rights and obligations by attaching the correspondent "sticky" preference. Obligations are enforced by reacting to external and scheduled events. Before an action is performed on a collected PII, queries are evaluated against the attached preference. Services record privacy-relevant behaviour in execution traces.

Verifying compliance of traces. Execution traces can be used by internal or external auditors in order to check the behaviour of services. Traces are verified according to the trace semantics given in Section 5.

Our implementation of S4P is based on the SecPAL [8] evaluation engine implementation, extended with generic predicates and the may/will-constructs. The evaluation process begins by translating each assertion into constrained Datalog clauses. Queries against the resulting constrained Datalog program are evaluated using a resolution algorithm with tabling [17] in order to guarantee termination even with recursive facts in policies and preferences. The translation preserves S4P's query semantics: a query is true in the context of S4P's assertions iff the corresponding Datalog query evaluates to true against the Datalog program.

A successful query can be visualized by a proof viewer that graphically displays the deduction steps in a proof graph; a failed query can be analysed using our logical abduction tool [10]. In future work, we plan to adapt the tool to suggest modifications of privacy preferences in the case of non-satisfaction.

8   Evaluating S4P's Design

This section briefly discusses S4P's language design with regards to the six design goals listed in Section 1.

Generality and abstractness. Abstractness avoids premature commitment to a limited set of features suitable for one particular application domain, but not necessarily for another. It allows concrete ontologies and semantic specifications to be plugged in flexibly, depending on the context and needs. Abstractness is thus conducive to a modular language design, simplifying formal reasoning. As we have showed in this paper, useful correctness properties can be established with relatively little effort, without having to instantiate the temporal and stateful semantics of behaviours.

S4P is abstract in several aspects. First, the vocabulary is kept abstract. Even though most websites' natural language privacy statements have a common structure (e.g. adhering to the Safe Harbor Privacy Principles), with details on notification, user choice, third party disclosure, user access, and security, their vocabularies vary greatly, especially across different application domains.

Second, we have kept the semantics of behaviours abstract by assuming a mapping from traces to behaviour atoms. In most cases it is sufficient to agree on the semantics of behaviours only informally, especially for behaviours involving human interaction. Our framework facilitates such partial informality by providing the abstract level of behaviour atoms. If a more formal treatment is needed, our framework can be used to concretize the meaning of behaviours to any desired level. Complex privacy obligations [22] and temporal logic to express trace constraints [4] are examples of how our abstract notion of behaviour could be concretized.

Third, we are not tied to a specific compliance enforcement model. In practice, automatically enforcing compliance is unfeasible or unnecessary; instead, informal methods such as auditing are used. To automate enforcement, the most direct way is to implement a reference monitor for dynamically checking the permissions, accompanied by an obligation monitoring system [12,19]. For simple systems, it may be possible to enforce compliance by static analysis, as has been done for cryptographic protocols and access control policies [11].

Uniform treatment of preferences and policies. In S4P, both preferences and policies are uniformly expressed as assertions and queries in a single language. Satisfaction checking between policies and preferences reduces to simple query evaluation.

Support for both permissions and obligations. S4P introduces two modal verbs for specifying upper bounds (may) and lower bounds (will) on service behaviours. This minimal syntactic construct is sufficient for expressing permissions, promises, and obligations, as formalized in Section 5.

Human-readable syntax. The case study from Section 4 showed that real-world online policy statements in natural language can be translated into S4P fairly directly in a way that preserves human readability to a reasonable degree. This is achieved by S4P's infix notation for phrases and the restriction of assertions to essentially the Horn logic fragment, which can be written as if-clauses.

Expressiveness. S4P's relatively high expressiveness compared to other privacy languages is mainly due to its abstractness, but also to a number of language features. First, the application-specific predicates are parameterized, which allows the modelling of arbitrary relations. Second, the if-conditions of assertions are recursive, which is necessary for transitive trust relations. And third, the where-clause may contain arbitrary application-specific constraints, including arithmetic and string ones, and functions for retrieving environmental data.

Support for delegation. The need for trust policies has been long recognized in authorization logics, which has led to the development of language construct for delegation of authority. But trust and delegation is equally important in privacy policies (see e.g. Section 4). S4P supports delegation by qualifying all statements with the says-modality and providing the can say primitive to allow utterances to be dependent on other principals' utterances.

Conclusion. Summarizing, we believe that the abstractness of S4P, in conjunction with the other design goals from Section 1, makes it a particularly attractive privacy language in terms of expressiveness, applicability, usability, and for formal analysis.

References

1. Antón, A., Earp, J., Bolchini, D., He, Q., Jensen, C., Stufflebeam, W., et al.: The lack of clarity in financial privacy policies and the need for standardization. In: IEEE Symposium on Security & Privacy, pp. 36–45 (2004)
2. Ardagna, C.A., Cremonini, M., di Vimercati, S.D.C., Samarati, P.: A privacy-aware access control system. Journal of Computer Security 16(4), 369–397 (2008)
3. Ashley, P., Hada, S., Karjoth, G., Powers, C., Schunter, M.: Enterprise Privacy Authorization Language (EPAL 1.2). Technical report, IBM (November 2003)
4. Barth, A., Datta, A., Mitchell, J., Nissenbaum, H.: Privacy and contextual integrity: Framework and applications. In: IEEE Symposium on Security and Privacy (2006)
5. Barth, A., Mitchell, J.: Enterprise privacy promises and enforcement. In: Proceedings of the 2005 Workshop on Issues in the Theory of Security, pp. 58–66. ACM, New York (2005)
6. Beatty, P., Reay, I., Dick, S., Miller, J.: P3P adoption on e-Commerce web sites: a survey and analysis. IEEE Internet Computing, 65–71 (2007)
7. Becker, M.Y.: SecPAL formalisation and extensions. Technical Report MSR-TR-2009-127, Microsoft Research (2009)
8. Becker, M.Y., Fournet, C., Gordon, A.D.: Design and semantics of a decentralized authorization language. In: IEEE Computer Security Foundations Symposium (2007)
9. Becker, M.Y., Malkis, A., Bussard, L.: S4P: A Generic Language for Specifying Privacy Preferences and Policies. Technical Report MSR-TR-2010-32, Microsoft Research (2010)
10. Becker, M.Y., Nanz, S.: The role of abduction in declarative authorization policies. In: Hudak, P., Warren, D.S. (eds.) PADL 2008. LNCS, vol. 4902, pp. 84–99. Springer, Heidelberg (2008)
11. Bengtson, J., Bhargavan, K., Fournet, C., Gordon, A.D., Maffeis, S.: Refinement types for secure implementations. In: Computer Security Foundations Symposium (2008)
12. Bettini, C., Jajodia, S., Wang, X., Wijesekera, D.: Obligation monitoring in policy management. In: Policies for Distributed Systems and Networks (2002)
13. Blaze, M., Feigenbaum, J., Lacy, J.: Decentralized trust management. In: IEEE Symposium on Security and Privacy, pp. 164–173 (1996)
14. Casassa Mont, M., Beato, F.: On parametric obligation policies: Enabling privacy-aware information lifecycle management in enterprises. In: IEEE International Workshop on Policies for Distributed Systems and Networks, pp. 51–55 (2007)

15. Cranor, L., Dobbs, B., Egelman, S., Hogben, G., Humphrey, J., Langheinrich, M., Marchiori, M., Presler-Marshall, M., Reagle, J., Schunter, M., Stampley, D.A., Wenning, R.: The Platform for Privacy Preferences 1.1 (P3P1.1) Specification. W3C (November 2006)
16. Cranor, L., Langheinrich, M., Marchiori, M.: A P3P Preference Exchange Language 1.0. W3C (April 2002), http://www.w3.org/TR/P3P-preferences
17. Dietrich, S.W.: Extension tables: Memo relations in logic programming. In: Furukawa, K., Fujisaki, T., Tanaka, H. (eds.) Logic Programming 1987. LNCS, vol. 315, pp. 264–272. Springer, Heidelberg (1988)
18. Hochheiser, H.: The platform for privacy preference as a social protocol: An examination within the U.S. policy context. ACM Transactions on Internet Technologys 2(4) (2002)
19. Irwin, K., Yu, T., Winsborough, W.H.: On the modeling and analysis of obligations. In: Computer and Communications Security (2006)
20. Itai, A., Makowsky, J.A.: Unification as a complexity measure for logic programming. Journal of Logic Programming 4(2) (1987)
21. Jensen, C., Potts, C.: Privacy policies as decision-making tools: an evaluation of online privacy notices. In: Human Factors in Computing Systems (2004)
22. Ni, Q., Bertino, E., Lobo, J.: An obligation model bridging access control policies and privacy policies. In: Access Control Models and Technologies (2008)
23. OASIS. eXtensible Access Control Markup Language (XACML) Version 2.0 core specification (2005), http://www.oasis-open.org/committees/xacml/
24. Stufflebeam, W.H., Antón, A.I., He, Q., Jain, N.: Specifying privacy policies with P3P and EPAL: lessons learned. In: Workshop on Privacy in the Electronic Society (2004)

Efficient Detection of the Return-Oriented Programming Malicious Code

Ping Chen, Xiao Xing, Hao Han, Bing Mao, and Li Xie

State Key Laboratory for Novel Software Technology, Nanjing University
Department of Computer Science and Technology, Nanjing University, Nanjing 210093
{chenping,xingxiao,hanhao}@sns.nju.edu.cn,
{maobing,xieli}@nju.edu.cn

Abstract. Return-Oriented Programming (ROP) is a code-reuse technique which helps the attacker construct malicious code by using the instruction snippets in existing libraries/executables. Such technique makes the ROP program contain no malicious instructions. Moreover, in recent research, Return-Oriented Programming without returns has been proposed, which can be used to mount an attack without any independent return instructions, therefore, ROP malicious code circumvents the existing defenses which are based on the assumption that the ROP malicious code should use the `ret` without corresponding `call`. In this paper, we found the intrinsic feature of the ROP shellcode, and proposed an efficient method which can detect the ROP malicious code (including the one without returns). Preliminary experimental results show that our method can efficiently detect ROP malicious code and have no false positives and negatives.

1 Introduction

Return-Oriented Programming(ROP) was introduced by Shacham [27] on the x86 architecture. Later, it was mounted on other modern architectures [5, 15, 19, 8, 17]. Different from the traditional code-injection techniques, ROP allows the attacker to launch an attack by using short instruction sequences in existing libraries/executables, without injecting malicious code. Traditionally, ROP uses the so-called gadgets which are the instruction sequences ending with `ret`. The behavior that `ret` drives the flow from one sequence to the next in ROP, is different from the instruction stream executed by legitimate programs: first, ROP uses an abundant return instructions with just a few instructions apart; second, ROP executes return instructions without the corresponding `call`; third, the ROP programs are totally installed on the stack. There are three mechanisms proposed by researchers for detecting and defeating return-oriented attacks.

The first method suggests a defense that looks for frequent instruction streams with returns. Davi et al. [11] and Chen et al. [9] detect ROP based on the assumption that ROP leverages the gadget which contains no more than 5 instructions, and the number of contiguous gadgets is no less than 3. The second approach proposes a defense which is based on the fact that return-oriented instructions produce an imbalance in the ratio of executed `call` and `ret` instructions on x86. Francillon et al. [14] proposes a hardware-based method by using a return-address shadow stack to detect ROP. With the same idea, ROPdefender [12] alternatively uses a software-based method. The third

S. Jha and A. Maturia (Eds.): ICISS 2010, LNCS 6503, pp. 140–155, 2010.
© Springer-Verlag Berlin Heidelberg 2010

mechanism proposes a return less kernel [18]. It recommends a compiler which eliminates the `ret` instruction.

However, the property of the ROP malicious code (using the return instructions) has been broken by recent works [30, 7]. Checkoway et al. [7] suggests that the ROP malicious code could be constructed without the return instructions, and they use the `pop-jmp` instructions to chain gadgets together. Bletsch et al. [30] suggests the concept of Jump-Oriented Programming (JOP), and uses so-called *Dispatcher Gadgets* to chain the gadgets together. These two works demonstrate the fact that the gadgets ending in `jmp` instruction are Turing-complete. In this paper, we investigate the diversity of the gadget's ending instructions as well as its abnormal behavior in ROP malicious code, and further we introduce the more intrinsic property of the ROP, based on which we propose a new method to detect the ROP malicious code.

Our paper makes three major contributions:

- We select the gadgets from `libc-2.3.5.so` and `libgcj.so.5.0.0`, and the gadgets end with the diverse instructions:`ret`, `call` and `jmp`, then we leverage the gadgets to rewrite the 130 x86 shellcode on milw0rm [22] by ROP techniques.
- We propose the common property of the ROP malicious code, compared with existing ROP defenses, our tool does not rely on the assumption that ROP malicious codes use the gadgets ending in `ret`.
- We develop an effective tool to detect the ROP attack, which to the best of our knowledge, is the first one for detecting ROP attacks that use `jmp` and `call` as the ending instruction. Experimental results show that our tool can efficiently detect all the ROP malicious code, and the performance overhead is acceptable.

2   Feature of ROP Malicious Code

In practical writing the ROP malicious code, we find that, ROP malicious code can be written by either the traditional gadgets ending in `ret` [27] or the new gadgets ending in `jmp` and `call` [7, 30]. In order to extract the intrinsic property of ROP malicious code, we should not focus on the specific instruction used by the gadget (e.g.,the frequency analysis of `ret`, `call` and `jmp`), because the attacker can construct the ROP malicious code in any shape by using the diverse ending instructions. In order to understand the abnormal behavior of ROP, we firstly review the normal behavior of the legitimate program. As we know a *function* combines a block of programs to be executed into one logical unit. On x86 architecture, `ret`, `call` and `jmp` can drive the control flows within one function or among different functions. All the three instructions have their own manipulation rules: `ret` uses the return address to roll back to the *caller* at the epilogue of *callee*; `call` transfers the control flow to the prologue of *callee*[1], and save the return address on the stack; `jmp` can be divided into the intra-procedure `jmp` instruction and the inter-procedure `jmp` instruction. The most commonly used `jmp` instruction is the intra-procedure `jmp` instruction, which is used to jump within the same function,

---

[1] There are some exceptions, for example, in certain cases, the "call" instruction only stores the address of the next instruction on the stack for later usage.

and the inter-procedure `jmp` instruction, which is used to jump among the different functions, often has its specific purpose. We will discuss it in Section 4.4.

Figure 1 shows the legitimate control flow during normal program's execution as well as the control flow during ROP malicious code's execution. The difference between legitimate program control flow and ROP control flow is that: In ROP control flow, `call` and `ret` instructions (④ and ⑤ in Figure 1 (b)) do not manipulate the function, instead, they are used to chain the gadgets which are often located in the middle of the functions; whereas `call` and `ret` instructions (① and ② in Figure 1 (a)) represent the prologue and epilogue of the function in the normal program. In ROP control flow, `jmp` instruction (⑥ in Figure 1 (b))jumps between the different library functions or even different libraries. Note that as the gadgets selected by the attacker may be *unintended* instruction sequence, this kind of gadget with the *unintended* behavior is quite different from the normal program execution. For example, in the middle of the function, if there is a gadget ending in `jmp`. It will change the control flow to the next gadget, which often does not locate in the same function; whereas `jmp` instruction (③ in Figure 1 (a)) in the normal program execution often jumps within the same function.

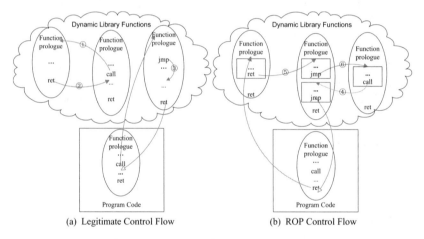

(a) Legitimate Control Flow   (b) ROP Control Flow

Fig. 1. Legitimate Control Flow and ROP Control Flow

3   Overview

In order to efficiently detect the ROP malicious code, we focus on three control flow sensitive instructions: `call`, `ret`, `jmp`. Based on the feature of the ROP malicious code, we propose the *function granularity sensitive control flow monitoring*:

– **Ret instruction.** The `ret` instruction is used at the epilogue of the function in normal program, and there should be a corresponding `call` instruction. Thus it is very easy to detect the gadget ending in `ret` instruction by maintaining a return-address shadow stack for the program. When an independent `ret` instruction occurs, there should be a ROP attack.

– **Call instruction.** The `call` instruction is often leveraged to invoke a function, and it should jump to the prologue of the function. Function can be divided into two categories, frame function and non-frame function, and their features are mentioned in [29]. Fixed instruction sequences are located at the beginning of the two kinds of functions, which is shown as below. Based on the observation, we check whether the target instructions of `call` matches the beginning instructions of either frame function or non-frame function, if not, we regard it as a ROP attack.

```
non-frame function:  sub esp, value
                     . . .
frame function:      push ebp
                     mov ebp,esp
                     . . .
```

– **Jmp instruction.** Generally speaking, the `jmp` instruction can be divided into direct `jmp` and indirect `jmp`. Because the target address of the direct `jmp` is hardcoded, the attacker can not leverage it to launch the attack. ROP attacker leverages the indirect `jmp` instruction to launch an attack by preparing the value of the register which is used in the indirect `jmp` instruction. Indirect `jmp` instruction is often leveraged to do some specific work, such as dynamic function relocation and hook function for debugging. We find that, in normal programs, the indirect `jmp` instructions can not be used to jump from one library function to another. Thus we monitor the indirect `jmp` instruction and its target address, if it jumps among the different library functions, it should be a ROP attack.

Figure 2 shows the overall architecture of our work. The tools can be divided into three parts. The first part is the *Pre-processing* component, the second part is the *Run-time Monitoring* component, and the third part is *ROP Signature* component. The *Pre-processing* component is used to analyze the binary executable file and the dynamic

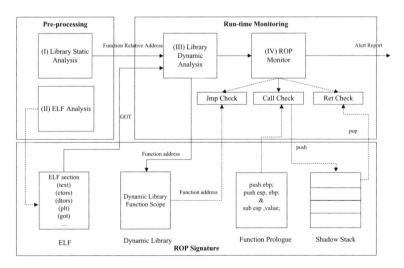

Fig. 2. Architecture of Our Work

library. More detailed, *ELF Analysis* analyzes the GOT/PLT/CTORS/DTORS/TEXT segments of the ELF format file, the result is served as part of *ROP signature* for the *Run-time Monitoring* to detect the ROP attack. In addition, *Library Static Analysis* analyzes the dynamic libraries used by the application, and finds the memory scope of each library functions. It provides the relative address of the library functions to the *Library Dynamic Analysis*, which then leverages GOT to find the base address of dynamic library, and computes the address of the library function as part of the *ROP signature*. *ROP signature* component contains two additional information, one is the function prologue, the other is the return-address shadow memory which is maintained at runtime. Based on the *ROP signature*, *ROP monitor* dynamically instruments the program, and checks the three instructions: jmp, call and ret. The return-address shadow stack can be leveraged to detect the ret instruction without the corresponding call instruction. For detecting the gadget ending in call instruction, we check whether the target instruction of the call instruction is the "push ebp; mov ebp,esp" (frame function) or the "sub esp, value" (non-frame function). If not, it must be a gadget ending in call, which transfers the control flow to the next gadget. For detecting the jmp instruction, we check the address of the jmp instruction and the target address of it. If these two addresses are in the different dynamic library functions, there should be a gadget ending in jmp.

Figure 3 shows the work flow of the *ROP monitor* component. As we can see that, the dynamic instrumentation tools monitor three instructions, call, ret and jmp. When we recognize the call instruction, we push the return address onto the *shadow stack*, then we check the target instruction. If the instruction is neither "push ebp;mov ebp,esp" nor "sub esp, value", we assume it is a ROP attack. When we recognize the ret instruction, we pop up the address from the *shadow stack*, and check

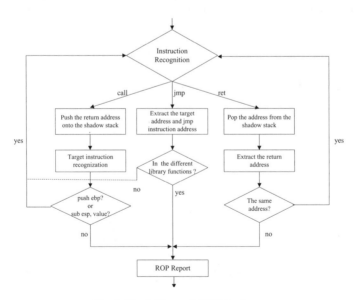

Fig. 3. Work Flow of ROP Monitor

whether return address matches the one from the shadow stack, if not, we assume it is a ROP attack. When we recognize an indirect jmp instruction, we check whether the address of the instruction and the target address locate in the different library functions, if so, we assume there is a ROP attack.

4   Implementation Details

Our system is implemented on dynamical binary instrumentation tool PIN-2.6 [21], the disassembler IDA Pro-5.2 [10], and Readelf-2.17 [25]. We use the Readelf to analyze the segments in ELF files, and the IDA Pro to disassemble the library code, and get the relative address of the library function, which is the function of *Library Static Analysis*. In addition, we implement the *Library Dynamic Analysis* and *ROP Monitor* on the PIN. We will introduce our implementation in details in the section.

4.1   ELF Analysis

In current implementation, we use Readelf to statically analyze ELF structure in the ELF header. We focus on the start address and the size of the segments, including text, GOT. "Text" can be used to determine the first instruction in the program code. "GOT" can be leveraged to find the base address of dynamic library. The "GOT[1]" is filled with the "link_map" list address by the loader, and each dynamic library is in the form of the structure "link_map", which is defined in link.h in linux-2.6.15. All the dynamic libraries are chained together in the "link_map" list. "link_map" contains the field "l_addr", which is the base address of the dynamic library. If we traverse through the "link_map" list, all the library base address can be extracted.

4.2   Library Static Analysis

We use the IDA Pro to statically analyze the dynamic library which is used by the program. For each library, we write a plug-in to extract the relative address of the library function from the analysis result of the IDA Pro, and the information includes the library name, function name, start address of the function and the end address of the function.

4.3   Library Dynamic Analysis

Library Dynamic Analysis is the component which retrieves the base address of each library. As mentioned above, the information of the library is stored at the structure link_map, which is written during the loading time before the program code executed. Figure 4 shows that, each node in the form of the structure link_map represents one dynamic library, and link_map constructs the double link. In each node, there are two important fields: l_addr and l_name. l_addr is the base address of the dynamic library, and l_name is the name of the dynamic library. As the address of the link_map list is located at GOT[1] [28], we can traverse through the double link to find each dynamic library's base address. Combined with the relative address of the library function which is analyzed by *Library Static Analysis*, we can compute the memory scope of each library function at runtime, including the start address and the end address.

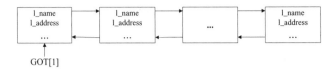

Fig. 4. Dynamic library link information

4.4 ROP Monitor

The ROP Monitor Component is the key of our system. It leverages the library information (section 4.2 and section 4.3) and ELF information (section 4.1) to check whether there are exceptions of the control flow sensitive instructions (ret, call and jmp). Further, we design different mechanisms for monitoring them.

- *Ret Integrity Check*
  In order to check the integrity of the ret instruction, we maintain a *shadow stack*. When executing the call/ret instruction, we update the *shadow stack*. For call instruction, we push the address onto the *shadow stack*, whereas for ret instruction, we pop the address from the *shadow stack*, and check whether the address matches with the one poped up by the ret instruction. If the addresses are different, we report that it is a ROP attack. However, there exists the exception when the program leverages the system calls setjmp and longjmp. As they may skip several stack frames, and make the *shadow stack* and program stack contain the different return address. To solve the problem, we set flag for the setjmp and longjmp, and pops up the return addresses which are saved between setjmp and longjmp from the *shadow stack* when executing *longjmp*. This mechanism can guarantee the program stack and *shadow stack* contain the same return addresses, and avoid the false positives. *Ret Integrity Check* is able to defend the ROP attack which leverages the gadget ending in ret without corresponding call instruction, but it can not prevent the ROP attack which leverages the call gadgets and jmp gadgets.
- *Call Integrity Check*
  In the C/C++ Programming, the function can be divided into the frame function and the non-frame function. The fixed instructions of the function prologue is that, "push ebp;mov ebp,esp" for frame function, and "sub esp, value" for non-frame function. As we know that, the target address of the call instruction is the entry of the function. Therefore, the next instruction of it should be either "push ebp" or "sub esp, value". If the program does not obey the rule, we suspect it could be ROP attack which uses the gadget ending in call instruction. This mechanism can be used to detect the ROP attack which uses the gadget ending in call instruction or the *combinational gadgets* which use the "*call-jmp*" instruction sequence(call is used to invoke another instruction sequence ending in ret and jmp is used to chain the next gadget). But it cannot prevent the ROP attack which uses merely the gadget ending in jmp instruction.
- *Jmp Integrity Check*
  Direct jmp instruction cannot be used to chain the gadgets because it can not be controlled by the attacker, therefore, we regard the direct jmp instruction is benign.

Jmp Integrity Check monitors the indirect jmp instruction, which uses the register as the address or the pointer to the memory. During the program running, we record the address of the indirect jmp instruction and the target address it will jump to. Then we check whether the two addresses locate in the different library functions. This mechanism is based on the assumption that all the jmp instructions in the dynamic library should jump within the same library function. In fact, in practical analysis, we find that the indirect jmp instructions are often used in some specific cases. For example, when evoking the dynamic library function, it uses the indirect jmp instruction to jump from the PLT to GOT. Another example is that, when executing the "longjmp", it uses the "jmp edx" to jump back to the point set by "setjmp". Note that "longjmp" and "setjmp" may cause the false positive because they are used to do the inter-function jmp. In practice, we pay special attention on them, and avoid the exception.

5   Evaluation

In this section, we choose a large number of normal programs and ROP malicious code to evaluate the effectiveness of our tools. In order to test the ability of our tool, we rewrite about 130 malicious code on milw0rm [22] into the Return-Oriented Programming shellcode, and we divide these ROP shellcode by two categories, including the traditional ROP shellcode which uses the gadget ending in ret instruction and the new ROP shellcode which uses the gadgets ending in jmp and the *combinational gadgets*. All the gadgets are extracted from two widely used libraries, libc-2.3.5.so (C library) and libgcj.so.5.0.0 (a Java runtime library).

In order to test the false positives of our tool, we select several commonly used softwares to validate the three assumption our tool based on: (1) ret instruction has the corresponding call instruction. (2) the target instructions of call is either "push ebp" or "sub esp, value". (3) the address of jmp instruction and its target address are in the same library function. In our current experiment, we select the typical dynamic library libc-2.3.5 to test the normal jmp execution, because all of the softwares we test use libc dynamic library. In addition, we use the same softwares to test the call instruction. Since our strategy of detecting the violation of call instruction does not use the information of library, we test all the call instructions which are not specifically localized in the dynamic library. The evaluation is performed on an Intel Pentium Dual E2180 2.00GHz machine with 2GB memory and Linux kernel 2.6.15. Tested programs are compiled by gcc-4.0.3 and linked with glibc-2.3.5.

Finally we evaluate the performance overhead of our tool. In this section, we first evaluate the normal applications with its dynamic libraries, as well as the number of library functions in these libraries. Then we test the false positives and the false negatives of our tool. Finally, we test the performance overhead of our tool.

5.1   Dynamic Library Analysis

In current implementation, we choose several libraries to do the static and dynamic analysis. We leverage the IDA pro-5.2 [10] and PIN-2.6 [21] to analyze the function information of certain library, including the number of function, function name, the start

Table 1. Dynamic Library and its Functions

Number	Library Name	LOC (K)	Number of Functions	Number	Library Name	LOC (K)	Number of Functions
1	libc-2.3.5	199.8	3071	2	libm-2.3.6	1489.6	414
3	ld-2.4	121.4	163	4	libgdbm.so.2.0.0	25.6	119
5	libwrap.so.0	30.2	253	6	libpam.so.0	45.6	182
7	libdl.so.2	9.5	48	8	libresolv.so.2	69.7	236
9	libcrypto.so.0.9.8	1344.3	3760	10	libutil.so.1	9.5	74
11	libz.so.1	81.6	175	12	libselinux.so.1	104.1	456
13	libgssapi_krb5.so.2	109.7	461	14	libkrb5.so.3	496.1	1708
15	libk5crypto.so.3	152.9	306	16	libkrb5support.so.0	11.7	48
17	libcom_err.so.2	9.4	82	18	libsepol.so.1	239.5	563
19	libnsl.so.1	77.8	376	20	libcrypt.so.1	37.4	66
21	libaprutil-1.so.0	95.7	721	22	libexpat.so.0	125.2	252
23	libapr-1.so.0	135.6	998	24	librt.so.1	29.9	185
25	libpthread.so.0	112.2	523				

Table 2. Application and its Dynamic Libraries

Prog.	LOC (K)	Benchmark	Dynamic Libraries	Library Name
bzip2-1.0.5	236.6	Compress the 1.7M file	2	1,3
slocate-2.7	89.2	Search patterns in 87K database	2	1,3
gzip-1.2.4	278.2	Uncompress the 55M file	2	1,3
bc-1.06	375.9	Finds primes between 2 and limits	2	1,3
gcc-4.2.4	4060.4	Compile 1KB source code	2	1,3
man-1.6c	248.5	Open the message catalog for ls	3	1,3,4
gocr-0.46	823.6	Process JPG file	3	1-3
grep-2.5.1	904.1	Find pattern in 1.9 MB file	2	1,3
openssh-2.2.1	976.8	Login in using user name	18	1,3,5-20
httpd-2.2.0	9883.7	ab	10	1-3,7,20-25

address and the end address of certain function. Take the libc-2.3.5 for example, IDA pro reports that there are total 3071 functions in it, and it statistically analyzes the start address and end address of each function. Based on the relative address of the library function, further, we use the method which we mentioned in section 4.3 to get the base address of the dynamic library. Then we add the base address to the relative function address to compute the linear address at runtime, which is the basis of our detection tool. We select ten normal programs and statistically analyze the information of the dynamic libraries. Table 1 shows the function number of 25 dynamic libraries, which are used by the ten test applications in Table 2. Table 2 shows the ten test applications with their dynamic libraries, including the number of libraries and the library name. Note that, to be brief, we use the library index in Table 1 to represent the library name.

5.2   False Negatives and False Positives

We choose 130 Linux x86 shellcode from milw0rm [22], and all these types of shellcode are rewritten by ROP to evaluate the effectiveness of our tool. The code base contains two libraries: libc-2.3.5.so and libgcj.so.5.0.0. The gadgets ending in ret are extracted merely from libc-2.3.5.so and the gadgets ending in call and jmp are extracted from libc-2.3.5.so and libgcj.so.5.0.0. Based on these gadgets, we rewrite each shellcode into two kinds of shellcode: ROP shellcode uses only the gadgets ending in ret, ROP shellcode without returns which uses the gadgets ending in jmp and the *combinational gadgets* ending in call and ret to invoke the system call. For this purpose, we select the following couple of gadgets: "gadget-a"

Table 3. ROP shellcode Tested by our Tool and DROP

Number	Size (Bytes)	Description	Gadgets jmp	call	ret	DROP	Our Tool
1	30	chmod("//etc/shadow",666) exit(0)	5	2	2	×	✓
2	34	killall5 shellcode	5	2	2	×	✓
3	30	PUSH reboot()	5	2	2	×	✓
4	40	/sbin/iptables -F	7	3	3	×	✓
5	45	execve(rm -rf /) shellcode	9	4	4	×	✓
6	25	execve("/bin//sh")	5	2	2	×	✓
7	34	setreuid(getuid(),getuid()),execve("/bin//sh",0,0)	24	3	3	×	✓
8	86	edit /etc/sudoers for full access	30	4	4	×	✓
9	45	system-beep shellcode	20	2	2	×	✓
10	12	iopl(3); asm(cli); while(1)	8	1	1	×	✓
11	7	forkbomb	5	1	1	×	✓
12	36	write(0,"Hello core!",12)	16	2	2	×	✓
13	40	eject cd-rom (follows /dev/cdrom symlink) + exit()	22	3	3	×	✓
14	39	anti-debug trick (INT 3h trap) + execve /bin/sh	8	1	1	×	✓
15	12	set system time to 0 and exit	10	2	2	×	✓
16	11	kill all processes	8	1	1	×	✓
17	16	re-use of /bin/sh string in .rodata shellcode	6	1	1	×	✓
18	18	File unlinker	10	2	2	×	✓
19	15	dup2(0,0); dup2(0,1); dup2(0,2);	21	1	1	×	✓
20	56	Ho' Detector	22	3	3	×	✓
21	5	normal exit w/ random return value	3	1	1	×	✓
22	25	Radically Self Modifying Code	18	0	0	×	✓
23	30	chmod("//etc/shadow",666) exit(0)	0	0	8	✓	✓
24	34	killall5 shellcode	0	0	15	✓	✓
25	30	PUSH reboot()	0	0	8	✓	✓
26	40	/sbin/iptables -F	0	0	19	✓	✓
27	45	execve(rm -rf /) shellcode	0	0	29	✓	✓
28	25	execve("/bin//sh")	0	0	8	✓	✓
29	34	setreuid(getuid(),getuid()),execve("/bin//sh",0,0)	0	0	21	✓	✓
30	86	edit /etc/sudoers for full access	0	0	32	✓	✓
31	45	system-beep shellcode	0	0	23	✓	✓
32	12	iopl(3); asm(cli); while(1)	0	0	9	✓	✓
33	7	forkbomb	0	0	4	✓	✓
34	36	write(0,"Hello core!",12)	0	0	18	✓	✓
35	40	eject cd-rom (follows /dev/cdrom symlink) + exit()	0	0	28	✓	✓
36	39	anti-debug trick (INT 3h trap) + execve /bin/sh	0	0	23	✓	✓
37	12	set system time to 0 and exit	0	0	13	✓	✓
38	11	kill all processes	0	0	12	✓	✓
39	16	re-use of /bin/sh string in .rodata shellcode	0	0	8	✓	✓
40	18	File unlinker	0	0	13	✓	✓
41	15	dup2(0,0); dup2(0,1); dup2(0,2);	0	0	25	✓	✓
42	56	Ho' Detector	0	0	34	✓	✓
43	5	normal exit w/ random return value	0	0	3	✓	✓
44	25	Radically Self Modifying Code	0	0	19	✓	✓

(libgcj.so.5.0.0) and "gadget-b" (libc-2.3.5.so). The work flow of the *combinational gadget* is that, gadget-a can call gadget-b, which will return to gadget-a's jmp instruction, and then it jumps to next gadget. We regard the combinational gadgets as one call gadget and one ret gadget. For the JOP shellcode, its number of ret gadget equals to the number of system call in the original shellcode.

```
1   call [esi+54h]  (a)       1   call large dword ptr gs:10h   (b)
2   jmp  [ebp-18h]             2   ret
```

Table 3 shows 44 ROP shellcode we rewrite, the first 22 ROP shellcode use the gadgets ending in jmp and the combinational gadgets; the last 22 ROP shellcode use the gadgets ending in ret. In table 3, column 1 represents the index of the ROP shellcode, column 2 represents the size of original shellcode, column 3 illustrates the function of the shellcode, column 4-6 refer to the number of gadgets ending in `jmp`, `call`, and `ret` respectively, column 7 represents whether the ROP shellcode can be detected by DROP [9], and column 8 represents whether the ROP shellcode can be detected by our tool. Note that the 22th ROP shellcode in Table 3 merely use the gadgets ending in `jmp` instruction. In experiment, we evaluate our tool from three aspects: `ret` checking, `call` checking, and `jmp` checking. We use the first 22 ROP shellcode to test `jmp` and `call` checking. Note that, we can either use the `call` checking or `jmp` checking to detect the first 21 ROP shellcodes. Because the 22th ROP shellcode only uses the gadgets ending in `jmp` instruction, we can only use the `jmp` checking to detect it. In addition, we use the last 22 ROP shellcode to test the `ret` checking. Experimental results shows that our tool can efficiently detect all the ROP shellcode. Table 3 shows that previous tool DROP [9] can not detect the ROP shellcode which uses the `jmp` gadget and *combinational gadgets* because it assumes that ROP shellcode should continuously use the gadget ending in `ret`. By contrast, our tool does not rely on the assumption, and find the more intrinsic feature of ROP shellcode: there are abnormal usages of `ret`,`call` or `jmp` instruction, thus it can detect all the ROP shellcode.

In order to test the false positives of our tool, we choose hundreds of applications to test the feature of normal programs' execution, and the sizes of these applications range from 10K to 100M. These tested programs cover major categories of common programs such as Database, Media Player, Web Server. Experimental results show our tool has no false positives. Table 4 lists the statistical results of ten programs with its execution of jmp instruction in libc-2.3.5. The fourth column is the number of the indirect `jmp` in libc whose target address is also in libc. The fifth column is the number of `jmp` instruction whose target address and its address are in the same libc function. The sixth column is the number of the indirect `jmp` in libc whose target address and its address are in the different library functions. We can see from Table 4 that, the indirect `jmp` instructions in libc-2.3.5.so are all *"intra-function"* `jmp` instructions, when they are executed by the normal programs. We find that other dynamic libraries all fits with the rule.

Table 5 lists the statistical results of ten programs with its execution of call instruction. The fourth column in Table 5 is the number of call instruction; the fifth column in Table 5 is the number of `call` instruction whose next instruction is `push esp`, and the sixth column in Table 5 is the number of `call` instruction whose next instruction is

Table 4. Statistical result of jmp execution in libc

Software	LOC (K)	Benchmark	jmp instruction in libc	intra-procedure jmp	inter-procedure jmp
bzip2-1.0.5	236.6	Compress the 1.7M file	2	2	0
slocate-2.7	89.2	Search patterns in 87K database	2	2	0
gzip-1.2.4	278.2	Uncompress the 55M file	0	0	0
bc-1.06	375.9	Finds primes between 2 and limits	2	2	0
gcc-4.2.4	4060.4	Compile 1KB source code	8	8	0
man-1.6c	248.5	Open the message catalog for ls	5	5	0
gocr-0.46	823.6	Process JPG file	2	2	0
grep-2.5.1	904.1	Find pattern in 1.9 MB file	2	2	0
openssh-2.2.1	976.8	Login in using user name	11	11	0
httpd-2.2.0	9883.7	ab	3	3	0
Average			4	4	0

Table 5. Statistical result of call execution in normal programs

Software	LOC (K)	Benchmark	call instruction	frame call	non-frame call	other call
bzip2-1.0.5	236.6	Compress the 1.7M file	27	12	15	0
slocate-2.7	89.2	Search patterns in 87K database	30	13	17	0
gzip-1.2.4	278.2	Uncompress the 55M file	12	4	8	0
bc-1.06	375.9	Finds primes between 2 and limits	20	9	11	0
gcc-4.2.4	4060.4	Compile 1KB source code	22	10	12	0
man-1.6c	248.5	Open the message catalog for ls	2	2	0	0
gocr-0.46	823.6	Process JPG file	27	12	15	0
grep-2.5.1	904.1	Find pattern in 1.9 MB file	16	7	9	0
openssh-2.2.1	976.8	Login in using user name	46	21	25	0
httpd-2.2.0	9883.7	ab	122	31	91	0
Average			32	12	20	0

Table 6. Performance Overhead

Prog.	LOC (K)	Benchmark	Native Run	Under Our tool	Under DROP	Under Our tool	DROP
bzip2-1.0.5	236.6	Compress the 1.7M file	1.347s	4.311s	17.107s	3.2X	12.7X
slocate-2.7	89.2	Search patterns in 87K database	0.096s	0.336s	0.593s	3.5X	6.2X
gzip-1.2.4	278.2	Uncompress the 55M file	2.457s	6.142s	10.839	2.5X	4.4X
bc-1.06	375.9	Finds primes between 2 and limits	0.125s	0.163s	2.628s	1.3X	21.0X
gcc-4.2.4	4060.4	Compile 1KB source code	0.078s	0.273s	0.748s	3.5X	9.6X
man-1.6c	248.5	Open the message catalog for ls	0.188s	0.451s	1.234s	2.4X	6.6X
gocr-0.46	823.6	Process JPG file	0.136s	0.449s	1.868s	3.3X	13.7X
grep-2.5.1	904.1	Find pattern in 1.9 MB file	0.958s	3.066s	9.753s	3.2X	10.2X
openssh-2.2.1	976.8	Login in using user name	4.626s	17.579s	14.803s	3.8X	3.2X
httpd-2.2.0	9883.7	ab	1.019s	5.299s	5.208s	4.9X	5.1X
Average			1.103s	3.807s	6.478s	3.5X	5.8X

`sub esp, value`. The seventh column in Table 5 is the number of `call` instruction which is different from the one in column fifth and the one in column sixth.

Note that the rest of programs we analyzed also come up to the average statistical result listed in Table 4 and Table 5.

5.3 Performance Evaluation

We used the ten normal applications listed in Table 6 to measure the performance overhead of our tool. For each program, we tested the performance overhead when the program runs natively, under DROP [9] and under our tool. From Table 6, we can see the average performance overhead of our tool (3.5 X) is down sharply compared with DROP (5.8 X), although it monitors larger categories of the ROP shellcode. There are two reasons. First, our tool is implemented on more efficient dynamic instrumentation framework PIN [21], which is 3.3x faster than Valgrind [24]. Second, our tool only monitors the specific instruction `call`, `ret` and indirect `jmp`. In the ten tested applications, the number of the monitored instructions only 10-250, which account for 0.068%. By contrast, DROP monitors all the executed instructions, and it counts the number of instructions between the `ret` instruction. In Table 6, we can see that the performance overhead of our tool for protecting openssh-2.2.1 and httpd-2.2.0 are higher than others, because there are more `jmp`, `call` and `ret` instructions when executing the two applications, and our tool should take more time to monitor these instructions.

6 Discussion

Currently, our work has several limitations. First, our tool assumes the `call` and `ret` instruction in normal program will occur in pairs. However, there are several exceptions. For example, PIC (Position Independent Code) code uses a relative address-based `call` to the next instruction, and then to pop the return address off the stack in order to compute the absolute code address. PIC code leverages this technique to compute the location of its static variables from the base address of its code. If this technique was used by a compiler to generate PIC code, it would break our technique. Another problem with the return address matching approach arises with C++ code, because exception handling can lead to non-matching calls and returns. Second, compilers may perform what is called a tail-call optimization, where, if the last operation is a function call, then the compiler replaces it with a jump. If this call happens to use a function pointer, then the jump would correspondingly become an indirect jump. In this case, it would be a jump that cross function boundaries, and hence raise a false alarm.

7 Related Work

7.1 Traditional Code Injection Defenses

One method is the malicious code scanners [26, 31], which detect the context of input, and check whether there are malicious code. Currently, malicious code scanners detect the malicious code by using pattern matching. As ROP malicious code contains the address and data of the gadgets, malicious code scanners will be ineffective for detecting ROP attack. $W \oplus X$ (e.g., PAX [1]) is another method which enforces the property that no memory location in a process image is marked with both writable ("W") and executable ("X"). However, ROP attack executes the existing code in the libraries or executables, and thus it cannot be detected by $W \oplus X$. Address Space Randomization techniques [1, 3] prevent the attacker from predicting the base address of the libraries or other executable code, and they not only make the code injection more difficulty, but also hamper the return-into-libc or ROP attack which uses the code in the libraries. However, several anti-randomization techniques [23, 13] have been proposed to help the attacker to evade the protection. Other techniques (e.g. CFI [2]) can be used to prevent the illegal program control flow transfer, which is the precondition to launch the code injection attack and ROP attack. However, these defenses are rely on complex program analysis, thereby hard to be applied to the programs with a large code. Also, it is difficult to guarantee no bugs existing in the program so that the attacker still has chance to hijack the control flow and achieve the ROP attack.

7.2 Other Code-Reuse Techniques

Most recently, researchers propose many interesting code-reuse methods to construct the attack. For example, Caballero et al. [6] proposed a binary code reuse method, which extracts a function from a malware and re-uses it later. In addition, Kolbitsch et al. [16] developed Inspector, which generates a so-called gadget from a binary and reuses it to achieve specific malicious behavior. Lin et al. [20] proposed a new trojan construction method which re-uses malicious function in a legitimate binary code and performs malicious activities. All the works mentioned above use the existing binary code, and try to find the useful code snippet to do malicious behavior. Dion [4] proposes a method which uses the code generated by flash VM to construct the shellcode. The flash engine can be coerced into generate the malicious code by the definition of the object, which is introduced by the adversary. The code-reuse techniques are still the open problem for researchers to solve.

8   Conclusion

In this paper, we have studied Return-Oriented Programming(ROP) and wrote several ROP malicious code by using this technique. In addition, we conclude the intrinsic feature of the ROP malicious code, which can use three kinds of the control flow sensitive instruction(`call`, `ret`, `jmp`), all the three instructions are distinguished from the normal usage in the program. Based on the observation, we statically analyze the ELF file and the dynamic libraries, and determine the scope of each dynamic library function, and further, based on the information, we check the integrity of the `call`, `ret` and `jmp` instructions. We have implemented our approach on the dynamic instrumentation framework PIN and applied it to analyze a number of ROP malicious code on x86 architecture. These ROP malicious codes use the mixed gadgets which are ending in `call`, `ret` and `jmp` instruction. Preliminary experimental results show that our approach is highly effective and practical, and has no false positives and negatives.

Acknowledgements

This work was supported in part by grants from the Chinese National Natural Science Foundation (60773171, 61073027, 90818022, and 60721002), the Chinese National 863 High-Tech Program (2007AA01Z448), and the Chinese 973 Major State Basic Program(2009CB320705).

References

1. The pax project (2004), http://pax.grsecurity.net/
2. Abadi, M., Budiu, M., Ligatti, J.: Control-flow integrity. In: Proceedings of the 12th ACM Conference on Computer and Communications Security (CCS), pp. 340–353. ACM, New York (2005)
3. Bhatkar, E., Duvarney, D.C., Sekar, R.: Address obfuscation: an efficient approach to combat a broad range of memory error exploits. In: Proceedings of the 12th USENIX Security Symposium, pp. 105–120 (2003)
4. Blazakis, D.: Interpreter exploitation: pointer inference and jit spraying. BHDC (2010), http://www.semantiscope.com/research/BHDC2010/BHDC-2010-Paper.pdf
5. Buchanan, E., Roemer, R., Shacham, H., Savage, S.: When good instructions go bad: generalizing return-oriented programming to risc. In: Proceedings of the 15th ACM Conference on Computer and Communications Security (CCS), pp. 27–38 (2008)

6. Caballero, J., Johnson, N.M., McCamant, S., Song, D.: Binary code extraction and interface identification for security applications. In: Proceedings of the 17th Annual Network and Distributed System Security Symposium (2010)
7. Checkoway, S., Davi, L., Dmitrienko, A., Sadeghi, A.R., Shacham, H., Winandy, M.: Return-oriented programming without returns. In: Proceedings of the 17th ACM Conference on Computer and Communications Security, CCS (2010)
8. Checkoway, S., Feldman, A.J., Kantor, B., Halderman, J.A., Felten, E.W., Shacham, H.: Can dres provide long-lasting security? the case of return-oriented programming and the avc advantage. In: Proceedings of EVT/WOTE 2009. USENIX/ACCURATE/IAVoSS (2009)
9. Chen, P., Xiao, H., Shen, X., Yin, X., Mao, B., Xie, L.: Drop: Detecting return-oriented programming malicious code. In: Prakash, A., Sen Gupta, I. (eds.) ICISS 2009. LNCS, vol. 5905, pp. 163–177. Springer, Heidelberg (2009)
10. Datarescue: Interactive disassembler (ida) pro (2008), http://www.datarescue.com
11. Davi, L., Sadeghi, A.R., Winandy, M.: Dynamic integrity measurement and attestation: towards defense against return-oriented programming attacks. In: Proceedings of the 2009 ACM Workshop on Scalable Trusted Computing, pp. 49–54 (2009)
12. Davi, L., Sadeghi, A.R., Winandy, M.: Ropdefender: A detection tool to defend against return-oriented programming attacks. Technical Report HGI-TR-2010-001 (2010), http://www.trust.rub.de/home/_publications/LuSaWi10/
13. Durden, T.: Bypassing pax aslr protection. Phrack Magazine (2002)
14. Francillon, A., Perito, D., Castelluccia, C.: Defending embedded systems against control flow attacks. In: Proceedings of the First ACM Workshop on Secure Execution of Untrusted Code, SecuCode 2009, pp. 19–26. ACM, New York (2009)
15. Francillon, A., Castelluccia., C.: Code injection attacks on harvard-architecture devices. In: Syverson, P., Jha, S. (eds.) Proceedings of CCS 2008 (2008)
16. Kolbitsch, C., Holz, T., Kruegel, C., Kirda, E.: Inspector gadget: Automated extraction of proprietary gadgets from malware binaries. In: Proceedings of the 30th IEEE Symposium on Security and Privacy (2010)
17. Kornau, T.: Return oriented programming for the arm architecture. Master's thesis, Ruhr-Universitat Bochum (2010)
18. Li, J., Wang, Z., Jiang, X., Grace, M., Bahram, S.: Defeating return-oriented rootkits with "return-less" kernels. In: Proceedings of the 5th European Conference on Computer Systems, EuroSys 2010, pp. 195–208. ACM, New York (2010)
19. Lidner, F.F.: Developments in cisco ios forensics. CONFidence 2.0, http://www.recurity-labs.com/content/pub/FX_Router_Exploitation.pdf
20. Lin, Z., Zhang, X., Xu, D.: Reuse-oriented camouflaging trojan: Vulnerability detection and attack construction. In: Proceedings of the 40th DSN-DCCS (2010)
21. Luk, C.K., Cohn, R., Muth, R., Patil, H., Klauser, A., Lowney, G., Wallace, S., Reddi, V.J., Hazelwood, K.: Pin: building customized program analysis tools with dynamic instrumentation. In: Proceedings of the 2005 ACM SIGPLAN Conference on Programming Language Design and Implementation, pp. 190–200. ACM, New York (2005)
22. milw0rm, http://www.milw0rm.com/shellcode/linux/x86
23. Nergal: The advanced return-into-lib(c) exploits (pax case study). Phrack Magazine (2001), http://www.phrack.com/issues.html?issue=58&id=4
24. Nethercote, N., Seward, J.: Valgrind: a framework for heavyweight dynamic binary instrumentation. In: Proceedings of the 2007 PLDI Conference, vol. 42(6), pp. 89–100 (2007)
25. Readelf, http://sourceware.org/binutils/docs/binutils/readelf.html
26. Roesch, M.: Snort - lightweight intrusion detection for networks. In: Proceedings of the 13th USENIX Conference on System Administration, pp. 229–238. USENIX Association, Berkeley (1999)

27. Shacham, H.: The geometry of innocent flesh on the bone: return-into-libc without function calls (on the x86). In: Proceedings of the 14th ACM Conference on Computer and Communications Security (CCS), pp. 552–561. ACM, New York (2007)
28. Symantec: Dynamic linking in linux and windows, part one (2006),
    `http://www.symantec.com/connect/articles/`
    `dynamic-linking-linux-and-windows-part-one`
29. Team, P.: What the future holds for pax (2003), `http://pax.grsecurity.net/`
    `docs/pax-future.txt`
30. Bletsch, T., Jiang, X., Freeh, V.: Jump-oriented programming: A new class of code-reuse attack. Technical Report TR-2010-8 (2010)
31. Wang, X., Pan, C.C., Liu, P., Zhu, S.: Sigfree: A signature-free buffer overflow attack blocker. IEEE Transactions on Dependable and Secure Computing 99(2) (2006)

ValueGuard: Protection of Native Applications against Data-Only Buffer Overflows

Steven Van Acker, Nick Nikiforakis, Pieter Philippaerts,
Yves Younan, and Frank Piessens

IBBT-Distrinet
Katholieke Universiteit Leuven
3001 Leuven
Belgium
Steven.VanAcker@student.kuleuven.be,
{Nick.Nikiforakis,Pieter.Philippaerts,yvesy,frank}@cs.kuleuven.be

Abstract. Code injection attacks that target the control-data of an application have been prevalent amongst exploit writers for over 20 years. Today however, these attacks are getting increasingly harder for attackers to successfully exploit due to numerous countermeasures that are deployed by modern operating systems. We believe that this fact will drive exploit writers away from classic control-data attacks and towards data-only attacks. In data-only attacks, the attacker changes key data structures that are used by the program's logic and thus forces the control flow into existing parts of the program that would be otherwise unreachable, e.g. overflowing into a boolean variable that states whether the current user is an administrator or not and setting it to "true" thereby gaining access to the administrative functions of the program.

In this paper we present ValueGuard, a canary-based defense mechanism to protect applications against data-only buffer overflow attacks. ValueGuard inserts canary values in front of all variables and verifies their integrity whenever these variables are used. In this way, if a buffer overflow has occurred that changed the contents of a variable, ValueGuard will detect it since the variable's canary will have also been changed. The countermeasure itself can be used either as a testing tool for applications before their final deployment or it can be applied selectively to legacy or high-risk parts of programs that we want to protect at run-time, without incurring extra time-penalties to the rest of the applications.

Keywords: buffer overflows, non-control-data attacks, canary.

1 Introduction

The buffer overflow is probably the most widely known programming error. It has been used by attackers for over 20 years to exploit programs that do poor handling of user input. The most known computer worms, Morris Worm [31], Code Red [23] and SQL Slammer [22] all used a buffer overflow in vulnerable

S. Jha and A. Maturia (Eds.): ICISS 2010, LNCS 6503, pp. 156–170, 2010.
© Springer-Verlag Berlin Heidelberg 2010

software as their primary way of attacking and infecting new hosts. Even though the attack is well understood and many solutions have been proposed over the years, buffer overflows continue to plague modern and legacy software, which is written in unsafe languages. SANS application security blog currently ranks the "classic buffer overflow" as third in their list of twenty-five most dangerous programming errors [29].

Buffer overflows are commonly associated with an attacker placing code of his choice in a variable of the vulnerable program and then using the overflow itself to overwrite a memory location that is used to dictate the control-flow of the running program. Such memory locations are return-addresses, saved base pointers, function pointers and so on. These attacks are called control-data attacks since they target data that is used to control the application's behavior. Since these attacks are the most prevalent, academics and the programming industry itself has focused most of their efforts in protecting the control-data of an application. Stackguard [12] and DEP [21], two widely used countermeasures in modern operating systems are geared towards protecting control-data attacks. The former protects the return address in each stack-frame from overwrites by placing a canary in-front of it and checking its integrity before the function is allowed to return. The latter tries to stop an attacker by marking the stack and the heap memory pages of the current running process as non-executable. Even if an attacker somehow manages to gain control of the execution-flow of the process, he can no longer execute code that he earlier injected.

Since successful exploitation of control-data attacks is becoming harder by the day, it is reasonable to assume that attackers will change their focus into a new exploiting technique that will give them as much control as the old ones. Data-only, or non-control data, attacks fit this description. In non-control data attacks, the attacker is no longer trying to inject and execute his own code. He identifies the existing portions of a program that are of interest to him (e.g. the functions that are allowed to run by an administrator) and he changes the values of data structures in the program that will enable him to access functionality that he normally couldn't (e.g. change the boolean value of a variable that encodes whether the current user is an administrator). Many of the countermeasures proposed to mitigate classic control-data attacks cannot detect non-control data attacks (including the aforementioned Stackguard and DEP).

In this paper we present ValueGuard, a countermeasure specifically geared towards preventing non-control data attacks. ValueGuard identifies all variables in the source code of a program and protects each one individually by placing a random value, a canary, in-front of it. If an attacker uses a buffer-overflow to change the contents of a variable, he will inevitably overwrite over the canary before writing into the variable itself. ValueGuard checks the integrity of a variable's canary before any expression that uses the value of that variable. If the canary has been changed, it is a sign of a non-control data attack and ValueGuard forces the process to terminate, effectively stopping the attack.

Depending on how critical an application is, ValueGuard can be used either as a testing tool to find vulnerabilities before the actual deployment or as a run-time protection tool which will detect and stop data-only buffer overflows in time. While testing the effectiveness of our system, we discovered a heap-based buffer overflow vulnerability in the Olden benchmark suite that was previously unreported.

The rest of this paper is structured as follows. In Section 2 we describe the different categories of non-control data that an attacker can misuse followed by an example program vulnerable to a non-control data attack. In Section 3 we present the design of our countermeasure and in Section 4 we give details concerning our specific implementation. In Sections 5 and 6 we evaluate the security of ValueGuard and the performance of our prototype. Related work is discussed in Section 7 and we conclude in Section 8.

2   Data-Only or Non-control-Data Attacks

In this section we present the different data structures that a non-control data attack may target and we give an example of a program vulnerable to such an attack.

2.1   Critical Data Structures

Chen et. al [9] were among the first researchers to point out that non-control data attacks can be as dangerous as control data attacks. In their paper, they experimented with real-world applications and they showed that an attacker trying to conduct a non-control data attack, has a number of critical data structures at his disposal which he can overwrite to compromise a running application. Their study showed that these data structures can be categorized in four different types:

Configuration data
> Data stored in a process's memory that was read from e.g. a configuration file. The process expects this data to be specified by the system administrator. If an attacker can overwrite such data, the process's behavior can change in ways the system administrator could not foresee.

User identity data
> Data that identifies a user after e.g. a login, is typically used to enforce access to resources. If this data is altered, an attacker could impersonate another user and get unauthorized access to the user's resources.

User input string
> User input validation ensures that user input conforms to the format a program expects when handling it. If an attacker manages to change the input string after it has been validated, then the program will consider the input safe while it is not.

Decision making data
> Overwriting data used to make decisions can obviously have disastrous consequences. Our example attack in Section 2.2 targets decision making data.

It is clear that at least a subset of these types of data structures is present in any useful real-world application. While their exploitation is not as straight-forward as in control-data attacks and the attacker needs to be able to at least partially understand the semantics of a program, Chen et. al showed that it can be done. We argue that today, Chen's observation that "non-control data attacks are realistic threats" is as relevant as ever. A program which would otherwise be not exploitable because of the deployed countermeasures may be vulnerable to a non-control data attack.

2.2   Non-control Data Attack

```
1  int main(int argc, char **argv) {
2      char pass[40];
3      int authenticated = 0;
4      char buffer[30];
5      char *p;
6
7      readPassFile(PASSFILE, pass, sizeof(pass));
8
9      printf("Enter password: ");
10     fgets(buffer, sizeof(pass), stdin);
11
12     if (!strcmp(buffer, pass)) { authenticated = 1; }
13
14     if (authenticated) {
15         printf("Yes!\n");
16         execl("/bin/sh", "sh", NULL);
17     }
18
19     return 0;
20 }
```

Fig. 1. Example code of a data-only vulnerability

Consider the program listed in Figure 1. The purpose of the program is to authenticate a user. If the user supplies the correct password, he is given a shell else the program exits. The `main()` function contains a call to the `fgets()` function to read a line of text from the user, on line 10. While `fgets()` is considered a safe function since its second argument states the maximum number of characters to be read, the programmer misused the argument and instead of providing `fgets()` with the size of `buffer`, it provided the size of `pass`. So `fgets()` will read up to 40 characters, which is 10 more than the size of `buffer`. This is a typical example of a buffer overflow.

When this program is compiled with stack smashing protection in place ([12,14,30]), this vulnerability can not be exploited to initiate a control-data attack. However, when the `buffer` variable is overflowed the `authenticated` variable is overwritten since the two variables are adjacent on the stack. This variable is normally set by the program when the authentication was successful. An attacker could overflow this value and set it to a non-zero value. The program will think that authentication succeeded, even though it didn't, and it will execute the /bin/sh shell.

3   ValueGuard Design

The design of ValueGuard is based on the concepts introduced by StackGuard and extends them to cover all variables instead of only protecting the return address. Naturally, this will result in a higher performance overhead, but this way one can reliably detect bugs or attacks that corrupt only part of the stack or heap.

During the compilation of a program, the ValueGuard framework rewrites the source code of the application and encapsulates all variables into *protection structures*. A protection structure is implemented as C struct that consists of two items: the original variable and a canary value. When a variable is allocated, either on the stack or heap, the canary value is initialized to a random value that changes on every run of the application. The application is further modified to detect when every variable is used, and additional canary checks are inserted accordingly.

Pointer Support. An important requirement is to detect changes to variables that are used indirectly through pointers. Figure 2 shows an application that complicates the verification of the canary of the 'important' variable, because it is accessed through a pointer. Figure 3 shows the stack contents for the program during a normal run. If an attacker manages to abuse the call to *strcpy* to overwrite the value (and canary) of the 'important' variable, this will not be detected. When the pointer variable 'p' is dereferenced, a check will be executed that verifies the canary of 'p' itself, which was unchanged in the attack - Fig. 4.

The source of the problem is that a variable is used through a pointer, without first checking the integrity of the canary in front of that variable. The detection mechanism of ValueGuard solves this by adding checks for each pointer

```
1  int main(int argc, char **argv) {
2      int important = 123;
3      char buffer[80];
4      int *p = &important;
5
6      strcpy(buffer, argv[1]);
7      printf("%d\n", *p);
8
9      return 0;
10 }
```

Fig. 2. An example that shows how pointer de-references can complicate canary verification

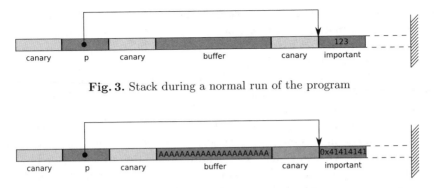

Fig. 3. Stack during a normal run of the program

Fig. 4. Stack after malicious `strcpy()`

dereference that looks up and verifies the canary of the dereferenced variable. This lookup is necessary because the pointers may point to objects that are un-predictable (or un-decidable) at compile-time.

ValueGuard uses a memory map to store information about all the registered objects in memory space. When objects are created, they are registered in this memory map. On each pointer dereference, the corresponding memory object can be looked up and the associated canary can be verified.

Compatibility. Not all code in a process can be assumed to have been instrumented. Code in shared libraries will not be aware of the use of canaries. ValueGuard, unlike similar countermeasures [16,4,15], does not change the representation of pointers or the calling conventions of functions and thus remains fully compatible with existing code. This also implies that ValueGuard supports being used selectively. Developers can choose to protect only (potentially crucial) parts of an application with ValueGuard, thereby limiting the total overhead.

ValueGuard does not change the layout of structures that are defined by the programmer, because many programmers rely on the exact layout of objects in memory. As a result of this, ValueGuard cannot insert canaries in-between the different fields of a structure. Hence, buffer overflows that corrupt data inside a single structure are not detected. This is a limitation of most existing defense mechanisms.

4   Prototype Implementation

4.1   Canaries

Our implementation makes use of the CIL framework ([24]) to transform C-code. During this transformation, modifications are made to the code through a custom CIL plugin.

Canaries are implemented as integers that are encapsulated in a struct, together with the variable they protect. An array of random canary values is initialized at program start. Each canary is initialized with a value from that table and the indices into the canary table are determined at compile-time. During the code transformation, canary verification calls are inserted in front of statements that use protected variables. If a verification fails, the program is forced to terminate with a segmentation fault.

Several optimizations are introduced to reduce overhead. First, safe variables are grouped together and protected by a single canary. Safe variables are those variables whose addresses are never used. Arrays and variables used with the address operator (&) are therefore unsafe. Second, multiple canary verification calls can be made in sequence, all verifying the same canaries. These are obviously grouped together in a single call. Third, verification calls preceded by safe statements are shifted upwards so that they are grouped. Safe statements are the kind of statements that do not threaten the integrity of any canaries, for example assigning the result of a calculation to a variable. Last, safe functions are not instrumented with extra code. A safe function is one that only uses safe statements and local variables.

4.2 Memory Map

The memory map stores the start addresses of memory objects. For every block of 2^k bytes in the memory space, there is an entry in the memory map that holds the start address of the memory object it holds. Memory objects must be aligned to and be a multiple of 2^k bytes. To handle registration of memory objects on the heap, the memory allocator functions `malloc`, `calloc`, `realloc` and `free` are overridden with a wrapper. The wrapper functions allocate extra memory for a canary value, initialize the canary and register the memory object with the memory map. An extra verification call is inserted in front of every pointer dereference. The pointer is looked up in the memory map. If it points to a protected object, the associated canary is verified. Just as for failed regular canary verification, the process is terminated if the canary can not be verified.

5   Security Evaluation

In this section we evaluate the security provided by ValueGuard and we present cases that show that ValueGuard can detect attacks in real-world scenarios.

5.1   Effectiveness

ValueGuard's effectiveness in detecting data-only buffer overflows lies in the accurate detection of a modified canary. As explained in Section 4 the canary of each variable is a random integer number chosen at the runtime of the protected program. In order for an attacker to evade detection while using a buffer overflow to conduct a non-control data attack, he must be able to restore the canary to its original contents. This can be done by a) brute-forcing the canary or b) finding out the value of the canary through a memory leakage attack.

Brute-forcing: When ValueGuard detects a modified canary, it terminates the running process. This means that for a canary of 4 bytes (standard integer size) the attacker must make, for the worst-case scenario, 2^{32} attempts before finding out the correct value. Accordingly, ValueGuard will terminate the process $2^{32} - 1$ times before the attacker succeeding. We believe that a system's administrator is likely to notice that an attack is taking place well before the exhaustion of 4 billion attempts.

Memory Leakage: Strackx et. al [33] have shown how certain programming errors can reveal to the attacker parts of memory that he can use to de-randomize countermeasures that rely on secret data. While this attack is possible we believe that its exploitation in the case of ValueGuard is not probable since the attacker must find the canary for the specific variables that he can overflow and not just any secret canary. That is because ValueGuard uses multiple canaries and thus the compromise of one canary doesn't necessarily lead to a compromise of the whole countermeasure.

In total, practice shows that the randomness provided by 32 bits of data is enough to ensure security. While some may argue that bounds-checkers provide better security guarantees since their detection is not related with random values, we would like to point out that in our case, ValueGuard will detect overflows occurred while in third-party code (such as libraries) while bounds-checkers will not. This is because bounds-checkers can detect overflows only in code that they have instrumented and thus can't protect variables when third-party code (such as external libraries) accesses them. ValueGuard on the other hand, will be able to detect that an overflow occurred since the variable's canary will have been changed regardless of where the overflow happened.

5.2   Real World Test

The defense mechanism was tested in the real world at the Hackito Ergo Sum 2010 conference in Paris. During a 3 day period, a hacker wargame was hosted which contained a program compiled with the described defense mechanism. The program contained a data-only vulnerability that could lead to a root-compromise. After the conference, the wargame was moved to the OverTheWire ([26]) wargame network where it still resides. Despite the numerous attempts, the program was not exploited.

The techniques used in the attacks were closely observed. We found out that most attackers un-successfully tried to circumvent the countermeasure by the means of guessing the values generated by the random number generator.

5.3   Heap Overflow in em3d

During the benchmarks, a heap overflow was detected by the defense mechanism in the em3d test of the Olden benchmarks. The overflow occurs in the `initialize_graph` function in `make_graph.c`: The assignment `retval->e_nodes[i] = local_node_r;` is executed for `i = 1 to NumNodes` where NumNodes is a command-line parameter, while the e_nodes array in retval only has room for a fixed amount of values (determined by the PROCS constant in em3d.h)

The discovery of this heap overflow in a commonly used benchmark suite like Olden, is further validation that ValueGuard can detect and stop non-control data attacks. To our knowledge, no other defense mechanism has detected this overflow before.

6   Performance Evaluation

The extra calls to verify the integrity of canaries, have an impact on runtime and memory usage. To measure this effect, two benchmark suites were run: Olden and SPEC CPU2000. All benchmarks were run on Dell GX755 machines with each an Intel Core 2 Duo CPU (E6850) running at 3.00GHz and 4GB of memory, running Ubuntu GNU/Linux 8.04 LTS with kernel 2.6.24-27-server.

Each benchmark was compiled with 5 "compilers":

gcc. The GNU C compiler, version 4.2.4 (Ubuntu 4.2.4-1ubuntu4)
cilly. Transformation with the CIL driver w/o any modules, compilation with gcc.
vg_baseline
   Using the ValueGuard plugin, but with all flags turned off. This is basically the same as the cilly compiler without any modules.
vg_stackdatabss
   Using the ValueGuard plugin, but with the memory map disabled. Only the stack, data and BSS variables are protected.
vg_all
   Using the full defense mechanism.

Some tests from the two benchmark suits were ommited either because they were not compatible with the CIL transformation framework or because ValueGuard detected an overflow (see Section 5.3) and terminated the running test. The runtime and memory usage results for Olden and SPEC CPU2000 can be found in Figures 5, 6, 7 and 8.

	gcc	cilly	vg_baseline	vg_stackdatabss	vg_all
bh	101.12 (±7.03)	100.24 (±4.97)	100.64 (±5.74)	153.36 (±9.03)	282.00 (±13.10)
bisort	23.63 (±0.21)	23.69 (±0.20)	23.67 (±0.21)	28.40 (±0.27)	43.04 (±0.47)
health	3.40 (±0.10)	3.40 (±0.09)	3.41 (±0.08)	3.80 (±0.09)	10.84 (±0.13)
mst	4.69 (±0.08)	4.70 (±0.07)	4.70 (±0.08)	7.14 (±0.09)	10.52 (±0.16)
perimeter	1.12 (±0.03)	1.06 (±0.03)	1.05 (±0.03)	1.31 (±0.03)	2.15 (±0.04)
treeadd	21.94 (±0.23)	21.84 (±0.07)	24.42 (±0.46)	24.30 (±0.44)	37.68 (±0.49)
tsp	22.76 (±0.10)	22.76 (±0.12)	22.82 (±0.19)	25.27 (±0.11)	29.10 (±0.17)
Average	25.52	25.39	25.82	34.80	59.33

Fig. 5. Olden benchmarks: runtime results in seconds. Lower is better. The values in between brackets are the standard deviation.

	gcc	cilly	vg_baseline	vg_stackdatabss	vg_all
bh	70.47 70.49		70.49	70.50	128.79
bisort	128.43 128.44		128.45	128.45	640.48
health	147.25 147.27		147.27	147.27	657.47
mst	312.72 312.74		312.74	312.74	391.51
perimeter	171.09 171.10		171.10	171.10	533.80
treeadd	256.43 256.44		256.44	256.44	1280.51
tsp	320.49 320.51		320.51	320.51	960.58
Average	200.98 201.00		201.00	201.00	656.16

Fig. 6. Olden benchmarks: memory usage in MiB. Lower is better.

	gcc	cilly	vg_baseline	vg_stackdatabss	vg_all
164.gzip	99.68 ($\pm$0.14)	98.07 ($\pm$0.17)	98.71 ($\pm$0.08)	183.77 ($\pm$0.64)	188.83 ($\pm$0.28)
181.mcf	55.77 ($\pm$0.26)	55.55 ($\pm$0.39)	55.43 ($\pm$0.05)	91.87 ($\pm$0.66)	171.11 ($\pm$0.48)
196.parser	1046.60 ($\pm$37.57)	1014.33 ($\pm$7.62)	1003.64 ($\pm$12.64)	1082.86 ($\pm$1.37)	1307.27 ($\pm$14.65)
254.gap	48.01 ($\pm$0.18)	50.62 ($\pm$0.21)	49.62 ($\pm$0.09)	145.44 ($\pm$0.27)	410.74 ($\pm$1.01)
256.bzip2	78.45 ($\pm$0.19)	78.70 ($\pm$0.20)	79.09 ($\pm$0.30)	176.36 ($\pm$1.43)	277.06 ($\pm$0.41)
300.twolf	113.43 ($\pm$0.39)	116.52 ($\pm$0.12)	116.90 ($\pm$0.17)	394.75 ($\pm$10.38)	539.25 ($\pm$10.25)
177.mesa	89.36 ($\pm$0.76)	80.22 ($\pm$0.26)	81.41 ($\pm$0.95)	120.44 ($\pm$0.31)	472.93 ($\pm$6.97)
179.art	77.68 ($\pm$0.40)	78.06 ($\pm$0.26)	77.73 ($\pm$0.72)	139.63 ($\pm$0.54)	294.25 ($\pm$3.31)
183.equake	56.97 ($\pm$0.13)	55.95 ($\pm$0.02)	56.15 ($\pm$0.03)	91.35 ($\pm$0.01)	483.01 ($\pm$4.62)
Average	185.11	180.89	179.85	269.61	460.50

Fig. 7. SPEC CPU2000 benchmarks: runtime results in seconds. Lower is better. The values in between brackets are the standard deviation.

	gcc	cilly	vg_baseline	vg_stackdatabss	vg_all
164.gzip	2712.27 2712.51		2712.52	2713.04	3391.16
181.mcf	232.13 232.19		232.19	232.23	357.70
197.parser	76.62 76.68		76.66	77.07	100.23
254.gap	579.10 579.13		579.13	580.61	728.34
256.bzip2	1666.35 1666.50		1666.52	1666.84	2083.29
300.twolf	12.05 12.09		12.11	12.96	36.09
177.mesa	27.09 27.13		27.14	27.50	46.45
179.art	22.84 22.96		22.96	23.05	39.26
183.equake	125.84 125.90		125.90	125.98	390.69
Average	606.03 606.12		606.13	606.59	797.02

Fig. 8. SPEC CPU2000 benchmarks: memory usage results in MiB. Lower is better.

When not using the memory map, the results show 25% and 100% average runtime overhead for the Olden and SPEC CPU2000 benchmarks. The memory overhead is negligible in this case (0% for Olden, 1% for SPEC CPU2000).

Using the memory map comes at a cost. For the Olden benchmarks, the overhead increases to 114% and for SPEC CPU2000 it increases to 351% overhead. Likewise, the memory usage due the memory map increases as well: 238% overhead for Olden and 79% for SPEC CPU2000. We believe that developers can use the full version of ValueGuard while testing their applications before deployment and the basic version (ValueGuard without the memory map) after deployment. This will allow them to detect and correct as many programming errors as possible while at development phase where the performance of applications doesn't matter. For deployed applications, the basic mode of ValueGuard can be chosen to protect the running applications with an acceptable performance cost.

7   Related Work

Many approaches exist that try and protect against buffer overflow attacks. In this section we will briefly discuss the most important types of countermeasures. A more extensive discussion can be found in [38,13,37].

7.1   Bounds Checkers

[18,32,4,16,20,25,27] is a better solution to buffer overflows, however when implemented for C, it has a severe impact on performance and may cause existing code to become incompatible with bounds checked code. Recent bounds checkers [3,41] have improved performance somewhat, but one major limitation of these bounds checkers compared to ValueGuard is that they do not detect buffer overflows in code that has not been protected even if the data is used in protected code. ValueGuard will detect changes to data even if it has been overwritten by unprotected code, as soon as the data is used in protected code.

7.2   Probabilistic Countermeasures

Many countermeasures make use of randomness when protecting against attacks. Canary-based countermeasures [12,14,19,28] use a secret random number that is stored before an important memory location: if the random number has changed after some operations have been performed, then an attack has been detected. Memory-obfuscation countermeasures [11,7] encrypt (usually with XOR) important memory locations or other information using random numbers. Memory layout randomizers [34,6,36,8] randomize the layout of memory: by loading the stack and heap at random addresses and by placing random gaps between objects. Instruction set randomizers [5,17] encrypt the instructions while in memory and will decrypt them before execution.

While our approach is also probabilistic, it is aimed at protecting locations from non-control-data attacks, while most of the above approaches are aimed at protecting either control data or preventing the attacker from injecting code, neither of which are useful for non-control data attacks.

An exception is DSR [7], which protects against non-control-data attacks but requires that all code is aware of the data obfuscation, hindering the use of third party libraries.

7.3   Separation and Replication of Information

Countermeasures that rely on separation or replication of information will try to replicate valuable control-flow information [35,10] or will separate this information from regular data [39,40]. This makes it harder for an attacker to overwrite this information using an overflow. Some countermeasures will simply copy the return address from the stack to a separate stack and will compare it to or replace the return addresses on the regular stack before returning from a function. These countermeasures are easily bypassed using indirect pointer overwriting where an attacker overwrites a different memory location instead of the return address by using a pointer on the stack. More advanced techniques try to separate all control-flow data (like return addresses and pointers) from regular data, making it harder for an attacker to use an overflow to overwrite this type of data [40].

While these techniques can efficiently protect against buffer overflows that try to overwrite control-flow information, they do not protect against non-control-data attacks.

7.4   Runtime Enforcement of Static Analysis Results

In this section we describe two countermeasures that provide runtime enforcement of results of static analysis.

Control-flow integrity [1] determines a program's control flow graph beforehand and ensures that the program adheres to it. It does this by assigning a unique ID to each possible control flow destination of a control flow transfer. Before transferring control flow to such a destination, the ID of the destination is compared to the expected ID, and if they are equal, the program proceeds as normal. This approach, while strong, does not protect against non-control data attacks.

WIT [2] discusses a very efficient technique to check whether instructions write to valid memory location. Their technique is based on static analysis that does a points-to analysis of the application. This analysis is then used to assign colors to memory locations and instructions. Each instruction has the same color as the objects it writes to. Then runtime checks are added to ensure that these colors are the same. This prevents instructions from writing to memory that they cannot normally write to. This technique depends on a static points-to analysis, which can result in false negatives where an instruction is determined to be safe when it is not or it can assign an instruction or object a color that allows an unsafe instruction access to the object. Also, static alias analysis could confuse objects, allowing instructions access to multiple objects.

8   Conclusion

The increased difficulty of reliably exploiting control data attacks in modern operating systems is likely to shift the attention of attackers to other attack vectors. We believe that data-only attacks is such a vector since its successful exploitation can provide the attacker with as much leverage as traditional control-data attacks.

In this paper we presented ValueGuard, a countermeasure for data-only attacks caused by buffer overflows. ValueGuard's detection technique consists of inserting canary values in front of all memory objects and verifying them when the objects are used. Our countermeasure operates on the source code level and does not require any modifications to the target platform. In addition, Value-Guard can be used either as a testing tool by developers before deployment of an application or as a run-time protection monitor for critical applications.

Using ValueGuard we found a previously unreported buffer overflow in the Olden benchmark suite and we showed that ValueGuard can detect and stop data-only attacks that many other generic countermeasures cannot.

Acknowledgments

This research is partially funded by the Interuniversity Attraction Poles Programme Belgian State, Belgian Science Policy, and by the Research Fund K.U.Leuven.

References

1. Abadi, M., Budiu, M., Erlingsson, U., Ligatti, J.: Control-flow integrity. In: 12th ACM Conference on Computer and Communications Security (2005)
2. Akritidis, P., Cadar, C., Raiciu, C., Costa, M., Castro, M.: Preventing memory error exploits with WIT. In: IEEE Symposium on Security and Privacy (2008)
3. Akritidis, P., Costa, M., Castro, M., Hand, S.: Baggy bounds checking: An efficient and backwards-compatible defense against out-of-bounds errors. In: 18th USENIX Security Symposium (2009)
4. Austin, T.M., Breach, S.E., Sohi, G.S.: Efficient detection of all pointer and array access errors. In: ACM Conference on Programming Language Design and Implementation (1994)
5. Barrantes, E.G., Ackley, D.H., Forrest, S., Palmer, T.S., Stefanović, D., Zovi, D.D.: Randomized Instruction Set Emulation to Disrupt Binary Code Injection Attacks. In: 10th ACM Conference on Computer and Communications Security (2003)
6. Bhatkar, S., DuVarney, D.C., Sekar, R.: Address Obfuscation: An Efficient Approach to Combat a Broad Range of Memory Error Exploits. In: 12th USENIX Security Symposium (2003)
7. Bhatkar, S., Sekar, R.: Data space randomization. In: 5th Conference on Detection of Intrusions and Malware & Vulnerability Assessment (2008)
8. Bhatkar, S., Sekar, R., DuVarney, D.C.: Efficient techniques for comprehensive protection from memory error exploits. In: 14th USENIX Security Symposium (2005)
9. Chen, S., Xu, J., Sezer, E.C., Gauriar, P., Iyer, R.K.: Non-control-data attacks are realistic threats. In: 14th USENIX Security Symposium (2005)
10. Chiueh, T., Hsu, F.: RAD: A compile-time solution to buffer overflow attacks. In: 21st International Conference on Distributed Computing Systems (2001)
11. Cowan, C., Beattie, S., Johansen, J., Wagle, P.: PointGuard: Protecting Pointers From Buffer Overflow Vulnerabilities. In: 12th USENIX Security Symposium (2003)
12. Cowan, C., Pu, C., Maier, D., Hinton, H., Walpole, J., Bakke, P., Beattie, S., Grier, A., Wagle, P., Zhang, Q.: StackGuard: Automatic Adaptive Detection and Prevention of Buffer-Overflow Attacks. In: 7th USENIX Security Symposium (1998)

13. Erlingsson, U., Younan, Y., Piessens, F.: Low-level software security by example. In: Handbook of Information and Communication Security. Springer, Heidelberg (2010)
14. Etoh, H., Yoda, K.: Protecting from stack-smashing attacks. Tech. rep., IBM Research Divison, Tokyo Research Laboratory (2000)
15. Jim, T., Morrisett, G., Grossman, D., Hicks, M., Cheney, J., Wang, Y.: Cyclone: A safe dialect of C. In: USENIX Annual Technical Conference (2002)
16. Jones, R.W.M., Kelly, P.H.J.: Backwards-compatible bounds checking for arrays and pointers in C programs. In: 3rd International Workshop on Automatic Debugging (1997)
17. Kc, G.S., Keromytis, A.D., Prevelakis, V.: Countering Code-Injection Attacks With Instruction-Set Randomization. In: 10th ACM Conference on Computer and Communications Security (2003)
18. Kendall, S.C.: Bcc: Runtime Checking for C Programs. In: USENIX Summer Conference (1983)
19. Krennmair, A.: ContraPolice: a libc Extension for Protecting Applications from Heap-Smashing Attacks (2003)
20. Lhee, K.S., Chapin, S.J.: Type-Assisted Dynamic Buffer Overflow Detection. In: 11th USENIX Security Symposium (2002)
21. Microsoft Coorporation: Detailed description of the Data Execution Prevention
22. Moore, D., Paxson, V., Savage, S., Shannon, C., Staniford, S., Weaver, N.: Inside the slammer worm. IEEE Security and Privacy 1(4), 33–39 (2003)
23. Moore, D., Shannon, C., Claffy, K.: Code-red: a case study on the spread and victims of an internet worm. In: 2nd ACM Workshop on Internet Measurment (2002)
24. Necula, G.C., McPeak, S., Rahul, S.P., Weimer, W.: CIL: Intermediate language and tools for analysis and transformation of C programs. In: CC 2002. LNCS, vol. 2304, p. 213. Springer, Heidelberg (2002)
25. Oiwa, Y., Sekiguchi, T., Sumii, E.: Fail-Safe ANSI-C Compiler: An Approach to Making C Programs Secure. In: Okada, M., Babu, C. S., Scedrov, A., Tokuda, H. (eds.) ISSS 2002. LNCS, vol. 2609, pp. 133–153. Springer, Heidelberg (2003)
26. OverTheWire: The OverTheWire hacker community, http://www.overthewire.org/
27. Patil, H., Fischer, C.N.: Low-Cost, Concurrent Checking of Pointer and Array Accesses in C Programs. Software: Practice and Experience 27(1) (1997)
28. Robertson, W., Kruegel, C., Mutz, D., Valeur, F.: Run-time Detection of Heap-based Overflows. In: 17th Large Installation Systems Administrators Conference (2003)
29. SANS: Top 25 Most Dangerous Programming Errors
30. Solar Designer: Non-executable stack patch (1997)
31. Spafford, E.H., Spafford, E.H.: The internet worm program: An analysis. Computer Communication Review 19 (1988)
32. Steffen, J.L.: Adding Run-Time Checking to the Portable C Compiler. Software: Practice and Experience 22(4) (1992)
33. Strackx, R., Younan, Y., Philippaerts, P., Piessens, F., Lachmund, S., Walter, T.: Breaking the memory secrecy assumption. In: 2nd European Workshop on System Security (2009)
34. The PaX Team: Documentation for the PaX project
35. Vendicator: Documentation for Stack Shield (2000)
36. Xu, J., Kalbarczyk, Z., Iyer, R.K.: Transparent Runtime Randomization for Security. In: 22nd International Symposium on Reliable Distributed Systems (2003)

37. Younan, Y.: Efficient Countermeasures for Software Vulnerabilities due to Memory Management Errors. Ph.D. thesis, Katholieke Universiteit Leuven (2008)
38. Younan, Y., Joosen, W., Piessens, F.: Code injection in C and C++: A survey of vulnerabilities and countermeasures. Tech. Rep. CW386, Departement Computer-wetenschappen, Katholieke Universiteit Leuven (2004)
39. Younan, Y., Joosen, W., Piessens, F.: Efficient protection against heap-based buffer overflows without resorting to magic. In: Ning, P., Qing, S., Li, N. (eds.) ICICS 2006. LNCS, vol. 4307, pp. 379–398. Springer, Heidelberg (2006)
40. Younan, Y., Joosen, W., Piessens, F.: Extended protection against stack smashing attacks without performance loss. In: 22nd Annual Computer Security Applications Conference (2006)
41. Younan, Y., Philippaerts, P., Cavallaro, L., Sekar, R., Piessens, F., Joosen, W.: PAriCheck: an efficient pointer arithmetic checker for c programs. In: ACM Symposium on Information, Computer and Communications Security (2010)

Mining RBAC Roles under Cardinality Constraint

Ravi Kumar, Shamik Sural, and Arobinda Gupta

School of Information Technology
Indian Institute of Technology, Kharagpur, 721302, India
kumarravi.iitkgp@gmail.com,
{shamik,agupta}@sit.iitkgp.ernet.in

Abstract. Role Based Access Control (RBAC) is an effective way of managing permissions assigned to a large number of users in an enterprise. In order to deploy RBAC, a complete and correct set of roles needs to be identified from the existing user permission assignments, keeping the number of roles low. This process is called *role mining*. After the roles are mined, users are assigned to these roles. While implementing RBAC, it is often required that a single role is not assigned a large number of permissions. Else, any user assigned to that role will be overburdened with too many operations. In this paper, we propose a heuristic bottom-up constrained role mining scheme that satisfies a cardinality condition that no role contains more than a given number of permissions. We compare its results with eight other recently proposed role mining algorithms. It is seen that the proposed scheme always satisfies the cardinality constraint and generates the least number of roles among all the algorithms studied.

Keywords: RBAC, Role Engineering, Role Mining, Cardinality Constraint.

1   Introduction

In any organization, an access control mechanism is implemented to protect the confidentiality and integrity of applications and associated data. In traditional access control methods, user access is granted by adding necessary permissions to each individual resource. The set of users with their assigned permissions can be represented by a user-permission assignment matrix (UPA), where the rows represent users, the columns represent permissions, and an entry in a particular cell represents the permission assigned to the corresponding user. With increase in the number of users and permissions, the size of the UPA matrix becomes quite large and hence, difficult to manage. Since an individual user is assigned individual permissions to access the resources, the process of administering access permissions involving many users and several different applications becomes difficult and ineffective.

An alternative approach is to assign users and permissions to *roles*. A *role* is the set of permissions that a user acquires when he is assigned to the role. Any

S. Jha and A. Maturia (Eds.): ICISS 2010, LNCS 6503, pp. 171–185, 2010.
© Springer-Verlag Berlin Heidelberg 2010

change in the user's position or needs can be handled by assigning the user to another role. Accessing the system based on assigning permissions and users to roles is known as *Role Based Access Control* (*RBAC*). In RBAC, each user has a utilization profile that defines his roles in an enterprise. To implement RBAC in an organization, roles have to be first identified. The process of identification of roles is known as role-engineering [1] and can be done by top-down or bottom-up approaches [1][2]. Bottom-up identification of roles from the UPA matrix is known as *RoleMining*. However, the problem of finding the minimum number of roles satisfying a given user-permission assignment has been shown to be NP-complete [3].

Role mining identifies a set of roles, *ROLES*, from the UPA matrix. After the roles are mined, the users and permissions are assigned to these roles. The user-role assignment and permission-role assignment relations are represented by Boolean matrices UA and PA respectively. In UA, a 1 in cell $\{i, j\}$ indicates the assignment of role j to user i. Similarly, in PA, a 1 in cell $\{m, n\}$ indicates the assignment of permission n to role m. When the user-permission assignments available to users described through UA and PA matrices are exactly the same as that described by the given UPA, then the UA and PA matrixes are said to be 0-consistent with the given UPA [3]. Formally the Role Mining Problem (RMP) can be stated as follows [3]:

[Role Mining Problem]

Given a set of users USERS, a set of permissions PRMS, and a user permission assignment matrix UPA, find a set of roles, ROLES, a user-to-role assignment UA, and a role-to-permission assignment PA, that is 0-consistent with the given UPA and has the minimum number of roles.

An organization, while implementing the RBAC infrastructure, may desire to impose a restriction on the maximum number of permissions in a role. The primary motivation for this is that the roles should not get overburdened by a large number of permissions. We refer to this as the *cardinality constraint*. Various RBAC models proposed in the literature [4][5] discuss the possibility of placing some constraints on roles like *separation of duty, cardinality constraint*, etc. However, none of the existing role mining algorithms satisfy any given cardinality constraint.

We implemented some of the recently proposed role mining algorithms, namely, PairCount (*PC*) [18], CompleteMiner (*CM*) [14] and FastMiner (*FM*) [14] and executed them on the datasets mentioned in Section 4. It was observed that, for all the algorithms, a significant number of mined roles contain a substantially large number of permissions. In this paper, we propose a heuristic algorithm called Constrained Role Miner (CRM) for the role mining problem that satisfies a given cardinality constraint and the number of generated roles is comparable with that of the other existing algorithms.

The rest of the paper is organized as follows. In Section 2, we discuss the background and related work in this area. We bring out the limitations of the existing work along with the objective of the current work. Section 3 presents our approach of constrained role mining. In Section 4, the results of running the algorithm on real world datasets are presented. Comparative summary of the results for different role mining algorithms is also discussed. Finally, Section 5 presents the conclusion drawn from this work with future scope of work.

2 Related Work

Role engineering approaches can be broadly classified as top-down and bottom-up. A top-down approach requires a detailed analysis of business processes for identifying which permissions are necessary to carry out a specific set of tasks. It may ignore the existing assigned permissions. A bottom-up approach mines the roles from an existing UPA matrix ignoring the business functions of the organizations [1]. A combination of the two can be incorporated into a hybrid approach [24].

Coyne [1], the first to introduce the top down approach, proposed to identify roles based on users' activities. It was an analytical approach and lacked practicality for a large enterprise. The work in [7] proposed the use-case approach to group actions to be performed in a procedure into a role. Roeckle et al. [8] proposed a process-oriented approach for role-finding and suggested a data model which integrates business processes, role based security administration and access control. Newmann and Strembeck [9] proposed a scenario-driven approach to formulate the task using a collection of scenarios and each scenario is decomposed into a set of steps. The limitation of this approach is that it only derives the functional roles. Several other references [10][11][23] exist on the use of top-down approach for role identification.

The bottom-up approach [12] basically applies a data mining technique on the UPA matrix and facilitates the automated discovery of roles. Schlegelmilch and Steffens proposed the ORCA [13] role mining tool, which is a hierarchical agglomerative clustering algorithm on permissions, and forms a hierarchy of permission clusters. A drawback of this algorithm is a strict partitioning of the permissions set, i.e., no overlapping of permissions among roles that are not hierarchically related. The work in [14] uses subset enumeration, which starts with clustering users who have the same or similar permissions. Then it generates a set of candidate roles, computing all possible intersections among permissions possessed by the users. It removes the drawbacks of ORCA and can produce roles with overlapping permission sets. The work in [3] proposed the Largest Uncovered Tile Mining (LUTM) algorithm, which uses the notion of database tiling [15] to generate the approximate minimum number of roles required to completely cover the UPA matrix. A unified framework for modeling the optimal binary matrix decomposition and its variants (basic Role Mining Problem (RMP), database tiling, etc.) using binary integer programming is given in [16]. The work in [17] implements role mining without considering the whole permission assignments, i.e., leaving out some permissions so that the quality of the resulting roles gets improved or more practical roles can be mined. Thus, instead of identifying all possible roles within a particular infrastructure, it identifies and analyzes roles that cover the largest portion of permission assignments.

Zhang et al. have presented a heuristic algorithm for role mining to optimize a graph representing an RBAC state [19]. The algorithm starts with an initial RBAC state and iteratively improves the states by identifying pairs of roles such that merging or splitting of two roles results in a lower cost graph.

The main limitation of all the cited role mining approaches is that none of the approaches have dealt with the cardinality constraint issue. Some have discussed that if the cardinality constraint is incorporated in their role-mining algorithm, then it would produce more number of roles as compared to that without having any constraints. However, to the best of our knowledge, no work has been done to show the change in the number of roles and other metrics when the cardinality constraint is introduced.

3   Constrained Role Miner (CRM)

We use a combination of clustering and constrained permission set mining to obtain the roles that satisfy a given cardinality constraint. The algorithm along with an illustrative example is described below.

ORCA [13] first implemented a clustering algorithm in which every permission is divided into clusters and the clusters are merged based on the members of the clusters. Due to the drawback of their clustering approach, the roles mined from their algorithm suffered from practical realization of the generated roles in an organization. Unlike the clustering method of ORCA, our proposed CRM algorithm starts by taking similar permission assignments of different users and makes clusters based on the users' permissions. It places users who have the same set of permissions in the same cluster. The rest of the algorithm works on this initial set of clusters. Algorithm 1 shows the Constrained Role Miner algorithm in detail.

We illustrate our clustering method on the UPA matrix shown in Table 1. Since there are 5 users each with a unique permission set (i.e., no two users have the same permission set assigned to them), initially there are 5 clusters as shown in Table 2. With each cluster, we have the count of users (*user count*) associated with the cluster as well as the unique permissions (*permissions*) found in that cluster. On this initial set of clusters, permission set mining is performed. Line 1 of Algorithm 1 shows this clustering method.

In the next phase, the CRM algorithm identifies all the roles satisfying the given cardinality constraint, say k, that are consistent with the given UPA matrix. This phase starts by arranging the initial clusters in decreasing order of the count of unique permissions assigned to them.

In this example, we arrange the clusters in Table 2 in the order c1, c2, c3, c5, c4 as shown in Table 3. We represent the unique permission count value of the clusters in the column named as *unvisited permission count* (*UC*). Algorithm 1, line 7 describes the arranging of clusters in decreasing order of the count of unique permissions assigned to each cluster.

```
Input: UPA matrix
Input: cardinality constraint k
P(c) = Cluster c's visited or non-visited permissions.
count_u(c) = number of users of cluster c.
count_p(c) = Cluster c's non-visited permissions count.
status(c, p) = status of the permission p of cluster c.
R(x) = role consisting of a set of permissions x.
roles(c) = set of roles assigned to cluster c.
1  {Group users into the initial clusters based on the exact match of the set of permissions}.
   The set of clusters are, Clusters = {c1, c2...cm}.
2  FinalRoles ← {} ;
   {Set the status value of each permission of each cluster as 1}
3  forall c ∈ Clusters do
4      roles(c) ← {} ;
5      forall p ∈ P(c) do
6          status(c, p) ← 1 ;
7  {Sort the clusters in descending order based on their count_p(c)}
8  maxUser ← 0 ;
9  select ← 0 ;
10 forall (i | i ∈ Clusters) ∩ (count_p(i) ≤ k) do
11     Users_i ← count_u(i) ;
12     Clusters ← Clusters − i ;
13     forall j ∈ Clusters do
14         if Q(i) ⊆ P(j) then
15             Users_i ← Users_i + count_u(j) ;
16     if maxUser < Users_i then
17         maxUser ← Users_i ;
18         select ← i ;
19     Clusters ← Clusters ∪ i ;
20 FinalRoles ← FinalRoles ∪ R{Q(select)} ;
21 roles(select) ← roles(select) ∪ R{Q(select)} ;
22 Clusters = Clusters − select ;
23 forall i ∈ Clusters do
24     if Q(select) ⊆ P(i) then
25         count ← 0 ;
26         forall p ∈ Q(select) do
27             if status(i, p) = 1 then
28                 status(i, p) ← 0;
29                 count ← count + 1;
30         count_p(i) ← count_p(i) − count ;
31         roles(i) ← roles(i) ∪ R{Q(select)} ;
32 count_p(select) ← 0 ;
33 if Clusters ≠ {} then
34     {then repeat from step 7} ;
```

Algorithm 1. Constrained Role Miner (CRM)

Table 1. UPA Matrix

	p1	p2	p3	p4	p5
u1	1	1	1	1	1
u2	0	1	1	1	1
u3	1	1	0	0	1
u4	0	0	1	1	0
u5	1	1	1	0	0

Initially, for each cluster, a binary valued parameter called *status* is associated with each permission, with its value set as 1 (Algorithm 1, lines 3 to 6). This parameter indicates in the later stages of the algorithm if any permission has

Table 2. Initial clusters with their permissions

cluster	user count	permissions
c1	1(u1)	p1,p2,p3,p4,p5
c2	1(u2)	p2,p3,p4,p5
c3	1(u3)	p1,p2,p5
c4	1(u4)	p3,p4
c5	1(u5)	p1,p2,p3

Table 3. Clusters in descending order of unvisited permission count UC

cluster	user count	permissions	unvisited permission count (UC)
c1	1(u1)	p1,p2,p3,p4,p5	5
c2	1(u2)	p2,p3,p4,p5	4
c3	1(u3)	p1,p2,p5	3
c5	1(u5)	p1,p2,p3	3
c4	1(u4)	p3,p4	2

already been visited in the earlier stages of the algorithm. A value of 1 indicates that this permission has not been visited and 0 indicates that the permission has been visited.

Next the clusters which have their permission count satisfying the cardinality constraint are considered. For each such cluster the total number of users that have the cluster's permission set as the subset of permissions assigned to them is computed. The cluster with the highest user count in the UPA matrix is selected (Algorithm 1, lines 10 to 19). Once such a cluster whose set of permissions has the highest number of users in the whole UPA database is determined, a *role* is created having the permissions of the selected cluster. An entry of the created role is added in the set of final roles named *FinalRoles* (Algorithm 1, line 20).

The permission count of those clusters which have the set of permissions as a superset of that of the selected *role*, are decremented by the count of the number of permissions of the selected *role* which have the *status* value set as 1 in the cluster. Since some of the permissions of the clusters are covered by the permissions of the created *role*, hence, the *status* values of the covered permissions in the clusters are set as 0, indicating that these permissions have already been visited (Algorithm 1, lines 23 to 31).

An entry of the created *role* is made in each cluster whose permissions are covered by the created *role's* permissions. In this way the clusters get their roles and the users of the clusters also keep on getting the roles assigned to them. Once a cluster's permission count reaches 0, it means that the roles have been mined for that cluster and that cluster will not be considered again in the successive steps of the algorithm.

Continuing with the example, suppose the cardinality constraint is $k = 3$. In the clusters shown in Table 3, only clusters c3, c5 and c4 satisfy the constraint. From these clusters, the cluster c3's unvisited permission set {p1, p2, p5} is the subset of the permission set of cluster c1. Therefore, the total user count

Table 4. Roles mined for clusters in iteration 1

cluster	user count	permissions	UC	Roles
c1	1(u1)	p1,p2,p5, [p3, p4]	5-2=3	{r1}
c3	1(u3)	p1,p2,p5	3	{}
c5	1(u5)	p1,p2,p3	3	{}
c2	1(u2)	p2,p5, [p3, p4]	4-2=2	{r1}
c4	1(u4)	[p3, p4]	2-2=0	{r1}

of permission set {p1, p2, p5} is 2. Similarly, for c5{p1, p2, p3}, it is 2 and for c4{p3, p4} it is 3. Since c4{p3, p4} has the maximum user count value, we select the cluster c4, group its permissions as role r1 (r1{p3, p4}) and remove all its permissions from other clusters (i.e., we mark them as visited permissions). After modifying the UC values and arranging the clusters with their users and roles in descending order of UC, we are left with the situation as shown in Table 4. In the table, the roles assigned to clusters are also added.

The clusters are recursively sorted based on their remaining unvisited permission count and the algorithm is applied again on this reduced number of clusters. It may be noted that the sorting is done based on the *UC* of the clusters only, whereas to find the cluster that has the superset of the permission set to be searched for, all the visited as well as non-visited set of permissions for the cluster are considered.

Continuing further with the example, after iteration 1 with the remaining clusters in Table 4, the clusters having non-zero values in the UC column are c1{p1, p2, p5}, c3{p1, p2, p5}, c5{p1, p2, p3} and c2{p2, p5}. In these, all the clusters satisfy the cardinality constraint. We see the total user count of unvisited permissions of the clusters as:

c2{p2, p5}: total user count = 3 (in c1, c3, c2);
c5{p1, p2, p3}: total user count = 2 (in c1, c5);
c3{p1, p2, p5}: total user count = 2 (in c1, c3);
c1{p1, p2, p5}: total user count = 2 (in c1, c3);

Cluster c2's unvisited permission set {p2, p5} has the maximum user count value. Therefore, we select it as role r2 (r2{p2, p5}), shown in Table 5, and mark the permissions of c2 as visited in the remaining clusters which have their permissions as the superset of the remaining permissions of c2{p2, p5}.

Now clusters c5, c1 and c3 satisfy the constraint and the unvisited permission p1 of c1 and c3 has the user count as 3. Therefore, we select role 3 as (r3{p1}) and mark p1 as visited in the remaining clusters. At this stage, only cluster c5 is left, having unvisited permissions as p2, p3. Therefore, we take it as role r4 (r4{p2, p3}). After taking this role, all the permissions of all the clusters have been visited and the algorithm terminates. The final set of four roles is shown in Table 6.

In Algorithm 1, line 10, if we do not have any cluster which has the unvisited permission count satisfying the constraint, then there is no specific initial choice

Table 5. After iteration 2, after sorting

cluster	user count	permissions	UC	Roles
c5	1(u5)	p1,p2,p3	3	{}
c1	1(u1)	p1, [p2,p5] , [p3,p4]	3-2=1	{r1} {r2}
c3	1(u3)	p1, [p2,p5]	3-2=1	{r2}
c2	1(u2)	[p2,p5] , [p3,p4]	2-2=0	{r1} {r2}
c4	1(u4)	[p3,p4]	2-2=0	{r1}

Table 6. Clusters with all the roles assigned

cluster	user count	permissions	UC	Roles
c5	1(u5)	[p1] , [p2,p3]	0	{r3} {r4}
c1	1(u1)	[p1] , [p2,p5], p3,p4]	0	{r1}{r2} {r3}
c3	1(u3)	[p1] , [p2,p5]	0	{r2} {r3}
c2	1(u2)	[p2,p5][p3,p4]	0	{r1}{r2}
c4	1(u4)	[p3,p4]	0	{r1}

to start the algorithm. This exceptional case is handled using the algorithm shown in Algorithm 2. In this case, we take the cluster c having the lowest value of $count\_p(c)$, say n (Algorithm 2, line 1), i.e., the last cluster arranged in descending order of $count\_p(c)$. We compute all possible intersections of $Q(c)$ with all the other clusters' non-visited permissions sets (Algorithm 2, line 2). The intersected permissions are collected as the set of roles $S(Q(c))$. The intersection is performed in the same way as done in the *CompleteMiner* (*CM*) algorithm [14].

We select the role from the set $S(Q(c))$, with the largest number of users having this permission set (role) as the subset of the permissions assigned to them (Algorithm 2, lines 3 to 13) and repeat the main CRM algorithm. If the set $S(Q(c))$ is found to be empty, i.e., no user is found with this selected cluster c's combination of permissions as the subset of their assigned permissions, then it means that this cluster's permissions do not occur in any other cluster. Then, (according to the cardinality constraint specified) the unvisited permission set of this cluster is broken into roles, which are assigned to the cluster as well as the users of this cluster (Algorithm 2, lines 14 to 16). For example, if the cardinality constraint is 4, we encounter a cluster that has 10 unvisited permissions, and none of the permission sets of roles in $S(Q(c))$ are subsets of any other remaining cluster's unvisited permission set, then we break these 10 permissions of the cluster in 3 roles containing 4, 4 and 2 permissions, respectively. We then assign these three roles to the cluster and repeat this step on the remaining clusters.

$S(Q(c))$ = a set containing the sets of all possible roles obtained by computing all possible intersections of $Q(c)$ with all the other clusters' non-visited permission sets.
$perms(r)$ = a set of permissions of role r, one from the set $S(Q(c))$ of roles.
$count(r)$ = number of permissions in role r.

{Select cluster c having the least value of count_$p(c)$}
1   $n \leftarrow count\_p(c)$;
2   {Generate all possible set of roles $S(Q(c))$, by computing all possible intersections of $Q(c)$ with the clusters having non-zero value of non-visited permissions}
3   $Clusters \leftarrow Clusters - c$;
4   $maxUser \leftarrow 0$;
5   $select \leftarrow 0$;
6   forall $r \in S(Q(c))$ do
7       $Users_r \leftarrow 0$;
8   forall $j \in Clusters$ do
9   if $perms(r) \subseteq P(j)$ then
10              $Users_r \leftarrow Users_r + count\_u(j)$;
11   if $maxUser < Users_r$ then
12          $maxUser \leftarrow Users_r$;
13          $select \leftarrow r$;
14 if $select = 0$ then
15   {Partition the unvisited permissions of cluster c into roles based on k and add the role entry into the cluster c as well as into the set $FinalRoles$}
16      $Clusters = Clusters - c$; continue from line 33 ;
17 $count\_p(c) \leftarrow count\_p(c) - count(select)$;
18 $FinalRoles \leftarrow FinalRoles \cup R\{perms(select)\}$;
19 $roles(c) \leftarrow roles(c) \cup R\{perms(select)\}$;
20 forall $p \in R\{perms(select)\}$ do
21      $status(c, p) \leftarrow 0$;
22 forall $i \in Clusters$ do
23   if $R\{perms(select)\} \subseteq P(i)$ then
24          $count \leftarrow 0$;
25   forall $p \in perms(select)$ do
26   if $status(i, p) = 1$ then
27                  $status(i, p) \leftarrow 0$;
28                  $count \leftarrow count + 1$;
29          $count\_p(i) \leftarrow count\_p(i) - count$;
30          $roles(i) \leftarrow roles(i) \cup R\{perms(select)\}$;
31 if $count\_p(c) \neq 0$ then
32      $Clusters = Clusters \cup c$;
33 if $Clusters \neq \{\}$ then
34   {start from line 7 of Algorithm 1} ;

Algorithm 2. An Exceptional Case of CRM

4   Experimental Results

As the input data, all of the role mining algorithms use user-permission information as an access control configuration. In [21], several real-world datasets have been considered for comparing different role mining algorithms. We take the same datasets ([21] also considers another dataset called University, which is not readily available and hence, was not considered in our study) to show the results of CRM algorithm as well as to compare its performance with the algorithms mentioned in [21]. These datasets are listed in Table 7. |USERS| represents the number of users in the organization. |PRMS| represents the total number of permissions. |UPA| is the total number of permissions assigned to all the users in the given system. Density represents what percentage of total assignable permissions is actually assigned to the users of the system in the UPA.

4.1   Performance of CRM

We ran the CRM algorithm on all the datasets presented in Table 7. In Figures 1(a)-(b) and 2(a)-(b), we present the variation of the number of roles and the size of (|UA|+|PA|) (on the y-axis), by varying the constraint value (on the x-axis). Due to page limitation, we only show the variation on 2 datasets (*Healthcare* and *EMEA*). It was observed that the *Domino* dataset has a variation similar to *EMEA* whereas all the other datasets have similar variation as *Healthcare*. The results demonstrate that as we tighten the cardinality constraint, the number of roles increases as expected. However, the CRM algorithm adjusts the permissions in the best possible way which results in, for some cardinality constraint, similar number of roles as that without considering the constraint. It is only when the allowed number of permissions is too low that the number of roles increases by a large extent.

An important observation from Figures 2(a)-(b) for dataset *EMEA* is that on reducing the allowed number of permissions per role, although the number of mined roles goes on increasing or remains the same, the value of (|UA|+|PA|) decreases by a considerable extent. If we take the optimizing criteria as (Number of roles + |UA| + |PA|), we observe that it is through the implementation of constraint on the roles that one can achieve a lower value of the optimization variables. Similar observation was made for the *Domino* dataset also.

One important result that we observe while experimenting with the CRM algorithm is that, with several other large sized UPA matrices, it is not always the case that on decreasing the number of permissions per role the number of mined roles goes on increasing rapidly. Sometimes the number of roles decreases, stays the same, or increases only very slightly. We find this as an important point to work on since other earlier works [17] have pointed out that implementing the cardinality constraint on their algorithm would always increase the number of roles.

Table 7. Real-world datasets with their sizes

Datasets	|USERS|	|PRMS|	|UPA|	Density
Healthcare	46	46	1486	70%
Domino	79	231	730	4%
EMEA	35	3046	7220	6.8%
APJ	2044	1164	6841	0.3%
Firewall 1	365	709	31951	12.3%
Firewall 2	325	590	36428	19%
Americas	3477	1587	105205	1.9%

4.2   Comparison of CRM with Other Role Mining Algorithms

In this sub-section, we give the comparative results of CRM with eight other role mining algorithms that have been evaluated in [18]. These are PairCount (PC) [18], DynamicMiner (DM) [20], HierarchicalMiner (HM) [22], ORCA [13], HProles (HPr) [21], HP edge minimization (HPe) [21], Graph Optimization (GO) [19] and CompleteMiner (CM) [14].

The results for different metrics on different datasets are shown in Tables 8 to 14. The results of first three rows, in which the numbers are written, are obtained by minimizing three role mining metrics [18]: (i) Number of roles

(|ROLES|), (ii) Size of (|UA|+|PA|+|RH|) without direct user-permission assignment (DUPA) denoted as |S1|. RH represents the role-hierarchy and (iii) Size of (|ROLES|+|UA|+|PA|+|RH|) with DUPA denoted as |S2|.

The last row represents the percentage of DUPA for which the value of $|UA| + |PA| + |RH| + |DUPA|$ comes out to be the minimum. For the CRM algorithm, this value is 0. Allowing direct user permissions will result in a lower value of |UA|+|PA|+|RH|+|DUPA|. The results from all the algorithms are shown without any cardinality constraint. The values for all the columns except CRM have been taken directly from [18]. It is observed that the number of roles mined by the CRM algorithm is the lowest among all the algorithms. However, it is very close to that for the HPr algorithm. Although for some of the datasets the number of roles for CRM and HPr matches, for some of the other datasets (*APJ* and *Americas*) the value of |UA|+|PA|+|RH| is significantly less for CRM. For the *Americas* dataset this difference is quite large, indicating that CRM produces the lowest possible number of roles and along with it also tries to optimize the other role mining parameters (for example |UA|+|PA|+|RH|) in the best possible way.

The work in [18] discussed a method to rank the performance by optimizing different criteria of each algorithm over all the datasets. We implemented the same ranking method and recomputed the rankings for different metrics. The rankings of different algorithms for different metrics are shown in Table 15. As discussed previously, for some of the datasets, on reducing the allowed number of permissions per role, the value of |UA|+|PA|+|RH| decreases in case of CRM.

As seen from the table, CRM produces the least number of roles. Although the value of HPr comes out to be second (very close) in minimizing the number of roles, yet CRM mines the roles such that the roles of CRM produce better ranking in terms of all the other metrics as compared to HPr.

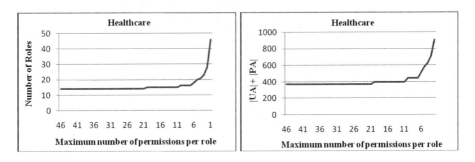

Fig. 1. (a) Number of Roles generated by CRM (b) Size of |UA|+|PA| generated by CRM v/s constraint value for the Healthcare dataset

Table 8. Comparative results of algorithms for Healthcare

Metrics	PC	DM	HM	ORCA	HPr	HPe	GO	CM	CRM
|ROLES|	24	27	17	46	14	15	16	31	14
|S1|	189	390	144	225	288	185	162	30	370
|S2|	148	325	146	223	298	210	136	64	384
|DUPA|/|UPA|	0.02	0	0.01	0	0.04	0.04	0.01	0.02	0

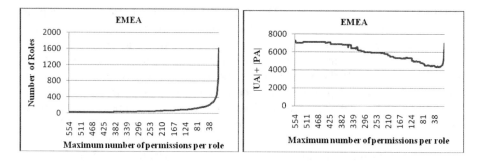

Fig. 2. (a) Number of Roles generated by CRM (b) Size of |UA|+|PA| generated by CRM v/s constraint value for the EMEA dataset

Table 9. Comparative results of algorithms for Domino

Metrics	PC	DM	HM	ORCA	HPr	HPe	GO	CM	CRM
|ROLES|	64	31	31	231	20	27	20	62	20
|S1|	573	733	411	703	741	402	517	549	741
|S2|	501	553	376	659	723	389	476	495	732
|DUPA|/|UPA|	0.18	0.61	0.26	0.6	0.97	0.25	0.24	0.22	0

Table 10. Comparative results of algorithms for EMEA

Metrics	PC	DM	HM	ORCA	HPr	HPe	GO	CM	CRM
|ROLES|	242	37	115	3046	34	176	34	674	34
|S1|	9439	7264	4120	7468	7246	3930	8118	12025	7246
|S2|	5811	7105	4482	6915	7214	4508	4926	6364	7222
|DUPA|/|UPA|	0.75	0.97	0.34	0.94	1	0.4	0.33	0.86	0

Table 11. Comparative results of algorithms for APJ

Metrics	PC	DM	HM	ORCA	HPr	HPe	GO	CM	CRM
|ROLES|	779	655	549	1164	455	477	475	764	453
|S1|	5674	5349	3794	5152	4876	3910	13029	5971	4587
|S2|	4733	4207	3904	4608	4867	3951	3987	4985	5040
|DUPA|/|UPA|	0.36	0.36	0.32	0.45	0.41	0.31	0.33	0.66	0

Table 12. Comparative results of algorithms for Firewall 1

Metrics	PC	DM	HM	ORCA	HPr	HPe	GO	CM	CRM
|ROLES|	248	219	111	709	65	78	71	278	66
|S1|	2558	4490	1411	13295	3037	1611	3172	1919	3072
|S2|	2258	4869	1456	22101	2932	1723	2554	2678	3138
|DUPA|/|UPA|	0.03	0.12	0.01	0.48	0.02	0	0.01	0.03	0

Table 13. Comparative results of algorithms for Firewall 2

Metrics	PC	DM	HM	ORCA	HPr	HPe	GO	CM	CRM
|ROLES|	14	13	11	590	10	12	10	21	10
|S1|	986	1075	952	29232	1554	1053	1008	1000	1554
|S2|	992	998	959	30789	1562	1067	981	995	1564
|DUPA|/|UPA|	0	0	0	0.77	0	0	0	0	0

Table 14. Comparative results of algorithms for Americas

Metrics	PC	DM	HM	ORCA	HPr	HPe	GO	CM	CRM
|ROLES|	1778	829	428	1587	206	317	225	2672	199
|S1|	17657	18783	6779	41264	16235	8143	10459	19276	9647
|S2|	16647	18557	6756	43156	16376	8394	9721	29926	9846
|DUPA|/|UPA|	0.08	0.12	0	0.36	0	0	0.01	0.22	0

Table 15. Comparative rankings of algorithms over all datasets using constraint

Metrics	PC	DM	HM	ORCA	HPr	HPe	GO	CM	CRM
|ROLES|	7.29	5.79	4.93	8.71	1.79	4.29	2.71	7.86	1.64
|S1|	5.29	7	1.29	7.14	5.93	2.29	5.29	6	4.79
|S2|	4.43	6.71	1.14	7.57	7.14	3	3	5.57	6.43
|DUPA|/|UPA|	5.14	6.14	3.86	7.29	6.5	4	3.93	6.21	1.93

If we allow direct user-permission assignments (DUPA) for CRM also, the ranking for the parameter $|ROLES|+|UA|+|PA|+|RH|+|DUPA|$ can improve further.

5 Conclusion and Future Work

We have presented a new algorithm named *Constrained RoleMiner (CRM)* for mining roles from existing user-permissions available in an organization. Variation of the number of roles and other metrics in CRM with variation in the allowed number of permissions per role has been studied. We also compared our work with other recently proposed role-mining algorithms using real datasets. We looked at the comparative results produced by all these algorithms to demonstrate the strengths and weaknesses of these algorithms. It has been observed that CRM generates the least number of roles.

There are still a few interesting issues to be considered for future work. The elimination strategy being used in CRM might result in roles having skewed number of permissions. Placing a lower bound on the allowable minimum number of permissions per role could mine a more practical set of roles. Also, CRM can be generalized to deal with other constraints such as maximum number of roles per user and maximum number of users per role. Adding other RBAC constraints like role hierarchies and separation of duty can result in optimizing the number of roles and other metrics in the mined set of roles.

Acknowledgement

This work is partially supported by a grant from the Department of Science and Technology, Govt. of India, under Grant No. SR/S3/EECE/ 082/2007.

References

1. Coyne, E.J.: Role engineering. In: Proceedings of the 1st ACM Workshop on Role Based Access Control, USA, pp. 15–16 (1995)
2. Vanamali, S.: WHITE PAPER: Role engineering and RBAC, Role engineering: The cornerstone of role based access control. In: CISA, CISSP, pp. 1–3 (2008)

3. Vaidya, J., Atluri, V., Guo, Q.: The Role Mining Problem: Finding a minimal descriptive set of roles. In: The 12th ACM Symposium on Access Control Models and Technologies, France, pp. 175–184 (2007)
4. Sandhu, R.S., Coyne, E.J., Feinstein, H.L., Youman, C.E.: Role based access control models. IEEE Computer 29(2), 38–47 (1996)
5. Ferraiolo, D.F., Sandhu, R., Gavrila, S., Kuhn, D.R., Chandramouli, R.: Proposed NIST standard for role-Based access control. ACM Transactions on Information and System Security 4(3), 224–274 (2001)
6. Goh, C., Baldwin, A.: Towards a more complete model of role. In: Proceedings of the 3rd ACM Workshop on Role Based Access Control, USA, pp. 55–62 (1998)
7. Fernandez, E.B., Hawkins, J.C.: Determining role rights from use cases. In: Proceedings of the 2nd ACM Workshop on Role Based Access Control, USA, pp. 121–125 (1997)
8. Rockle, H., Schimpf, G., Weidinger, R.: Process-oriented approach for role-finding to implement role-based security administration in a large industrial organization. In: Proceedings of the 5th ACM Workshop on Role Based Access Control, Germany, pp. 103–110 (2000)
9. Neumann, G., Strembeck, M.: A scenario-driven role engineering process for functional RBAC roles. In: Proceedings of the 7th ACM Symposium on Access Control Models and Technologies, USA, pp. 33–42 (2002)
10. Shin, D., Ahn, G.J., Cho, S., Jin, S.: On modeling system-centric information for role engineering. In: Proceedings of the 8th ACM Symposium on Access Control Models and Technologies, Italy, pp. 169–178 (2003)
11. Kern, A., Kuhlmann, M., Schaad, A., Moffett, J.: Observations on the role life-cycle in the context of enterprise security management. In: Proceedings of the 7th ACM Symposium on Access Control Models and Technologies, USA, pp. 43–51 (2002)
12. Kuhlmann, M., Shohat, D., Schimpf, G.: Role mining - revealing business roles for security administration using data mining technology. In: Proceedings of the 8th ACM Symposium on Access Control Models and Technologies, Italy, pp. 179–186 (2003)
13. Schlegelmilch, J., Steffens, U.: Role mining with ORCA. In: Proceedings of the 10th ACM Symposium on Access Control Models and Technologies, Sweden, pp. 168–176 (2005)
14. Vaidya, J., Atluri, V., Warner, J.: RoleMiner: Mining roles using subset enumeration. In: Proceedings of the 13th ACM Conference on Computer and Communications Security, USA, pp. 144–153 (2006)
15. Geerts, F., Goethals, B., Mielikainen, T.: Tiling databases. In: Suzuki, E., Arikawa, S. (eds.) DS 2004. LNCS (LNAI), vol. 3245, pp. 278–289. Springer, Heidelberg (2004)
16. Lu, H., Vaidya, J., Atluri, V.: Optimal Boolean matrix decomposition: Application to role engineering. In: Proceedings of the 24th IEEE International Conference on Data Engineering, USA, pp. 297–306 (2008)
17. Zhang, D., Ramamohanarao, K., Ebringer, T., Yann, T.: Permission set mining: Discovering practical and useful roles. In: Proceedings of the 2008 Annual Computer Security Applications Conference, USA, pp. 247–256 (2008)
18. Molloy, I., Li, N., Li, T., Mao, Z., Wang, Q., Lobo, J.: Evaluating role mining algorithms. In: Proceedings of the 14th ACM Symposium on Access Control Models and Technologies, Italy, pp. 95–104 (2009)
19. Zhang, D., Ramamohanarao, K., Ebringer, T.: Role engineering using graph optimization. In: Proceedings of the 12th ACM Symposium on Access Control Models and Technologies, France, pp. 139–144 (2007)

20. Molloy, I., Chen, H., Li, T., Wang, Q., Li, N., Bertino, E., Calo, S., Lobo, J.: Mining roles with multiple objectives. In: Review
21. Ene, A., Horne, W., Milosavljevic, N., Rao, P., Schreiber, R., Tarjan, R.E.: Fast exact and heuristic methods for role minimization problems. In: Proceedings of the 13th ACM Symposium on Access Control Models and Technologies, USA, pp. 1–10 (2008)
22. Molloy, I., Chen, H., Li, T., Wang, Q., Li, N., Bertino, E., Calo, S., Lobo, J.: Mining roles with semantic meanings. In: Proceedings of the 13th ACM Symposium on Access Control Models and Technologies, USA, pp. 21–30 (2008)
23. Colantonio, A., Pietro, R.D., Verde, N.V., Ocello, A.: A formal framework to elicit roles with business meaning in RBAC Systems. In: Proceedings of the 14th ACM Symposium on Access Control Models and Technologies, Italy, pp. 85–94 (2009)
24. Fuchs, L., Pernul, G.: HyDRo - Hybrid development of roles. In: Sekar, R., Pujari, A.K. (eds.) ICISS 2008. LNCS, vol. 5352, pp. 287–302. Springer, Heidelberg (2008)

Specification of History Based Constraints for Access Control in Conceptual Level*

Fathiyeh Faghih, Morteza Amini, and Rasool Jalili

Dept. of Comp. Eng., Sharif University of Technology
Tehran, Iran
{faghih@ce,m_amini@ce,jalili}@sharif.edu

Abstract. An access control model for Semantic Web should take the semantic relationships among the entities, defined in the abstract conceptual level (i.e., ontology level), into account. Authorization and policy specification based on a logical model let us infer implicit security policies from the explicit ones based on the defined semantic relationships in the domains of subjects, objects, and actions. In this paper, we propose a logic based access control model for specification and inference of history-constrained access policies in conceptual level of Semantic Web. The proposed model (named TDLBAC-2) enables authorities to state policy rules based on the history of users' accesses using a temporal description logic called $\mathcal{DLR}_{US}$. The expressive power of the model is shown through seven different patterns for stating history-constrained access policies. The designed access decision algorithm of the model leverages the inference services of $\mathcal{DLR}_{US}$, which facilitates the implementation of an enforcement system working based on the proposed model. Sound inference, history-awareness, ability to define access policies in conceptual level, and preciseness are the main advantages of the proposed model.

1 Introduction

A proper access control model for a semantic-aware environment like Semantic Web should consider the semantic relationships among entities in the subject, object, and action domains. The relationships are defined as ontologies in Semantic Web, and should be utilized in inferring the authorized accesses from the explicit policy rules. On the other hand, considering the history of accesses may be important in access control in many modern applications such as e-banking systems. To consider these two aspects, we propose an access control model based on a temporal description logic ($\mathcal{DLR}_{US}$).

An access control model named as SBAC (Semantic Based Access Control) is introduced in [1] for Semantic Web, with the aim of taking semantic relationships into account . The SBAC model is extended in [2] to express policies with constraints on history of users' accesses in the past. TDLBAC in [3] tries to remove

---

* Thanks to ITRC (Iran Telecommunication Research Center) for partial support of this work.

S. Jha and A. Maturia (Eds.): ICISS 2010, LNCS 6503, pp. 186–200, 2010.
© Springer-Verlag Berlin Heidelberg 2010

two limitations of this extension. The first one is its restriction to the policies at the level of individuals. Therefore, security authorities are unable to state policies at the concept level. The second limitation is that the extension utilizes a formal language without proof theory that is only used for stating policy constraints. TDLBAC improves this model through a logical framework. Expressing security policy rules is possible using a logic-based language in TDLBAC.

Logic-based access control has many advantages including abstraction from implementation, expressiveness, and verifiability [4,5]. For Semantic Web, using logic can help to infer implicit authorized accesses from defined policies based on defined relationships among entities. On the other hand, description logic (DL) has always been considered as the foundation of Semantic Web for definition, integration, and maintenance of ontologies [6]. Accordingly, DL is chosen as a basis for proposing an access control model for Semantic Web in TDLBAC.

The other aspect in designing TDLBAC is access control with constraints on history of users' accesses. DLs in their standard forms are unable to state dynamic aspects. In order to state the history constrained policies, a temporal extension of a DL, named $\mathcal{TL}\text{-}\mathcal{ALCF}$ is used in TDLBAC. The underlying logic in TDLBAC ($\mathcal{TL}\text{-}\mathcal{ALCF}$) limits it to expression of a special pattern of policy rules with history based constraints. In this paper, we improve TDLBAC by changing the underlying logic to $\mathcal{DLR}_{US}$, which enables us to express various patterns of policy rules with constraints on history of accesses.

The proposed model in this paper is named TDLBAC-2. The model is introduced with its components and the procedure for storing the history of users' accesses. The access control algorithm is designed based on the inference services of $\mathcal{DLR}_{US}$. It enables us to discuss the complexity of the algorithm based on the inference services. It will be also helpful in implementation of the model using an available theorem prover for the $\mathcal{DLR}_{US}$ logic.

The rest of the paper is organized as follows: In section 2, TDLBAC-2 is introduced with its components, and the patterns for definition of security rules. Section 3 explains the access control procedure. Section 4 is a brief discussion on the complexity of the access control algorithm. Section 5 evaluates TDLBAC-2 focusing on its comparison with TDLBAC. Section 6 reviews the related work to the paper, and section 7 concludes the paper.

2   TDLBAC-2

2.1   Preliminaries

In this section, we briefly introduce the employed logic, $\mathcal{DLR}_{US}$. It is a temporal description logic proposed by Artale et al. in [7], [8]. The logic is based on the decidable DL, $\mathcal{DLR}$. There are efficient and complete algorithms for this logic which are used in the real applications. Considering the desirable characteristics of $\mathcal{DLR}$, Artale et al. tried to add the temporal extension to this logic.

$\mathcal{DLR}_{US}$ is designed as a combination of $\mathcal{DLR}$ and propositional linear temporal logic with the operators *Since* and *Until*. In this logic, temporal operators are applied to all syntactical expressions including concepts, relations and schemas.

The previous attempts for adding temporal aspect include weaker languages in the family of DLs which contain only binary relations. In $\mathcal{DLR}_{US}$, the flow of time, $\mathcal{T} = \langle \mathcal{T}_p, < \rangle$, in which $\mathcal{T}_p$ is a set of temporal points, and $<$ is a binary relation over $\mathcal{T}_p$, is considered to be equivalent to $\langle \mathbb{Z}, < \rangle$. Each time point is representative of a time interval (between this point and the next one.)

$\mathcal{DLR}$ is the non-temporal fragment of $\mathcal{DLR}_{US}$. For entity and relation expressions, it includes all the Boolean expressions, as well as the selection and projection expressions. The selection expression $U_i/n : E$ states an n-ary relation in which the argument U_i is of type E. The parameter name can be used instead of stating its position. The projection expression $(\exists^{\leq k}[j]R)^{\mathcal{I}(t)}$ is a projection of the relation R over its jth argument with respect to the cardinality relation ($\leq k$). The basic syntactical types in $\mathcal{DLR}_{US}$ include concepts and n-ary relations for $n \geq 2$. The semantics of $\mathcal{DLR}_{US}$ includes the temporal models, which are the triples $\mathcal{I} \doteq \langle \mathcal{T}, \Delta^{\mathcal{I}}, .^{\mathcal{I}(t)} \rangle$. $\Delta^{\mathcal{I}}$ is a nonempty set of objects (the domain of $\mathcal{I}$) and $.^{\mathcal{I}}$ is an interpretation function such that for every $t \in \mathcal{T}$, every concept E, and every n-ary relation R, $E^{\mathcal{I}(t)} \subseteq \Delta^{\mathcal{I}}$ and $R^{\mathcal{I}(t)} \subseteq (\Delta^{\mathcal{I}})^n$. In the following you can see a part of the syntax and semantic of $\mathcal{DLR}_{US}$ as used in the design of TDLBAC-2. The intuitive meanings of $\Diamond^+$, $\Diamond^-$, and $\oplus$ are "sometime in the future", "sometime in the past", and "at the next moment". Note that $\top_n$ is the top n-ary relation.

$$(\top_n)^{\mathcal{I}(t)} \subseteq (\Delta^{\mathcal{I}})^n, R^{\mathcal{I}(t)} \subseteq (\top_n)^{\mathcal{I}(t)}, (\neg R)^{\mathcal{I}(t)} \subseteq (\top_n)^{\mathcal{I}(t)} \backslash R^{\mathcal{I}(t)}$$

$$(U_i/n : E)^{\mathcal{I}(t)} = \left\{ \langle d_1, ..., d_n \rangle \in (\top_n)^{\mathcal{I}(t)} | d_i \in E^{\mathcal{I}(t)} \right\}$$

$$(\Diamond^+ R)^{\mathcal{I}(t)} = \{ \langle d_1, ..., d_n \rangle \in (\top_n)^{\mathcal{I}(t)} | \exists v > t.(\langle d_1, ..., d_n \rangle \in R^{\mathcal{I}(v)}) \}$$

$$(\oplus R)^{\mathcal{I}(t)} = \{ \langle d_1, ..., d_n \rangle \in (\top_n)^{\mathcal{I}(t)} | \langle d_1, ..., d_n \rangle \in R^{\mathcal{I}(t+1)} \}$$

$$(\Diamond^- R)^{\mathcal{I}(t)} = \{ \langle d_1, ..., d_n \rangle \in (\top_n)^{\mathcal{I}(t)} | \exists v < t.(\langle d_1, ..., d_n \rangle \in R^{\mathcal{I}(v)}) \}$$

$$(\exists^{\leq k}[j]R)^{\mathcal{I}(t)} = \left\{ d \in \top^{\mathcal{I}(t)} | \#\{ \langle d_1, ..., d_n \rangle \in R^{\mathcal{I}(t)} | d_j = d \} \leq k \right\}$$

2.2   Overall TDLBAC-2 Model Description

TDLBAC-2 is an access control model based on the temporal description logic $\mathcal{DLR}_{US}$. The model includes two main DL components; TBox and ABox.

TBox contains statements expressing properties and relationships among entities. Considering the nature of subsumption relationship which is the essential operator in TBox, this component has a lattice structure [9]. ABox includes assertions about the real world instances.

Since TDLBAC-2 is a history based access control model, it contains two essential components from the "history based access control" point of view:

1. History Base (HB): contains the history of previous accesses. HB is stored as a part of ABox.
2. History-based Policy-Base (HPB): is a set of security policy rules with constraints on history of accesses. The rules of HPB are stored in TBox.

2.3   Model Terminology

In TDLBAC-2, the axioms related to the domain are stored in TBox. The axioms include the definition of different *concepts*, in addition to their semantic relationships. TBox contains three hierarchies of concepts:

1. Subjects: Instances of these concepts are potential active users/agents/ webservices that require to access the objects.
2. Objects: Instances of these concepts can be accessed by subjects.
3. Actions: Instances of these concepts identify different access types.

Each security rule is defined as a logical *relation* and is stored in TBox. Security rules are defined by specifying the sorts of the subjects that have permission of a special type of access on the specific objects. In TDLBAC-2, security rules are defined as ternary relations among subjects, objects and access types. To specify the type of each access parameter, the selection operator $(U_i/n : E)$ in $\mathcal{DLR}_{US}$ is utilized. The selection operator states an n-ary relation that one of its parameters, called $U_i(i \leq n)$ is of type E. Using this operator, we can specify the types of the three parameters of a security rule. The pattern for defining security rules in TDLBAC-2 is as follows:

$$(\text{policy-rule})_i \equiv (\text{PS}_1/3 : \text{SType}) \sqcap (\text{PO}_2/3 : \text{OType}) \sqcap (\text{PA}_3/3 : \text{AType})$$

In this pattern, $(\text{policy-rule})_i$ is a name given to the defined security rule. SType is a concept in the hierarchy of subjects, OType is a concept in the objects hierarchy, and AType belongs to the actions hierarchy.

TDLBAC-2 is an access control model which allows stating the history constrained policy rules. Therefore, in TDLBAC-2, there is a history of accesses similar to the policy rules. Each access logged in the history is a ternary relation between specific types of subjects, objects, and actions. To define the types of an access parameters, the selection operator $(U_i/n : E)$ is utilized in the access definition. The parameters of accesses are named as AS, AO, and AA. The pattern for access definition in TDLBAC-2 is as follows:

$$\text{access}_i \equiv (\text{AS}_1/3 : \text{SType}) \sqcap (\text{AO}_2/3 : \text{OType}) \sqcap (\text{AA}_3/3 : \text{AType})$$

access_i is a name given to the logged access. In this paper, we simply only use the name of the argument and omit the indexes (for example, AS instead of AS_1).

2.4   Ground Assertions

In a DL based system, ground assertions are stored in ABox. These facts are grouped into three categories in TDLBAC-2:

– The assertions which state correspondence of instances to the concepts defined in subjects, objects, and actions hierarchies.
– The assertions which state the users' previous accesses and are stored in HB as a part of ABox. These assertions are utilized for checking the history based constraints of security policy rules in the access control procedure. These assertions are added to ABox after granting each request.

- The assertions which are related to the type of requester in each request. They are added to ABox based on the certificates that the requester attaches to her request. This is discussed in Section 3 in details.

2.5   Security Policy Rules Definition

TDLBAC-2 allows security authorities to define history constrained policy rules. These rules specify the authorized types of subjects, objects, and actions, as well as the constraints defined over the previous accesses. In most of the access control systems based on the history of accesses (like e-government systems), the constraints are enforced on the history of subjects' accesses. For instance, consider a security rule which gives the right of attending in the second round of the election to those who have voted in the first round. The idea of expressing history constrained policy rules in TDLBAC-2 is stating the history based constraint of the rule besides the permitted type of the subject. The history based constraints are stated using the operators defined in the syntax of $\mathcal{DLR}_{US}$ logic. The operator which is utilized the most in stating the history constrained policy rules is $\Diamond^-$. The informal meaning of this operator is "sometime in the past".

To limit the subjects of a security rule to those who had a special access in past, the projection expression is used. As seen in the semantics, the interpretation of the projection expression is a set of instances for which the number of relations of type R having these instances as their ith argument, satisfies the specified relation with k (equals, less than or greater than). This operator can be used to specify the number and type of users' accesses.

2.6   Patterns of History Constrained Policy Rules

The main purpose of this paper is investigation into the specification of history constrained policies in conceptual level using $\mathcal{DLR}_{US}$. Therefore, in this section, different patterns to define possible security policy rules in TDLBAC-2 (based on $\mathcal{DLR}_{US}$) are introduced:

Pattern 1. Pattern 1 is used to state the rules which authorize those users who had special accesses in the past. In the other words, special accesses have been registered by these users in the history base (HB). The pattern of stating such policy rules is as follows:

$$(\text{policy-rule})_i \equiv (\text{PS}/3 : (\text{SType} \sqcap \Diamond^- \exists^{\geqslant 1}[\text{AS}](\text{access}_i))) \sqcap (\text{PO}/3 : \text{OType}) \sqcap (\text{PA}/3 : \text{AType})$$

$(\text{policy-rule})_i$ is a policy rule that gives the SType users, the permission of AType accesses to objects of type OType with the constraint of having an access of type access_i in the past. The constraint on the existing an access of type access_i is defined by $(\Diamond^- \exists^{\geqslant 1}[\text{AS}](\text{access}_i))$ in this rule. This condition is conjuncted to the other condition of the subject on its type (i.e., SType). To clarify the meaning, let's take a look at the semantics of the history based constraint in this pattern:

$$(\lozenge^- \exists^{\geqslant 1}[AS]access_i)^{\mathcal{I}(t)} = \left\{ d \in (\top)^{\mathcal{I}(t)} | \exists v < t.d \in (\exists^{\geqslant 1}[AS]access_i)^{\mathcal{I}(v)} \right\} =$$
$$\left\{ d \in (\top)^{\mathcal{I}(t)} | \exists v < t.\# \left\{ \langle d_{AS}, d_{AO}, d_{AA} \rangle \in (access_i)^{\mathcal{I}(v)} | d_{AS} = d \right\} \geqslant 1 \right\}$$

Interpretation of the constraint at time t contains instances (in the domain of $\mathcal{I}$) which are the AS argument of one or more relations of type $access_i$ in a time point less than t.

As an example of this pattern, suppose the security rule in a second round election which gives the permission of voting to the residents of the country (instances of type resident). Moreover, the right of voting is limited to those who have voted in the first round. The security policy rule for this election can be stated as follows:

$$\text{vote-policy-2nd} \equiv PS/3:(\text{Resident} \sqcap \lozenge^- \exists^{\geqslant 1}[AS](\text{vote-1st}))$$
$$\sqcap PO/3:\text{election-system} \sqcap PA/3:\text{vote}$$

vote-1st is a relation which specifies the type of an access. Regarding this policy rule, a requester is authorized, if he/she is the AS argument (subject) of an access of type *vote-1st*, which can be defined in TBox as follows:

$$\text{vote-1st} \equiv AS/3:\text{resident} \sqcap AO/3:\text{election-system} \sqcap AA/3:\text{vote}$$

Pattern 2. Pattern 2 is used to state the policy rules which authorize the subjects who had a given number of accesses of special type.

$$(\text{policy-rule})_i \equiv PS/3:(\text{SType} \sqcap \exists^{\leqslant n}[AS](\lozenge^- access_i)) \sqcap PO/3:\text{OType} \sqcap PA/3:\text{AType}$$

The cardinality in the projection expression is utilized to express the limitation on the number of accesses (equals, less than, or greater than a given number). To clarify, let us take a look at the semantics of the constraint in this pattern:

$$(\exists^{\leqslant n}[AS](\lozenge^- access_i))^{\mathcal{I}(t)} =$$
$$\left\{ d \in (\top)^{\mathcal{I}(t)} | \# \left\{ \langle d_{AS}, d_{AO}, d_{AA} \rangle \in (\lozenge^- access_i)^{\mathcal{I}(t)} | d_{AS} = d \right\} \leqslant n \right\} =$$
$$\left\{ d \in (\top)^{\mathcal{I}(t)} | \# \left\{ \begin{array}{c} \langle d_{AS}, d_{AO}, d_{AA} \rangle \in (\top_3)^{\mathcal{I}(t)} | \exists v < t. \\ \langle d_{AS}, d_{AO}, d_{AA} \rangle \in (access_i)^{\mathcal{I}(v)} \wedge d_{AS} = d \end{array} \right\} \leqslant n \right\}$$

For example, the permission of taking the entrance exam can be given to those who took it less than "y" times.

Pattern 3. Pattern 3 is used to state the policy rules which give the permission to the subjects who had accesses in some time interval in the past for specified number of times. As mentioned in "Preliminaries" section, time in $\mathcal{DLR}_{US}$ is considered as a partial order, $\mathcal{T} = \langle \mathcal{T}_p, < \rangle$, in which $\mathcal{T}_p$ is a set of time points. Moreover, each time point is representative of a time interval defined in the logic semantics. The pattern for stating such policy rules is as follows:

$$(\text{policy-rule})_i \equiv PS/3:(\text{SType} \sqcap \lozenge^- \exists^{\leqslant n}[AS](access_i)) \sqcap PO/3:\text{OType} \sqcap PA/3:\text{AType}$$

To clarify, let us take a look at the semantics of the constraint defined in the above rules:

$$(\Diamond^- \exists^{\leq n}[AS]access_i)^{\mathcal{I}(t)} = \left\{ d \in (\top)^{\mathcal{I}(t)} | \exists v < t.d \in (\exists^{\leq n}[AS]access_i)^{\mathcal{I}(v)} \right\} =$$

$$\left\{ d \in (\top)^{\mathcal{I}(t)} | \exists v < t.\# \left\{ \langle d_{AS}, d_{AO}, d_{AA} \rangle \in (access_i)^{\mathcal{I}(v)} | d_{AS} = d \right\} \leqslant n \right\}$$

So an authorized subject has been the subject of a special kind of relations (actions) for more or less than a specified number of times in a specific time interval (the time point v is representative of this interval) . As an example, we can state a policy rule which gives the permission of undertaking a special kind of projects to those, who have the record of doing more than two projects in a year (in a model that each time point is representative of a year).

Pattern 4. Pattern 4 is used to state the policy rules which give a permission to ones who had accesses in some consecutive intervals. The pattern is as follows:

$$(policy\text{-}rule)_i \equiv PS/3{:}(SType \sqcap \Diamond^-(\exists^{\geq 1}[AS]access_i \sqcap \exists^{\geq 1}[AS] \oplus access_j$$
$$\sqcap \exists^{\geq 1}[AS] \oplus \oplus access_k \sqcap ...)) \sqcap PO/3{:}OType \sqcap PA/3{:}AType$$

$access_i$, $access_j$, and $access_k$ are representatives of three accesses in three consecutive intervals in the past. The semantics of the constraint on history of accesses in this pattern is as follows:

$$(\Diamond^-(\exists^{\geq 1}[AS]access_i \sqcap \exists^{\geq 1}[AS] \oplus access_j \sqcap \exists^{\geq 1}[AS] \oplus \oplus access_k))^{\mathcal{I}(t)} =$$

$$\left\{ d{\in}(\top)^{\mathcal{I}(t)} | \exists v<t.d{\in}(\exists^{\geq 1}[AS]access_i \sqcap \exists^{\geq 1}[AS] \oplus access_j \sqcap \exists^{\geq 1}[AS] \oplus \oplus access_k)^{\mathcal{I}(v)} \right\}$$

$$= \left\{ d{\in}(\top)^{\mathcal{I}(t)} | \exists v<t. \left\{ \begin{array}{l} \#\{\langle d_{AS}, d_{AO}, d_{AA} \rangle \in (access_i)^{\mathcal{I}(v)} | d_{AS} = d\} \geqslant 1 \\ \wedge \#\{\langle d_{AS}, d_{AO}, d_{AA} \rangle \in (access_j)^{\mathcal{I}(v+1)} | d_{AS} = d\} \geqslant 1 \\ \wedge \#\{\langle d_{AS}, d_{AO}, d_{AA} \rangle \in (access_k)^{\mathcal{I}(v+2)} | d_{AS} = d\} \geqslant 1 \end{array} \right\} \right\}$$

The pattern is extensible for more consecutive intervals in a similar way. As an example, using this pattern, we can define a policy rule which gives the permission of using insurance services to those, who have paid the insurance fee for at least three consecutive months.

Pattern 5. Pattern 5 is used to state the policy rules which give permission to those who had special accesses with a certain order in the past.

$$(policy\text{-}rule)_i \equiv PS/3{:}(SType \sqcap \Diamond^-(\exists^{\geq 1}[AS]access_i \sqcap \Diamond^+ \exists^{\geq 1}[AS]access_j))$$
$$\sqcap PO/3{:}OType \sqcap PA/3{:}AType$$

In this pattern, the history constraint is defined over the subjects, in the way that it should be the instance of two access types, $access_i$ and $access_j$. Moreover, the $access_i$ instance should precede the $access_j$ instance. By nesting the $\Diamond^+$ and $\Diamond^-$ operators in this way, we can provide the concept of precedence relation between the accesses in the past, since $\Diamond^+$ shows "sometime in the future", relative to "sometime in the past", which is provided by $\Diamond^-$. Let us take a look at the semantics of the constraint on the history of accesses in this pattern:

$$(\Diamond^-(\exists^{\geqslant 1}[AS]access_i \sqcap \Diamond^+\exists^{\geqslant 1}[AS]access_j))^{\mathcal{I}(t)} =$$

$$\left\{ d \in (\top)^{\mathcal{I}(t)} | \exists v < t.d \in (\exists^{\geqslant 1}[AS]access_i \sqcap \Diamond^+\exists^{\geqslant 1}[AS]access_j)^{\mathcal{I}(v)} \right\} =$$

$$\left\{ d \in (\top)^{\mathcal{I}(t)} | \exists v < t. \left\{ \begin{array}{l} \# \left\{ \begin{array}{l} \langle d_{AS}, d_{AO}, d_{AA} \rangle \in \\ (access_i)^{\mathcal{I}(v)} | d_{AS} = d \end{array} \right\} \geqslant 1 \wedge \exists v < w. \\ \# \left\{ \begin{array}{l} \langle d'_{AS}, d'_{AO}, d'_{AA} \rangle \in \\ (access_j)^{\mathcal{I}(w)} | d'_{AS} = d \end{array} \right\} \geqslant 1 \end{array} \right\} \right\}$$

As an example of this pattern, access to the electronic payment page of a banking system is allowable, only if the client has accessed an online store, and then inserted the information of her credit card.

Meta Pattern 6. Definition of different accesses separately may cause TBox to be extremely large in some systems. Meta pattern 6 is a method to alleviate this problem. We explain this pattern with its application to pattern 3:

$$(\text{policy-rule})_i \equiv PS/3:(SType \sqcap \exists^{\leqslant n}\Diamond^-[AS](accesss_i \sqcap AS/3:S''Type$$
$$\sqcap AO/3:O''Type \sqcap AA/3:A''Type)) \sqcap PO/3:OType \sqcap PA/3:AType$$

$$access_i \equiv AS/3:S'Type \sqcap AO/3:O'Type \sqcap AA/3:A'Type$$

In this pattern, $access_i$ is defined as an access with general types of access parameters. In the definition of $(\text{policy-rule})_i$, the types of subject, object, and action are defined more specifically. In this pattern, the relation between S''Type, O''Type, and A''paType with S'Type, O'Type, and A'Type is as follows:

$$(S''Type \sqcap S'Type \neq \varnothing) \wedge (O''Type \sqcap O'Type \neq \varnothing) \wedge (A''Type \sqcap A'Type \neq \varnothing)$$

This way, we can save the volume of the ontology related to the definition of accesses. This meta pattern can be similarly applied to other patterns too. For example, consider the action of repaying a loan in a banking system as follows:

$$\text{repay-loan} \equiv AS/3:\text{account-holder} \sqcap AO/3:\text{loan} \sqcap AA/3:\text{repay}$$

Now, consider a security rule, which gives the permission of getting the secured loan to those who already repaid at least three unsecured loans. The security loan policy rule can be defined as follows:

$$\text{secured-loan-policy} \equiv PS/3 : (\text{account-holder} \sqcap \Diamond^-\exists^{\geqslant 3}[AS](\text{repay-loan}$$
$$\sqcap AO/3 : \text{unsecured-loan})) \sqcap PO/3:\text{secured-loan} \sqcap PA/3:\text{get}$$

"$AO/3$: unsecured-loan" expresses the relations in which the AO parameter is of type unsecured-loan. This condition is conjuncted to the "repay-loan" access type, which is itself a relation.

Meta Pattern 7. Meta Pattern 7 is used to state the negation of history based constraints. The pattern might be applied to patterns 1 to 4 as follows:

- Applying pattern 7 to pattern 1 is as follows:

$$(\text{policy-rule})_i \equiv PS/3{:}(STy pe \sqcap \neg \Diamond^- \exists^{\geqslant 1}[AS](access_i)) \sqcap PO/3{:}OType \sqcap PA/3{:}AType$$

For example, using this pattern, we can state the policy rule which gives the permission of getting the loan to those who have not already got any loan.
- Applying pattern 7 to pattern 2 is as follows:

$$(\text{policy-rule})_i \equiv PS/3{:}(STy pe \sqcap \neg \exists^{\leqslant n}[AS](\Diamond^- access_i)) \sqcap PO/3{:}OType \sqcap PA/3{:}AType$$

As an example of this pattern, we can mention a policy rule, which gives the permission of registration in an education system to those who have not already registered more than 11 times in the system.
- Applying pattern 7 to pattern 3 is as follows:

$$(\text{policy-rule})_i \equiv PS/3{:}(STy pe \sqcap \neg \Diamond^- \exists^{\leqslant n}[AS](access_i)) \sqcap PO/3{:}OType \sqcap PA/3{:}AType$$

As an example, consider a rule in a banking system, based on which only those who have not withdrawn from their accounts more than five times in any of the previous years can fill loan application forms.
- Applying pattern 7 to pattern 4 is as follows:

$$(\text{policy-rule})_i \equiv PS/3{:}(STy pe \sqcap \neg \Diamond^- \exists^{\geqslant 1}[AS](access_i \sqcap \oplus access_j \sqcap \oplus ...))$$
$$\sqcap PO/3{:}OType \sqcap PA/3{:}AType$$

For example, consider a rule in an education system for students who want to register as teaching assistantships. This rule might restrict the permission to those who did not pass two consecutive terms with GPA lower than 16.

To clarify the meaning of pattern 7, the semantics of the history constraint $(\neg \exists^{\geqslant n}[AS](\Diamond^- access_i))$ in application of this pattern to pattern 2 is formalized:

$$(\neg \exists^{\leqslant n}[AS](\Diamond^- access_i))^{\mathcal{I}(t)} = \top^{\mathcal{I}(t)} \backslash (\exists^{\leqslant n}[AS](\Diamond^- accesss_i))^{\mathcal{I}(t)} =$$

$$\top^{\mathcal{I}(t)} \backslash \left\{ d \in \top^{\mathcal{I}(t)} | \#\{\langle d_1,...,d_n \rangle \in (\Diamond^- accesss_i)^{\mathcal{I}(t)} | d_{AS} = d \} \leqslant n \right\} =$$

$$\top^{\mathcal{I}(t)} \backslash \left\{ \begin{array}{l} d \in \top^{\mathcal{I}(t)} | \#\{\langle d_1,...,d_n \rangle \in (\top_n)^{\mathcal{I}(t)} | \exists v < t. \langle d_1,...,d_n \rangle \in (accesss_i)^{\mathcal{I}(v)} \\ \wedge d_{AS} = d \} \leqslant n \end{array} \right\}$$

The permission is given to those who did not have $\leqslant n$ access(es) of type $access_i$.

3 Access Control Procedure

A formal procedure for handling an access request in TDLBAC-2 is as follows.

An access request is interpreted as a triple (s_r, o_r, a_r), where s_r is the subject of the request, o_r is the object , and a_r is the requested access type. Two conditions should be satisfied for applicability of a security rule in HPB to a request:

- **Type Compatibility Condition:** The types of the access request parameters should be compatible with the types of the parameters specified in the the policy rule. Suppose, sc_r, oc_r, and ac_r are the types of the subject, object, and action parameters in the request, and sc_p, oc_p, and ac_p are the types of the corresponding parameters in the policy rule. A policy rule is applicable to an access request, if: $sc_r \sqsubseteq sc_p \wedge oc_r \sqsubseteq oc_p \wedge ac_r \sqsubseteq ac_p$
  In other words, the types of the parameters in the request should be subsumed by the types of the corresponding parameters in the security rule.
- **History Constraint:** The history constraint in the policy rule definition should be satisfied w.r.t. the facts inserted to the history base.

In the following, we first discuss how to store the history of accesses. Then, the proposed algorithm for access control is described. To clarify the whole procedure, an example is used.

Example: Consider an election system in a country. The election-system is a concept in the objects hierarchy in TBox. This concept has an instance in each city which can be accessed via the web. Suppose that the system is used in a presidential election in the second round. The security rule is to limit the voters to a group of the residents who voted in the first round. *Resident* is a concept in the subjects hierarchy. The security rule can be stated in HPB as follows:

$$\text{vote-policy-2nd} \equiv \text{PS}/3{:}(\text{resident} \sqcap \Diamond^{-}\exists^{\geq 1}[\text{AS}](\text{vote-1st})) \sqcap \text{PO}/3{:}\text{election-system} \sqcap \text{PA}/3{:}\text{vote}$$

The concept of vote-1st is defined in TBox as follows:

$$\text{vote-1st} \equiv \text{AS}/3{:}\text{resident} \sqcap \text{AO}/3{:}\text{election-system} \sqcap \text{AA}/3{:}\text{vote}$$

3.1   Storing the History of Accesses in HB

To describe the process of storing the history of accesses in HB, we use the election system example. The requests for voting in the first round are processed with respect to the security rules in HPB. For every request granted by the system, the facts related to the corresponding access will be inserted to ABox.

Suppose that "John Day" has a request for voting in the first round of presidential election in an instance of the election-system concept, named as election-sub20. The request is granted after being processed by the access control system. The next step is to store the access in HB. To store the access with its parameters, this statement is inserted to ABox: vote-1st(12345,election-sub20,v_1,t_1). v_1 is an instance of the vote action which is delivered to the system as a parameter of the request. The point is that we have *UNA* (Unique Name Assumption) for subjects in TDLBAC-2, similar to the case in TDLBAC. Therefore, the uniqueness of the subjects in storing and retrieving is guaranteed. For instance, in the example of the election system, the national ID of people is used for this purpose. In the stored statement, 12345 is considered as John's national ID. The parameter t_1 in the stored statement is the time of granting the access request. Using this parameter in storing an instance in ABox is necessary in $\mathcal{DLR}_{US}$.

Generally speaking, suppose that acc is the name of the relation related to the performed access, and s_r, o_r, and a_r are the instances forming the subject, object, and action parameters of the access request respectively. To store the access occurred in t_1, this statement is inserted to ABox: $acc(s_r,o_r,a_r,t_1)$. Using this technique, each access could be distinguished by its four parameters in ABox.

3.2   Access Control Algorithm

To clarify the proposed algorithm, we continue with the election system example. Suppose that "John Day" wants to vote in the second round of the presidential election. Instances of the object and action are known in the server side. However, all the potential users are not known by the access control system. Subject identification is based on the certificates that the user attaches to her request. The system is able to map the requester to the concepts in the hierarchy of subjects using the delivered certificates. For instance, "John Day" might be mapped to the *resident* concept by one of his certificates, and to the *graduate* concept by the other one. It is important that a unique certificate be included in the attached certificates, so that *UNA* can be satisfied. Corresponding statements are inserted to ABox to be used in the access control procedure. For example, using 12345 as John's national ID, the statements resident($12345,t_2$) and graduate($1234,t_2$) are inserted to ABox before starting the access control procedure (in t_2).

Checking the applicability of each security rule with respect to the access request is performed using *instance checking* inference service. In our proposed algorithm, this service checks whether the triple related to the requested access is a member of the relation defined with respect to a security rule or not. Suppose, in the election system example, the parameters of the access request (voting in the second round) are 12345, election-sub30, and v_2 respectively. In this case, to check the applicability of the security rule "vote-policy-2nd" to the access request, the *instance checking* inference service will be used to check the satisfiability of vote-policy-2nd(12345,election-sub30,v_2,t_3).

Generally speaking, if s_r, o_r, and a_r are the parameters of the access request, and (policy-rule)$_i$ is the security rule, the access control algorithm will be performed using the (policy-rule)$_i$(s_r,o_r,a_r,t) inference service. If this inference service returns true, the two following conditions of compatibility between the security rule and the access request are satisfied:

1. **Type Compatibility Condition:** The *instance checking* inference service returns true, if the three type conditions of (policy-rule)$_i$ i.e., (PS/3:SType ⊓ PO/3:OType ⊓ PA/3:AType) are satisfied with respect to the three parameters of the access request, (s_r,o_r,a_r). The facts related to the types of the object and access parameters are already in ABox. The facts related to the type of the subject parameter have been inserted to ABox with respect to the attached certificates.

2. **History Constraint:** The *instance checking* inference service returns true, if the history constraint in the definition of (policy-rule)$_i$ is satisfied w.r.t. the facts in ABox and parameters of the request.

Using the above procedure, each access request can be checked against each policy rule. The algorithm is terminated in one of the two following scenarios:

- An applicable security policy rule to the access request is found; the request is granted by the access control system.
- None of the security policy rules has the required conditions for granting the request; the request is rejected by the system.

4   Complexity of the Access Control Algorithm

Full $\mathcal{DLR}_{US}$, even restricted to atomic formulas, turns out to be undecidable [7]. $\mathcal{DLR}_{US}^-$ is a decidable fragment of $\mathcal{DLR}_{US}$, in which the temporal operators are applied only to the concepts and formulas. In other words, in this decidable fragment, the temporal operators can not be applied to n-ary relations (n$\geqslant$2). The computational behavior of $\mathcal{DLR}_{US}^-$ can be summarized as follows [7]:

- The logical implication problem in $\mathcal{DLR}_{US}^-$, when restricted to atomic formulas, is EXPTIME-complete.
- The formula satisfiability problem (and the logical implication) in $\mathcal{DLR}_{US}^-$ is 2EXSPACE-complete.
- The problem of query containment for non-recursive Datalog queries in $\mathcal{DLR}_{US}^-$ is decidable in 2EXPTIME and is EXSPACE-hard.

As mentioned before, policy rules are expressed as logical relations in TDLBAC-2. The only pattern that can not be stated under $\mathcal{DLR}_{US}^-$ constraints is pattern 2, since the temporal operator $\diamondsuit^-$ is applied to the ternary relation in this pattern. Therefore, we study the complexity of the access control algorithm without considering pattern 2. Note that undecidability of the underlying logic should not be considered as a great weakness for pattern 2. With further research in this area, decidable algorithms might be found for a larger fragment of $\mathcal{DLR}_{US}$ that includes such formulae.

The algorithm of access control in TDLBAC-2 in the worst case will include an *instance checking* inference service for each security rule. The *instance checking* inference service can be expressed as the problem of answering (boolean) conjunctive queries [10]. It is proved in [11] that query answering under DL constraints can be reduced to query containment. On the other hand, The problem of query containment for non-recursive Datalog queries in $\mathcal{DLR}_{US}^-$ is decidable in 2EXP-TIME and is EXSPACE-hard [7]. Since the problem of query answering is reducible to the problem of query containment, 2EXP-TIME can be considered as the upper bound for this problem. In the access control procedure, the service is performed for all the security rules in the worst case. Since there is a limited number of security rules, the upper bound of complexity of the algorithm will remain 2EXP-TIME in the worst case.

Note that we investigated the upper bound of the algorithm based on the known complexity of inference services. The point of this section is proof of the algorithm decidability. In future, efficient algorithms and reasoners might be developed for the logic that can lead to an efficient implementation of TDLBAC-2.

5   Evaluation and Comparison

TDLBAC [3] and TDLBAC-2 are two access control models based on a temporal extension of DLs for expressing the history constrained security rules in Semantic Web. In this section, we compare these two models from different points of view.

5.1   The Applied Logic

The logic used for stating the security policy rules in TDLBAC is $\mathcal{TL\text{-}ALCF}$, while TDLBAC-2 uses $\mathcal{DLR}_{US}$. $\mathcal{TL\text{-}ALCF}$ is an interval-based temporal extension of the DL $\mathcal{ALCF}$, while $\mathcal{DLR}_{US}$ is a point-based temporal extension of the DL $\mathcal{DLR}$. One of the advantages of $\mathcal{DLR}_{US}$ over $\mathcal{TL\text{-}ALCF}$ is its ability to state n-ary relations ($n \geqslant 2$). n-ary relations ($n \geqslant 2$) in $\mathcal{DLR}_{US}$ allows us to define a 3-ary relation for each access and policy rule, instead of defining a concept and three binary relations as in TDLBAC. Similarly, to store the history of accesses in HB, one statement is enough for each access. However, in TDLBAC four statements are registered for each access. It is obvious that stating security rules and accesses is easier in TDLBAC-2. Moreover, the size of HB in TDLBAC-2 is smaller in comparison to TDLBAC in similar conditions. This can reduce the problem of size for large history bases. Moreover, it can help the access control procedure to be more efficient.

5.2   Expressiveness

To compare TDLBAC and TDLBAC-2 from the expressiveness point of view, we take a look at the ability of TDLBAC to state the patterns used in TDLBAC-2.

TDLBAC is able to state policy rules in pattern 1. However, it is not able to state policy rules of pattern 2, since there is no operator for stating the cardinality in the syntax of $\mathcal{TL\text{-}ALCF}$. In TDLBAC, it is not also possible to state policy rules of patterns 3,4, and 5. The reason is the interval based nature of the temporal part of $\mathcal{TL\text{-}ALCF}$. In TDLBAC, for each access, a separate concept should be defined, and it does not propose a method for decreasing the ontology size like meta pattern 6. Application of meta pattern 7 is not also possible using the $\neg$ operator in TDLBAC.

6   Related Work

Logical ideas and tools have been used since late 90's by many researchers to state different kinds of security rules. Kolaczek in [4] employs Deontic Logic to propose a new formal model for role-based access control. Deontic Logic is used as a language for specification of security policies, which helps to automate the implementation of policies. Chae in [5] uses a a modal logic to propose a a kind of role-based access control model. The novelty of this model is to perform authorization at the level of classes, instead of individual objects, which leads to more flexibility in security management.

The other related works include the works for expressing the security rules based on the past events. Among those, Chinese Wall Security Policy in [12] and Deeds system in [13] can be mentioned. These works focus on collecting a selective history of sensitive access requests and using this information to constrain future access requests. Abadi in [14] uses a different approach which considers the history of control transfers, rather than a history of sensitive requests. None of these works considers access control in a semantic-based environment, as well as conceptual-level policy specification and inference. Bertino in [15] presents a language to express both static and dynamic authorization constraints as clauses in a logic program. This work considers the execution history of the workflow for workflow management systems. Our schema differs from the above approach in employing a temporal description logic to propose a model suitable for Semantic Web. We also provide seven patterns for expressing different kinds of history-based policy rules.

With the growth of Semantic Web, access control for these environments have been extensively investigated. An access control model for a semantic-aware environment should consider the defined semantic relationships among entities to infer the authorized accesses from the defined policy rules. Several efforts as in [1] have been put into designing access control models for semantic-aware environments such as Semantic Web. The important novelty of the proposed model in [1], named SBAC, is reducing semantic relationships (defined as ontologies in three domains of access control) to subsumption. This approach reduces the temporal and spatial complexities, and simplifies the authorization propagation. TSBAC [2] is an extension of the SBAC model [1], which allows expressing the policies with the constraints on history of users' accesses. TDLBAC is proposed in [3] to remove two weaknesses of TSBAC; Restriction to the security policies in the level of individuals, and Lack of proof theory in the formal language.

TDLBAC tries to improve TSBAC with a logical foundation to take advantage of a logic-based model. In this model, it is possible to state the history-constrained policy rules in conceptual (ontology) level. TDLBAC is restricted to a special pattern for stating the policy rules. In this paper, we tried to improve this work using another temporal extension of DLs for our proposed model.

7   Conclusions

In this paper, we proposed an access control model based on a temporal description logic, $\mathcal{DLR}_{US}$, for Semantic Web. The main characteristic of the proposed model is its ability to express historical constraints in policy specification in conceptual or ontology level. To show how the model can be used in practice, seven usage patterns are introduced in the paper. The expressive power of the proposed model enables it to be used in different applications such as banking and insurance systems, elections systems, and education systems. The examples of such usages are presented in this paper after introducing each usage pattern. The inference ability, which is embedded in the access control procedure of the proposed model (using the inference services of the underlying logic), enables it to infer implicit security policies from the explicit ones based on the defined semantic relationships in the conceptual abstract layer of Semantic Web.

References

1. Javanmardi, S., Amini, M., Jalili, R., GanjiSaffar, Y.: SBAC: A Semantic–Based Access Control Model. In: Proceedings of the 11th Nordic Workshop on Secure IT-Systems, NordSec2006, Linkping, Sweden:[sn], pp. 157–168 (2006)
2. Ravari, A.N., Amini, M., Jalili, R.: A Semantic Aware Access Control Model with Real Time Constraints on History of Accesses. In: International Multiconference on Computer Science and Information Technology, pp. 827–836 (2008)
3. Faghih, F., Amini, M., Jalili, R.: A Temporal Description Logic Based Access Control Model for Expressing History Constrained Policies in Semantic Web. In: Proceedings of the 2009 IEEE International Symposium on Policies for Distributed Systems and Networks, pp. 142–149. IEEE Computer Society, Los Alamitos (2009)
4. Kołaczek, G.: Application of Deontic Logic in Role–Based Access Control. Int. J. Appl. Math. Comput. Sci. 12(2), 269–275 (2002)
5. Chae, J.: Towards Modal Logic Formalization of Role-Based Access Control with Object Classes. In: Derrick, J., Vain, J. (eds.) FORTE 2007. LNCS, vol. 4574, p. 97. Springer, Heidelberg (2007)
6. Baader, F., Horrocks, I., Sattler, U.: Description logics as ontology languages for the semantic web. LNCS (LNAI), pp. 228–248. Springer, Heidelberg (2005)
7. Artale, A., Franconi, E., Wolter, F., Zakharyaschev, M.: A temporal description logic for reasoning over conceptual schemas and queries. LNCS, pp. 98–110. Springer, Heidelberg (2002)
8. Artale, A., Franconi, E., Mosurovic, M., Wolter, F., Zakharyaschev, M.: The DLRUS temporal description logic. In: Proceedings of the 2001 Description Logic Workshop (DL 2001), Citeseer, pp. 96–105 (2001)
9. Baader, F., Calvanese, D., McGuinness, D.L., Patel-Schneider, P., Nardi, D.: The description logic handbook: theory, implementation, and applications. Cambridge Univ. Pr., Cambridge (2003)
10. Calvanese, D., De Giacomo, G., Lembo, D., Lenzerini, M., Rosati, R.: Data complexity of query answering in description logics. In: Proc. of the 10th Int. Conf. on the Principles of Knowledge Representation and Reasoning (KR 2006), pp. 260–270 (2006)
11. Calvanese, D., De Giacomo, G., Lenzerini, M.: Conjunctive query containment and answering under description logic constraints. ACM Transactions on Computational Logic (TOCL) 9(3), 22 (2008)
12. Brewer, D.F.C., Nash, M.J.: The Chinese wall security policy. In: Proceedings of the 1989 IEEE Symposium on Security and Privacy, Citeseer, pp. 206–214 (1989)
13. Edjlali, G., Acharya, A., Chaudhary, V.: History-based access control for mobile code. In: Proceedings of the 5th ACM Conference on Computer and Communications Security, pp. 38–48. ACM, New York (1998)
14. Abadi, M., Fournet, C.: Access control based on execution history. In: Proceedings of the 10th Annual Network and Distributed System Security Symposium, Citeseer, pp. 107–121 (2003)
15. Bertino, E., Ferrari, E., Atluri, V.: The specification and enforcement of authorization constraints in workflow management systems. ACM Transactions on Information and System Security (TISSEC) 2(1), 104 (1999)

Abstracting Audit Data for Lightweight Intrusion Detection

Wei Wang[1], Xiangliang Zhang[2], and Georgios Pitsilis[3]

[1] Interdisciplinary Centre for Security, Reliability and Trust (SnT Centre),
Université du Luxembourg, Luxembourg
wwangemail@gmail.com
[2] Mathematical and Computer Sciences and Engineering Division,
King Abdullah University of Science and Technolgy (KAUST), Saudi Arabia
[3] Faculty of Science, Technology and Communication,
Université du Luxembourg, Luxembourg

Abstract. High speed of processing massive audit data is crucial for an anomaly Intrusion Detection System (IDS) to achieve real-time performance during the detection. Abstracting audit data is a potential solution to improve the efficiency of data processing. In this work, we propose two strategies of data abstraction in order to build a lightweight detection model. The first strategy is exemplar extraction and the second is attribute abstraction. Two clustering algorithms, Affinity Propagation (AP) as well as traditional k-means, are employed to extract the exemplars, and Principal Component Analysis (PCA) is employed to abstract important attributes (a.k.a. features) from the audit data. Real HTTP traffic data collected in our institute as well as KDD 1999 data are used to validate the two strategies of data abstraction. The extensive test results show that the process of exemplar extraction significantly improves the detection efficiency and has a better detection performance than PCA in data abstraction.

1 Introduction

Computer network security has become more and more important as computer networks have heavily been involved in people's daily life and in all business processes within most organizations. As an important technique in the defense-in-depth network security framework, intrusion detection has become a widely studied topic in computer networks in recent years.

The techniques for intrusion detection can be categorized as signature-based detection and anomaly detection. Signature-based detection (e.g., Snort [1]) relies on a database of signatures from known malicious threats. Anomaly detection, on the other hand, defines a profile of a subject's normal activities and attempts to identify any unacceptable deviation as a potential attack. Any observable behavior of a system, e.g., a network's traffic [2–4], a host's operating system [5–8] and audit logs [9], can be used as the subject information.

Anomaly detection has a potential to detect unforeseen attacks and thus attracts a lot of attention from the research communities. An ideal anomaly IDS

S. Jha and A. Maturia (Eds.): ICISS 2010, LNCS 6503, pp. 201–215, 2010.
© Springer-Verlag Berlin Heidelberg 2010

(Intrusion Detection System) can be considered as a black box. It learns normal activities of a subject in an automated fashion. Security officers and system administrators thus have no need to manually analyze a large amount of applications. In practice, data in intrusion detection is massive and high dimensional in nature. In the experiments for collecting HTTP traffic on the main web server of our institute, for example, we have collected 1.45 million HTTP requests (561 MB) in only 3 days. High-speed processing of high dimensional massive audit data in most cases is essential for a practical IDS so that potential attacks can be identified and actions in response can be taken as soon as possible.

In general, there are four steps in anomaly intrusion detection: *collecting data, constructing attributes* (a.k.a. feature), *building normal models* and *detecting anomalies*. Many methods [3, 4, 10–14] have been employed for anomaly intrusion detection and most of them mainly focus on attribute construction or detection algorithms. In this paper, we aim at building a lightweight IDS by enhancing its capability of data processing. Intuitively, the most direct way of high-speed processing massive audit data in intrusion detection is to reduce the data. In this paper, we propose to abstract audit data and add a step "*abstracting data*" between the step "constructing attributes" and the step "building normal models". The process of abstracting data is based on the training data. It extracts a smaller representative data set from the large amount of training data, so that the training is based on a smaller set and the detection is based on a compressed model. The performance of an IDS is thus significantly improved in the process of training and detection.

There are generally two strategies to achieve the goal of data abstraction. The first is attribute abstraction after the attributes have been constructed. In this paper, we use Principal Component Analysis (PCA) to transform audit data in a high-dimensional space onto a space of fewer dimensions. The transformed attributes in the low-dimensional space are not part of the original ones. Different from attribute abstraction, in this paper, we propose to develop the second strategy that finds a subset of original data and we call this process as *exemplar* extraction. An *exemplar* refers to a factual data item (e.g., a HTTP request, a network connection) that represents a number of similar data items. Comparing to randomly sampling data items (e.g., Netflow based network intrusion detection [15, 16]), *exemplars* summarize massive audit data and thus better represents the audit data for anomaly detection. In this paper, we used two clustering methods, a newly developed Affinity Propagation (AP) [17] as well as traditional k-means [18], to cluster the original training data before the detection model is built. After the clustering process is finished, each cluster can be represented by an exemplar for AP, and by a mean center for k-means. We then use the exemplars or the cluster centers as the data input for building the detection models. In this way, data are largely reduced while the valuable information is kept in the exemplars, so that a lightweight detection model is built since there are only fewer exemplars remained.

Our contributions of this paper are summarized in the following aspects:

- We propose two different strategies of data abstraction for lightweight intrusion detection. The first strategy is *exemplar extraction* and the second is *attribute abstraction*. We employed two data clustering algorithms, the newly developed AP as well as traditional k-means, to extract exemplars from the massive training data, and use PCA to abstract important attributes from the data. A lightweight IDS is thus built since the training is based on a smaller data set and the detection is based on a compressed model. To the best of our knowledge, this is the first time *factual **exemplar extraction*** is used for anomaly detection.
- We compare the detection performance with AP against with k-means in exemplar extraction. We also compare the above mentioned techniques with each other along with attribute abstraction using PCA.
- We use two different types of data to validate the two strategies of data abstraction for intrusion detection. The extensive test results provide a reference for data abstraction in intrusion detection.

The remainder of this paper is organized as follows. Section 2 briefly introduces the related work. Section 3 describes the two strategies of data abstraction for anomaly intrusion detection. Extensive experiments and comparative results are reported in Section 4. Concluding remarks follow in Section 5.

2   Related Work

Anomaly intrusion detection has been an active research area. Its history dates back to Denning's seminal paper [19] on intrusion detection. Early studies [20] on anomaly detection mainly focused on modeling system or user behavior from monitored system log or accounting log data, including CPU usage, time of login, and names of files accessed.

System call sequences can also be used as a data source for detection of anomalous program behavior. In 1996, Forrest et al. [5] introduced an anomaly detection method called time-delay embedding (tide), based on monitoring system calls invoked by active and privileged processes. Liao et al. [8] used k-Nearest Neighbor (k-NN) classifier for intrusion detection based on system call data to model program behavior and classification.

Network traffic has been widely used for anomaly intrusion detection. Wang et al. [3] used payload of network traffic to detect anomalies. Cretu et al. [21] tried to sanitize training network traffic to obtain a clean training data set by combining the "micro-model" in a voting scheme by which some attacks in the training data can be discovered and filtered out. Krüegel and Vigna [12] are the first who used HTTP traffic for web attack detection. They investigated client queries with the parameters contained in these queries to detect potential attacks by six methods (e.g., length and structure of the parameters). Ingham and Inoue [11] collected a set of HTTP attacks and introduced a framework to compare different anomaly detection techniques for HTTP. Song et al. [13] used a mixture-of-markov-chains model for anomaly detection in web traffic.

Based on the 1998 DARPA Intrusion Detection Evaluation Program, Lee et al. [2] extracted 41 attributes for each network connection and formed a well known KDD Cup 1999 data [22]. The attributes of each network connection include basic attributes (e.g., protocol type), content attributes (e.g., number of "root" accesses) and traffic attributes (e.g., percentage of connections to the same service in a two-second time window). Many research groups [2, 10, 23] have used the KDD 1999 data to validate their detection methods.

Most existing anomaly detection methods mainly focus on attribute construction or on detection algorithms. They use all the attributes constructed from audit data or use all the original data to build the detection models. For example, most network intrusion detection methods that have used KDD 1999 data as data source utilized all the 41 attributes for the detection. However, some of the attributes may be redundant or may even be the effect of noise and therefore may decrease the performance of an IDS. Moreover, many data may be very similar or even exactly the same, using all the data hence decreases the efficiency of building the detection models.

There is related work regarding data reduction for intrusion detection. Sung and Mukkamala [24] used Artificial Neural Networks (ANN) and SVM to identify some important attributes based on the performance comparison. In our previous work [25], we used Information Gain (IG) and the combination of Bayesian Networks and decision tree classifiers to select some key subsets from the 41 attributes. We also used Principal Component Analysis (PCA) to reduce the dimensions of the audit data for intrusion detection [10]. Li et al. [26] employed Fuzzy C-Means to select a limited size of data items from the original ones for network intrusion detection. Fuzzy C-Means is like k-means in that each cluster centroid is a averaged one. Each data item has a degree of belonging to clusters. In their work, they select the items having large degrees (notable items or obscure items) as the training data for building the detection models. However, the items selected may also be redundant or duplicates, since many items belonging to a cluster may be selected. In Netflow based network anomaly detection, many methods sampled data with a certain probablity in order to deal with the massive traffic [15]. However, the randomly sampled traffic (e.g., flow or packet) is inherently a lossy process, discarding potentially useful information.

Different from attribute selection [25] and from random data sampling [15], in this paper, we developed a strategy that finds *exemplars* from original data and then uses the exemplars for training and detection. In order to facilitate comparison, we used PCA to abstract attributes from the same set of training data.

3   Abstracting Audit Data for Intrusion Detection

We used PCA for attribute abstraction as this is a widely used attribute transformation algorithm. In fact, PCA can be considered itself as an anomaly intrusion detection method. For exemplar extraction, we employ Affinity Propagation (AP) [17] and k-means [18]. We used k-Nearest Neighbor(NN) [27] and one class Support Vector Machine (SVM) [28] for anomaly detection, as both the two methods have been shown effective for intrusion detection [27, 29]. Both k-NN and one class SVM are used for building normal models (using attack-free data for training the model) based on which anomalies can be detected.

3.1   No Data Abstraction: Direct Use of k-NN and One Class SVM

k-NN based anomaly intrusion method. k-NN is a method for classifying objects by finding the closest training examples in the feature space. It uses the class labels of the k most nearest neighbor to predict the class of the test vector. A data vector normally consists of attributes. It represents an event or an object (e.g., a http request, a network connection) that needs to detect whether it is normal or not. In the remainder of this paper, *data item* and *data vector* are used interchangeably. Euclidean distance is usually used for measuring the similarity between two vectors: $d(T, X_i) = \| T - X_i \| = \sqrt{\sum_{i=1}^{m}(t_i - x_{ij})^2}$, where t_i is the value of i-th attribute in the test vector T; X_j is the vector j in the training data set and x_{ij} is the value of i-th attribute in sequences X_j.

Given a test vector T, the Euclidean distance between the test vector and each vector in the training data set is calculated. The k nearest neighbor of the test vector is chosen to determine whether the test vector is normal or not. In anomaly detection, we define the averaged k closest distance score that we call *anomaly index*. If the *anomaly index* of a test sequence vector is above a threshold, the test vector is then classified as abnormal. Otherwise it is considered as normal.

One class SVM based anomaly intrusion method. In this paper for our comparison, we use one class SVM that was proposed by Schölkopf et al. [28]. One class SVM algorithm maps the data into a feature space using an appropriate kernel function, and then separates the mapped vectors from the origin with maximum margin. The algorithm returns a function f that takes the value $+1$ in a "small" region capturing most of the data vectors (e.g., training data), and -1 elsewhere [30].

Given training vectors $X_1, X_2, ..., X_l$ belonging to normal class, the primal form of quadratic programming problem is $min \frac{1}{2}\|\omega\|^2 + \frac{1}{vl}\sum_{i=1}^{l}\xi_i - \rho$, subject to $(\omega \cdot \Phi(X_i)) \geq \rho - \xi_i$, where Φ is a kernel map that transforms the training examples into another space.

After the appropriate ω and ρ are found to solve the problem, the decision function is

$$f(x) = sgn((\omega \cdot \Phi(X)) - \rho) \tag{1}$$

In anomaly detection, we use the normal data to build the normal model. If the decision function gives a positive value for a test vector T, the test data is then classified as normal. Otherwise, it is considered as anomalous.

3.2   Attribute Abstraction and Intrusion Detection with PCA

Principal Component Analysis (PCA) [31] is based on transforming a relatively large number of variables into a *smaller* number of uncorrelated variables by finding a few orthogonal linear combinations of the original variables with the largest variance.

Given a set of original observations be $X_1, ..., X_i$, and suppose each observation is represented by a row vector of length m (the number of attributes), then the data set can be represented by a matrix $X_{n \times m}$. The average observation is defined as $\mu = \frac{1}{n} \sum_{i=1}^{n} X_i$. The observation deviation from the average is defined as $\Phi_i = X_i - \mu$. The sample covariance matrix of the data set is defined as $C = \frac{1}{n} \sum_{i=1}^{n} (X_i - \mu)(X_i - \mu)^T$.

Suppose $(\lambda_1, \mu_1), (\lambda_2, \mu_2), ..., (\lambda_m, \mu_m)$ are m eigenvalue-eigenvector pairs of the sample covariance matrix C, we choose k eigenvectors having the largest eigenvalues. Often there are just few large eigenvalues. This implies that k is the inherent dimensionality of the subspace governing the "signal", while the remaining $(m - k)$ dimensions generally contain noise. The dimensionality of the subspace k can be determined by $\frac{\sum_{i=1}^{k} \lambda_i}{\sum_{i=1}^{m} \lambda_i} \geq \alpha$, where α is the ratio of variation in the subspace to the total variation in the original space. We form a $(m \times k)$ (usually $k \ll m$ for data reduction) matrix U whose columns consist of the k eigenvectors. The representation of the data by principal components consists of projecting the data onto the k-dimensional subspace according to the rule $Y_i = (X_i - \mu)U = \Phi U$.

The number of principal eigenvectors $U_1, U_2, ..., U_k$, used to represent the distribution of the original data, is determined by α. They can also be regarded as the attributes abstracted from the original data attributes.

For anomaly detection, given an incoming vector T that represents a test sample, we project it onto the k-dimensional subspace representing the normal behavior. The distance between the test data vector Φ and its reconstruction onto the subspace Φ_r is the distance between the mean-adjusted input data vector $\Phi = T - \mu$ and $\Phi_r = (T - \mu)UU^T = \Phi UU^T$ [10]. If the test data vector is normal, that is, if the test data vector is very similar to the training vectors corresponding to normal behavior, the test data vector and its reconstruction should be very similar with each other and therefore the distance between them should be small. Our intrusion identification model is based on this property. As PCA seeks a projection that best represents the data in a least-square sense, we use the squared Euclidean distance in the experiments to measure the distance between these two vectors: $\varepsilon = \parallel \Phi - \Phi_r \parallel^2$. ε is characterized as the *anomaly index*. If ε is below a predefined threshold, the vector is then identified as normal. Otherwise it is identified as anomalous.

3.3   Exemplar Extraction

AP based exemplar extraction. AP is a newly developed exemplar-based clustering algorithm [17]. Let $\mathcal{E} = \{e_1, ..., e_N\}$ be a set of data items, and let $d(e_i, e_j)$ denote the distance (e.g., an Euclidean distance) between items e_i and e_j: $d(e_i, e_j) = \|e_i - e_j\|$.

The fitness function is defined by:

$$\mathbf{E}(c) = \sum_{i=1}^{n} S(e_i, e_{c(i)}) \tag{2}$$

where $c(i)$ is the index of the exemplar representing the item e_i in a cluster; $S(e_i, e_j)$ is set to $-d(e_i, e_j)^2$ if $i \neq j$, and otherwise is set to a small constant $-s^*$ $(s^* \geq 0)$. $-s^*$ represents a preference that e_i itself be chosen as an exemplar. AP finds the mapping $\mathbf{c}$ that maximizes the fitness function $\mathbf{E}(c)$ defined by (2) to cluster the data items. The resolution of this optimization problem is achieved by a message passing algorithm [17].

In practical use, there may be some items that are exactly the same in the audit data. In our study, we used Weighted AP (WAP) [32] that adds more weights to the multiple-appear items so as to let one of them have more probability to be an exemplar. Let data set $\mathcal{E}' = \{(e_i, n_i)\}$ involve n_i copies of item e_i, for $i = 1, \ldots, L$. WAP considers the similarity metric defined as:

$$S'(e_i, e_j) = \begin{cases} -n_i d(e_i, e_j)^2 & \text{if } i \neq j \\ -s^* & \text{otherwise} \end{cases}$$

Unlike k-means or k-centers, AP has no need to pre-define how many exemplars or clusters exist in the data. Instead, AP specifies the penalty s^* for allowing an item to become an exemplar. Note that for $s^* = 0$, the best solution is the trivial one, selecting every item as an exemplar.

k-means based exemplar extraction. Given a set of observations $(X_1, X_2, \ldots, X_n)$, where each observation is a real attribute vector, k-means clustering aims to partition the n observations into k sets $(k < n)$ $S = \{S_1, S_2, \ldots, S_k\}$ so as to minimize the within-cluster sum of squares

$$\sum_{i=1}^{k} \sum_{x_j \in s_i} \| X_j - \mu_i \|^2 \tag{3}$$

where μ_i is the mean of points in S_i. It is clear that k-means can only generate mean cluster centroids other than real exemplars.

4 Experiments and Comparative Results

4.1 Data

In the experiments, we used two different types of data for the evaluation. The first is real HTTP traffic[1] collected from the main HTTP server of our institute. The second is the benchmark KDD 1999 intrusion detection data [22]. Although the KDD 1999 data has been criticized [33] for having some flaws, the data set is so far probably the only large-size, available and well labeled network data source in public. The results can thus be compared with those obtained by other methods.

---

[1] All the preprocessed data as well as the programs used in this paper are available from the first author upon request.

HTTP data streams. We used HTTP traffic for detection of web attacks. The traffic is well labeled. The attacks in the traffic mainly include JS XSS attacks, SQL-injection attacks and PHP remote file inclusion attacks. In detail, the traffic contains 239 attacks in more than 1.4 million requests. The HTTP traffic is described in Table 1.

Table 1. Quantitative data of HTTP traffic

Before Filtering		After Filtering		# normal	# attack	Duration
File size	# requests	File size	# requests	requests	requests	
561.2MB	1,449,379	9.5MB	40,095	39,856	239	3 days 3 hrs

Our method examines individual HTTP requests and models the content of script inputs. In order to reduce noise contained in the data streams, we filtered out most static requests (e.g., .html, .wav, .txt, .pdf, .swf) as well as widely known search engine robots (e.g., googlebot, Msnbot) before the detection, because a static request cannot be an attack to the server. Note that we only filter out widely known attack-free static requests to guarantee that no attack is removed from the data. The data is largely reduced by the filtering and as shown in Table 1, only 2.77% of the original requests finally remained.

In the experiments, we used the character distribution of each path source in HTTP requests as the attribute. Character distribution was first introduced for anomaly detection by Krüegel and Vigna [12] who computed them in a coarse way. The test results in [12] showed that even the attributes of coarse character distribution can detect most web attacks. Wang et al. [3] used full character distribution of payload of network traffic for anomaly network detection and the results also showed its effectiveness.

There are 256 instances of ASCII code in total but only 95 instances of ASCII code (between 33 and 127) appear in the HTTP request. The character distribution is computed as the frequency of each ASCII code in the path source of HTTP requests. As a consequence, each HTTP request (data item) is represented by a vector of 95 dimensions. The intrusion detection aims at identifying whether an item is normal or anomalous.

KDD 1999 data. In order to extensively evaluate our methods, we also used KDD 1999 data in the experiments. The raw KDD 1999 data contains traffic in a simulated military network that consists of hundreds of hosts. It has been processed into about 5 million connection records by Lee et al. [2] as part of the UCI KDD archive [22]. A connection is a sequence of TCP packets starting and ending at some well defined times, between which data flows from a source IP address to a target IP address under some well defined protocol [22]. In the data set, each network connection is labeled as either normal, or as an exactly one specific kind of attack. The network connection data contains 41 attributes among which 34 are numeric and 7 are alphanumeric. Only the 34 numeric attributes were used in the experiments. Each connection in the data set is thus transformed into a 34-dimensional vector as data input for detection.

4.2   Experiment Settings

For exemplar extraction, in order to generate different number of exemplars, the preference parameter $(-s^*)$ of AP needs to be set to various values. In the experiments, we set $(l * N^2)$-th largest value of the N^2 similarities between all pairs of items as $-s^*$ and set $l = 1/2, 1/4, 1/8, 1/16, 1/32, 1/64$, respectively. For k-means, to facilitate comparison, we set k as the same number of exemplars generated by AP to generate clusters. For attribute abstraction with PCA, we used ratio α as 99.9%, as it is most desirable based on our previous findings in [10]. For k-NN, we set $k = 1$ as it is a good choice for the detection [27] and it is thus the *de facto* Nearest Neighbor (NN). We made our own MATLAB programs for all the algorithms except SVM for which LibSVM tools [34] were used.

The two data sets, the number of exemplars generated with AP as well as the number of attributes abstracted with PCA from their corresponding training data are described in Table 2. In this paper, we report the exemplars extracted, detection speed as well as the detection accuracy.

Table 2. Two data sets and their exemplars generated from training data with AP

Data	# training items	# test items	# attributes origin	with PCA	# exemplars $l = 1/2$	$l = 1/4$	$l = 1/8$	$l = 1/16$	$l = 1/32$	$l = 1/64$
HTTP	7000	33095	95	66	420	529	613	692	781	975
KDD99	7000	93576	34	23	191	327	614	1172	/	/

4.3   Exemplars Extracted

For AP based exemplar extraction, an exemplar is a factual data item (i.e., a http request). For example, two exemplars extracted by AP based on the HTTP traffic are shown as:

```
1. /ariana/download_publications.php?type=article&reference=lafarge_sfpt05&file=pdf
2. /acacia/project/edccaeteras/wakka.php?wiki=ActionOrphanedPages/referrers
```

The two exemplars are clearly shown to represent a set of similar http requests in the training data. The attributes abstracted by PCA, however, are not the original ones as they represent attributes in a new feature space.

4.4   Detection Efficiency

For exemplar extraction, the computation time for generating exemplars, for training the models and for the detection is summarized in Table 3. All the experiments were carried out on a machine with Intel Dual Core 2.80GHz and memory 4GB.

Table 3. The computing time (sec.) for anomaly detection **with or without exemplar extraction process** (AP and k-means)

Data set	training data	time for generating exemplars		time for anomaly detection		
		AP	k-means	k-NN	PCA	SVM
HTTP	7000 items	/	/	592	29	101
	420 exemplars	139	190	29	0.3	5
	529 exemplars	141	365	38	0.3	6
	613 exemplars	158	215	45	0.3	8
	692 exemplars	158	408	48	0.3	8
	781 exemplars	176	495	56	0.3	10
	975 exemplars	162	307	67	0.7	12
KDD99	7000 items	/	/	989	11	74
	191 exemplars	548	302	27	0.3	2
	327 exemplars	557	414	46	0.3	3
	614 exemplars	611	603	83	0.3	6
	1172 exemplars	753	1023	153	0.6	12

It is seen from Tables 3 that the detection efficiency for all the detection algorithms is significantly improved by the process of exemplar extraction. For example, while using all the data for building the detection models, k−NN needed 592 seconds for the detection of web attacks, however, it only required 29 seconds for the detection using AP for extracting 420 exemplars out of 7000 items. In most cases AP is more efficient than k-means for generating exemplars.

4.5   Comparative Results on HTTP Traffic

The comparative results on http traffic are shown in Figures 1 in terms of ROC (Receiver Operating Characteristic) Curves. There is a tradeoff between the detection rates and false positive rates, the pairs of which are obtained by adjusting the threshold for *anomaly index* computed in each intrusion detection methods. It is seen that using a smaller set of exemplars, the detection accuracy remains similar, and even improves in many cases. Normally as the number of exemplar increases, the detection accuracy is improved too. However, as shown in the Figure, selecting approximately 10 percent of the total number of data items as exemplars gives satisfied detection results. In many cases it performs better than using all the data.

AP has similar performance with k-means in exemplar extraction for anomaly intrusion detection. Regarding the three detection methods, k-NN is shown to be more effective than PCA and SVM for the detection on HTTP traffic.

4.6   Comparative Results on KDD 1999 Data

The comparative results on KDD 1999 data are shown in Figure 2. It is observed from the Figure that exemplar extraction is a good tool. Selecting a smaller set of exemplars for training does not affect detection accuracy and in some cases it even improves the detection accuracy. The results on KDD 1999 data are

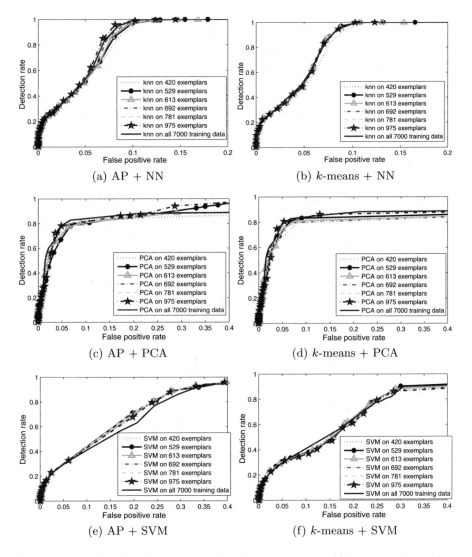

(a) AP + NN

(b) k-means + NN

(c) AP + PCA

(d) k-means + PCA

(e) AP + SVM

(f) k-means + SVM

Fig. 1. Competitive Results on http traffic with exemplar extraction and with attribute abstraction

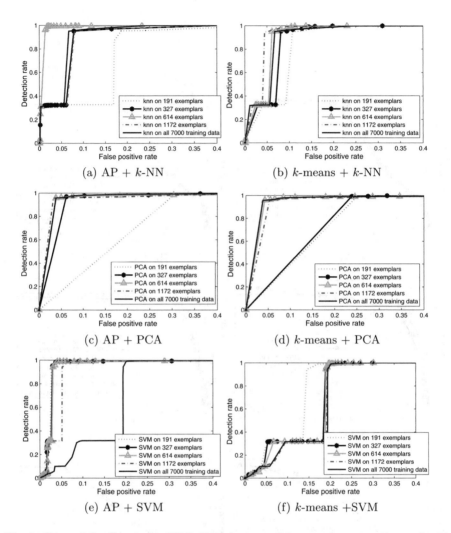

Fig. 2. Competitive Results on KDD 1999 data set with exemplar extraction and with attribute abstraction

consistent with those on HTTP traffic. It is also shown that k-NN is better than PCA and SVM for anomaly detection.

5   Concluding Remarks

Data for intrusion detection becomes increasingly massive. Building a lightweight intrusion detection model to achieve real-time detection therefore becomes an important challenge. In this paper, we abstract audit data by finding a small set of representative exemplars from a large set of original data. The exemplars are then fed as data input for training the detection models. The detection efficiency is hence significantly improved for two reasons: first, because only a smaller set of data needs to be processed for the training, and second, because the detection process only needs to be based on a compressed model. In order to have a comparative view of different strategies of data abstraction in intrusion detection, in this paper we also introduced PCA to abstract attributes for anomaly detection.

PCA is a widely used attribute abstraction algorithm which performs a coordinate rotation that aligns the transformed axes with the directions of maximum variance. The new coordinates can be regarded as the new attributes abstracted from the original ones. However, PCA is effective only when the observed data has a high signal-to-noise ratio that the principal components with larger variance correspond to interesting dynamics and lower ones correspond to noise. Therefore it does not work in cases where the data items are all centralized into a circle. For such circumstances, exemplar extraction can be more suitable as it works through clustering. By this, similar data items are grouped together and form a cluster in which the most representative factual data item is selected as an exemplar.

Exemplar extraction is necessary for intrusion detection, as it not only reduces reduplicate data items that usually exist in the original data set, but also reduces similar ones. In this way detection efficiency is significantly improved. To give a figure of the existed duplicates in the data sets we used in our experiments, in KDD 1999 data, there were only 1172 unique data items out of 7000 training items. Similarly in HTTP traffic data, the number of unique items were 2308 out of 7000. In this paper, we employed a newly developed clustering algorithm Affinity Propagation (AP) [17] to extract real exemplars from original data and used traditional k-means clustering method to generate average exemplars.

A real HTTP traffic data set collected in our institute as well as KDD 1999 data have been used to validate the two strategies of data abstraction. The extensive experimental results confirm that both AP and k-means improve the detection performance in terms of efficiency and effectiveness through exemplar extraction. In addition, AP compared to k-means has two major advantages. First, AP extracts factual exemplars from the data while k-means can only generate averaged ones. This is important because an exemplar has a physical significance in many cases, which in practice means, a set of real HTTP requests can be extracted directly and replaced the original ones. Second, AP does not need to define the number of clusters (exemplars) beforehand while k-means does. This is an important advantage because it is often difficult to have *a priori* knowledge for the data, especially for a very large amount of streaming data like HTTP traffic. The process of exemplar extraction behaves more robust than attribute abstraction with PCA. In order to enhance the detection performance, exemplar extraction is suggested to be made before building the detection models.

Our future work is summarized in two aspects: (1) using more attributes of the http traffic to improve the detection performance; (2) dealing with the problem of "concept drift" in audit data.

Acknowledgements

The authors thank European Research Consortium for Informatics and Mathematics (ERCIM) fellowship programme for the support.

References

1. Beale, J., Baker, A.R., Caswell, B.: Snort 2.1 Intrusion Detection, 2nd edn. Syngress Press (2004)
2. Lee, W., Stolfo, S.J., Mok, K.W.: A data mining framework for building intrusion detection models. In: IEEE S&P (1999)
3. Wang, K., Stolfo, S.J.: Anomalous payload-based network intrusion detection. In: Jonsson, E., Valdes, A., Almgren, M. (eds.) RAID 2004. LNCS, vol. 3224, pp. 203–222. Springer, Heidelberg (2004)
4. Wang, K., Cretu, G.F., Stolfo, S.J.: Anomalous payload-based worm detection and signature generation. In: Valdes, A., Zamboni, D. (eds.) RAID 2005. LNCS, vol. 3858, pp. 227–246. Springer, Heidelberg (2006)
5. Forrest, S., Hofmeyr, S.A., Somayaji, A., Longstaff, T.A.: A sense of self for unix processes. In: IEEE S&P (1996)
6. Guan, X., Wang, W., Zhang, X.: Fast intrusion detection based on a non-negative matrix factorization model. J. Network and f Applications 32(1), 31–44 (2009)
7. Wang, W., Guan, X., Zhang, X., Yang, L.: Profiling program behavior for anomaly intrusion detection based on the transition and frequency property of computer audit data. Computers & Security 25(7), 539–550 (2006)
8. Liao, Y., Vemuri, V.R.: Using text categorization techniques for intrusion detection. In: USENIX Security Symposium (2002)
9. Schonlau, M., Theus, M.: Detecting masquerades in intrusion detection based on unpopular commands. Inf. Process. Lett. 76(1-2) (2000)
10. Wang, W., Guan, X., Zhang, X.: Processing of massive audit data streams for real-time anomaly intrusion detection. Computer Communications 31(1), 58–72 (2008)
11. Ingham, K.L., Inoue, H.: Comparing anomaly detection techniques for http. In: Kruegel, C., Lippmann, R., Clark, A. (eds.) RAID 2007. LNCS, vol. 4637, pp. 42–62. Springer, Heidelberg (2007)
12. Krügel, C., Vigna, G.: Anomaly detection of web-based attacks. In: ACM CCS (2003)
13. Song, Y., Keromytis, A.D., Stolfo, S.J.: Spectrogram: A mixture-of-markov-chains model for anomaly detection in web traffic. In: NDSS (2009)
14. Robertson, W.K., Vigna, G., Krügel, C., Kemmerer, R.A.: Using generalization and characterization techniques in the anomaly-based detection of web attacks. In: NDSS
15. Brauckhoff, D., Salamatian, K., May, M.: A signal-processing view on packet sampling and anomaly detection. In: INFOCOM (2010)
16. Brauckhoff, D., Tellenbach, B., Wagner, A., Lakhina, A., May, M.: Impact of packet sampling on anomaly detection metrics. In: Internet Measurement Conference, IMC (2006)
17. Frey, B.J., Dueck, D.: Clustering by passing messages between data points. Science 315(5814), 972–976 (2007)

18. MacQueen, J.B.: Some methods for classification and analysis of multivariate observations. In: Proceedings of 5th Berkeley Symposium on Mathematical Statistics and Probability (1967)
19. Denning, D.E.: An intrusion-detection model. IEEE Trans. Software Eng. 13(2), 222–232 (1987)
20. Smaha, S.E.: Haystack: An intrusion detection system. In: Proceedings of the IEEE Fourth Aerospace Computer Security Applications Conference (1988)
21. Cretu, G.F., Stavrou, A., Locasto, M.E., Stolfo, S.J., Keromytis, A.D.: Casting out demons: Sanitizing training data for anomaly sensors. In: IEEE S&P (2008)
22. KDD-Data: Kdd cup 1999 data (1999),
    http://kdd.ics.uci.edu/databases/kddcup99/kddcup99.html
    (retrieved March 2009)
23. Shyu, M., Chen, S., Sarinnapakorn, K., Chang, L.: A novel anomaly detection scheme based on principal component classifier. In: IEEE Foundations and New Directions of Data Mining Workshop (2003)
24. Sung, A.H., Mukkamala, S.: Feature selection for intrusion detection using neural networks and support vector machines. In: 82nd Annual Meeting of the Transportation Research Board (2003)
25. Wang, W., Gombault, S., Guyet, T.: Towards fast detecting intrusions: using key attributes of network traffic. In: ICIMP (July 2008)
26. Li, Y., Lu, T.B., Guo, L., Tian, Z.H., Qi, L.: Optimizing network anomaly detection scheme using instance selection mechanism. In: Proceedings of the 28th IEEE Conference on Global Telecommunications, GLOBECOM 2009, Piscataway, NJ, USA, pp. 425–431. IEEE Press, Los Alamitos (2009)
27. Wang, W., Zhang, X., Gombault, S.: Constructing attribute weights from computer audit data for effective intrusion detection. J. Sys. and Soft. 82(12) (2009)
28. Schölkopf, B., Platt, J.C., Shawe-Taylor, J., Smola, A.J., Williamson, R.C.: Estimating the support of a high-dimensional distribution. Neural Computation 13(7), 1443–1471 (2001)
29. Liao, Y., Vemuri, V.R., Pasos, A.: Adaptive anomaly detection with evolving connectionist systems. J. Network and Computer Applications 30(1) (2007)
30. Manevitz, L.M., Yousef, M.: One-class svms for document classification. Journal of Machine Learning Research 2, 139–154 (2001)
31. Jolliffe, I.T.: Principal Component Analysis, 2nd edn. Springer, Berlin (2002)
32. Zhang, X., Furtlehner, C., Sebag, M.: Data streaming with affinity propagation. In: Daelemans, W., Goethals, B., Morik, K. (eds.) ECML PKDD 2008, Part II. LNCS (LNAI), vol. 5212, pp. 628–643. Springer, Heidelberg (2008)
33. McHugh, J.: Testing intrusion detection systems: a critique of the 1998 and 1999 darpa intrusion detection system evaluations as performed by lincoln laboratory. ACM Trans. Inf. Syst. Secur. 3(4), 262–294 (2000)
34. Chang, C.C., Lin, C.J.: LIBSVM: a library for support vector machines (2001), Software available at http://www.csie.ntu.edu.tw/~cjlin/libsvm

A Persistent Public Watermarking
of Relational Databases

Raju Halder and Agostino Cortesi

Dipartimento di Informatica
Università Ca' Foscari di Venezia, Italy
{halder,cortesi}@unive.it
http://www.unive.it

Abstract. In this paper, we propose a novel fragile and robust persistent watermarking scheme for relational databases that embeds both private and public watermarks where the former allows the owner to prove his ownership, while the latter allows any end-user to verify the correctness and originality of the data in the database without loss of strength and security. The public watermarking is based on a part of the database state which remains invariant under processing of the queries associated with the database, whereas the private watermarking is based on an appropriate form of the original database state, called *abstract database*, and the *semantics-based properties* of the data which remain invariant under processing of the associated queries.

Keywords: Watermarking, Databases, Abstraction.

1 Introduction

Most of the existing watermarking techniques [1,4,10,16] in the literature are private, meaning that they are based on some private parameters (*e.g.* a secret key). Only the authorized people (*e.g.* database owners) who know these private parameters are able to verify the watermark and prove their ownership of the database in case of any illegal redistribution, false ownership claim, theft etc. However, private watermarking techniques suffer from disclosure of the private parameters to dishonest people once the watermark is verified in presence of the public. With access to the private parameters, attackers can easily invalidate watermark detection either by removing watermarks from the protected data or by adding a false watermark to the non-watermarked data. In contrast, in public watermarking techniques [9,15], any end-user can verify the embedded watermark as many times as necessary without having any prior knowledge about any of the private parameters to ensure that they are using correct (not tampered) data coming from the original source. For instance, when a customer uses sensitive information such as currency exchange rates or stock prices, it is very important for him to ensure that the data are correct and coming from the original source.

S. Jha and A. Maturia (Eds.): ICISS 2010, LNCS 6503, pp. 216–230, 2010.
© Springer-Verlag Berlin Heidelberg 2010

There are many applications that need to provide both private and public watermarks so that the owner can verify any suspicious database to claim his ownership, while at the same time any end-user can verify the originality and integrity of the data without exposing any private parameters. However, the existing techniques in the literature are unable to provide both.

Digital watermarking for integrity verification is called fragile watermarking as compared to the robust watermarking for copyright protection [11]. Fragileness of public watermarking must be maintained when any end-user wants to verify the correctness of the data through it. Since the location of public watermark in the host data is public, robustness of it is a prime concern too. However, there exist no watermarking scheme in the literature that can provide both of robustness and fragileness.

The watermark verification phase in the existing techniques [4,10,15,16] completely relies on the content of the database. In other words, the success of the watermark detection is content dependent. *Benign Updates* or any other intensional processing of the database content may damage or distort the embedded watermark that results into an unsuccessful watermark detection. For instance, suppose a publisher is offering a 20% discount on the price of all articles. The modification of the price information may make the watermark detection phase almost infeasible if the price values are marked at bit-level or if any information (*viz*, hash value) is extracted based on this price information and used in the embedding phase. Therefore, most of the previous techniques are designed to face *Value Modification Attacks*, but are unable to resolve the persistency of the watermark under intentional allowed modifications.

In our previous work [6], we already introduced the notion of persistent watermark and discussed how to improve the existing techniques in terms of persistency of the watermark that serves as a way to recognize the integrity and ownership proof of the database bounded with a set of queries Q while allowing the evaluation of the database by queries in Q. In this paper, we go one step further, and we propose a novel fragile and robust persistent watermarking scheme that embeds both private and public watermarks where the former allows the owner to prove his ownership, while the latter allows any end-user to verify the correctness and originality of the data in the database without loss of strength and security. The public watermarking is based on a part of the database state which remains invariant under processing of the queries associated with the database, whereas the private watermarking is based on an appropriate form of the original database state, called *abstract database*, and the *semantics-based properties* of the data which remain invariant under the processing of the associated queries.

The structure of the paper is as follows: Section 2 recalls some basic concepts. In Section 3, we propose a combined persistent public and private watermarking scheme. In Section 4, we provide a brief discussions about the complexity of our algorithms and the relations with the existing techniques in the literature. Finally, we draw our conclusions in Section 5.

2   Basic Concepts

In this Section some basic concepts are recalled from the literature [5,6,8].

Persistent Watermark: Given a database dB and a set of applications interacting with the dB. Let Q be the set of queries issued by these applications. We denote the database model by a tuple $\langle dB, Q \rangle$. We do not make any restrictions on the operations used in Q (SELECT, UPDATE, DELETE, INSERT).

Let the initial state of dB be d_0. For the sake of simplicity, we assume that there is a unique sequence $d_1, d_2 \ldots, d_{n-1}$ of valid states of the dB reached when executing the queries of Q. Let W be the watermark that is embedded in state d_0. The watermark W is persistent $w.r.t.$ Q if we can extract and verify it blindly from any of the following $n - 1$ states successfully.

Definition 1 (Persistent Watermark)
Let $\langle dB, Q \rangle$ be a database model where Q is the set of queries associated with the database dB. Suppose the initial state of dB is d_0. The processing of the queries in Q over d_0 yield to a set of valid states $d_1, \ldots, d_{n-1}$. A watermark W embedded in state d_0 of dB is called persistent $w.r.t.$ Q if

$$\forall i \in [1..(n-1)], \quad verify(d_0, W) = verify(d_i, W)$$

where $verify(d, W)$ is a boolean function such that the probability of "$verify(d, W) = true$" is negligible if and only if W is not the watermark embedded in d.

Static versus Non-static Database States: Consider a database model $\langle dB, Q \rangle$ where Q is the set of queries associated with the database dB. For any state d_i, $i \in [0..(n-1)]$, we can partition the data cells in d_i into two parts $w.r.t.$ Q: *Static* and *Non-Static*. Static part contains those data cells of d_i that are not affected by the queries in Q at all, whereas the data cells in non-static part of d_i may change under processing of the queries in Q.

Let $CELL_{d_i}$ be the set of cells in state d_i of dB. We denote the set of static cells of d_i $w.r.t.$ Q by $STC_{d_i}^Q \subseteq CELL_{d_i}$. For each tuple $t \in d_i$ we denote the static part of it by $STC_t^Q \subseteq STC_{d_i}^Q$. Thus, $STC_{d_i}^Q = \bigcup_{t_j \in d_i} STC_{t_j}^Q$.

Now we discuss how to identify the static and non-static part of d_i $w.r.t.$ Q. As SELECT and INSERT statements in Q do not affect the existing data cells of d_i, they do not take part in determining static/non-static part at all. However, DELETE statement may delete some data cells form static or non-static part, resulting into a subset of it. Thus, if $STC_{d_i}^Q$ and $(CELL_{d_i} - STC_{d_i}^Q)$ represent static and non-static part of d_i $w.r.t.$ Q respectively, a subset of it remains invariant over all the n valid states $d_0, d_1, \ldots, d_{n-1}$ under processing of DELETE statements in Q. The UPDATE statements modify values of the data cells in non-static part only. Let ATT^{update} be the set of attributes of dB that are targeted by the UPDATE statements. Thus we can identify the set of cells $STC_{d_i}^Q$, $i \in [0..(n-1)]$ in state d_i corresponding to the attributes not in ATT^{update}, which remains invariant over all the n valid states.

Semantics-based Properties: Given a database state d_i, $i \in [0..(n-1)]$ of dB associated with a set of queries Q, we can identify some semantics-based properties of the data in d_i w.r.t. Q. These properties include $Intra-cell$ (IC), $Intra-tuple$ (IT) or $Intra-attribute\ among-tuples$ (IA) properties.

Intra-cell (IC) property: In this case individual data cells of a database state represents some specific properties of interests. Let the possible values of a cell corresponding to a attribute Z be $a \leq Z \leq b$ over all the valid states, where a and b represent integer values. The IC property can be represented by $[a, b]$ from the domain of intervals.

Intra-tuple (IT) property: An IT property is a property which is extracted based on inter-relationship between two or more attribute values in the same tuple. As an example, we may consider inter-relation between two attributes $basic\_price$ and $total\_price$ of a database containing commodity information where $total\_price$ includes $basic\_price$ plus a percentage of VAT of the $basic\_price$. This can be abstracted by a relational abstract domain, like the domain of octagons [13].

Intra-attribute among-tuples (IA) property: The IA property is obtained from the set of independent tuples in a relation. Examples of such property are: (i) in an employee database $\#male\ employee = \#female\ employee \pm 1$, where $\#$ denotes cardinality of a set, (ii) the average salary of male employees is greater than the average salary of female employees, (iii) the total number of female employees is greater than 3, etc. The first two can be abstracted by relational abstract domain, whereas the last one can be represented by interval $[3, +\infty]$.

We denote the set of semantics-based properties obtained this way from state d_i w.r.t. Q by $P_{d_i}^Q$. For each tuple $t \in d_i$ we denote the set of IC, IT properties by $P_t^Q = IC_t^Q \cup IT_t^Q \subseteq P_{d_i}^Q$. Note that IA property can not be determined at tuple level. Thus, $P_{d_i}^Q = \{\bigcup_{t_j \in d_i} (IC_{t_j}^Q \cup IT_{t_j}^Q)\} \cup IA_{d_i}^Q$, where $IA_{d_i}^Q$ represents $Intra-attribute\ among-tuples$ (IA) property in state d_i w.r.t. Q. Observe that $P_{d_i}^Q$ remains invariant over all the n valid states $d_0, d_1, \ldots, d_{n-1}$.

Abstract Database: In [5,8], we proposed a sound approximation technique for database query languages based on the Abstract Interpretation framework where the values of the concrete database are replaced by abstract values from abstract domains representing some specific properties of interests, resulting into an abstract database. We may distinguish partially abstract databases in contrast to fully abstract one, as in the former case only a subset of data in the database is abstracted. The abstract database provides a partial view of the data by disclosing properties rather than their exact content. Consider the employee database in Table 1(a) that consists of a single table emp. Table 1(b) depicts a partially abstract database consisting of $emp^\sharp$ which is obtained by abstracting basic and gross salaries of the employees in emp by elements from the domain of intervals.

Table 1. Concrete and corresponding partially abstract employee database

(a) The concrete table emp

eID	Name	Basic Sal (euro)	Gross Sal (euro)	Age	DNo
E001	Bob	1000	1900	48	2
E002	Alice	900	1685	29	1
E003	Matteo	1200	2270	58	2
E004	Tom	600	1190	30	2
E005	Marry	1350	2542.5	55	1

(b) The abstract table $emp^\sharp$

eID$^\sharp$	Name$^\sharp$	Basic Sal$^\sharp$ (euro)	Gross Sal$^\sharp$ (euro)	Age$^\sharp$	DNo$^\sharp$
E001	Bob	[1000, 1300]	[1900, 2470]	48	2
E002	Alice	[900, 1170]	[1685, 2190.5]	29	1
E003	Matteo	[1200, 1560]	[2270, 2951]	58	2
E004	Tom	[600, 780]	[1190, 1547]	30	2
E005	Marry	[1350, 1755]	[2542.5, 3305.25]	55	1

Definition 2 (Abstract Database). *Let dB be a database. The database $dB^\sharp = \alpha(dB)$ where α is the abstraction function, is said to be an abstract version of dB if there exist a representation function γ, called concretization function such that for each tuple $\langle x_1, x_2, \ldots, x_n \rangle \in dB$ there exist a tuple $\langle y_1, y_2, \ldots, y_n \rangle \in dB^\sharp$ such that $\forall i \in [1 \ldots n]$, $x_i \in \gamma(y_i) \vee x_i \in id(y_i)$.*

Watermarking based on partially abstract databases which are obtained by abstracting the data cells in non-static part $(CELL_d - STC_d^Q)$ only, results into a content-independent persistent watermark. This is because although the exact values in $(CELL_d - STC_d^Q)$ may change under processing of the queries in Q, their properties represented by abstract values remain invariant.

3   Persistent Public/Private Watermarking

In the rest of the paper, we do not restrict ourself to any particular data type of the attributes. Attributes of any type including numeric, boolean, character, or any other can play roles in the public as well as private watermarking phase. Consider a database $dB(PK, A_0, A_1, A_2, \ldots, A_{\beta-1})$ in state d associated with a set of queries Q, where PK is the primary key. We divide the attribute set $\{A_0, A_1, A_2, \ldots, A_{\beta-1}\}$ into two parts *w.r.t.* Q: *Static attribute set* $A_{static}^Q = \{A_0^s, A_1^s, \ldots, A_{p-1}^s\}$ and *Non-static attribute set* $A_{var}^Q = \{A_0^v, A_1^v, \ldots, A_{q-1}^v\}$, where $p + q = \beta$. The set of static data cells STC_d^Q corresponds to static attribute set A_{static}^Q, whereas the set of non-static data cells $(CELL_d - STC_d^Q)$ corresponds to non-static attribute set A_{var}^Q. Although the primary key PK may be static in nature, we exclude it from the set A_{static}^Q and mention it separately in the rest of the paper. Of course, any change on the values of the primary key will be detected in the verification phase.

Public watermark is embedded into a known location of the host data with known methods to guarantee its public detectability. We identify most significant bit (MSB) positions of the data cells in STC_d^Q as the location for public watermark. We avoid non-static data cells because their values keep changing under processing of the queries in Q. This ensures the persistency of the public watermark. Since the public watermark in the host data is visible to all end-users, it is highly possible that attackers try to remove or distort it. We achieve robustness of the public watermark by choosing only the most significant bit positions of the host data as the location for public watermark: any major malicious change of the static portion of the database will be detected in the verification phase. Moreover, our scheme is designed to be fragile by using a cryptographic hash value of each tuple so as to detect and locate any modification when attackers try to modify the data in the database while keeping the watermark untouched.

The **private watermarking** is based on two invariants of the database states: *semantics-based properties* and *partially abstract database*, so as to maintain the persistency of the watermark under processing of the queries associated with the database. The security of private watermarking relies on the secret key as well as the level of abstraction used. Attackers do not know which properties are used to abstract the database. In addition, private watermarking is also based on MSBs of the attribute values. We assume the secret key to be large enough to thwart Brute force attack.

It is worthwhile to mention that, unlike existing techniques [1,16,9,2], the verification phase of the proposed scheme is deterministic. Since the watermarking does not introduce any distortion to the underlying data, it is distortion-free. However, in our scheme we do not allow any schema transformations.

3.1 Public Watermarking

The overall architecture of the public watermarking phase is depicted in Figure 1. It consists of a single procedure, called **GenPublicKey**. The inputs of **GenPublicKey** are the database $dB(PK, A_0, A_1, A_2, \ldots, A_{\beta-1})$ in state d associated with a set of queries Q, the signature S of the database owner which is known to all end-users, and a parameter ξ representing the number of most significant bits (MSBs) available in attributes. The procedure generates a table $B(PK, b_0, \ldots, b_{p-1})$ where PK is the primary key, p is the number of attributes in A_{static}^Q and $\forall j \in [0..(p-1)]$: b_j contains either 1 or 0. The binary table B is treated as public key and made available to all end-users. Later, when any end-user wants to verify the source of a suspicious database, he uses B as the public key to generate and verify the embedded signature S.

The algorithm of **GenPublicKey** is depicted in Figure 2. Let us describe it in details.

Let $|S|$ be the length of the signature S in binary form. We divide S into m blocks $\{S_0, S_1, \ldots, S_{m-1}\}$ each of length p, where p is the number of attributes in A_{static}^Q and $m = \lceil \frac{|S|}{p} \rceil$. If the length of the last block is less than p, we append 0s to make it of length p.

For each tuple $t \in d$, the algorithm generates an hash value h in binary form of length p from its primary key and its static part $STC_t^Q = \{t.A_0^s, \ldots, t.A_{p-1}^s\}$. We exclude the dynamic part of the tuples in computing hash because it keeps

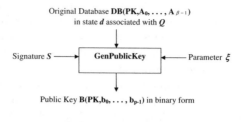

Performed by: Database Owner

Fig. 1. Overall architecture of Public Watermarking Phase

changing under processing of the queries. While computing hash, we assume that it is almost infeasible to generate same hash value from two different messages.

The $HASH$ function we might use takes a parameter p and generates a binary hash value of length p: we can use Merkle-Damgård's Meta method [12] where the length of the initial hash value and the length of each block of the binary string obtained from "$t.PK||t.A_0^s||\ldots||t.A_{p-1}^s$" (where $||$ stands for concatenation operation) is considered to be p.

Algo:	GenPublicKey
Input:	Database $dB(PK, A_0, A_1, A_2, \ldots, A_{\beta-1})$ in state d associated with a set of queries Q, Owner's signature S, Parameter ξ representing the no. of MSBs available in attributes.
Output:	A publicly available binary table $B(PK, b_0, \ldots, b_{p-1})$.
1.	Identify $A_{static}^Q = \{A_0^s, A_1^s, \ldots, A_{p-1}^s\}$
2.	Compute $m = \lceil \frac{|S|}{p} \rceil$, where $|S|$ denotes length of signature S in binary form and p=no. of attributes in A_{static}^Q
3.	Split the signature S into m blocks $\{S_0, S_2, \ldots, S_{m-1}\}$ where $|S_i| = p$
4.	FOR each tuples $t \in d$ DO
5.	$\quad h = HASH(t.PK||t.A_0^s||\ldots||t.A_{p-1}^s,\ p)$
6.	$\quad i = PRSG(t.PK)\%m$
7.	$\quad w = h \otimes S_i$
8.	$\quad$ Generate a binary tuple r in $B(PK, b_0, \ldots, b_{p-1})$ with $r.PK = t.PK$
9.	$\quad$ FOR $j = 0 \ldots p-1$ DO
10.	$\quad\quad k = HASH(t.PK||t.A_j^s)\%\xi$
11.	$\quad\quad r.b_j = k^{th}$ MSB of $t.A_j^s \otimes w[j]$
12.	$\quad$ END FOR
13.	END FOR
14.	Return B

Fig. 2. Algorithm for Signature Embedding and Public Key Generation

Using pseudorandom sequence generator $PRSG$ (*e.g.* Linear Feedback Shift Register [7]) seeded by tuple's primary key, we identify which group the tuple belongs to. If the tuple t belongs to i^{th} group, we compute $w = h \otimes S_i$ where h is the binary hash value of length p and S_i is the ith block of the binary signature S.

In other words, we embed i^{th} block S_i of signature S into all tuples that belong to i^{th} group. This ensures the existence of the signature during verification phase if there exist at least one marked tuple in each group after processing of DELETE operations. Observe that w is of length p.

Corresponding to tuple t, we now create a binary tuple r in $B(PK, b_0, \ldots, b_{p-1})$ whose primary key is same as that of t, $i.e.$ $r.PK = t.PK$. For each static attribute $A_j^s \in A_{static}^Q$ where $j = 0, \ldots, (p-1)$, we obtain a MSB bit position k in the corresponding data cell $t.A_j^s$ by computing $k = HASH(t.PK \| t.A_j^s)\%\xi$ where ξ is the number of MSBs available in A_j^s. The value of the jth attribute b_j of r is, thus, $r.b_j = k^{th}$ MSB of $t.A_j^s \otimes w[j]$.

We perform similar operations for all tuples in state d of dB, and finally we get a binary table $B(PK, b_0, \ldots, b_{p-1})$ consisting of a set of binary tuples generated this way. This binary table B is then made publicly available and treated as public key which is later used by any end-user to verify the embedded signature S.

Signature Verification. Figure 3 depicts the overall architecture of signature verification phase performed by end-users. The procedure **PublicVerify** takes a suspicious database $dB(PK, A_0, \ldots, A_{\beta-1})$ in a different state d' as input, and generates an intermediate binary table $B'(PK, a_0, \ldots, a_{p-1})$. Based on this intermediate binary table $B'(PK, a_0, \ldots, a_{p-1})$ and the public key $B(PK, b_0, \ldots, b_{p-1})$ which is generated by the database owner in watermarking phase, the procedure **ExtractSig** extracts a signature S'. Finally, **MatchSig** compares S' with the original signature S. If it matches, the verification claim is true, otherwise false.

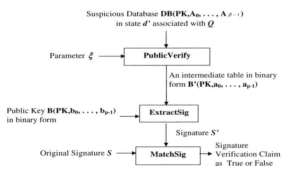

Fig. 3. Overall architecture of publicly Signature Verification phase

The algorithms of the procedures **PublicVerify** and **ExtractSig** are depicted in Figure 4 and 5 respectively. For each tuple $t' \in d'$, the algorithm **PublicVerify** generates a binary tuple r' in $B'(PK, a_1, \ldots, a_{p-1})$ whose primary key is equal to the primary key of t', $i.e.$ $r'.PK = t'.PK$. The binary values of the attributes a_j, $j \in [0..(p-1)]$ in r' are obtained as follows: (i) Compute binary hash value

h of length p from the primary key $t'.PK$ and static part $STC_{t'}^Q = \{t'.A_0^s,$
$\ldots, t'.A_{p-1}^s\}$ in similar way as in algorithm **GenPublicKey**, (ii) Extract k^{th}
MSB from $t'.A_j^s$ in similar way as in algorithm **GenPublicKey**, (iii) Compute
$a_j = k^{th}$ MSB of $t'.A_j^s \otimes h[j]$, where $h[j]$ represents j^{th} bit of h. In this way,
the algorithm generates a set of binary tuples from the tuples in state d', and
collection of these binary tuples forms the table B'.

Algo:	**PublicVerify**
Input:	Database $dB(PK, A_0, A_1, A_2, \ldots, A_{\beta-1})$ in state d' associated with Q, Parameter ξ, Public key $B(PK, b_0, \ldots, b_{p-1})$, Owner's Signature S.
Output:	Signature Verification Claim as True or False.

1.	Identify $A_{static}^Q = \{A_0^s, A_1^s, \ldots, A_{p-1}^s\}$
2.	FOR each tuples $t' \in d'$ Do
3.	$\quad h = HASH(t'.PK || t'.A_0^s || \ldots || t'.A_{p-1}^s, p)$
4.	$\quad$ Construct a tuple r' in $B'(PK, a_0, \ldots, a_{p-1})$ such that $r'.PK = t'.PK$
5.	$\quad$ FOR $j = 0 \ldots p-1$ DO
6.	$\quad\quad k = HASH(t'.PK, t'.A_j^s) \% \xi$
7.	$\quad\quad r'.a_j = k^{th}$ MSB in $t'.A_j^s \otimes h[j]$
8.	$\quad$ END FOR
9.	END FOR
10.	$S' = \textbf{ExtractSig}(B, B')$
11.	Return **MatchSig**(S, S')

Fig. 4. Algorithm to Extract and verify Signature

Procedure **PublicVerify** then calls another procedure **ExtractSig**, and
passes the binary table B' and the public key B (generated by the owner in
watermarking phase). **ExtractSig** finds the pairs of tuples (r, r') where $r \in B$
and $r' \in B'$ such that their primary keys are same $i.e.$ $r.PK = r'.PK$. It then
performs attribute-wise XOR $i.e.$ $r.b_j \otimes r'.a_j$ for all $j \in [0..(p-1)]$, excluding
the primary key attribute, and concatenate them to obtain a binary string str.
If the tuple r and r' belongs to i^{th} group which is determined from the pseudo
random sequence generator $PRSG$ seeded by $r.PK$ or $r'.PK$, the corresponding
str denotes i^{th} block S_i' of a signature S'. This way we can collect all strings str
from the tuples belonging to the ith group and put them into the buffer buff$[i]$.
If no tampering occurred, all strings in buff$[i]$ will be same and represent S_i'.
However, when data is tampered, some strings str in buff$[i]$ may be different
from the others. In such case, function $MajorityVote()$ returns the string with
maximum match. In this way, we can determine $S_0', \ldots, S_{m-1}'$ by extracting str
from the tuples belonging to m different groups. By concatenating them, finally
we get a signature S'. The procedure **MatchSig** returns true when S' matches
with the original signature S, otherwise it returns False.

Example 1. Consider the employee database of Table 1(a) where eID is the
primary key. Suppose the set of queries Q associated with the database are only
able to increase the basic and gross salary of employees by at most 30%. As only

Algo:	ExtractSig
Input:	Public key $B(PK, b_0, \ldots, b_{p-1})$ and Binary table $B'(PK, a_0, \ldots, a_{p-1})$
Output:	Signature S'.
1.	Find binary tuple $r \in B$ and $r' \in B'$ such that $r.PK == r'.PK$
2.	FOR all pair (r, r') DO
3.	$\quad str = NULL$
4.	$\quad$ For $j = 0 \ldots p-1$ DO
5.	$\quad\quad$ Perform $str = str \| r.b_j \otimes r'.a_j$
6.	$\quad i = PRSG(r.PK)\%m$
7.	$\quad \text{buff}[i] \leftarrow str$
8.	END FOR
9.	FOR $i = 0 \ldots m-1$ DO
10.	$\quad S'_i = MajorityVote(\text{buff}[i])$
11.	END FOR
12.	Return $S' = S'_0 \| S'_1 \| \ldots \| S'_i \| \ldots \| S'_{m-1}$

Fig. 5. Algorithm to Extract Signature

the basic and gross salary can possibly be modified by the queries, we get A^Q_{static} = {*Name, Age, Dno*} and A^Q_{var}={*Basic Sal, Gross Sal*}.

Let the signature of the database owner be S = "RAJU" which is public and known to all end-users. By concatenating the ASCII codes of the characters in S, we get the binary representation of S as 01010010010000010100101001010101. Since $|S| = 32$ and the number of static attributes in A^Q_{static} is p=3, we divide S into $m = \lceil \frac{|S|}{p} \rceil = \lceil \frac{32}{3} \rceil = 11$ blocks each of length 3, *i.e.* 010 100 100 100 000 101 001 010 010 101 010. Since the last block contains only 2 bit, we append a 0 to make it of length 3.

Consider the tuple $t = \langle E001, Bob, 1000, 1900, 48, 2 \rangle$. The primary key of t is $t.eID = E001$ and the static part of t is $STC^Q_t = \langle t.Name, t.Age, t.Dno \rangle = \langle Bob, 48, 2 \rangle$. By following Step 5 of the algorithm **GenPublicKey**, let the hypothetical binary hash value of length $p = 3$ be $h = HASH(E001 \| Bob \| 48 \| 2, 3) = 001$, obtained from its primary key $t.eID$ and its static part STC^Q_t. Based on the random value generated from $PRSG$ seeded by $t.eID$ (Step 6), suppose we determine that t belongs to the second group *i.e.* $i = 2$. Therefore, we compute $w = h \otimes S_2 = 001 \otimes 100 = 101$ in Step 7.

In Step 8, corresponding to t we create a binary tuple r in $B(PK, b_0, b_1, b_2)$ with $r.PK = t.eID = E001$. Suppose in Step 10, for each of the three static attribute values $t.Name$ = "Bob", $t.Age$ = "48" and $t.Dno$ = "2" we get the value of k as 2, 3 and 1 respectively (assuming ξ equal to 4). Let 0, 1 and 1 be the 2nd MSB of "Bob", the 3rd MSB of "48" and the 1st MSB of "2" respectively. Therefore in Step 11, we compute $r.b_0 = 0 \otimes 1 = 1$, $r.b_1 = 1 \otimes 0 = 1$ and $r.b_2 = 1 \otimes 1 = 0$. This way we get the binary tuple $r = \langle E001, 1, 1, 0 \rangle$. We do the same for other tuples in state d, and finally we obtain a binary table B which is then made publicly available.

Now we illustrate the verification phase. Consider the tuple $t' = \langle E001, Bob, 1000, 1900, 48, 2 \rangle$. In Step 3 of the algorithm **PublicVerify**, we compute a binary

Algo:	**PrivateWatermark**
Input:	Database $dB(PK, A_0, \dots, A_{\beta-1})$ in state d bounded with a set of queries Q, Secret key K, Abstraction function α.
Output:	A private binary watermark $PW(PK, c_0, \dots, c_{\beta-1}, p_0, p_1, p_2)$.
1.	Obtain Partially Abstract Database $dB^\sharp(PK^\sharp, A_0^\sharp, \dots, A_{\beta-1}^\sharp)$ in state $d^\sharp$ by abstracting non-static part $(CELL_d - STC_d^Q)$ only
2.	Determine $IA_{d^\sharp}^Q$
3.	FOR each tuple $t^\sharp \in d^\sharp$ DO
4.	Construct tuple r in PW with primary key $r.PK = t^\sharp.PK^\sharp$
5.	Determine $IC_{t^\sharp}^Q$, $IT_{t^\sharp}^Q$
6.	$r.p_0 = g_{encode}^p(IC_{t^\sharp}^Q)$
7.	$r.p_1 = g_{encode}^p(IT_{t^\sharp}^Q)$
8.	$r.p_2 = g_{encode}^p(IA_{d^\sharp}^Q)$
9.	FOR (i=0; i< β; i=i+1) DO
10.	val= $G_i(K \circ t^\sharp.PK^\sharp \circ t^\sharp.A_0^\sharp \circ \dots \circ t^\sharp.A_{\beta-1}^\sharp)$
11.	$j = val\%(no.\ of\ attributes\ in\ t^\sharp)$
12.	$r.c_i$= (MSB of jth attribute in $t^\sharp$)
13.	delete the jth attribute from $t^\sharp$
14.	END FOR
15.	END FOR
16.	Return PW;

Fig. 6. Private Watermarking Algorithm

hash value h of length $p = 3$ in similar way, and we obtain $h = 001$. We now construct a binary tuple r' in $B'(PK, a_0, a_1, a_2)$ as follows: (i) $r'.PK = t'.eID = E001$, (ii) for attribute values "Bob", "48" and "2", we get MSB position k as 2, 3 and 1 respectively. Thus, $a_0=0 \otimes 0 = 0$, $a_1=1 \otimes 0 = 1$ and $a_2=1 \otimes 1 = 0$, and the binary tuple r' in $B'(PK, a_0, a_1, a_2)$ is $\langle E001, 0, 1, 0 \rangle$.

When we call the procedure **ExtractSig**, it finds two binary tuples $r = \langle E001, 1, 1, 0 \rangle \in B$ and $r' = \langle E001, 0, 1, 0 \rangle \in B'$, and it generates the string $str = 1 \otimes 0 || 1 \otimes 1 || 0 \otimes 0 = 100$. Since the tuples r and r' belong to the 2nd group which is determined from the pseudorandom sequence generator seeded by $r.PK = E001$, we get that the string $str = 100$ represents the 2nd block S_2' of a signature S'. In similar way we can extract all 11 blocks $S_0', \dots, S_{10}'$ of S' from the tuples in d' belonging to 11 different groups, and by concatenating them we get 01010010010000010100101001010101010 which is same as the original signature $S = $ "RAJU".

3.2   Private Watermarking

The private watermarking algorithm **PrivateWatermark** is depicted in Figure 6. The inputs of the algorithm are the original database $dB(PK, A_0, A_1, \dots, A_{\beta-1})$ in state d bounded with a set of queries Q, a secret key K, and the abstract function α. It generates a private binary watermark PW whose schema is $PW(PK, c_0, \dots, c_{\beta-1}, p_0, p_1, p_2)$.

The algorithm generates a partially abstract database state $d^\sharp$ from the original state d by abstracting the data cells belonging to the non-static part $(CELL_d - STC_d^Q)$ only. For each tuple $t^\sharp \in d^\sharp$, the algorithm generates a tuple r in $PW(PK, c_0, \ldots, c_{\beta-1}, p_0, p_1, p_2)$ whose primary key is equal to the primary key of $t^\sharp$ just to identify the tuples in PW uniquely and to perform matching in the verification phase. Note that as the primary key attribute is static in nature we never abstract its values. The algorithm, then, adds three values for the attributes p_0, p_1 and p_2 in r that correspond to the encoded values of IC, IT properties for $t^\sharp$ and encoded value of IA property for the whole database state $d^\sharp$, where g^p_{encode} represents an encoding function (e.g. minimal perfect hash function). G_i represents a pseudorandom sequence generator that returns i^{th} random value val when it is seeded by the attribute values of $t^\sharp$ including its primary key, and the secret key K. For all i from 0 to $\beta - 1$, val chooses an attribute randomly in $t^\sharp$ excluding the primary key and consider its MSB as the binary value for c_i in r. While computing the seed value for G_i or extracting MSBs, if there is any problem with abstract form of the values we can use its encoded form too. For instance, we can encode any interval by using the Chinese Remainder Theorem [14].

Observe that since the binary tuples in PW are constructed from semantics-based properties and partially abstract database information, the private watermark PW is invariant under processing of the queries in Q. The inputs of the verification algorithm are the database in state d' bounded with Q, the secret key K, the abstract function α, and the output is a binary table PW'. We use a boolean function $match(PW, PW')$ to compare PW' with the original private watermark PW which is obtained in the private watermarking phase. Note that the function $match(PW, PW')$ compares tuple by tuple taking into account the primary key of the tuples in PW and PW'. As tuples may be deleted from or added to the initial state d and yield to a different state d', only those tuples whose primary keys are common in both PW and PW' are compared. If $match(PW, PW') = True$, then the claim of the ownership is true, otherwise it is false. Observe that the verification phase is deterministic rather than probabilistic [9], as we compare and verify tuples in PW' against the tuples in PW with the same primary key only, and the binary values of the attributes in PW are invariant. Observe that there is an obvious tradeoff between the level of abstraction of the non-static part and the strength of the robustness of the private watermarking.

Example 2. Consider the database consisting of table emp with eID as the primary key in Table 1(a) where we determine that $A^Q_{static} = \{Name, Age, Dno\}$ and $A^Q_{var} = \{Basic\ Sal, Gross\ Sal\}$ w.r.t. the queries that are only able to increase the basic and gross salary of employees by at most 30%.

The partially abstract table $emp^\sharp$ is shown in Table 1(b) where data cells corresponding to the non-static attribute set A^Q_{var} are abstracted by elements from the domain of intervals. Consider an abstract tuple $t^\sharp$, say, $\langle E002, Alice,$ $[900, 1170], [1685, 2190.5], 29, 1\rangle$ in $emp^\sharp$. Corresponding to $t^\sharp$ we create a tuple r in watermark table $PW(PK, c_0, \ldots, c_{\beta-1}, p_0, p_1, p_2)$ with $r.PK = E002$.

In $t^\sharp$, the abstract values of the basic and gross salary are $[900, 1170]$ and $[1685, 2190.5]$ respectively. These abstract values represent IC properties for $t^\sharp$. The relation between two attributes $Basic\ Sal^\sharp$ and $Gross\ Sal^\sharp$ can be represented, for instance, by the following inequation: $Gross\ Sal^\sharp \geq \frac{(165 \times Basic\ Sal^\sharp)}{100} +$ 200, assuming that $Gross\ Sal^\sharp$ includes $Basic\ Sal^\sharp$, 65% of the $Basic\ Sal^\sharp$ as PF, HRA etc and minimum of 200 euro as incentive. Thus, the IT property can be obtained by abstracting the above relation by the elements from the domain of polyhedra [3] $i.e.$ by the linear equation just mentioned. The IA property may be: "The number of employees in every department is more than 2". This can also be represented by $[3, +\infty]$ in the domain of intervals. Suppose after encoding these three properties, we obtain the encoded values k_1, k_2, k_3. Therefore, the values of the attributes p_0, p_1, p_2 in r will be k_1, k_2, k_3 respectively.

Suppose the random selection of the attributes in $t^\sharp$ based on the random value generated by the pseudorandom sequence generator yields to the selection order as follows: $\langle [1685, 2190.5], 1, 29, [900, 1170], Alice \rangle$. We choose MSB from these attribute values in this order. Note that for abstract values (represented by intervals) we may extract MSB from its encoded values obtained by using Chinese Remainder Theorem. Let the extracted MSBs be 0, 1, 1, 0, 1 respectively. Thus the tuple r in PW would be $\langle E002, 0, 1, 1, 0, 1, k_1, k_2, k_3 \rangle$.

After performing similar operations for all the tuples, the watermark PW is generated.

4   Discussions

The time complexity to generate the public key B depends only on the number of tuples in the original database linearly, whereas the time complexity to generate the private watermark PW depends on the the number of tuples in the original database as well as the complexity of the abstraction operation used in private watermarking phase. That is, the time complexity of the algorithms **GenPublicKey** and **PrivateWatermark** are $O(\eta)$ and $O(\eta \times \mu)$ respectively, where η is the number of tuples in the original database and μ is the complexity of the abstraction operation applied to tuples' values.

Given a database $dB(PK, A_0, A_1, A_2, \ldots, A_{\beta-1})$, the number of attributes in public watermark B is $p + 1$, where p is the cardinality of A_{static}^Q. Suppose η is the number of tuples in the original database state. The total number of cells in public watermark B is, thus, $(p + 1) \times \eta$. If σ is the number of bits required to represent the primary key, the total number of bits in B is $(\sigma + p) \times \eta$. Thus, the space complexity can be represented by $O(\eta)$.

Similarly we can show that the total number of bits in the private watermark PW is $(\nu + \beta) \times \eta$ where ν is the total number of bits required to represent the primary key and the three semantics-based properties p_0, p_1, p_2, and η is the number of tuples in the original database state. Thus, in this case also the space complexity can be represented by $O(\eta)$.

Before concluding, let us briefly discuss the properties of our proposal and relate them with the existing techniques in the literature.

Our proposed public and private watermarking scheme has the following properties: (i) It is blind, (ii) It does not introduce any distortions to the underlying data, and thus never degrades the usability of the data in the database, (iii) It preserves the persistency of both public and private watermarks, (iv) Public watermarking is robust as well as fragile, (v) There is no need of recomputation when tuples are updated by the queries associated with the database. (vi) The verification phase is deterministic rather than probabilistic and can, thus, reduce false positive and false negative.

Although the public watermarking algorithm of [9] is robust, it is not fragile: attackers can easily tamper the data by keeping the MSBs unchanged. Observe that our scheme uses cryptographic hash value obtained from the static part of each tuple. Any modification of the static part, thus, reflects to the hash value and makes the signature extraction from that tuple unsuccessful. In other words, any modification is narrowed down to each tuple.

The watermark embedding phase in [4,10,15,16] is content-dependent. Any intentional processing of the database content may damage or distort the existing watermark, resulting the persistency of it into a risk. Our scheme is designed in such a way to preserve the persistency of the watermark by exploiting invariants of the database state.

The watermark detection algorithm of [1,2,9,16] is parameterized with a threshold value. The lower the value of the threshold, the higher is the probability of a successful verification. We strictly improve on these techniques by exploiting invariants of the database state and by keeping the identity of the binary tuples in public key B and in private watermark PW. This makes the verification phase in both cases deterministic.

5   Conclusions

In this paper, we proposed a novel persistent watermarking scheme that embeds both private and public watermarks. Public watermarking is based on static data cells, whereas private watermarking is based on partially abstract database and semantics-based properties of the data. This ensures the persistency of both watermarks under processing of the queries associated with the database. We use cryptographic hash function and most significant bit positions for the location of public watermark to defeat any malicious attempt by the attackers.

Acknowledgement. Work partially supported by Italian MIUR COFIN'07 project "SOFT" and by RAS project TESLA - Tecniche di enforcement per la sicurezza dei linguaggi e delle applicazioni.

References

1. Agrawal, R., Haas, P.J., Kiernan, J.: Watermarking relational data: framework, algorithms and analysis. The VLDB Journal 12(2), 157–169 (2003)
2. Bhattacharya, S., Cortesi, A.: A generic distortion free watermarking technique for relational databases. In: Prakash, A., Sen Gupta, I. (eds.) ICISS 2009. LNCS, vol. 5905, pp. 252–264. Springer, Heidelberg (2009)

3. Chen, L., Miné, A., Cousot, P.: A sound floating-point polyhedra abstract domain. In: Ramalingam, G. (ed.) APLAS 2008. LNCS, vol. 5356, pp. 3–18. Springer, Heidelberg (2008)

4. Guo, H., Li, Y., Liua, A., Jajodia, S.: A fragile watermarking scheme for detecting malicious modifications of database relations. Information Sciences 176, 1350–1378 (2006)

5. Halder, R., Cortesi, A.: Abstract interpretation for sound approximation of database query languages. In: Proceedings of the IEEE 7th International Conference on INFOrmatics and Systems (INFOS 2010), Advances in Data Engineering and Management Track, Cairo, Egypt, March 28-30, pp. 53–59. IEEE Catalog Number: IEEE CFP1006J-CDR (2010)

6. Halder, R., Cortesi, A.: Persistent watermarking of relational databases. In: Proceedings of the IEEE International Conference on Advances in Communication, Network, and Computing (CNC 2010), October 4-5. IEEE CS, Calicut (2010)

7. Halder, R., Dasgupta, P., Naskar, S., Sarma, S.S.: An internet-based ip protection scheme for circuit designs using linear feedback shift register (lfsr)-based locking. In: Proceedings of the 22nd ACM/IEEE Annual Symposium on Integrated Circuits and System Design (SBCCI 2009), August 31-September 3. ACM Press, Natal (2009)

8. Halder, R., Cortesi, A.: Observation-based fine grained access control for relational databases. In: Proceedings of the 5th International Conference on Software and Data Technologies (ICSOFT 2010), July 22-24, vol. 24, pp. 254–265. INSTICC, Athens (2010)

9. Li, Y., Deng, R.H.: Publicly verifiable ownership protection for relational databases. In: Proceedings of the ACM Symposium on Information, Computer and Communications Security (ASIACCS 2006), pp. 78–89. ACM, Taiwan (2006)

10. Li, Y., Guo, H., Jajodia, S.: Tamper detection and localization for categorical data using fragile watermarks. In: Proceedings of the 4th ACM Workshop on Digital Rights Management (DRM 2004), pp. 73–82. ACM, Washington (2004)

11. Lin, E., Delp, E.: A review of fragile image watermarks. In: Proceedings of the Multimedia and Security Workshop (ACM Multimedia 1999), Orlando, pp. 25–29 (1999)

12. Menezes, A.J., Vanstone, S.A., Oorschot, P.C.V.: Handbook of Applied Cryptography. CRC Press, Inc., Boca Raton (1996)

13. Miné, A.: The octagon abstract domain. Higher Order Symbol. Comput. 19(1), 31–100 (2006)

14. Rivest, R., Adleman, L., Dertouzos, M.: On data banks and privacy homomorphisms. In: Foundations of Secure Computation, pp. 169–180. Academic Press, New York (1978)

15. Tsai, M.H., Tseng, H.Y., Lai, C.Y.: A database watermarking technique for temper detection. In: Proceedings of the 2006 Joint Conference on Information Sciences (JCIS 2006), October 8-11. Atlantis Press, Kaohsiung (2006)

16. Zhang, Y., Niu, X., Zhao, D., Li, J., Liu, S.: Relational databases watermark technique based on content characteristic. In: First International Conference on Innovative Computing, Information and Control (ICICIC 2006), October 16, pp. 677–680. IEEE CS, Beijing (2006)

Security Rules *versus* Security Properties

Mathieu Jaume

SPI – LIP6 – University Pierre & Marie Curie,
4 Place Jussieu, 75252 Paris Cedex 05, France
Mathieu.Jaume@Lip6.fr

Abstract. There exist many approaches to specify and to define security policies. We present here a framework in which the basic components of security policies can be expressed, and we identify their role in the description of a policy, of a system and of a secure system. In this setting, we formally describe two approaches to define policies, and we relate them: the rule-based approach consists of specifying the conditions under which an action is granted and, the property-based approach consists of specifying the security properties the policy aims to enforce. We also show how a policy can be applied to constrain an existing system, and how a secure system can be defined from a security policy.

Keywords: Security policies, security properties, security rules, systems.

1 Introduction

Security has become a major issue in computer science and there exists now a large collection of literature on this topic. In this context, many security policies have been introduced, describing, in a more or less formal way, within a particular specification language, a notion of information system, suitable in a particular context, and/or the specification of granted actions in this system, and/or the specification of secure states of this system. A classification of these approaches can be obtained by considering two main criteria. The first one is the language used to describe the policy. Specification languages can be natural languages, XACML, logic, reduction systems, automata, etc. Of course, a formal language, based on a clear syntax and semantics, allows a clear meaning of the described policy, and also allows to reason about its properties in a mathematical setting. Furthermore, depending on the language used to specify a policy, an operational mechanism, allowing to enforce the policy on a system, can be more or less difficult to develop. The second criterion is the definition of what is a security policy. Is it a specification of secure states of the system? is it an operational mechanism allowing to grant or to revoke actions on the system? does this mechanism take into account how the system is transformed by the actions, or is it just based on the name of actions? what is a security information? is it an information that the policy aims to control or is it an information that the policy uses to control a system? what is a security configuration? can a security configuration be modified during the lifetime of a system? is there

S. Jha and A. Maturia (Eds.): ICISS 2010, LNCS 6503, pp. 231–245, 2010.
© Springer-Verlag Berlin Heidelberg 2010

a (administrative) policy to control changes of security configurations? does a policy take into account a notion of environment? are the systems on which policies apply and the policies independent, or do they share some entities? In this paper, we provide a formal framework allowing to specify and to define security policies by following several approaches and we show how to relate them. In this setting, we focus on two approaches to define policies: the rule-based approach consists of specifying the conditions under which an action is granted, and the property-based approach consists of specifying the security properties the policy aims to enforce. As we will see, while property-based policies can be expressed as rule-based policies, there exist some rule-based policies which cannot be expressed as property-based policies. Indeed rule-based policies allow to specify some behaviours which cannot be enforced by property-based policies. This is the main difference between the two approaches. However, we give here a formal characterization of the class of rule-based policies which can be expressed as property-based policies. Moreover, we also present how to apply a policy to constrain an existing system to get a secure system according to the policy, and how to define a secure system from a policy. Last, we give some equivalence results about the executions of such systems. Our framework does not correspond to the definition of a language to deal with security policies but aims to define what are the components needed to specify security policies, what are their roles and, depending on the considered approach, what can be done with a security policy. Using such a framework provides several benefits. Firstly, policies developed within this framework can be easily reused when considering new policies or even variant of these policies. Secondly, we think that this framework provides some methodological guidelines allowing to specify security policies. Finally, it is convenient to deal with a generic formal framework in which many policies can be expressed in order to perform analysis of these policies and to define operations over these policies (such as comparison or composition of policies).

2 Systems

This section introduces the basic notions related to labelled transition systems (LTS) together with their notations. A LTS $\mathbb{S}$ is a tuple $(\Sigma, \Sigma^0, L, \delta)$ where Σ is a set of states, $\Sigma^0 \subseteq \Sigma$ is a set of initial states, L is a set of labels, and $\delta \subseteq \Sigma \times L \times \Sigma$ is a transition relation. Often, we will write $\sigma_1 \xrightarrow{l}_\delta \sigma_2$ instead of $(\sigma_1, l, \sigma_2) \in \delta$. Furthermore, we will write $\overrightarrow{l}$ a sequence $(l_1, \cdots, l_n)$ of labels in L and, when it is defined, we will write $\sigma_1 \xrightarrow{\overrightarrow{l}}{}^\star_\delta \sigma_{n+1}$ the sequence:

$$\sigma_1 \xrightarrow{l_1}_\delta \sigma_2 \xrightarrow{l_2}_\delta \cdots \xrightarrow{l_{n-1}}_\delta \sigma_n \xrightarrow{l_n}_\delta \sigma_{n+1}$$

of transitions. From an operational point of view, we can require that the relation δ of a LTS defines a deterministic and left-total relation:

$$\forall \sigma, \sigma_1, \sigma_2 \in \Sigma \; \forall l \in L \; (\sigma \xrightarrow{l}_\delta \sigma_1 \wedge \sigma \xrightarrow{l}_\delta \sigma_2) \Rightarrow \sigma_1 = \sigma_2$$
$$\forall \sigma_1 \in \Sigma \; \forall l \in L \; \exists \sigma_2 \in \Sigma \; \sigma_1 \xrightarrow{l}_\delta \sigma_2$$

We write $\Gamma(\mathbb{S})$ the set of states that are reachable by "applying" a finite number of times δ from a state in Σ^0. We also define the set $Exec(\mathbb{S}) \subseteq \Sigma^+$ (where Σ^+ is the set of non-empty finite sequences of states) of executions of $\mathbb{S}$ as follows:

$$Exec(\mathbb{S}) = \{(\sigma_1, \cdots, \sigma_n) \mid n \geq 1 \wedge \sigma_1 \in \Sigma^0 \wedge \forall i \; \exists l \in L \; \sigma_i \xrightarrow{l}_\delta \sigma_{i+1}\}$$

Example 1. We define the system $\mathbb{S}_{ac} = (\Sigma_{ac}, \Sigma_{ac}^0, L_{ac}, \delta_{ac})$ allowing to add or to release accesses done by active entities, the subjects in $\mathcal{S}$, over passive entities, the objects in $\mathcal{O}$, according to access modes in $\mathcal{A}$ (for example, read, write, etc). A state is represented by a function $\alpha : \mathcal{S} \to \wp(\mathcal{O} \times \mathcal{A})$ such that $(o, a) \in \alpha(s)$ means that s has an access over o according to the access mode a. Hence, $\Sigma_{ac} = \{\alpha : \mathcal{S} \to \wp(\mathcal{O} \times \mathcal{A})\}$. We define $\Sigma_{ac}^0 = \{\alpha_0 \mid \forall s \in \mathcal{S} \; \alpha_0(s) = \emptyset\}$ expressing that no access is done in the initial state. By considering the set of labels $L_{ac} = \{\langle +, s, o, a\rangle, \langle -, s, o, a\rangle \mid s \in \mathcal{S}, \; o \in \mathcal{O}, \; a \in \mathcal{A}\}$, where $\langle +, s, o, a\rangle$ (resp. $\langle -, s, o, a\rangle$) allows to add (resp. to release) the access done by s over o according to a, we define the transition relation δ_{ac} by:

$$\left\{ \begin{array}{l} \alpha \xrightarrow{\langle +, s, o, a\rangle}_{\delta_{ac}} \alpha[s \leftarrow \alpha(s) \cup \{(s, o, a)\}] \\ \alpha \xrightarrow{\langle -, s, o, a\rangle}_{\delta_{ac}} \alpha[s \leftarrow \alpha(s) \backslash \{(s, o, a)\}] \end{array} \right\} \text{ where } f[x \leftarrow v](y) = \left\{ \begin{array}{l} f(y) \text{ if } x \neq y \\ v \quad\;\; \text{if } x = y \end{array} \right.$$

We introduce now the notion of interpretation of the states of a system: an interpretation $I_\Sigma^{\mathbb{D}}$ of Σ based on the domain $\mathbb{D}$ is a mapping from Σ to $\mathbb{D}$. We write $[\![\sigma]\!]_{I_\Sigma^{\mathbb{D}}}$ the interpretation of σ, and we extend this definition for subsets Σ' of Σ as follows: $[\![\Sigma']\!]_{I_\Sigma^{\mathbb{D}}} = \{[\![\sigma]\!]_{I_\Sigma^{\mathbb{D}}} \mid \sigma \in \Sigma'\}$. The interpreted system is defined by $[\![\mathbb{S}]\!]_{I_\Sigma^{\mathbb{D}}} = ([\![\Sigma]\!]_{I_\Sigma^{\mathbb{D}}}, [\![\Sigma^0]\!]_{I_\Sigma^{\mathbb{D}}}, L, \delta^{I_\Sigma^{\mathbb{D}}})$ where $\delta^{I_\Sigma^{\mathbb{D}}} = \{([\![\sigma_1]\!]_{I_\Sigma^{\mathbb{D}}}, l, [\![\sigma_2]\!]_{I_\Sigma^{\mathbb{D}}}) \mid \sigma_1 \xrightarrow{l}_\delta \sigma_2\}$.

Example 2. We can change the representation of states of $\mathbb{S}_{ac}$ by considering the interpretation $I_{\Sigma_{ac}}^{\mathbb{A}_{ac}}$ of Σ_{ac} where $\mathbb{A}_{ac} = \wp(\mathcal{S} \times \mathcal{O} \times \mathcal{A})$ and:

$$\forall \alpha \in \Sigma_{ac} \quad [\![\alpha]\!]_{I_{\Sigma_{ac}}^{\mathbb{A}_{ac}}} = \bigcup_{s \in \mathcal{S}} \bigcup_{(o,a) \in \alpha(s)} \{(s, o, a)\}$$

In this way, states of the interpreted system are sets of accesses.

Intuitively, interpretations will be useful when applying security policies over systems: an interpretation can provide the information that a policy aims to control. Indeed, thanks to interpretations, it will be possible to apply a policy on a system even if the policy and the system do not share the same entities or representations. For example, by considering an interpretation whose mapping provides the information flows generated by a set of accesses, it is possible to apply a flow policy over an access system such as $\mathbb{S}_{ac}$. Furthermore, considering a composition operator over the domain of an interpretation allows to define a semantics over executions of a system. This can be useful to check that even if each transition of a sequence is secure according to a policy, the sequence is also secure according to the policy. Such property does not always hold. For example, when dealing with a flow policy over an access system, some sequences of legal sets of accesses (e.g. sets of accesses generating legal flows according to the policy) may generate, by composition of flows generated by each element of the sequence, some illegal flows. Later, when defining sytems from policies, a transition will be labelled both by a request submitted to the system and by the answer given by the policy to this request. We write $\mathcal{R}$ for the set of requests, and $\mathcal{D}$ for the set of possible answers. The semantics of $\mathcal{R}$ and $\mathcal{D}$ is defined by a relation $[\![\mathcal{R}]\!]^{\mathcal{D}}_{\Sigma} \subseteq \Sigma \times (\mathcal{R} \times \mathcal{D}) \times \Sigma$. $(\sigma_1, (R, d), \sigma_2) \in [\![\mathcal{R}]\!]^{\mathcal{D}}_{\Sigma}$ means that when the system is in the state σ_1, if the request R is applied according to the answer d, then the system moves into the state σ_2. The notion of answers allows to consider policies specifying transformations that must be done over states when a request has not been accepted (this can be useful for policies that aim to control the number of times that an entity tries to perform an action that would lead to an insecure state). However, for many policies, the set of answers contains only two elements allowing to specify that the request is granted or not.

Example 3. We define the set $\mathcal{R}^{ac}$ as the set L_{ac} and the set $\mathcal{D} = \{\text{yes}, \text{no}\}$. The semantics of $\mathcal{R}^{ac}$ can be defined by:

$$(A_1, (\langle +, s, o, a\rangle, \text{yes}), A_2) \in [\![\mathcal{R}^{ac}]\!]^{\mathcal{D}}_{\mathbb{A}_{ac}} \Leftrightarrow A_2 = A_1 \cup \{(s, o, a)\}$$
$$(A_1, (\langle -, s, o, a\rangle, \text{yes}), A_2) \in [\![\mathcal{R}^{ac}]\!]^{\mathcal{D}}_{\mathbb{A}_{ac}} \Leftrightarrow A_2 = A_1 \backslash \{(s, o, a)\}$$
$$(A_1, (R, \text{no}), A_2) \in [\![\mathcal{R}^{ac}]\!]^{\mathcal{D}}_{\mathbb{A}_{ac}} \Leftrightarrow A_1 = A_2$$

3   Security Policies

Several points of view exist on security policies, among which two main approaches can be distinguished.

Property-based security policies. A property-based policy is a characterization of secure elements of a set according to some security information. Hence, specifying a property-based policy $\mathbb{P}$ first consists of defining a set $\mathbb{A}$ of "things" that the policy aims to control, called the security targets, in order to ensure the desired security properties (these "things" can be the actions simultaneously done in the system or some information about the entities of the system). Then, a set $\mathcal{C}$ of security configurations is introduced: configurations correspond to the information needed to characterize secure elements of $\mathbb{A}$ according to the policy. Last, a policy is defined by a relation $\Vdash$ between configurations and targets allowing to express that, given a configuration, a target satisfies the policy.

Definition 1. *A property-based security policy $\mathbb{P}$ is a tuple $\mathbb{P} = (\mathbb{A}, \mathcal{C}, \Vdash)$ where $\mathbb{A}$ is a set of security targets, $\mathcal{C}$ is a set of security configurations and $\Vdash \subseteq \mathcal{C} \times \mathbb{A}$ is a relation specifying secure targets according to configurations.*

Example 4. We consider here the HRU policy $\mathbb{P}_{\text{hru}} = (\mathbb{A}_{ac}, \mathcal{C}_{\text{hru}}, \Vdash_{\mathbb{P}_{\text{hru}}})$, introduced in [14], which is a discretionary access control policy, aiming to control accesses done in a system. The set of security targets is $\mathbb{A}_{ac}$ (defined in example 2) and the set of security configurations is $\mathcal{C}_{\text{hru}} = \mathbb{A}_{ac}$ (a configuration $m_D \in \mathcal{C}_{\text{hru}}$ specifies a set of granted accesses). Now we can define secure targets as sets of accesses which are granted: $m_D \Vdash_{\mathbb{P}_{\text{hru}}} A$ iff $A \subseteq m_D$.

In fact, within the property-based approach, a policy $\mathbb{P} = (\mathbb{A}_\mathbb{P}, \mathcal{C}_\mathbb{P}, \Vdash_\mathbb{P})$ can be viewed as the definition of a semantics for $\mathcal{C}$: each configuration c denotes the set of targets $[\![c]\!]_\mathbb{P} = \{A \in \mathbb{A}_\mathbb{P} \mid c \Vdash_\mathbb{P} A\}$ that c authorizes. Such definition is similar to the one introduced in [3], in the context of access control. For example, if we consider the HRU policy, we have $[\![m_D]\!]_{\mathbb{P}_{\text{hru}}} = \wp(m_D)$. Note that it may be useful to consider systems allowing to modify configurations. For these systems, we can also introduce a policy allowing to control the transformations of configurations. Hence, the "things" that this policy aims to control is defined by the set $\mathcal{C}_\mathbb{P}$. Such a policy is often called an administrative policy for $\mathbb{P}$ and is defined as a policy $\mathbb{P}_\mathbb{P} = (\mathcal{C}_\mathbb{P}, \mathcal{C}, \Vdash_{\mathbb{P}_\mathbb{P}})$. In the following, given a set $\mathcal{R}$ of requests together with its semantics $[\![\mathcal{R}]\!]_\mathbb{A}^\mathcal{D}$, a policy $\mathbb{P} = (\mathbb{A}, \mathcal{C}, \Vdash)$, and a configuration $c \in \mathcal{C}$, we write:

$$A_0 \xrightarrow{\ ((R_1,d_1),\cdots,(R_k,d_k))\ }_{[\![\mathcal{R}]\!]_\mathbb{A}^\mathcal{D},\mathbb{P},c}^{\ \star\ } A_k$$

to express that there exist $A_1, \cdots, A_{k-1} \in \mathbb{A}$ such that:

$$A_0 \xrightarrow{(R_1,d_1)}_{[\![\mathcal{R}]\!]_\mathbb{A}^\mathcal{D}} A_1 \xrightarrow{(R_2,d_2)}_{[\![\mathcal{R}]\!]_\mathbb{A}^\mathcal{D}} \cdots \xrightarrow{(R_k,d_k)}_{[\![\mathcal{R}]\!]_\mathbb{A}^\mathcal{D}} A_k \text{ and } \forall i\ (0 \leq i \leq k)\ c \Vdash A_i$$

Rule-based security policies. A security policy can also be viewed as a description of the conditions under which an action is permitted or forbidden. We extend here such an approach by considering an arbitrary set of answers. As before, a policy is defined from a set $\mathbb{A}$ of security targets and a set $\mathcal{C}$ of security configurations. Furthermore, to define a policy by specifying a set of authorized actions, we introduce a set $\mathcal{R}$ of requests (corresponding to names of actions) and a set $\mathcal{D}$ of answers (corresponding to different authorizations). Now, the policy is defined by a relation $\Vdash \subseteq (\mathcal{C} \times \mathbb{A}) \times (\mathcal{R} \times \mathcal{D})$, where $(c, A) \Vdash (R, d)$ means that when the current configuration is c and the current target is A, the action R can be performed according to the answer d.

Definition 2. *A rule-based security policy $\mathfrak{P}$ is a tuple $\mathfrak{P} = (\mathbb{A}, \mathcal{C}, \mathcal{R}, \mathcal{D}, \Vdash)$ where $\mathbb{A}$ is the set of security targets, $\mathcal{C}$ is the set of security configurations, $\mathcal{R}$ is the set of requests, $\mathcal{D}$ is a set of answers and $\Vdash \subseteq (\mathcal{C} \times \mathbb{A}) \times (\mathcal{R} \times \mathcal{D})$ is a relation specifying which (and how) actions can be performed.*

Example 5. The HRU policy can be defined as the rule-based policy $\mathfrak{P}_{\text{hru}} = (\mathbb{A}_{ac}, \mathcal{C}_{\text{hru}}, \mathcal{R}^{ac}, \mathcal{D}, \Vdash_{\mathfrak{P}_{\text{hru}}})$ where $\mathcal{D} = \{\text{yes}, \text{no}\}$ and $(m_D, A) \Vdash_{\mathfrak{P}_{\text{hru}}} (R, d)$ iff:

$$(R = \langle -, s, o, a \rangle \wedge d = \text{yes}) \vee (R = \langle +, s, o, a \rangle \wedge d = \text{yes} \wedge (s, o, a) \in m_D)$$
$$\vee (R = \langle +, s, o, a \rangle \wedge d = \text{no} \wedge (s, o, a) \notin m_D)$$

Hence, when $\mathcal{D} = \{\text{yes}, \text{no}\}$, given a pair (c, A), the set of granted (resp. forbidden) actions is the set $\{R \in \mathcal{R} \mid (c, A) \Vdash (R, \text{yes})\}$ (resp. $\{R \in \mathcal{R} \mid (c, A) \Vdash (R, \text{no})\}$). Such definition is similar to the one introduced in [6], where a policy is defined in terms of authorized actions, and can be extended by considering the set $[\![c, A]\!]_\mathfrak{P} = \{(R, d) \in \mathcal{R} \times \mathcal{D} \mid (c, A) \Vdash (R, d)\}$. Here again, administrative policies can be defined for rule-based policies. More generally, an administrative policy for a (rule-based or property-based) security policy whose set of security configurations is $\mathcal{C}$ can be a (rule-based or property-based) policy whose set of security targets is $\mathcal{C}$. Given a policy $\mathfrak{P} = (\mathbb{A}, \mathcal{C}, \mathcal{R}, \mathcal{D}, \Vdash)$, a security configuration $c \in \mathcal{C}$, and a relation $[\![\mathcal{R}]\!]_{\mathbb{A}}^{\mathcal{D}}$ specifying the semantics of requests, we write:

$$A_0 \xrightarrow[{[\![\mathcal{R}]\!]_{\mathbb{A}}^{\mathcal{D}}, \mathfrak{P}, c}]{(R,d)} A_1 \qquad \left(\text{resp. } A_0 \xrightarrow[{[\![\mathcal{R}]\!]_{\mathbb{A}}^{\mathcal{D}}, \mathfrak{P}, c}]{((R_1,d_1), \cdots, (R_k,d_k))}{}^{\star} A_k \right)$$

to express that:

$$A_0 \xrightarrow[{[\![\mathcal{R}]\!]_{\mathbb{A}}^{\mathcal{D}}}]{(R,d)} A_1 \text{ and } (c, A_0) \Vdash (R, d)$$

$$\left(\text{resp. } \left(\begin{array}{c} \exists A_1, \cdots, A_{k-1} \in \mathbb{A} \\ A_0 \xrightarrow[{[\![\mathcal{R}]\!]_{\mathbb{A}}^{\mathcal{D}}}]{(R_1,d_1)} A_1 \xrightarrow[{[\![\mathcal{R}]\!]_{\mathbb{A}}^{\mathcal{D}}}]{(R_2,d_2)} \cdots \xrightarrow[{[\![\mathcal{R}]\!]_{\mathbb{A}}^{\mathcal{D}}}]{(R_k,d_k)} A_k \\ \wedge \; \forall i \; (0 \leq i \leq k-1) \; (c, A_i) \Vdash (R_{i+1}, d_{i+1}) \end{array} \right) \right)$$

Within the rule-based approach, when $\mathcal{D} = \{\mathsf{yes}, \mathsf{no}\}$, two main issues must be handled. Given a current configuration and target, for each request, the policy must provide one answer (is the action permitted or forbidden?) and only one answer (no action can be both permitted and forbidden):

- $\mathfrak{P}$ is complete iff: $\forall R \in \mathcal{R} \; \exists d \in \mathcal{D} \quad (c, A) \Vdash (R, d)$
- $\mathfrak{P}$ is consistent iff: $((c, A) \Vdash (R, d_1) \wedge (c, A) \Vdash (R, d_2)) \Rightarrow d_1 = d_2$

For example, $\mathfrak{P}_{\mathsf{hru}}$ is both complete and consistent. When considering an arbitrary set of answers, only the first issue must be handled: the policy must provide an answer for each request, but several answers can be given to this request, all of them corresponding to authorized ways of applying the request (in practice, a mechanism allowing to specify which answer must be considered when several answers are given by the policy can be introduced, for example, an order relation over $\mathcal{D}$). The relation $\Vdash$ characterizes "secure" pairs (R, d) by considering a pair (c, A) describing the current state of a system. For a class of policies, $\Vdash$ can be defined only from the configuration c. For example, this is the case for the HRU policy for which deciding if a request is granted or not can be done by only considering the set m_D of authorized accesses. We call such policies free policies. Note that there exist non-free policies, such as MLS (MultiLevel Security) access control policies for which deciding if adding an access is granted or not is done by considering both the configuration (to ensure that the security level of the subject authorizes the access over the object according to its security level) and the current security target (to ensure that the new access won't generate an illegal information flow between objects, according to security levels of objects). Formally, a rule-based policy $\mathfrak{P} = (\mathbb{A}, \mathcal{C}, \mathcal{R}, \mathcal{D}, \Vdash)$ is said to be free iff:

$$\forall c \in \mathcal{C} \; \forall R \in \mathcal{R} \; \forall d \in \mathcal{D} \; \forall A_1, A_2 \in \mathbb{A} \quad (c, A_1) \Vdash (R, d) \Leftrightarrow (c, A_2) \Vdash (R, d)$$

Note that some frameworks, like in [6], only allow to consider free policies. We introduce now a property, based on the semantics of requests. Intuitively, this property holds iff for all reachable targets A_1 and A_2, according to the policy, if the semantics of $\mathcal{R}$ contains a transition allowing to transform A_1 into A_2, then this transformation is granted by the policy. More formally, given a relation $[\![\mathcal{R}]\!]_{\mathbb{A}}^{\mathcal{D}}$ specifying the semantics of $\mathcal{R}$, and a set $\mathscr{I} \subseteq \mathcal{C} \times \mathbb{A}$ containing pairs (c, A) such that A is assumed to be secure according to c, $\mathfrak{P} = (\mathbb{A}, \mathcal{C}, \mathcal{R}, \mathcal{D}, |\!|\!\vdash)$ satisfies the switching property according to $[\![\mathcal{R}]\!]_{\mathbb{A}}^{\mathcal{D}}$ and $\mathscr{I}$ iff:

$$\forall (c, A_0), (c, A_0') \in \mathscr{I} \ \forall A, A' \in \mathbb{A} \ \forall (R, d) \in \mathcal{R} \times \mathcal{D} \ \forall \overrightarrow{(R_1, d_1)}, \overrightarrow{(R_2, d_2)} \in (\mathcal{R} \times \mathcal{D})^\star$$
$$\left(A_0 \xrightarrow{\overrightarrow{(R_1, d_1)}}{}^\star_{[\![\mathcal{R}]\!]_{\mathbb{A}}^{\mathcal{D}}, \mathfrak{P}, c} A \wedge A_0' \xrightarrow{\overrightarrow{(R_2, d_2)}}{}^\star_{[\![\mathcal{R}]\!]_{\mathbb{A}}^{\mathcal{D}}, \mathfrak{P}, c} A' \wedge A \xrightarrow{(R, d)}{}_{[\![\mathcal{R}]\!]_{\mathbb{A}}^{\mathcal{D}}} A' \right)$$
$$\Rightarrow (c, A) |\!|\!\vdash (R, d)$$

For example, the policy $\mathfrak{P}_{\mathsf{hru}}$ satisfies the switching property. Of course, there exist some policies for which the switching property does not hold. This is the case for some policies aiming to control the order of actions.

Property-based policies *versus* Rule-based policies. We relate here the two approaches introduced above by showing how to obtain a property-based policy from a rule-based policy and *vice-versa* and we prove some equivalence results.

Building a property-based policy from a rule-based policy leads to characterize secure elements of $\mathbb{A}$ from granted actions according to a security configuration. To achieve this goal, both the semantics of requests and a set $\mathscr{I}$ of "initial" pairs of the form (c, A) considered as secure must be provided. In this way, a secure target A according to a configuration c is a reachable target by applying $\rightarrow_{[\![\mathcal{R}]\!]_{\mathbb{A}}^{\mathcal{D}}, \mathfrak{P}, c}$ from an element A_0 such that $(c, A_0) \in \mathscr{I}$. More formally, let $\mathfrak{P} = (\mathbb{A}, \mathcal{C}, \mathcal{R}, \mathcal{D}, |\!|\!\vdash)$ be a rule-based policy, $[\![\mathcal{R}]\!]_{\mathbb{A}}^{\mathcal{D}}$ be a relation specifying the semantics of $\mathcal{R}$, and $\mathscr{I} \subseteq \mathcal{C} \times \mathbb{A}$ be a set of pairs (c, A). We define the $(\mathfrak{P}, [\![\mathcal{R}]\!]_{\mathbb{A}}^{\mathcal{D}}, \mathscr{I})$-policy as the property-based policy $\mathbb{P} = (\mathbb{A}, \mathcal{C}, |\!\vdash)$ where:

$$c |\!\vdash A \Leftrightarrow \left(\exists (c, A_0) \in \mathscr{I} \ \exists \overrightarrow{(R, d)} \in (\mathcal{R} \times \mathcal{D})^\star \ A_0 \xrightarrow{\overrightarrow{(R, d)}}{}^\star_{[\![\mathcal{R}]\!]_{\mathbb{A}}^{\mathcal{D}}, \mathfrak{P}, c} A \right)$$

For example, the policy $\mathbb{P}_{\mathsf{hru}}$ is the $(\mathfrak{P}_{\mathsf{hru}}, [\![\mathcal{R}^{ac}]\!]_{\mathbb{A}_{ac}}^{\mathcal{D}}, \mathscr{I})$-policy where $\mathscr{I} = \{(c, \emptyset) \mid c \in \mathcal{C}_{\mathsf{hru}}\}$. We prove now that, given a configuration, applying a granted action according to an answer over a secure target leads to a secure target, and conversely, given a configuration c, if the semantics of the language of requests contains a transition allowing to transform a secure target A_1 into a secure target A_2, then such a transformation is granted by the policy (in order to prove this property, we need to suppose that the rule-based policy satisfies the switching property).

Proposition 1. *Let* $\mathbb{P} = (\mathbb{A}, \mathcal{C}, |\!\vdash)$ *be the* $(\mathfrak{P}, [\![\mathcal{R}]\!]_{\mathbb{A}}^{\mathcal{D}}, \mathscr{I})$-*policy,* $c \in \mathcal{C}$, $A_0, A \in \mathbb{A}$ *and* $\overrightarrow{(R, d)} \in (\mathcal{R} \times \mathcal{D})^\star$.

1. *If* $(c, A_0) \in \mathscr{I}$ *and* $A_0 \xrightarrow{\overrightarrow{(R, d)}}{}^\star_{[\![\mathcal{R}]\!]_{\mathbb{A}}^{\mathcal{D}}, \mathfrak{P}, c} A$, *then* $A_0 \xrightarrow{\overrightarrow{(R, d)}}{}^\star_{[\![\mathcal{R}]\!]_{\mathbb{A}}^{\mathcal{D}}, \mathbb{P}, c} A$.
2. *If* $\mathfrak{P}$ *satisfies the switching property according to* $[\![\mathcal{R}]\!]_{\mathbb{A}}^{\mathcal{D}}$ *and* $\mathscr{I}$, *then:*

$$A_0 \xrightarrow{\overrightarrow{(R, d)}}{}^\star_{[\![\mathcal{R}]\!]_{\mathbb{A}}^{\mathcal{D}}, \mathbb{P}, c} A \Rightarrow A_0 \xrightarrow{\overrightarrow{(R, d)}}{}^\star_{[\![\mathcal{R}]\!]_{\mathbb{A}}^{\mathcal{D}}, \mathfrak{P}, c} A$$

Hence, a policy $\mathfrak{P}$, which does not satisfy the switching property, can be more restrictive than $\mathbb{P}$ and cannot be expressed as an "equivalent" property-based policy. However, by adding some information about "the past" into targets (for example the sequence of transformations that have been done from an initial target to obtain the current target), it becomes possible to solve this problem.

Building a rule-based policy from a property-based policy $\mathbb{P} = (\mathbb{A}, \mathcal{C}, \Vdash)$ leads to introduce a set $\mathcal{R}$ of requests together with its semantics $[\![\mathcal{R}]\!]_{\mathbb{A}}^{\mathcal{D}}$. We define the $(\mathbb{P}, [\![\mathcal{R}]\!]_{\mathbb{A}}^{\mathcal{D}})$-policy as the rule-based policy $\mathfrak{P} = (\mathbb{A}, \mathcal{C}, \mathcal{R}, \mathcal{D}, \Vvdash)$ where:

$$(c, A) \Vvdash (R, d) \Leftrightarrow (\exists A' \in \mathbb{A} \ A \xrightarrow{(R,d)}_{[\![\mathcal{R}]\!]_{\mathbb{A}}^{\mathcal{D}}} A' \wedge c \Vdash A')$$

For example, the $(\mathbb{P}_{\mathsf{hru}}, [\![\mathcal{R}^{ac}]\!]_{\mathbb{A}_{ac}}^{\mathcal{D}})$-policy is based on a relation $\Vvdash$ defined by:

$$\begin{aligned}
&(m_D, A) \Vvdash (R, d) \\
&\Leftrightarrow \left(\begin{array}{l}
(R = \langle +, s, o, a\rangle \wedge d = \mathsf{yes} \wedge A \subseteq m_D \wedge (s, o, a) \in m_D) \\
\vee \ (R = \langle +, s, o, a\rangle \wedge d = \mathsf{no} \wedge (A \nsubseteq m_D \vee (s, o, a) \notin m_D)) \\
\vee \ (R = \langle -, s, o, a\rangle \wedge d = \mathsf{yes} \wedge A\backslash\{(s, o, a)\} \subseteq m_D) \\
\vee \ (R = \langle -, s, o, a\rangle \wedge d = \mathsf{no} \wedge A\backslash\{(s, o, a)\} \nsubseteq m_D)
\end{array} \right)
\end{aligned}$$

This relation is slightly different from the relation $\Vvdash_{\mathfrak{P}_{\mathsf{hru}}}$ of the policy $\mathfrak{P}_{\mathsf{hru}}$ (example 5). However, the only difference is concerned with answers for requests when the current target is not secure according to the configuration. Hence, as we will see, when applied over a system whose initial states are secure, these two policies lead to the same secure states. Last, we state the following proposition.

Proposition 2. Let $\mathfrak{P} = (\mathbb{A}, \mathcal{C}, \mathcal{R}, \mathcal{D}, \Vvdash)$ be the $(\mathbb{P}, [\![\mathcal{R}]\!]_{\mathbb{A}}^{\mathcal{D}})$-policy, $A_0, A \in \mathbb{A}$, $c \in \mathcal{C}$ and $\overrightarrow{(R, d)} \in (\mathcal{R} \times \mathcal{D})^\star$.

1. $A_0 \xrightarrow{\overrightarrow{(R, d)}}{}^\star_{[\![\mathcal{R}]\!]_{\mathbb{A}}^{\mathcal{D}}, \mathbb{P}, c} A \Rightarrow A_0 \xrightarrow{\overrightarrow{(R, d)}}{}^\star_{[\![\mathcal{R}]\!]_{\mathbb{A}}^{\mathcal{D}}, \mathfrak{P}, c} A$

2. If $c \Vdash A_0$ and if $[\![\mathcal{R}]\!]_{\mathbb{A}}^{\mathcal{D}}$ is deterministic, then

$$A_0 \xrightarrow{\overrightarrow{(R, d)}}{}^\star_{[\![\mathcal{R}]\!]_{\mathbb{A}}^{\mathcal{D}}, \mathfrak{P}, c} A \Rightarrow A_0 \xrightarrow{\overrightarrow{(R, d)}}{}^\star_{[\![\mathcal{R}]\!]_{\mathbb{A}}^{\mathcal{D}}, \mathbb{P}, c} A$$

Note that, when $[\![\mathcal{R}]\!]_{\mathbb{A}}^{\mathcal{D}}$ is deterministic, rule-based policies obtained from property-based policies satisfy the switching property.

4   Security Policies and Systems

We describe here how a policy can be applied on an existing system in order to obtain a secure system, and how to obtain a secure system from a policy.

Property-based policies and systems. To apply a property-based policy on a system, we first have to define an interpretation of the states of the system, providing information on which the policy can apply (states of the system are interpreted as security targets of the policy). Then, applying a policy on a system leads to a system whose states are enriched with security configurations, whose initial states are secure initial states, and whose transition relation is obtained by removing all "illegal" transitions (e.g. transitions transforming a secure state into a non-secure state). During executions of this new system, security configurations are constant (labels are not concerned with configurations). Systems for which the configurations can evolve can be obtained by composition with a system on which an administrative policy can apply. In practice, applying a policy over a system may be done by considering a particular security configuration, or a particular set of configurations, to constrain the executions of the system.

Definition 3. *Let* $\mathbb{S} = (\Sigma, \Sigma^0, L, \delta)$ *be a system,* $\mathbb{P} = (\mathbb{A}, \mathcal{C}, \Vdash)$ *be a property-based security policy,* C *be a subset of* $\mathcal{C}$*, and* $I_\Sigma^\mathbb{A}$ *be an interpretation of* Σ*. We define the system* $\lfloor \mathbb{S} \rfloor_{\mathbb{P},C}^{I_\Sigma^\mathbb{A}} = (C \times \Sigma, \lfloor \Sigma^0 \rfloor_{\mathbb{P},C}^{I_\Sigma^\mathbb{A}}, L, \lfloor \delta \rfloor_{\mathbb{P},C}^{I_\Sigma^\mathbb{A}})$ *where:*

$$\lfloor \Sigma^0 \rfloor_{\mathbb{P},C}^{I_\Sigma^\mathbb{A}} = \{(c,\sigma) \mid \sigma \in \Sigma^0 \wedge c \in C \wedge c \Vdash \llbracket \sigma \rrbracket_{I_\Sigma^\mathbb{A}}\}$$

$$\lfloor \delta \rfloor_{\mathbb{P},C}^{I_\Sigma^\mathbb{A}} = \{((c,\sigma_1), l, (c,\sigma_2)) \mid \sigma_1 \xrightarrow{l}_\delta \sigma_2 \wedge c \in C \wedge (c \Vdash \llbracket \sigma_1 \rrbracket_{I_\Sigma^\mathbb{A}} \Rightarrow c \Vdash \llbracket \sigma_2 \rrbracket_{I_\Sigma^\mathbb{A}})\}$$

The use of an interpretation, which can be viewed as a kind of interface between the policy and the system, allows to apply a policy on several different systems.

Example 6. By considering $C = \mathcal{C}_\text{hru}$ and the interpretation $I_{\Sigma_{ac}}^{\mathbb{A}_{ac}}$ (introduced in example 2), applying the policy $\mathbb{P}_\text{hru}$ on the system $\mathbb{S}_{ac}$ leads to a system whose states belongs to $\mathcal{C}_\text{hru} \times \Sigma_{ac}$, whose labels are labels in L_{ac}, and defined by:

$$\lfloor \Sigma_{ac}^0 \rfloor_{\mathbb{P}_\text{hru},\mathcal{C}_\text{hru}}^{I_{\Sigma_{ac}}^{\mathbb{A}_{ac}}} = \bigcup_{m \in \mathcal{C}_\text{hru}} \{(m,\alpha) \mid \alpha \in \Sigma_{ac}^0\}$$

$$\lfloor \delta_{ac} \rfloor_{\mathbb{P}_\text{hru},\mathcal{C}_\text{hru}}^{I_{\Sigma_{ac}}^{\mathbb{A}_{ac}}} = \begin{cases} ((m,\alpha), \langle +, s, o, a \rangle, (m, \alpha[s \leftarrow \alpha(s) \cup \{(o,a)\}])) \mid \\ (\exists s' \in \mathcal{S}\, \exists o' \in \mathcal{O}\, \exists a' \in \mathcal{A}\ (o', a') \in \alpha(s') \wedge (s', o', a') \notin m) \vee (s, o, a) \in m \end{cases} \\ \cup \{((m,\alpha), \langle -, s, o, a \rangle, (m, \alpha[s \leftarrow \alpha(s) \backslash \{(s,o,a)\}]))\}$$

Such a construction allows to ensure that all reachable states of $\lfloor \mathbb{S} \rfloor_{\mathbb{P},C}^{I_\Sigma^\mathbb{A}}$ are secure with respect to the policy $\mathbb{P}$.

Proposition 3. $\forall (c,\sigma) \in \Gamma(\lfloor \mathbb{S} \rfloor_{\mathbb{P},C}^{I_\Sigma^\mathbb{A}})\ c \Vdash \llbracket \sigma \rrbracket_{I_\Sigma^\mathbb{A}}$

Defining a system from a property-based policy $\mathbb{P}$ can be done by considering a language of requests $\mathcal{R}$ together with its semantics $\llbracket \mathcal{R} \rrbracket_\mathbb{A}^\mathcal{D}$, and a subset $\mathbb{A}^0$ of $\mathbb{A}$, and by applying $\mathbb{P}$ (according to the interpretation $I_\mathbb{A}^\mathbb{A}$ of $\mathbb{A}$ such that $\llbracket A \rrbracket_{I_\mathbb{A}^\mathbb{A}} = A$) on the system $(\mathbb{A}, \mathbb{A}^0, \mathcal{R} \times \mathcal{D}, \llbracket \mathcal{R} \rrbracket_\mathbb{A}^\mathcal{D})$. For example, from the policy $\mathbb{P}_\text{hru}$, the set $\mathbb{A}_{ac}^0 = \{\emptyset\} \subseteq \mathbb{A}_{ac}$, and the set $\mathcal{R}^{ac}$ of requests together with its semantics $\llbracket \mathcal{R}^{ac} \rrbracket_{\mathbb{A}_{ac}}^\mathcal{D}$, we can define the system obtained in example 6 by applying $\mathbb{P}_\text{hru}$ on $\mathbb{S}_{ac}$. However, note that such a construction leads to consider all the correct transitions according to $\mathbb{P}$ and to $\llbracket \mathcal{R} \rrbracket_\mathbb{A}^\mathcal{D}$, and, in some situations, it can be useful to constrain the transition relation δ. For example, it can happen that a correct transition according to $\mathbb{P}$ does not belong to δ in order to avoid that some subjects perform some authorized actions. This is the case for some administrative policies where access rights over an object must be provided only by its owner. In this case, it suffices to consider a transition relation δ such that:

$$\delta \subseteq \left\lfloor [\![\mathcal{R}]\!]_{\mathbb{A}}^{\mathcal{D}} \right\rfloor_{\mathbb{P},\mathcal{C}}^{I_{\mathbb{A}}^{\mathbb{A}}}$$

Rule-based policies and systems. To apply a rule-based policy $\mathfrak{P}$ on a system $\mathbb{S}$, we have to define an interpretation $I_{\Sigma}^{\mathbb{A}}$ of the states of the system whose domain is the set of security targets of $\mathfrak{P}$. In addition, to characterize initial states of the system, the definition of a subset of $\mathcal{C} \times \mathbb{A}$ must be considered. Last, since $\mathfrak{P}$ is defined in terms of granted actions, the semantics of the language of requests of $\mathfrak{P}$ must be given. We introduce here two ways to apply a rule-based policy on a system. The first one consists in removing all transitions $(\sigma_1, l, \sigma_2) \in \delta$ such that $[\![\sigma_1]\!]_{I_{\Sigma}^{\mathbb{A}}} \neq [\![\sigma_2]\!]_{I_{\Sigma}^{\mathbb{A}}}$ and such that each transition labelled by a request allowing to transform $[\![\sigma_1]\!]_{I_{\Sigma}^{\mathbb{A}}}$ into $[\![\sigma_2]\!]_{I_{\Sigma}^{\mathbb{A}}}$ is not granted by $\mathfrak{P}$. The second one is similar but consists in considering "weak-simulations" of transitions of δ (e.g. a sequence of requests may be used to transform $[\![\sigma_1]\!]_{I_{\Sigma}^{\mathbb{A}}}$ into $[\![\sigma_2]\!]_{I_{\Sigma}^{\mathbb{A}}}$).

Definition 4. *Let* $\mathbb{S} = (\Sigma, \Sigma^0, L, \delta)$ *be a system,* $\mathfrak{P} = (\mathbb{A}, \mathcal{C}, \mathcal{R}, \mathcal{D}, \Vdash)$ *be a rule-based policy,* $C \subseteq \mathcal{C}$, $[\![\mathcal{R}]\!]_{\mathbb{A}}^{\mathcal{D}}$ *be a relation specifying the semantics of* $\mathcal{R}$, $I_{\Sigma}^{\mathbb{A}}$ *be an interpretation of* Σ, *and* $\mathscr{I}$ *be a subset of* $C \times \mathbb{A}$. *We define the systems:*

$$\lfloor \mathbb{S} \rfloor_{\mathfrak{P},C,[\![\mathcal{R}]\!]_{\mathbb{A}}^{\mathcal{D}},\mathscr{I}}^{I_{\Sigma}^{\mathbb{A}}} = \left(C \times \Sigma, \lfloor \Sigma^0 \rfloor_{\mathfrak{P},C,[\![\mathcal{R}]\!]_{\mathbb{A}}^{\mathcal{D}},\mathscr{I}}^{I_{\Sigma}^{\mathbb{A}}}, L, \lfloor \delta \rfloor_{\mathfrak{P},C,[\![\mathcal{R}]\!]_{\mathbb{A}}^{\mathcal{D}},\mathscr{I}}^{I_{\Sigma}^{\mathbb{A}}} \right)$$

$$\lfloor \mathbb{S}, \star \rfloor_{\mathfrak{P},C,[\![\mathcal{R}]\!]_{\mathbb{A}}^{\mathcal{D}},\mathscr{I}}^{I_{\Sigma}^{\mathbb{A}}} = \left((C \times \Sigma, \lfloor \Sigma^0 \rfloor_{\mathfrak{P},C,[\![\mathcal{R}]\!]_{\mathbb{A}}^{\mathcal{D}},\mathscr{I}}^{I_{\Sigma}^{\mathbb{A}}}, L, \lfloor \delta, \star \rfloor_{\mathfrak{P},C,[\![\mathcal{R}]\!]_{\mathbb{A}}^{\mathcal{D}},\mathscr{I}}^{I_{\Sigma}^{\mathbb{A}}} \right)$$

where:

$$\lfloor \Sigma^0 \rfloor_{\mathfrak{P},C,[\![\mathcal{R}]\!]_{\mathbb{A}}^{\mathcal{D}},\mathscr{I}}^{I_{\Sigma}^{\mathbb{A}}} = \{ (c, \sigma) \mid \sigma \in \Sigma^0 \wedge (c, [\![\sigma]\!]_{I_{\Sigma}^{\mathbb{A}}}) \in \mathscr{I} \}$$

$$\lfloor \delta \rfloor_{\mathfrak{P},C,[\![\mathcal{R}]\!]_{\mathbb{A}}^{\mathcal{D}},\mathscr{I}}^{I_{\Sigma}^{\mathbb{A}}}$$
$$= \left\{ \begin{array}{l} ((c, \sigma_1), l, (c, \sigma_2)) \mid (\sigma_1, l, \sigma_2) \in \delta \wedge c \in C \\ \wedge [\![\sigma_1]\!]_{I_{\Sigma}^{\mathbb{A}}} \neq [\![\sigma_2]\!]_{I_{\Sigma}^{\mathbb{A}}} \Rightarrow \exists (R, d) \in \mathcal{R} \times \mathcal{D} \; [\![\sigma_1]\!]_{I_{\Sigma}^{\mathbb{A}}} \xrightarrow{(R,d)}_{[\![\mathcal{R}]\!]_{\mathbb{A}}^{\mathcal{D}},\mathfrak{P},c} [\![\sigma_2]\!]_{I_{\Sigma}^{\mathbb{A}}} \end{array} \right\}$$

$$\lfloor \delta, \star \rfloor_{\mathfrak{P},C,[\![\mathcal{R}]\!]_{\mathbb{A}}^{\mathcal{D}},\mathscr{I}}^{I_{\Sigma}^{\mathbb{A}}} = \left\{ \begin{array}{l} ((c, \sigma_1), l, (c, \sigma_2)) \mid (\sigma_1, l, \sigma_2) \in \delta \wedge c \in C \\ \wedge \exists \overrightarrow{(R, d)} \in (\mathcal{R} \times \mathcal{D})^{\star} \; [\![\sigma_1]\!]_{I_{\Sigma}^{\mathbb{A}}} \xrightarrow{\overrightarrow{(R,d)}}_{[\![\mathcal{R}]\!]_{\mathbb{A}}^{\mathcal{D}},\mathfrak{P},c}^{\star} [\![\sigma_2]\!]_{I_{\Sigma}^{\mathbb{A}}} \end{array} \right\}$$

Example 7. By considering $[\![\mathcal{R}^{ac}]\!]_{\mathbb{A}_{ac}}^{\mathcal{D}}$, $\mathscr{I} = \mathcal{C}_{\mathsf{hru}} \times \{\emptyset\}$ and $I_{\Sigma_{ac}}^{\mathbb{A}_{ac}}$, applying $\mathfrak{P}_{\mathsf{hru}}$ on $\mathbb{S}_{ac}$ leads to a system whose states belongs to $\mathcal{C}_{\mathsf{hru}} \times \Sigma_{ac}$ and defined by:

$$\lfloor \Sigma_{ac}^0 \rfloor_{\mathfrak{P}_{\mathsf{hru}},\mathcal{C}_{\mathsf{hru}},[\![\mathcal{R}^{ac}]\!]_{\mathbb{A}_{ac}}^{\mathcal{D}},\mathscr{I}}^{I_{\Sigma_{ac}}^{\mathbb{A}_{ac}}} = \bigcup_{m \in \mathcal{C}_{\mathsf{hru}}} \{ (m, \alpha) \mid \alpha \in \Sigma_{ac}^0 \}$$

$$\lfloor \delta_{ac} \rfloor_{\mathfrak{P}_{\mathsf{hru}},\mathcal{C}_{\mathsf{hru}},[\![\mathcal{R}^{ac}]\!]_{\mathbb{A}_{ac}}^{\mathcal{D}},\mathscr{I}}^{I_{\Sigma_{ac}}^{\mathbb{A}_{ac}}} = \lfloor \delta_{ac}, \star \rfloor_{\mathfrak{P}_{\mathsf{hru}},\mathcal{C}_{\mathsf{hru}},[\![\mathcal{R}^{ac}]\!]_{\mathbb{A}_{ac}}^{\mathcal{D}},\mathscr{I}}^{I_{\Sigma_{ac}}^{\mathbb{A}_{ac}}} =$$
$$\{ ((m, \alpha), \langle +, s, o, a \rangle, (m, \alpha[s \leftarrow \alpha(s) \cup \{(s, o, a)\}])) \mid (s, o, a) \in m \}$$
$$\cup \{ ((m, \alpha), \langle -, s, o, a \rangle, (m, \alpha[s \leftarrow \alpha(s) \backslash \{(s, o, a)\}])) \}$$

Note that the system obtained in example 7 is slightly different from the system obtained in example 6. Indeed transition relations of systems obtained by applying a property-based policy are not constrained when a request is applied on a non-secure state, while transition relations of systems obtained by applying a rule-based policy allow to apply a request only if the conditions specified by the policy are satisfied. The following proposition states a result about executions of systems constrained by a rule-based policy.

Proposition 4.   *1.* $Exec\left(\lfloor \mathbb{S}\rfloor^{I_\Sigma^A}_{\mathfrak{P},C,\llbracket\mathcal{R}\rrbracket^{\mathcal{D}}_A,\mathscr{I}}\right) \subseteq Exec\left(\lfloor \mathbb{S},\star\rfloor^{I_\Sigma^A}_{\mathfrak{P},C,\llbracket\mathcal{R}\rrbracket^{\mathcal{D}}_A,\mathscr{I}}\right)$

2. If $\mathfrak{P}$ satisfies the switching property according to $\llbracket\mathcal{R}\rrbracket^{\mathcal{D}}_A$ and $\mathscr{I}$ and if:

$$\forall l \in L \; \forall \sigma_1, \sigma_2 \in \Sigma \quad \sigma_1 \xrightarrow{l}_\delta \sigma_2$$
$$\Rightarrow \left(\left(\exists (R,d) \in \mathcal{R}\times\mathcal{D} \; \llbracket\sigma_1\rrbracket_{I_\Sigma^A} \xrightarrow{(R,d)}_{\llbracket\mathcal{R}\rrbracket^{\mathcal{D}}_A} \llbracket\sigma_2\rrbracket_{I_\Sigma^A}\right) \vee \llbracket\sigma_1\rrbracket_{I_\Sigma^A} = \llbracket\sigma_2\rrbracket_{I_\Sigma^A}\right)$$

then $Exec\left(\lfloor \mathbb{S},\star\rfloor^{I_\Sigma^A}_{\mathfrak{P},C,\llbracket\mathcal{R}\rrbracket^{\mathcal{D}}_A,\mathscr{I}}\right) \subseteq Exec\left(\lfloor \mathbb{S}\rfloor^{I_\Sigma^A}_{\mathfrak{P},C,\llbracket\mathcal{R}\rrbracket^{\mathcal{D}}_A,\mathscr{I}}\right).$

Furthermore, we prove that each reachable state of a system constrained by $\mathfrak{P}$ can been obtained in a secure way according to the policy.

Proposition 5. *If $(c,\sigma) \in \Gamma\left(\lfloor \mathbb{S}\rfloor^{I_\Sigma^A}_{\mathfrak{P},C,\llbracket\mathcal{R}\rrbracket^{\mathcal{D}}_A,\mathscr{I}}\right)$ or $(c,\sigma) \in \Gamma\left(\lfloor \mathbb{S},\star\rfloor^{I_\Sigma^A}_{\mathfrak{P},C,\llbracket\mathcal{R}\rrbracket^{\mathcal{D}}_A,\mathscr{I}}\right)$,*

then $\exists (c,A_0) \in \mathscr{I} \; \exists \overrightarrow{(R,d)} \in (\mathcal{R}\times\mathcal{D})^\star \; A_0 \xrightarrow{\overrightarrow{(R,d)}}^\star_{\llbracket\mathcal{R}\rrbracket^{\mathcal{D}}_A,\mathfrak{P},c} \llbracket\sigma\rrbracket_{I_\Sigma^A}.$

Here again, defining a system from a rule-based policy $\mathfrak{P}$ can be done by considering $\mathcal{R}$ together with its semantics $\llbracket\mathcal{R}\rrbracket^{\mathcal{D}}_A$, and a subset $\mathscr{I}$ of $C \times \mathbb{A}$, and by applying $\mathfrak{P}$ (according to the interpretation $I_\mathbb{A}^A$ such that $\llbracket A\rrbracket_{I_\mathbb{A}^A} = A$) on the system $(\mathbb{A}, \mathbb{A}^0, \mathcal{R}\times\mathcal{D}, \llbracket\mathcal{R}\rrbracket^{\mathcal{D}}_A)$, where $\mathbb{A}^0 = \{A \in \mathbb{A} \mid \exists(c,A) \in \mathscr{I}\}$. For example, from the policy $\mathfrak{P}_{\text{hru}}$, the set $\mathscr{I} = C_{\text{hru}} \times \{\emptyset\}$, and the set $\mathcal{R}^{ac}$ together with its semantics $\llbracket\mathcal{R}^{ac}\rrbracket^{\mathcal{D}}_{\mathbb{A}_{ac}}$, we can define the system obtained in example 7 by applying $\mathfrak{P}_{\text{hru}}$ on $\mathbb{S}_{ac}$. Of course, the transition relation δ can also be constrained by defining a relation such that:

$$\delta \subseteq \left\lfloor \llbracket\mathcal{R}\rrbracket^{\mathcal{D}}_A \right\rfloor^{I_\Sigma^A}_{\mathfrak{P},C,\llbracket\mathcal{R}\rrbracket^{\mathcal{D}}_A,\mathscr{I}}$$

Equivalence results. We state here equivalence results about systems constrained by, or defined from, policies obtained with the constructions defined above. More precisely, we characterize the assumptions under which these systems have the same executions.

Proposition 6. *Let $\mathbb{P} = (\mathbb{A}, C, \Vdash)$ be the $(\mathfrak{P}, \llbracket\mathcal{R}\rrbracket^{\mathcal{D}}_A, \mathscr{I})$-policy.*

1. $Exec\left(\lfloor \mathbb{S}\rfloor^{I_\Sigma^A}_{\mathfrak{P},C,\llbracket\mathcal{R}\rrbracket^{\mathcal{D}}_A,\mathscr{I}}\right) \subseteq Exec\left(\lfloor \mathbb{S},\star\rfloor^{I_\Sigma^A}_{\mathfrak{P},C,\llbracket\mathcal{R}\rrbracket^{\mathcal{D}}_A,\mathscr{I}}\right) \subseteq Exec\left(\lfloor \mathbb{S}\rfloor^{I_\Sigma^A}_{\mathbb{P},C}\right)$

2. If the three following properties hold:

(a) $\forall (c, A_0) \in \mathscr{I} \ \forall A \in \mathbb{A} \ \forall \overrightarrow{(R,d)} \in (\mathcal{R} \times \mathcal{D})^{\star}$

$$\left(A_0 \xrightarrow{\overrightarrow{(R,d)}}_{[\![\mathcal{R}]\!]_{\mathbb{A}}^{\mathcal{D}}, \mathfrak{P}, c} A \wedge \left(\exists \sigma_0 \in \varSigma^0 \ A = [\![\sigma_0]\!]_{I_{\varSigma}^{\mathbb{A}}} \right) \right) \Rightarrow (c, A) \in \mathscr{I}$$

(b) $\forall l \in L \ \forall \sigma_1, \sigma_2 \in \varSigma \quad \sigma_1 \xrightarrow{l}_{\delta} \sigma_2$

$$\Rightarrow \left(\left(\exists (R,d) \in \mathcal{R} \times \mathcal{D} \ [\![\sigma_1]\!]_{I_{\varSigma}^{\mathbb{A}}} \xrightarrow{(R,d)}_{[\![\mathcal{R}]\!]_{\mathbb{A}}^{\mathcal{D}}} [\![\sigma_2]\!]_{I_{\varSigma}^{\mathbb{A}}} \right) \vee [\![\sigma_1]\!]_{I_{\varSigma}^{\mathbb{A}}} = [\![\sigma_2]\!]_{I_{\varSigma}^{\mathbb{A}}} \right)$$

(c) $\mathfrak{P}$ satisfies the switching property according to $[\![\mathcal{R}]\!]_{\mathbb{A}}^{\mathcal{D}}$ and $\mathscr{I}$

then $Exec \left(\lfloor \mathbb{S} \rfloor_{\mathbb{P},C}^{I_{\varSigma}^{\mathbb{A}}} \right) \subseteq Exec \left(\lfloor \mathbb{S} \rfloor_{\mathfrak{P},C,[\![\mathcal{R}]\!]_{\mathbb{A}}^{\mathcal{D}},\mathscr{I}}^{I_{\varSigma}^{\mathbb{A}}} \right) = Exec \left(\lfloor \mathbb{S}, \star \rfloor_{\mathfrak{P},C,[\![\mathcal{R}]\!]_{\mathbb{A}}^{\mathcal{D}},\mathscr{I}}^{I_{\varSigma}^{\mathbb{A}}} \right)$.

Proposition 7. *Let* $\mathbb{S} = (\varSigma, \varSigma^0, L, \delta)$, $\mathfrak{P} = (\mathbb{A}, \mathcal{C}, \mathcal{R}, \mathcal{D}, \Vdash)$ *be the* $(\mathbb{P}, [\![\mathcal{R}]\!]_{\mathbb{A}}^{\mathcal{D}})$- *policy,* $C \subseteq \mathcal{C}$, *and* $\mathscr{I}$ *be the set* $\{ (c, A) \mid c \Vdash A \wedge c \in C \wedge \exists \sigma \in \varSigma^0 \mid [\![\sigma]\!]_{I_{\varSigma}^{\mathbb{A}}} = A \}$.

1. *If* $[\![\mathcal{R}]\!]_{\mathbb{A}}^{\mathcal{D}}$ *is deterministic, then:*

$$Exec \left(\lfloor \mathbb{S} \rfloor_{\mathfrak{P},C,[\![\mathcal{R}]\!]_{\mathbb{A}}^{\mathcal{D}},\mathscr{I}}^{I_{\varSigma}^{\mathbb{A}}} \right) \subseteq Exec \left(\lfloor \mathbb{S}, \star \rfloor_{\mathfrak{P},C,[\![\mathcal{R}]\!]_{\mathbb{A}}^{\mathcal{D}},\mathscr{I}}^{I_{\varSigma}^{\mathbb{A}}} \right) \subseteq Exec \left(\lfloor \mathbb{S} \rfloor_{\mathbb{P},C}^{I_{\varSigma}^{\mathbb{A}}} \right)$$

2. *If the following property holds:*

$$\forall l \in L \ \forall \sigma_1, \sigma_2 \in \varSigma \quad \sigma_1 \xrightarrow{l}_{\delta} \sigma_2$$

$$\Rightarrow \left(\left(\exists (R,d) \in \mathcal{R} \times \mathcal{D} \ [\![\sigma_1]\!]_{I_{\varSigma}^{\mathbb{A}}} \xrightarrow{(R,d)}_{[\![\mathcal{R}]\!]_{\mathbb{A}}^{\mathcal{D}}} [\![\sigma_2]\!]_{I_{\varSigma}^{\mathbb{A}}} \right) \vee [\![\sigma_1]\!]_{I_{\varSigma}^{\mathbb{A}}} = [\![\sigma_2]\!]_{I_{\varSigma}^{\mathbb{A}}} \right)$$

then $Exec \left(\lfloor \mathbb{S} \rfloor_{\mathbb{P},C}^{I_{\varSigma}^{\mathbb{A}}} \right) \subseteq Exec \left(\lfloor \mathbb{S} \rfloor_{\mathfrak{P},C,[\![\mathcal{R}]\!]_{\mathbb{A}}^{\mathcal{D}},\mathscr{I}}^{I_{\varSigma}^{\mathbb{A}}} \right) \subseteq Exec \left(\lfloor \mathbb{S}, \star \rfloor_{\mathfrak{P},C,[\![\mathcal{R}]\!]_{\mathbb{A}}^{\mathcal{D}},\mathscr{I}}^{I_{\varSigma}^{\mathbb{A}}} \right)$.

5   Related Works

As we said, there exists now a large collection of literature describing how to define and to reason about policies. Without being exhaustive, we give in table 1 a classification of some of the most representative of the existing approaches.

Rule-based approaches. In [1], C-Datalog programs are used to specify some entities (subjects, authorizations, etc), their structure (hierarchies, roles, etc) and the relationships existing between them: the meaning of a policy is based on a stable semantics model of C-Datalog programs. Like in [15], such development aims to define an architecture within a particular authorization language. In [2,3], an access control policy is defined as a set authorizations: a policy is viewed as a configuration together with its semantics and only free policies can be expressed. Such framework is used to compose policies. In [5], a more general approach to compose policies is introduced and is based on the Belnap logic, used to resolve conflicts and unspecified answers. In [7], in the context of access control, a clear distinction is done between configurations and authorizations, but security targets are not introduced in an explicit way: a policy is defined by a set of configurations, a set of operations allowing to modify configurations, and a relation characterizing correct access judgements according to configurations.

Table 1. Related works

	Distinction betwween $\mathbb{A}$ and $\mathcal{C}$	Approach	Def. of $[\![\mathcal{R}]\!]_{\mathbb{A}}^{\mathcal{D}}$	Def. of a system from the policy	Application of policies over independent systems	$\mathcal{D}$
[1,2,3,13,18]	no	rules	no	no	no	$\{yes, no\}$
[4,9]	no	rules	yes	yes	no	arbitrary
[5]	no	rules	no	no	no	$\{yes, no, \top, \bot\}$
[6,7]	yes	rules	no	no	no	$\{yes, no\}$
[8]	no	rules	yes	yes	no	$\{yes, no\}$
[12]	yes	property	yes	yes	no	arbitrary
[17]	no	property	yes	yes	no	$\{yes, no\}$

Such an approach aims to compare policies in term of expressive power of the administrative language allowing to transform configurations and can only be used for free policies. A similar approach can be found in [6], where security engineering of lattice-based policies is considered. In [18], a finer comparison mechanism for rule-based policies (in term of expressive power of the administrative language) is introduced. In [13], a rule-based policy is defined as a conjunction of first-order logic formula, and the authors characterize fragments of logic for which $\Vdash$ is decidable. In [8], rule-based policies are expressed as Datalog programs and semantics of requests is considered. Such an approach is similar to the one introduced in section 4 to define a system from a rule-based policy. However, the system and the policy are defined over the same vocabulary. In [9], the authors represent rule-based access control policies as rewriting systems and use such an approach to compose policies. In [4], this approach is modified in order to make a clear distinction between the policy and the semantics of requests: such a development is close to the approach introduced in section 4 to define a system from a rule-based policy but the system and the policy share the same "actions" and are defined over the same signature. This framework is used to check security properties (such as confidentiality or integrity) *via* a notion of morphisms between environments (close to our notion of interpretation).

Property-based approaches. Property-based approaches are simpler than rule-based approaches and few generic frameworks allow to define them: defining a property-based policy can be easily done without a framework. A framework becomes useful when comparing or composing policies, or when dealing with a particular class of properties (information flows, etc). Hence, many policies are defined by following the property-based approach in an implicit way. The most famous property-based policy is the Bell and LaPadula policy [16], based on the MAC and MAC⋆ properties over sets of accesses. These developments specify security properties and define a transition system, which preserves these properties: this corresponds to the definition of a relation $\Vdash$ characterizing secure targets together with the (direct) definition of a secure system from the policy. Furthermore, note that many access control policies [1,15,2,3,5,7,18,13,8] are defined in term of sets of authorizations and could also be viewed as property-based policies: in this context, authorizations can be viewed as (parts of) secure targets, as well as granted access requests. In [12], property-based policies are defined and a comparison mechanism (based on simulation of the executions of secure systems obtained from policies) is introduced. A policy is defined by a predicate Ω over a set of states, describing both the targets and the configurations, and two mappings are introduced to distinguish targets and configurations: given a state σ, $\Lambda(\sigma)$ (resp. $\Upsilon(\sigma)$) denotes the target (resp. the configuration), and we have $\Upsilon(\sigma) \Vdash \Lambda(\sigma) \Leftrightarrow \Omega(\sigma)$. In [17], property-based policies are introduced and the framework is used to check that executions of a system are correct according to the policy. Other works aiming to formally characterize security properties preserved by executions of systems can be found in [10,11].

6   Conclusion

Security of information systems has become a well-established field of computer science. Hence many approaches dealing with security have been developed. In this paper, we have identified the components involved in these approaches and the role they play in the definition of a policy, a system and a secure system. Two main approaches have been considered here: the property-based approach is an abstract way to specify the security properties we want to enforce, while the rule-based approach specifies which actions are granted. Hence, rule-based policies allows a fine control over executions of a system that cannot always be ensured by a property-based policy. However, in most of cases, rule-based policies one can find in the literature satisfies the switching property and can be expressed as property-based policies. Moreover, it should be notice that when targets contain information about the past, defining property-based policies that aim to control sequences of actions becomes possible. In any case, rule-based and property-based approaches are not equivalent, and our results allow to enlighten differences between the two approaches, by characterizing some properties the policies have to satisfy to be equivalent, and by characterizing some properties the policies and the systems have to satisfy in order to have the same executions. Thanks to this study, it becomes possible to relate the different existing approaches, thus allowing to reuse policies in a particular context even if these policies have been defined by following another approach. Hence, this paper provides a generic formal framework in which many security policies and systems can be specified, implemented and proved correct according to some security properties. We think that using formal specifications is largely beneficial. Indeed, in the literature, one can find papers presenting a particular security mechanism through examples without any formalisation (or generalisation) of the concepts involved in the mechanism. Of course, such papers are very useful to understand how a particular mechanism works but they provide little help to implement it. We also think that genericity is important: it allows to have a common formalism (in which policies are described) thus allowing to characterize particular classes of policies and systems (such as free policies), to compare, to define operations (such as composition) and to reason in a generic way about policies and systems. The definition of such a framework contributes to a better understanding of what is a security policy. This framework has been successfully used to define and analyse classical access control policies (HRU, RBAC, Bell & LaPadula, Chinese Wall, Trust Management).

References

1. Bertino, E., Catania, B., Ferrari, E., Perlasca, P.: A logical framework for reasoning about access control models. In: SACMAT, pp. 41–52 (2001)
2. Bonatti, P., De Capitani di Vimercati, S., Samarati, P.: A modular approach to composing access control policies. In: ACM Conf. on Computer and Communications Security, pp. 163–173 (2000)
3. Bonatti, P., De Capitani di Vimercati, S., Samarati, P.: An algebra for composing access control policies. ACM Trans. on Inf. and Syst. Security 5(1), 1–35 (2002)
4. Bourdier, T., Cirstea, H., Jaume, M., Kirchner, H.: Rule-based Specification and Analysis of Security Policies. In: 5th International Workshop on Security and Rewriting Techniques, SECRET 2010 (2010)
5. Bruns, G., Huth, M.: Access-control policies via Belnap logic: Effective and efficient composition and analysis. In: Proc. of the 21st IEEE Computer Security Foundations Symposium, CSF 2008, pp. 163–176. IEEE Computer Society, Los Alamitos (2008)
6. Bryce, C.: Security engineering of lattice-based policies. In: Proc. of The 10th Computer Security Foundations Workshop. IEEE Computer Society Press, Los Alamitos (1997)
7. Chander, A., Mitchell, J.C., Dean, D.: A state-transition model of trust management and access control. In: Proceedings of the 14th IEEE Computer Security Foundation Workshop CSFW, pp. 27–43. IEEE Comp. Society Press, Los Alamitos (2001)
8. Dougherty, D.J., Fisler, K., Krishnamurthi, S.: Specifying and reasoning about dynamic access-control policies. In: Furbach, U., Shankar, N. (eds.) IJCAR 2006. LNCS (LNAI), vol. 4130, pp. 632–646. Springer, Heidelberg (2006)
9. Dougherty, D.J., Kirchner, C., Kirchner, H., Santana de Oliveira, A.: Modular access control via strategic rewriting. In: Biskup, J., López, J. (eds.) ESORICS 2007. LNCS, vol. 4734, pp. 578–593. Springer, Heidelberg (2007)
10. Gürgens, S., Ochsenschläger, P., Rudolph, C.: Abstractions preserving parameter confidentiality. In: di Vimercati, S.d.C., Syverson, P.F., Gollmann, D. (eds.) ESORICS 2005. LNCS, vol. 3679, pp. 418–437. Springer, Heidelberg (2005)
11. Gürgens, S., Ochsenschläger, P., Rudolph, C.: On a formal framework for security properties. Computer Standards & Interfaces 27(5), 457–466 (2005)
12. Habib, L., Jaume, M., Morisset, C.: Formal definition and comparison of access control models. J. of Information Assurance and Security 4(4), 372–381 (2009)
13. Halpern, J.Y., Weissman, V.: Using first-order logic to reason about policies. ACM Trans. Inf. Syst. Secur. 11(4) (2008)
14. Harrison, M., Ruzzo, W., Ullman, J.: Protection in operating systems. Communications of the ACM 19, 461–471 (1976)
15. Jajodia, S., Samarati, P., Subrahmanian, V.S., Bertino, E.: A unified framework for enforcing multiple access control policies. SIGMOD Record (ACM Special Interest Group on Management of Data) 26(2), 474–485 (1997)
16. LaPadula, L.J., Bell, D.E.: Secure Computer Systems: A Mathematical Model. Journal of Computer Security 4, 239–263 (1996)
17. Ligatti, J., Bauer, L., Walker, D.: Run-time enforcement of nonsafety policies. ACM Trans. Inf. Syst. Secur. 12(3) (2009)
18. Tripunitara, M.V., Li, N.: Comparing the expressive power of access control models. In: 11th ACM Conf. on Computer and Communications Security (2004)

Protecting and Restraining the Third Party in RFID-Enabled 3PL Supply Chains

Shaoying Cai[1], Chunhua Su[1], Yingjiu Li[1], Robert Deng[1], and Tieyan Li[2]

[1] Singapore Management University, 80 Stamford Road, Singapore
[2] Institute for Infocomm Research (I2R), 1 Fusionopolis Way, Singapore

Abstract. "Symmetric secret"-based RFID systems are widely adopted in supply chains. In such RFID systems, a reader's ability to identify a RFID tag relies on the possession of the tag's secret which is usually only known by its owner. If a "symmetric secret"-based RFID system is deployed in third party logistics (3PL) supply chains, all the three parties (the sender of the goods, the receiver of the goods and the 3PL provider) should have a copy of those tags' secrets to access the tags. In case the three parties in 3PL supply chain are not all honest, sharing the secrets among the three parties will cause security and privacy problems. To solve these problems, we firstly formalize the security and privacy requirements of RFID system for 3PL supply considering the existence of the internal adversaries as well as the external adversaries. Then we propose two different protocols which satisfy the requirements, one is based on aggregate massage authentication codes, the other is based on aggregate signature scheme. Based on the comparisons of the two protocols on performance and usability, we get the conclusion that overall the aggregate MAC-based solution is more applicable in 3PL supply chains.

1 Introduction

Radio Frequency IDentification (RFID) technology is an automatic identification technology that uses radio waves (wireless) to transmit the messages. RFID systems consist of two main components: tags and readers. Tags are radio transponders attached to physical objects, while radio transceivers, or readers, query these tags for identifying information about the objects to which tags are attached. RFID technology, when combined with internet and networking technology, enables product information to be collected, integrated, shared, and queried at various levels (e.g., item, pallet, case and container) in real time in a supply chain. Third party logistics (3PL) is one of the most dominating kind of supply chains, it has been widely adopted by many companies. The companies outsources part or all of their supply chains to professional logistics service provider to get better management efficiency and at same time reduce the cost.

RFID-based system's high efficiency is due to the contactless identifying property; however, this property also benefits the potential adversaries. Radio transmits through open air, then an adversary can eavesdrop or interfere

S. Jha and A. Maturia (Eds.): ICISS 2010, LNCS 6503, pp. 246–260, 2010.
© Springer-Verlag Berlin Heidelberg 2010

the communications between reader and tag without the awareness of the tag's owner. Dozens of cryptographic protocols have been proposed to provide secure and private identification and authentication of the tag (Sometimes the reader authentication is also required), such as the "hash-lock" protocol of Weis et al. [15], OSK protocol [11] of Ohkubo, Suzuki and Kinoshita, and the tree-based protocol of Molnar et al. [10]. There are also many works [9,14] et al. deal with the secure and private ownership transfer between two parties. Most of these solutions for authentication and ownership transfer are "symmetric secret"-based that an authorized reader shares a secret with each tag.

The "symmetric secret"-based solutions are designed to protect the system against external adversaries who do not know the secrets. However, in 3PL supply chains that three parties (the sender of the goods, the receiver of the goods and the 3PL provider) are involved in the processing of the tags, internal adversaries should be considered. In 3PL supply chains, all of the three parties need to access the tags, hence all of them should have a copy of the secret when a "symmetric secret"-based solution is deployed. With a tag's secret, any party can fabricate the tag. In case inside adversaries exist, disputes on the goods' originality will be hard to solve since all the three parties have the ability to fabricate the tags.

Currently, there does not exist any solution that is suitable for 3PL supply chains considering the exitance of internal adversaries. It does not mean that putting effort on 3PL supply chains is not necessary. 3PL has large market size, a study[1] shows that in U.S. the 3PL market gross revenues reached \$107.1 billion in 2009 and 8.3% growth is predicted for 2010. It is crucial to enhance the security and privacy level of RFID-enabled system for 3PL supply chains. We are the first ones to work on this new direction. Our contributions can be summarized as follows:

- We firstly formulate the security and privacy requirements of RFID system for 3PL supply chains with respect to both the internal and external adversaries.
- To execute the authentication of the tags in 3PL supply chains without revealing the secrets to the 3PL provider and the receiver of the goods, we provide two solutions that enable the tags' aggregate authentication on batch level. One solution is based on an aggregate Message Authentication Code(MAC), the other is based on an aggregate signature scheme.

Both the two solutions match the privacy and security requirements of 3PL supply chains. The comparisons on performance and usability between the two proposals show that the aggregate MAC-based solution is more applicable than the aggregate signature-based solution in 3PL supply chains.

The Organization of this paper. The rest of this paper is organized as follows. In Section 2, we model the 3PL supply chain and analyze the security and privacy requirements, introduce the motivation of our work in details. In Section

---

[1] http://www.prnewswire.com/news-releases/us-and-global-third-party-logistics-market-analysis-is-released-94771894.html

3 and Section 4, we respectively show our aggregate MAC-based solution and aggregate signature-based solution as well as the analysis on security and privacy. In Section 5, we compare the performance and usability of the two schemes. We review the related work in Section 6 and finally conclude in Section 7.

2   Third Party Logistics Supply Chain

In this section, we provide a brief review of 3PL supply chain. Then, we provide the attacking scenario of adversaries in 3PL supply chain and formulate the security and privacy requirements for preventing these attacks.

2.1   3PL Supply Chain

We depict the model of 3PL supply chains in Figure 1. A 3PL supply chain contains three parties. We denote the sender (customer A) who entrusts the transportation of goods to a 3PL provider as Party A, the 3PL provider as Party C and the receiver (customer B) of the goods as Party B[2]. The procedures in 3PL supply chains contain three steps:

1. *Ownership transfers from Party A to Party C*: Party A transfers the goods to Party C after the three parties have reached an agreement of the transaction.
2. *Party C' transports the goods*: Party C takes over the goods, and guarantees the goods' security during the transportation.
3. *Ownership transfers from Party C to Party B*: Party B verifies the goods, accepts them if the goods are intact, or denies the goods if the goods are not satisfactory.

A successful transaction is finished after Party B accepts the goods. Traditionally, when a party transfers goods to another party, the originality and the quantity of the goods are checked manually. However, when RFID system is deployed to enhance the efficiency of the supply chain, automatic identification replaces the manually checking. In RFID-enabled supply chains, the existence of the tags indicates the existence of the original goods[3].

2.2   Attacking Scenario of Adversaries

Different with the general adversary model which only considers the external adversaries, our adversary model for 3PL supply chain also considers the internal adversaries as well as the external adversaries. We analyze the potential dishonest behaviors of the three parties and the disputes that may happen on the ownership transfer between Party C and Party B as below. Note that we

---

[2] Party A and Party B can be the same entity in some occasions, eg. a factory entrusts a 3PL provider to transmit a batch of goods to its branch plant.

[3] Suppose each tag is imbedded in or stick on one item and it is hard to separate the tag from the item.

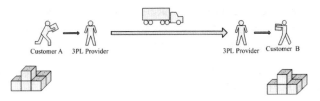

Fig. 1. 3PL Supply Chain Model

suppose ownership transfer from Party A to Party C is free of disputes. The reason is that a transaction will not begin unless Party A and Party C get into an agreement.

- *In case Party A is dishonest:* Party A sends a batch of low quality goods which do not satisfy Party B's requirements. When Party B refuses to accept the goods, Party A may claim that the goods are not original ones that it delivered, they have been replaced by Party C.
- *In case Party C is dishonest:* In case Party C loses or damages some goods during the transportation, to escape the compensation[4], Party C then fabricates the tags of the lost goods, and attaches them on fake goods. When Party B detects the replacements, Party C may claim that the faked goods came from Party A.
- *In case Party B is dishonest:* The dishonest Party B may intentionally refuse to accept the goods by claiming that goods do not satisfy the requirements.

2.3   Security and Privacy Requirements

Against internal adversaries. The major work for RFID system in 3PL supply chain is to facilitate Party C to transfer goods from Party A to Party B. The system should be able to detect Party C's malicious behavior. Inherently, we cannot prevent Party A (Party B) from cheating Party B (Party A), however, at least we should keep Party C away from Party A (Party B)'s malicious behavior. The requirements of the RFID system for 3PL supply chains against internal adversaries are listed as below:

- *Restrain dishonest Party C:* Party C should not be able to replace any goods without being detected. About privacy, in 3PL supply chain, Party A and Party B may not want to leak the goods' information to Party C. While the tags will be under Party C's control, the system should protect the tags' information leakage against Party C.

- *Protecting honest Party C:* If Party C honestly and successfully transfers the goods to Party B, Party B should accept the goods unconditionally, even if the goods do not meet the requirements, Party B should accept the goods (then Party B negotiates with Party A without involving Party C).

---

[4] Even worse, Party C replaces some goods and steals the original ones.

Against external adversaries. We assume that external adversaries only conduct the attacks during the transportation of goods.[5] The privacy and security requirements against external adversaries are listed as below.

- *Tag information privacy:* It means that external adversaries cannot get the information of the tags.
- *Tag location privacy:* If the responses of a tag are linkable to each other or distinguishable from those of other tags, then the location of a tag could be tracked by multiple collaborating tag readers. Tag location privacy means no one except the legitimate party can trace the tags.
- *Resistance of tag impersonation attack:* It means that the attacker impersonates a target tag without knowing the tag internal secrets and pass the authentication of the reader.
- *Resistance of replay attack:* It means that the attacker reuses communications from previous sessions to perform a successful authentication between a tag and a server.

2.4   Designing Principle

Adopting "symmetric secret"-based RFID systems in 3PL supply chains requires the three parties to share the secrets. Considering the existence of internal adversaries, sharing the secrets among three parties is problematic since having a tag's secret means having the ability to fabricate it. If all the three parties have the ability to fabricate the tags, disputes on the originality of the tags is difficult to solve.

Our method is to authorize each valid party with a credential instead of the secrets. The credential can be used by the authorized parties to check the status of the goods. At the same time the credential should not reveal any information about the tags. In a 3PL supply chain, Party A is the tags' owner. Only Party A possesses the tags' secrets. Party A grants a credential $credential_C$ to Party C so that Party C can check the tags' existing during the transportation. Party A grants a credential $credential_B$ to Party B, so that Party B can use it to verifies the goods. The construction and using is a subtle work.

Recalled that there are two requirements required against internal adversaries, namely, restraining Party C and protecting Party C. Restricting Party C requires that with $credential_C$, Party C cannot get any information of the tags. Protecting Party C requires that Party C should be able to confirm that the tags will pass the verification according to $credential_B$ before taking over the goods from Party A. Hence a systematic scheme should be designed for the three parties to make agreement on the credentials. And considering outside adversaries, the system should make sure that external adversaries cannot forge the tags that pass the verification according to the credentials.

---

[5] The two ownership transfer happens in relative secure environments that under two parties' surveillance.

The system will contain two parts: 1) designing a protocol that enable a authorized party to verify the tags with a credential; 2) designing a scheme that enables the three parties to make an agreement on the credentials. In this paper, we tackle the first part. We observe that in 3PL supply chains, normally, the goods are checked on batch level. In the following, we provide two group checking protocols to enable an authorized party verify the tags according to a credential on batch level based on two different credential designing schemes. While we focus on the originality checking of the tags, we suppose the number of the tags is stable, namely, if a malicious party take away one tag, he will replace it with a fake tag.

3   Solution Based on Aggregate MAC Scheme

Our first solution is based on an aggregate MAC scheme proposed in [7]. The intuition of this proposal is: each tag T_i (with k_i as its individual secret) is deployed with a MAC function. The authorized reader is granted with a credential that contains several couples of m_j and the aggregate MAC value $Agg(m_j)$ on m_j under each tag's key, where $1 \leq j \leq d$, d is the number of the pairs. The reader chooses an unused pair $(m, Agg(m))$, and uses m to query all the tags, each tag replies with the MAC value on m under its key. Upon receiving all tags' replies, the reader aggregates them and compares the aggregated value with $Agg(m)$, if they are the same, then the tags are intact, else, there are not all original ones.

3.1   Building Blocks of Our MAC-Based Solution

MAC: In cryptography, a message authentication code (MAC) is a short piece of information used to authenticate a message. A MAC algorithm, sometimes called a keyed (cryptographic) hash function $h_k(\cdot)$, it accepts the inputs as a secret key k and an arbitrary-length message m to be authenticated, and outputs a MAC tag $t = h_k(m)$ (sometimes known as a tag). The MAC value protects both the message's data integrity and its authenticity by allowing verifiers (who also possess the secret key) to detect any changes to the message content.

Aggregate MAC: In [7], Katz and Lindell proposed and investigated the notion of aggregate message authentication codes (MACs) which has the property that multiple MAC tags, computed by (possibly) different senders on multiple (possibly different) messages, can be aggregated into a shorter tag that can still be verified by a recipient who shares a distinct key with each sender. The aggregation is done by computing XOR of all the individual MAC tags. They proved that if the underlying MAC scheme is existentially unforgeable under an adaptive chosen-message attack and is deterministic, then the aggregate message authentication code generated by computing the XOR of every individual MAC values is secure.

3.2 Aggregate MAC-Based Solution

Requirements of the tags: The tags should be able to perform a MAC function $h_k(\cdot)$ under a key k stored in the tag. The tag should contain a random string generator.

Initialization: Party A initializes the tags. Suppose there are n tags in the system. Each tag T_i stores two secrets (b, k_i), $1 \leq i \leq n$, b is a common group secret that is shared by all the tags, and k_i is the tag T_i's individual secret.

Authorization to a valid party: Party A keeps k_i secret, and grants to a valid party the group secret b and a credential. d denotes the estimated upper bound of the number of times that the party will check the goods. The credential contains d pairs of $(m_j, Agg(m_j))$, $Agg(m_j) = \bigoplus_{i=1}^{n} h_{k_i}(m_j)$, for $1 \leq j \leq d$ and $1 \leq i \leq n$.

Group checking protocol for an authorized party: For each checking, the authorized party chooses an unused pair $(m_j, Agg(m_j))$ from the credential, then uses m_j to query all the tags. The details are depicted as below. Figure 2 illustrates the protocol.

1. *Reader $\rightarrow$ Tag T_i:* The reader sends m_j to the tag T_i.
2. *Tag $T_i \rightarrow$ Reader:* On receiving m_j, T_i chooses $r_2 \in_R \{0, 1\}^l$, l is the system parameter. T_i computes $M_1 = h_{k_i}(m_j) \oplus h(r_2)$, $M_2 = b \oplus r_2$, then sends (M_1, M_2) to the reader.
3. *Reader:* On receiving (M_1, M_2), the reader computes $r_2 = M_2 \oplus b$, and computes $t_i(m_j) = M_1 \oplus h(r_2)$. The reader stores the value of $t_i(m_j)$.

- After getting all the values $t_i(m_j)$, the reader checks whether $\bigoplus_{i=1}^{n} t_i(m_j) = Agg(m_j)$. If $\bigoplus_{i=1}^{n} t_i(m_j) = Agg(m_j)$, then the reader confirms the existing of the tags. If $\bigoplus_{i=1}^{n} t_i(m_j) \neq Agg(m_j)$, then the tags are not all the original ones.

Party A gives credentials $credential_B$ and $credential_C$ respectively to Party B and Party C. Party B uses $credential_B$ to verify the goods when taking over

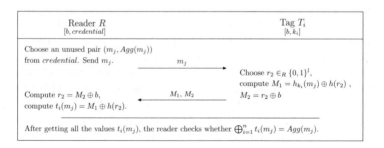

Fig. 2. Aggregate MAC-Based Solution

them from Party C. Party C uses $credential_C$ to verifying the tags during the transportation. In aggregate MAC-based scheme, Party B and Party C should keep its own credential in secret to each other, and $credential_B$ and $credential_C$ should not contain same $(m, Agg(m))$. Party C should make sure that the original tags will pass the verification using $credential_B$.

3.3   Analysis of the MAC-Based Solution

We first analyze the security and privacy properties of the MAC-based protocol against external adversaries.

- *Tag Information Privacy:* Without knowing b, the adversary cannot calculate the value of r_2. Without r_2, the adversary cannot get the value of $h_{k_i}(m_j)$. Then without $h_{k_i}(m_j)$, the adversary cannot get any information about k_i.
- *Tag location Privacy:* Without common secret b and individual secret of each tag, due to the cryptographic property of the MAC function $h_k(\cdot)$, the adversary cannot get any information of the tags through (M_1, M_2).
- *Resistance of tag impersonation attack:* Given (M_1, M_2), the adversary cannot retrieve any information of b and k_i. Without the knowledge of b and k_i, the adversary cannot retrieve any information about the tag. The probability that the adversary successfully impersonate a tag is equal to the probability that the adversary randomly chooses (M_1', M_2') and then (M_1', M_2') together with other valid tags' replies pass the verification.
- *Resistance replay attack:* The authenticated reader uses fresh pair of $(m_j, Agg(m_j))$ to verify the tags in each checking, so that the attacker cannot reuse the tags' replies from previous sessions.

Then we analyze the security and privacy properties of the MAC-based protocol against internal adversaries.

- *Protect Party C:* For Party C, given a tag T_i, with the common secret b, it can challenge the tag with arbitrary message m and get the MAC tag $t_i(m) = h^{k_i}(m)$ on m with T_i's secret k_i, however it cannot compute the value of k_i if the underlying MAC scheme is secure. While without the knowledge of k_i, based on the security of the aggregate MAC scheme, it is computational impossible to forge the tags so that given another message m', the aggregation of the tags' replies $\bigoplus_{i=1}^{n} t_i(m')$ equals $Agg(m') = \bigoplus_{i=1}^{n} h_{k_i}(m')$. Hence, if the tags pass the verification using Party B's credential, then Party B cannot deny that the tags are original ones.
- *Restrain Party C:* Providing some pairs of $(m, Agg(m))$, together with group secret s, Party C can verify the tags on batch level. However, given a tag T_i, although Party C can get the value $h_{k_i}(m)$ on any message m, it cannot compute the value k_i. Hence Party C cannot obtain any extra information of the tag.

4   Solution Based on Aggregate Signature Scheme

Another solution is based on aggregate signature scheme proposed in [1]. Party A authorizes the valid party with a credential that contains a value V. Each tag T_i is considered as a signature function with key k_i. Upon receiving a query m, tag T_i replies with the signature $\sigma_i(m)$ on m under its key. Then the reader aggregates the individual signatures $\sigma_i(m)$ for $1 \leq i \leq n$, verifies the aggregate signature using the value V.

4.1   Building Blocks of Our Aggregated Signature-Based Scheme

Bilinear Map: A bilinear map is a map $e : G_1 \times G_2 \rightarrow G_T$, where: (a) G_1 and G_2 are two (multiplicative) cyclic groups of prime order q; (b) $|G_1| = |G_2| = |G_T|$[6]; (c) g_1 is a generator of G_1 and g_2 is a generator of G_2. The bilinear map $e : G_1 \times G_2 \rightarrow G_T$ satisfies the following properties: (a) Bilinear: for all $x \in G_1, y \in G_2$ and $a, b \in \mathbb{Z}$, $e(x^a, y^b) = e(x, y)^{ab}$; (b) Non-degenerate: $e(g_1, g_2) \neq 1$.

Short Signature Scheme: Boneh, Lynh, and Shacham proposed the short signature scheme in [2] using the bilinear map. The system contains two groups G_1 and G_2 with prime order q, a full-domain hash function $H(\cdot) : \{0,1\}^* \rightarrow G_1$, and a bilinear map $e : G_1 \times G_1 \rightarrow G_2$. g is a generator of G. Each singer has public key $X = g^x$, where $x \in \mathbb{Z}_q$ is the corresponding private key. Signing a message M involves computing the message hash $h = H(M)$ and then the signature $\sigma = h^x$. To verify a signature one computes $h = H(M)$ and checks that $e(\sigma, g) = e(h, X)$.

Aggregate Signature Scheme: Aggregate signature scheme aggregates n signatures on n distinct messages from n distinct users to one signature. Any one should be able to do the aggregation without knowing the users' keys. Boneh and Gentry proposed a scheme [1] to aggregate BLS signatures. Given n individual signatures, one computes the aggregate signature as follows: $\sigma_{1,n} = \prod_{i=1}^{n} \sigma_i$, for $1 \leq i \leq n$, where σ_i corresponds to the user $user_i$'s signature on message M_i. Verification of an aggregate BLS signature $\sigma_{1,n}$ includes computing the product of all message hashes and verifying the following match: $e(\sigma_{1,n}, g) \stackrel{?}{=} \Pi_{i=1}^{n} e(h_i, X_i)$ where X_i is the public key of the signer who generates σ_i on message M_i.

ElGamal encryption scheme: ElGamal encryption system [4] is an public key encryption scheme based on the Diffie-Hellman problem. The scheme firstly chooses a multiplicative cyclic group G of order q with generator g. Each user $user_i$ chooses $x_i \in_R \mathbb{Z}_q$, sets x_i as the private key, then computes his public key $X_i = g^{x_i}$. To encrypt a message m to $user_i$, the sender converts his secret message m into an element m' of G, then chooses $r \in_R \mathbb{Z}_q$, computes $c_1 = g^r$ and $c_2 = m' \cdot X_i^r$, and then sends (c_1, c_2) to $user_i$. To decrypt the ciphertext (c_1, c_2), $user_i$ calculates $m' = c_2 \cdot s^{-1}$ which she then converts back into the plaintext message m.

---

[6] G_1 and G_2 can be the same group.

4.2   Basic Aggregate Signature-Based Solution

Requirements of the tags: The tags should be able to perform multiplication and addition on a multiplicative cyclic groups G_1 of prime order q. Each tag stores a secret.

Initialization: Suppose there are n tags in a batch, each tag is denoted as T_i, where $1 \leq i \leq n$. Let G_1, G_2 be cyclic groups of the order q. Then Party A chooses a bilinear map: $e : G_1 \times G_1 \rightarrow G_2$. For each tag T_i , Party A chooses a value $k_i \in_R \mathbb{Z}_q$ as the tag's individual secret. k_i is T_i 's individual secret. Then Party A generates the credentials. A credential contains a value V. V is computed to satisfy the following equation:

$$V = g^{\sum_{i=1}^{n} k_i} \tag{1}$$

where g is a generator of G_1.

Authorization to valid party: Party A keeps the tags' secrets and grants a credential to a valid party as well as the system parameters.

Group checking protocol for authorized party: The details of the protocol are shown below. Figure 3 depicts this solution.

1. *Reader* $\rightarrow$ *Tag* T_i: The reader firstly chooses a random number $r_i \in_R \mathbb{Z}_q$, computes $m_i = g^{r_i}$, sends m_i to the tag.
2. *Tag* T_i $\rightarrow$ *Reader*: After receiving m_i, T_i computes $\sigma_i = m_i^{k_i}$, then sends σ_i to the reader. For each tag T_i, the reader records the reply σ_i.

– After getting all the tags's replies σ_i, the reader checks whether $e(\prod_{i=1}^{n} \sigma_i, g) = e(g^{\sum_{i=1}^{n} r_i}, V)$. If the equation holds, the reader confirms that the tags are the original ones; else, the tags are not all original.

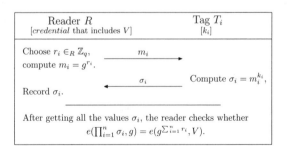

Fig. 3. Basic Aggregate Signature-Based Solution

4.3   Advanced Aggregate Signature-Based Solution

The basic aggregate signature-based scheme guarantees that the authorized party can check the tags without the secrets in batch level. However, it does not provide location privacy since a tag sends same reply to the same challenge in different sessions. To get the anti-tracing property, we randomize the tag's reply by using the ElGamal encryption scheme.

Requirements of the tags: Additional to the requirements in basic scheme, teach tag T_i stores a copy of a public key S, $S = g^s$, where s is the corresponding private key in advance.

Initialization: The same as the basic scheme except that the credential contains another value s.

Authorization to valid party: The same as the basic scheme.

Group checking protocol for authorized party: The details of the advanced aggregate signature based scheme are shown below. Figure 4 illustrates the proposal.

1. *Reader* $\rightarrow$ *Tag T_i*: The reader firstly chooses a random number $r_i \in_R \mathbb{Z}_q$, computes $m_i = g^{r_i}$, sends m_i to query T_i.
2. *Tag T_i* $\rightarrow$ *Reader*: After receiving m_i, T_i computes $\sigma_i = m_i^{k_i}$. Then T_i generates a random number $r_2 \in_R \mathbb{Z}_q$, computes $M_1 = \sigma_i \cdot S^{r_2}$, $M_2 = g^{r_2}$, namely T_i encrypts σ using the ElGamal encryption scheme. T_i sends (M_1, M_2) to the reader finally.
3. *Reader*: Receiving (M_1, M_2), the reader decrypts M_1, M_2, gets $v_i = M_1/M_2^s$. The reader records the value of σ_i.

- After getting all the tags's replies σ_i, the reader checks whether $e(\prod_{i=1}^{n} \sigma_i, g) = e(g^{\sum_{i=1}^{n} r_i}, V)$. If the equation holds, the reader confirms that the tags are the original ones, else the tags have been replaced.

Reader R		Tag T_i
[*credential* that contains V,s]		[k_i, S]
Choose $r_i \in_R \mathbb{Z}_q$, compute $m_i = g^{r_i}$.	$\xrightarrow{\quad m_i \quad}$	Compute $\sigma_i = m_i^{k_i}$. Choose $r_2 \in_R \mathbb{Z}_q$.
Compute $\sigma_i = M_1/M_2^s$, record it.	$\xleftarrow{\quad M_1, M_2 \quad}$	Compute $M_1 = \sigma_i \cdot S^{r_2}$, $M_2 = g^{r_2}$.
After getting all the values σ_i, the reader checks whether $e(\prod_{i=1}^{n} \sigma_i, g) = e(g^{\sum_{i=1}^{n} r_i}, V)$.		

Fig. 4. Advanced Aggregate Signature-Based Solution

Note that different with the aggregate MAC-Based scheme that each checking consumes a pair of $(m, Agg(m))$, in aggregate signature-based scheme, the value V is reusable. Given V, one cannot forge the tags. Hence, credentials for different parties include the same value V.

4.4   Analysis of the Aggregated Signature Based Solution

We first analyze the security and privacy properties of the advanced aggregate signature-based protocol against external adversaries.

- *Tag Information Privacy:* The security of ElGamal encryption scheme guarantees that only the authorized reader with s can decrypt the message (M_1, M_2), then get σ_i. For the authorized reader, with m_i and $\sigma_i(m_i)$, it is computational impossible for one to compute the value of k_i based on the hardness of Discrete Logarithm Problem. Hence our system guarantees tag information privacy.
- *Tag location Privacy:* Our system provides location privacy to external adversaries. Without knowing the secret s, the external adversaries cannot distinguish the two tags because ElGamal encryption introduces randomization.
- *Resistance of tag impersonation attack:* Based on the secure of the aggregate signature scheme, without the knowledge of the tags' keys, it is computational impossible for an adversary to forge the tags that pass the verification using the credential, even with the authorized parties' public key S.
- *Resistance of replay attack:* The authenticated reader uses fresh message m_i to query each tag. Hence, one cannot reuse the reply (M_1, M_2) that contains m_i's information as the response to another query m_i'.

Then we analyze the security and privacy properties of the aggregate signature-based protocol against internal adversaries.

- *Protect Party C:* The security of the aggregate signature scheme guarantees that without the knowledge of tags' secrets, Party C cannot forge the tags T_i' for $1 \leq i \leq n$ that satisfies $e(\prod_{i'=1}^{n} \sigma_i', g) = e(g^{\sum_{i=1}^{n} r_i}, V)$, where σ_i' corresponds to tag T_i''s signature on message m_i'. Hence if the tags pass the verification using V, no one can claim that Party C has replaced the tags.
- *Restrain Party C:* Since our system achieves the tag information private property and resist tag impersonation attack against the adversaries that do not know the tags' secret, Party C cannot gather any extra information of the tags and replace any of the tags.

5   Discussions

We provide two solutions to implement the group checking for the 3PL supply chains. One is aggregate MAC (AMAC)-based, the other is aggregate signature(AS)-based. As analyzed in Section 3 and Section 4, both the two proposals meet the requirements listed in Section 2, they achieve the same security and privacy level. In this section, we compare the two schemes' performances in Table 1 and their usability in Table 2. We realize the aggregate signature-based scheme on Elliptic Curves, more details on implementing Elliptic Curve Cryptography(ECC) on RFID chips can be found in [5]. Hence in aggregate signature-based solutions, operation · denotes point addition , operation / denotes point subtraction, exponential operations denotes point multiplication.

In the following tables, n denotes the number of tags in a batch. d denotes the number of $(m, Agg(m))$ pairs in a credential. We ignore the cheap operations $\oplus$, addition, subtraction and comparison of two values on calculating the computation consumptions on the reader side.

Table 1. Comparisons of the Two Schemes on Computation Performance

	AMAC-based solution	AS-based solution
Generation of a credential	$n \cdot d$ hash operations	1 point multiplication
Computations required on tag (running the protocol)	2 hash operations	3 point multiplications 1 point addition
Computations required on reader (running the protocol)	1 hash operation	2 point multiplications 1 point subtraction
Computations required on reader (Aggregation and verification)	none	2 paring operations 1 point multiplication

Table 2. Comparisons of the Two Schemes on Usability

	AMAC-based solution	AS-based solution
Computation capability (tag)	hash function, random number generator	operations on elliptic curve, random number generator
Storage requirements (tag)	2 values	2 values
Length of the credential	$O(d)$	$O(1)$
Restrictions on query	only allow to use a same pre-fixed value to query a batch of tags	allow to use arbitrary value to query each tag
Systematical support required	a scheme enables Party C to verify the validity of $credential_B$ without knowing the contents of $credential_B$	none

From above comparisons, we can find that the aggregate signature-based scheme is better compared to the aggregate MAC-based scheme. The reader can use arbitrary challenges to query the tags, while in aggregate MAC-based scheme, the reader should use a same pre-fixed value to query the whole batch of tags. The length of a credential is constant in the aggregate signature-based scheme while in aggregated MAC-based scheme, the length of the credential relates to the number of checking granted to a party. In aggregate signature-based scheme, $credential_B$ and $credential_C$ share the same value V, while in aggregate MAC-based scheme, $credential_B$ and $credential_C$ should not contain same $(m, Agg(m))$ pairs and additional scheme is required to convince Party C the validity of $credential_B$ without knowing the contents of $credential_B$.

Although aggregate signature-based scheme is more elegant, the aggregate MAC-based scheme overall takes more advantage since it requires much cheaper tag and performs more efficiently in running the protocol. Although the additional required systematical support will be counted on the reader side, since the efficiency bottleneck of the system is on the tag side, hence the aggregate MAC-based solution is more suitable for supply chains application.

6   Related Works

There is a concept called "grouping proof" proposed by Juels [6] which is similar with our "group checking". The pharmaceutical distribution example is used to illustrate how grouping proof protocols work. Yoking-proof would provide an evidence that each container of the medication was dispensed with a leaflet in case that a tag is embedded in the container and another tag is embedded in an accompanying leaflet. Yoking proof only enables two tags to prove their co-existence and is vulnerable to replay attack. Later works on grouping proof [13,12,3,8] support multiple tags and putting their efforts on improving the security and efficiency.

Both in the "grouping proof" scenario and "group checking" scenario, the readers are not trusted, they do not hold the secrets of the tags. In "grouping proof" scenario, the reader aims to prove to a verifier that the tags are processed together, in case the reader have the secrets, he can forge a proof using the keys. In "group checking" scenario, the reader should prove the tags' originality to another party, in case he has the secrets, he can forge the tags. Besides reading the tags in batch level without knowing the secrets. The two kinds of schemes work differently. In "group proof" scenario, the reader does not need to authenticate the tags. The reader only acts as a transfer stop in the grouping proof protocols in transmitting the messages among the tags. The whole tags generate a proof. While in "group checking" even without getting the secrets of the tags, the reader should have the ability to check the integrity and originality of a batch of tags. The reader interacts with the tags and verifies the tags' originality.

7   Conclusions

With the considerations of the internal adversaries as well as external adversaries, we analyzed the security and privacy requirements of RFID system for 3PL supply chains. We provided two "group checking" protocols to enable a reader to check the tags' existences and originality in batch level without knowing the secrets of the tags. One protocol is based on aggregate MAC scheme and the other is based on aggregate signature scheme. Both of the two protocols achieve the goals of protecting Party C and restraining Party C, and provide security and privacy guarantees. We compare the usability and performance of the two schemes, we can see that the aggregate MAC-based protocol outperforms the aggregate signature-based protocol. In the future, we will design a protocol that enables Party C to verify the validity of $credential_B$ without knowing the contents of $credential_B$. Then the system will achieve clear ownership transfers among the three parties.

Acknowledgement. This work is partly supported by A*Star SERC Grant No. 082 101 0022 in Singapore.

References

1. Boneh, D., Gentry, C.: Aggregate and verifiably encrypted signatures from bilinear maps. In: Biham, E. (ed.) EUROCRYPT 2003. LNCS, vol. 2656, pp. 416–432. Springer, Heidelberg (2003)
2. Boneh, D., Lynn, B., Shacham, H.: Short signatures from the weil pairing. J. Cryptology 17(4), 297–319 (2004)
3. Burmester, M., de Medeiros, B., Motta, R.: Provably secure grouping-proofs for rfid tags. In: Grimaud, G., Standaert, F.-X. (eds.) CARDIS 2008. LNCS, vol. 5189, pp. 176–190. Springer, Heidelberg (2008)
4. Gamal, T.E.: A public key cryptosystem and a signature scheme based on discrete logarithms. In: Blakely, G.R., Chaum, D. (eds.) CRYPTO 1984. LNCS, vol. 196, pp. 10–18. Springer, Heidelberg (1985)
5. Hein, D., Wolkerstorfer, J., Felber, N.: ECC is Ready for RFID A Proof in Silicon. In: RFIDSec 2008, Budapest, Hungary (July 2008)
6. Juels, A.: "Yoking-Proofs" for RFID Tags. In: Sandhu, R., Thomas, R. (eds.) PerSec 2004, Orlando, Florida, USA, pp. 138–143. IEEE Computer Society, Los Alamitos (March 2004)
7. Katz, J., Lindell, A.Y.: Aggregate message authentication codes. In: Malkin, T.G. (ed.) CT-RSA 2008. LNCS, vol. 4964, pp. 155–169. Springer, Heidelberg (2008)
8. Lin, C.C., Lai, Y.C., Tygar, J.D., Yang, C.K., Chiang, C.L.: Coexistence proof using chain of timestamps for multiple RFID tags. In: Chang, K.C.-C., Wang, W., Chen, L., Ellis, C.A., Hsu, C.-H., Tsoi, A.C., Wang, H. (eds.) APWeb/WAIM 2007. LNCS, vol. 4537, pp. 634–643. Springer, Heidelberg (2007)
9. Molnar, D., Soppera, A., Wagner, D.: A Scalable, Delegatable Pseudonym Protocol Enabling Ownership Transfer of RFID Tags. In: Preneel, B., Tavares, S. (eds.) SAC 2005. LNCS, vol. 3897, pp. 276–290. Springer, Heidelberg (2006)
10. Molnar, D., Wagner, D.: Privacy and Security in Library RFID: Issues, Practices, and Architectures. In: Pfitzmann, B., Liu, P. (eds.) CCS 2004, Washington, DC, USA, pp. 210–219. ACM Press, New York (October 2004)
11. Ohkubo, M., Suzuki, K., Kinoshita, S.: Cryptographic Approach to "Privacy-Friendly" Tags. In: RFID Privacy Workshop. MIT, Massachusetts (November 2003)
12. Piramuthu: On existence proofs for multiple rfid tags. In: PERSER 2006, Washington, DC, USA, pp. 317–320. IEEE Computer Society, Los Alamitos (2006)
13. Saito, J., Sakurai, K.: Grouping proof for rfid tags. In: AINA 2005, Washington, DC, USA, pp. 621–624. IEEE Computer Society, Los Alamitos (2005)
14. Song, B.: RFID Tag Ownership Transfer. In: RFIDsec 2008, Budaperst, Hungary (July 2008)
15. Weis, S.A., Sarma, S.E., Rivest, R.L., Engels, D.W.: Security and Privacy Aspects of Low-Cost Radio Frequency Identification Systems. In: Hutter, D., Müller, G., Stephan, W., Ullmann, M. (eds.) Security in Pervasive Computing. LNCS, vol. 2802, pp. 201–212. Springer, Heidelberg (2004)

Author Index

Printing: Mercedes-Druck, Berlin
Binding: Stein+Lehmann, Berlin